The Reach of Dialogue

Confirmation, Voice, and Community

THE HAMPTON PRESS COMMUNICATION SERIES

Communication Alternatives
Brenda Dervin, supervisory editor

Desert Storm and the Mass Media
Bradley S. Greenberg and Walter Gantz (eds.)

The Reach of Dialogue: Confirmation, Voice, and Community
Rob Anderson, Kenneth N. Cissna, and Ronald C. Arnett (eds.)

Forthcoming

Methodology Between the Cracks Volume One:
Sense-Making Theory and Method
Brenda Dervin

Methodology Between the Cracks Volume Two:
Sense-Making Issues, Explorations, Exemplars
Brenda Dervin

Ethical Communication and Risk Technologies:
Local and Global Concerns
James Jaksa and Michael Pritchard (eds.)

Glasnost U.S.A: Missing Political Themes in U.S. Media Discourse
Johan Galtung and Richard Vincent

Theorizing Fandom: Fans, Subcultures, and Identity
Cheryl Harris and Alison Alexander (eds.)

Nature Stories: Depictions of the Environment and Their Effects
James Shanahan

Public Intimacies: Talk Show Participants and Tell All TV
Pat Priest

The Reach of Dialogue

Confirmation, Voice, and Community

Rob Anderson
Saint Louis University

Kenneth N. Cissna
University of South Florida

Ronald C. Arnett
Duquesne University

HAMPTON PRESS, INC.
CRESSKILL, NEW JERSEY

Library of Congress Cataloging-in-Publication Data

The reach of dialogue: confirmation, voice, and community / [edited by] Rob Anderson, Kenneth N. Cissna, Ronald C. Arnett
        p.   cm. -- (The Hampton Press communication series)
    Includes bibliographical references and indexes
    ISBN 1-881303-00-4. -- ISBN 1-881303-01-2 (pbk.)
    1. Dialogue analysis. 2. Communication. I. Anderson, Rob, 1945- .
    II. Cissna, Kenneth N. III. Arnett, Ronald C., 1952- .
    IV. Series
    P95.455.R4 1994
    302.3'46--dc20   94-29161
                                                 CIP

Hampton Press, Inc.
23 Broadway
Cresskill, NJ 07626

Contents

Foreword

John Stewart

Rob Anderson, Ken Cissna, and Ron Arnett have gathered together in this volume readings that reflect both the historical richness and the current urgency of dialogue. Even more importantly, they have enriched and extended dialogue's contexts of application. Before this book, the term primarily described a communicative potential available to therapist and client, co-workers, friends, or family. Now, given Parts II and III of this work, dialogue's scope may also be seen to embrace political and scientific events of contact, meetings in cyberspace, and the connections that constitute ethnic, professional, social, and religious communities.

To the western reader at the end of the 20th century, this book addresses a daunting challenge: Can I acknowledge the poverty of the Cartesian-Kantian (and North American) view of the self-as-individual-consciousness and the connection between this version of hubris and the seemingly insurmountable problems of broken families, multiple addictions, homelessness, and political and professional immorality? Can I then move beyond acknowledgment to transform my comfort with individualism into a commitment to help speak and listen into being genuine contact, and even genuine community? As this challenge focuses specifically on communication, it may be articulated this way:

> Can I shift my orientation *from* my message behaviors that result from my perceptions of my agenda as I decide to adapt it to my perceptions of the other and his or her agenda *to* what happens when I let the other happen to me?

This, in a nutshell, is the challenge of moving from "rhetorical sensitivity" to dialogue.

In presenting its version of this challenge, *The Reach of Dialogue* joins good company; in addition to the authors excerpted here, many others are issuing their own versions of this call to change. For example, in two recent, widely cited works, sociologist Robert N. Bellah and his colleagues (1985, 1991) persuasively limn the dangers of America's misguided belief in singular selves and demonstrate the fundamental importance of interpersonal trust to healthy persons, groups, and organizations. Similarly, C. Roland Christensen and his colleagues (Christensen, Garvin, & Sweet, 1991) testify to the power of transforming classroom education from lecture to dialogue, and Faith Gabelneck and her colleagues (Gabelneck, MacGregor, Matthews, & Smith, 1990; Slavin, 1983, 1990) report on the revolutionary power of dialogically based collaborative learning groups and learning communities. On a broader scale, interpreters such as Georgia Warnke (1987), Susan Hekman (1986), and Michael Holquist (1990) clarify how virtually every person engaged in the human studies can profit from the dialogic perspectives of Hans-Georg Gadamer (1989a, 1989b) and Mikhail Bakhtin (1986).

Increasing numbers of communication and speech communication scholars are also urging moves to perspectives that echo central features of the dialogic approach developed here. Recently, Wendy Leeds-Hurwitz (1992a, 1992b) outlined some revolutionary "social" (which turn out in many ways to be "dialogic") approaches to interpersonal communication, and eight like-minded colleagues responded to her call to develop these approaches (Baxter, 1992; Bochner & Ellis, 1992; Carbaugh & Hastings, 1992; Jorgensen, 1992; Lannamann, 1992; Stewart, 1992). Klaus Krippendorff foregrounded similar concerns in his arguments against "message-driven" explanations of communication (1993) and for a dialogic/conversational view of communication theorizing (1994). Fourteen students of Norwegian communication scholar Ragnar Rommetveit also recently published *The Dialogical Alternative: Towards a Theory of Language and Mind* (Wold, 1992), which conceives of linguistic meaning as "open and dynamic, and constituted in the dialogic process of communication" (p. 1). And a consistent, albeit diverse, focus on aspects of dialogic praxis characterizes several of the most exciting current communication research programs that go under such headings as discourse analysis (e.g., Jacobs & Jackson, 1983), conversation analysis (e.g., Beach, 1989; Nofsinger, 1991) and ethnography of communication (e.g., Carbaugh, 1988; Philipsen, 1992).

As Anderson, Cissna, and Arnett emphasize, Martin Buber was one of the most influential progenitors of these efforts to rethink the nature of persons and reframe our understanding of the relationship among the individual, the social, and the interhuman. The editors of this volume consistently credit Buber for his pioneering insights; although Gadamer, Vygotsky, and especially Bakhtin are currently being cited by scholars with dialogic interests and inclinations, Buber remains the one author who initially did the most to describe dialogue and attempt to place it at the center of the human studies. As a result, it is altogether fitting that *The Reach of Dialogue* concludes with Buber's "Genuine Dialogue and the Possibilities of Peace." But the extended reflections that make up this book could, and perhaps most appropriately ought to, also *begin* with Buber's words.

If it were to do so, I can think of no more appropriate text than the opening two stanzas of Buber's classic, *I and Thou*. As Buber (1965a) explained it, the "dialogical principle" he announced in *I and Thou* was foreshadowed in the 18th-century writings of Friedrich Heinrich Jacobi, the 19th-century works of Ludwig Feuerbach and Sören Kierkegaard, Buber's own *Daniel: Dialogues on Realization* (1964), and neo-Kantian Hermann Cohen's *Religion of Reason Out of the Sources of Judaism* (1972), first published in 1919. But Buber's first, and ultimately most decisive, explication of the fundamental character of dialogue was completed in the spring of 1922 as the final draft of *I and Thou*. Much later, Buber commented that virtually everything he wrote between then and his old age was in some way an outgrowth of this work.

The first 13 sentences of *I and Thou* incisively sketch the primary features of Buber's view of dialogue. Thus I propose to unpack these lines here as a way of framing the reader's initial understanding of the broad-ranging discussions that make up *The Reach of Dialogue*. My goal is to contribute to the conception of dialogue developed in Rob, Ken, and Ron's work by enabling the reader to compare and contrast aspects of it with Buber's initial formulation.

Buber began *I and Thou*[1] with these words:

> The world is twofold for humans in accordance with their twofold orientation. The human orientation is twofold in accordance with the twofold nature of the basic words humans speak. The basic words are not single words but word pairs. One basic word is the word pair I-Thou The other basic word is the word pair I-It; but this basic word is not changed when He or She takes the place of It. Thus the I of the human is also twofold. For the I of the basic word I-Thou is a different I from that in the basic word I-It. Basic words do not state something that might exist outside them; by being spoken they establish a mode of existence. Basic words are spoken with one's being. When one says Thou, the I of the word pair I-Thou is said, too. When one says It, the I of the word pair I-It is said, too. The basic word I-Thou can only be spoken with one's whole being. The basic word I-It can never be spoken with one's whole being.

As I noted, most of the major elements of Buber's extensively developed and enormously influential approach to dialogue are present or nascent in this remarkable introduction. To begin, Buber's innocuous-sounding first sentence actually contains a revolutionary claim. Against all the philosophers who insisted, along with Descartes, Kant, and Husserl, that humans can only relate to what confronts them in *one*, subject-object

way, Buber boldly claimed in this sentence that the human's basic orientation is *two*fold. As he later testified, for example, in his dialogue with Carl
Rogers (Buber, 1965b), this conviction about the human potential for
relating grew out of Buber's own life experience. Over a 4-year period
which ended in May 1919, Buber reported that he experienced a mode of
contact that could not be explained in subject-object terms. As he put it,
"I had a decisive experience, experience of four years, many concrete
experiences, and from now on, I had to give something more than just my
inclination to exchange thoughts and feelings, and so on. I had to give
the fruit of an experience" (Buber, 1965b, p. 168).

At some points in his writing he labeled this experience "imagining the real of the other." It signaled a kind of human meeting which
heretofore had not, or had only incompletely, been recognized and
explained. *I and Thou*, and much of what Buber wrote between 1923 and
his death in 1965, were dedicated to describing this experience and artic-
ulating a philosophical anthropology rooted in it.

Perhaps only recently, with the growth of postmodern philosophy, has the full significance of the claim in this sentence begun to
emerge. Buber was one of the earliest thinkers who recognized that
Cartesian-Kantian analyses of humans were incomplete. Martin
Heidegger was another. Despite the many manifest dissimilarities between
Heidegger and Buber, Heidegger also challenged the adequacy of exclusively subject-object thinking. As Hubert Dreyfus (1991) explains,

> Since Descartes, philosophers have been stuck with the *epistemological*
> [emphasis in original] problem of explaining how the idea in our
> mind can be true of the external world. Heidegger shows that this
> subject/object epistemology presupposes a background of everyday
> practices into which we are socialized but that we do not represent in
> our minds. . . . [Heidegger asks] about the nature of this understand-
> ing of being that we do not *know*—that is not a representation in the
> mind corresponding to the world—but that we simply *are*. (p. 3)

Although Heidegger's and Buber's projects were very different, both recognized that subject-object thinking failed to do justice to the human condition. Edmund Husserl had moved in the direction of this insight when
he argued that the irreducible element of the fundamental process of
perception was neither the in-here noetic pole nor the out-there noemat-
ic pole, but the *relationship* or *encounter* between them.[2] But for Husserl
both the poles and the encounter remained "of" and "in" consciousness.
Buber, Heidegger, and most of the postmodern thinkers who follow some

---

[1]The translation is my own, which I developed from the German text (Buber,
1983) and the English translations by Ronald Gregor Smith (Buber, 1958) and
Walter Kaufmann (Buber, 1970).

features of Heidegger's lead, recognize the necessity of overcoming in a fundamental way this entire subject-object orientation.

Both Buber and Heidegger recognized that this overcoming could begin only with an explicit recognition of the connection between the human's orientation and his or her *world*. In Buber's case this connection was developed as he explained how humans inhabit not a "natural" or "objective" world, but what might be termed a world of *meaning*. As he later wrote,

> An animal in the realm of its perceptions is like a fruit in its skin; [the hu]man is, or can be, in the world as a dweller in an enormous building which is always being added to, and to whose limits he[/she] can never penetrate, but which [the human] can nevertheless know as one does know a house in which one lives—for [the human] is capable of grasping the wholeness of the building as such. (Buber, 1965b, p. 61)

In other words, humans do not live simply in a subject-object relation with their worlds; they *inhabit* them. And in the first sentence of *I and Thou*, Buber affirmed that this world of meaning is of two fundamental qualities "in accordance with" the twofold orientation humans may take toward it. One orientation, as many philosophers have noted, is subject-object. When this orientation dominates the world the human inhabits, whether made up of things, people, or spiritual beings, it is nonetheless a subject-object world. But, Buber testifies, there is another option. As Buber's voluminous writing and teaching ultimately demonstrated, this second option cannot be simply described or compactly defined. But it can be characterized and exemplified, and these were some of the central goals, not only of the remainder of *I and Thou*, but also of much of Buber's post-1922 works.

"The human orientation is twofold in accordance with the twofold nature of the basic words humans speak." This second sentence proclaims that this hitherto unforeseen second option is tied directly, not to genetic influences, psychological dynamics, or cognitive capacities, but to the human's speech communicating, "the basic words humans speak." Like the claim in the first sentence, this one moved Buber to the forefront of philosophical anthropology in the 1920s. Philosophers rooted in several other traditions were beginning at that time to take what is now known as *The Linguistic Turn* (Rorty, 1967). But their interests in language manifested in projects such as Bertrand Russell's logical atomism or the picture calculus Ludwig Wittgenstein (1961) attempted unsuccessfully to work out in the *Tractatus Logico-Philosophicus*. Buber's insight was anchored much more directly in the existential human experience of living language. The human's world, he wrote, is directly connected to

---

[2]I discuss this feature of Husserl's work in Stewart (1978).

human *speech*, oral-aural lived experience. Sixty years after *I and Thou*, Hans-Georg Gadamer (1984) captured a central part of this insight when he described for a class he was teaching the *logoi*, which, he argued, constituted the primary data for classical Greek thinkers. As Gadamer put it, Plato, Aristotle, and most of their colleagues were interested in "colloquial life as such. How in life things are shared. Life. *Speech*" (p. 9). This second sentence of *I and Thou* signaled that Buber's philosophy was centrally similar in that it was a *philosophy of speech communicating*.

In the third sentence Buber claimed that these spoken words that so materially influence the human's twofold world are not single words but "word pairs," and in this way he foreshadowed one of his most profound and difficult constructs—"the between." At the end of his monograph, "What is Man," Buber (1965a) called "the between" "a primal category of human reality," which, he admitted, was "conceptually still uncomprehended" (p. 203). This may still be true today. As I noted earlier, communication theorists, sociologists, educators, psychologists, and anthropologists continue to recognize that human understandings are co-created (Stewart & Thomas, 1990) and even human identities are co-constituted (Shotter, 1994). But despite this growing awareness, human scientists also still lack a simple vocabulary in which to discuss this collaborative, negotiated, transactional, relational set of realities. Buber did not solve this problem. But he was one of the first thinkers to foreground this feature of human life and to underscore its significance, and, in an attempt to articulate and explicate it, he created and described his construct—"the between."

The fourth sentence affirms that one fold of the twofold relational orientation that is accessible to humans manifests in the speaking of the word pair "I-Thou." Thus this line and the next claim that the dyad is the basic unit of the communicating that constitutes the human world. If Buber is right, no study of the ontological dimensions of human communication can focus only on "source variables" or "message sending," because these constructs highlight only one side of the event of contact. Speaking, says Buber, praxically implicates an Other.

The fifth sentence helps define by contrast the nature and significance of the word pair announced in the fourth sentence. First, it notes that the basic difference between the two folds of the human's orientation is captured in the difference, as expressed in Romance languages, between speaking the third person pronouns—he, she, it—and speaking the familiar form of the second person pronoun—*Du, tu,* or *thou.* Then this sentence reminds its reader that inanimate objects and nonhuman animals are only some of the phenomena that are made subject to objectifying speech. When this subject-object fold of the twofold orientation prevails, hes and shes can be as objectified as rocks and trees. As the editors of and contributors to *The Reach of Dialogue* recognize, Buber's interpersonal ethics is anchored in this insight.

The sixth and seventh sentences extend one implication of what has preceded them, and it is an implication that is centrally important to the philosophical anthropology Buber developed. Because the words are word pairs, claimed Buber, the human speaker is co-implicated in his or her speaking. *How one talks, in other words, affects who one becomes.* The fourth and fifth sentences address the significance of what might be thought of as the left-to-right action of the hyphen connecting the word pairs. They highlight how speaking helps constitute the other. Then the sixth and seventh sentences explain the right-to-left operation of the hyphen connecting the word pairs. They highlight how speaking helps constitute the speaker. Precisely because of the irreducibly relational, mutual, between nature of the word pairs, the I who speaks the basic word I-Thou becomes different in some very significant ways from the I who speaks I-It.

The eighth sentence reads, "Basic words do not state something that might exist outside them; by being spoken they establish a mode of existence." Here Buber generalized the conclusion from the previous four sentences and expressed this conclusion as a claim about the nature of language. As a result, this sentence rivals the first one in its revolutionary impact, especially considering that it was written in the second decade of the 20th century. In the first clause of this sentence, Buber distinguished the nature of the language he was discussing from that discussed by most language philosophers and theorists. Aristotle (1941) claimed in the first lines of *De Interpretatione* that "Spoken words are the symbols of mental experience and written words are the symbols of spoken words" (p. 16a). This was his way of describing the function of words, in Buber's words, "state [ing] something that might exist outside them." This part of Aristotle's philosophy of language captured a central feature of his teacher Plato's perspective, and it was echoed in the analyses of countless language philosophers who followed in their footsteps. It led to what I call the symbol model of language (Stewart, in press), the almost universally promulgated view that language is essentially a system made up of units—usually words—that function as signs or symbols to represent the objects, events, or meanings for which they stand. St. Augustine articulated this view of language in *De Dialectica* (1975) when he wrote,

> A word is a sign of any kind of thing, which can be understood by a hearer, and is uttered by a speaker. A thing is whatever is sensed or understood or is hidden. A sign is what shows both itself to the senses and something beyond itself to the mind. To speak is to give a sign by an articulate utterance. By articulate I mean one that can be comprised of letters. (5.7)

John Locke (1894) continued the tradition in his claim that "since the things the mind contemplates are none of them, beside itself, present to

the understanding, it is necessary that something else, as a sign or representation of the thing it considers, should be present to it: and these are
ideas" (p. IV. 21.4). Wittgenstein (1961) preserved the symbol model in his
description in the *Tractatus* of language as a logical system of words that
"picture" thought and in which "One name stands for one thing, another
for another thing, and they are combined with one another. In this way
the whole group—like a tableau vivant—presents a state of affairs" (p.
4.0311). In 1990, communication theorist Michael Motley illustrated that
the symbol model is alive and well when he claimed that the first of four
"extremely common, if not quite universal assumptions found in even the
most elementary discussions of communication" was that "communication
is characterized by symbolic behaviors, that is to say, that communication
involves the transmission and/or reception of symbols" (p. 2).

But by 1922 Buber had seen it otherwise. The spoken words on
which he focused, he claimed, did *not* signify, symbolize, or otherwise represent; they did not "state something that might exist outside them."
Instead of functioning semiotically, he argued, they function constitutive-
ly. *These* words bring something into being. "By being spoken they establish a mode of existence," a way of living. This speech, in other words,
cannot be understood epistemologically; that is, it is not a more or less
accurate representation of the previously existing, objectively describable
content it is "about." No subject-object reading can capture the force of
this living language, because this speech functions *ontologically.*

In this way Buber's earlier claim about the effects on the involved
persons of their ways of speech communicating became a claim about the
nature of language itself. As I noted earlier, subsequent theorists, among
them Gadamer (1989a, 1989b) and Bakhtin (1986; Volosinov, 1973), have
articulated complementary and even parallel claims. But none has
focused as directly as did Buber on dialogue as the oral-aural and ontological nexus between persons.

The final four sentences of the beginning of *I and Thou* extend
once more what has preceded them, and again underscore the focus of
this work in philosophical anthropology. The first two specify *how*, as the
seventh sentence claimed, the I of the basic word I-Thou is different from
that in the basic word I-It. As was noted, not only does the speech communicating that Buber described implicate its participants, but the mode of
being of the other that is present in and constituted by one's speech
implicates the one speaking. Thus when one says "Thou," in the full sense
of "saying" that Buber has in mind, one is available to the other as a corresponding Thou. Similarly, when one says "It," one offers him- or herself to
the other as a corresponding It. Continued communication may, of
course, change both these options. But this is what is initially implicated
in one's speech.

The final two sentences of these first stanzas foreground "wholeness," a construct that became an important element of Buber's subsequent discussions of dialogue. In "The Education of Character," for example, Buber (1965a) reminded teachers that their concern should "always [be] the person as a whole, both in the actuality in which he[/she] lives before you now and in his[/her] possibilities"(p. 104). In "Elements of the Interhuman," Buber (1965b) emphasized the importance of "the perception of one's fellow [hu]man as a whole, as a unity, and as unique, even if his [or her] wholeness, unity, and uniqueness are only partly developed" (p. 80). And when Buber (1965a) discussed the differences among observing someone, approaching him or her as an "onlooker," and genuinely "becoming aware," he emphasized how the latter experience is of the other person as a whole. "I cannot depict or denote or describe" the person about whom I become aware in this way. "Were I to attempt it, that would be the end of saying." Why? Because this person is not the object of my perception; rather, "I have got to do with him [or her]" (p. 10). In effect, *I let him or her happen to me.*

This is the dimension of experience pointed toward in the final two sentences. When I engage the I-Thou fold of the twofold orientation available to me, my world is populated by whole beings. When I engage the other fold, the world I inhabit is populated by beings who are less than whole.

What, then, is the picture of dialogue that emerges in these crucial first sentences of Buber's most important work? First, insofar as the term *dialogue* is taken to be a shorthand label for the speech communicating that manifests the second "fold" of Buber's twofold orientation, this term designates a *quality of contact between persons. Dialogue* is not simply a form of speech, and not every interaction or conversation between two persons is *dialogic* in this sense. Rather, the kind or quality of meeting that Buber labeled "dialogic" emerges *between* two or more persons when they are mutually and simultaneously willing to orient to one another in the second of the two ways accessible to them as humans and able to embody or manifest this willingness verbally and nonverbally in their speech.

Second, Buber's philosophical anthropology was concretely speech communicative. As he clarified in "On the Psychologizing of the World" (Buber, 1969), his focal interest was not on individual psychic dynamics, but on oral-aural articulate contact. This is why it is unfortunate that both Smith (Buber, 1958) and Kaufmann (Buber, 1970) translated *Verhalten* in the first two lines of *I and Thou* as "attitude." Buber was not concerned only, or even centrally, with attitude defined by psychologists as one's "predisposition to act," but with the vis-à-vis that is concretely embodied in verbal and nonverbal *speaking,* the quality of the communicator's ways-of-being-over-against one another that emerges in talk. This is why I believe *orientation* is preferable to *attitude.*

Third, the potential of dialogue is our birthright as humans.

Although future work with chimpanzees, whales, or extraterrestrials may belie this part of Buber's claim, he saw dialogue as a potential exclusively available in this world to humans and definitive of our uniquely human nature. The central implication of this ontological character of dialogue is that there is a direct relationship between the quality of human communication and the quality of human life. How we speech communicate, in other words, directly affects who we are and who we become. Communication is not just instrumental and expressive; it is also, and most importantly, person building (and can be person destroying).

Fourth, any conceptualization of dialogue consistent with Buber's insight must focus on the between. His is a relational perspective, one centrally concerned with collaboration and co-construction. This does not mean, as Buber often emphasized, that he was only interested in agreement. One of the greatest injustices that has been done to Buber is to reduce his work to a philosophy of "warm fuzzies." As his years of efforts toward Arab-Israeli understanding demonstrated, he was as interested in "the between" that emerged from age-old, violent conflict as he was in "the between" that may be built between teacher and student, therapist and client, or husband and wife. His point, which is being echoed by many of the contemporary thinkers cited at the beginning of this foreword, is that any adequate understanding of the human must take seriously the truism that we are *social* animals. We do not exist individually, but relationally. As Hugh Prather (1970) put it, "Nothing, including me, exists by itself—this is an illusion of words. I *am* a relationship, ever-changing." This feature of Buber's perspective is only now being taken seriously by scholars in speech communication, anthropology, sociology, and even psychology.

As the essays making up *The Reach of Dialogue* clearly demonstrate, Buber is not the only important dialogic theorist or practitioner. But his work sets the ground-tone for much of what follows. Thus it may be useful to hold his ideas in mind as one considers the upcoming discussions of "The Invitation to Dialogue," "The Arena of Dialogue," and "The Trust of Dialogue."

REFERENCES

Aristotle (1941). *De interpretatione* (E.M. Edghill, Trans.) *The basic works of Aristotle* (R. McKeon, Ed., pp. 40-61). New York: Random House
Augustine. (1975). *De dialectica* (J. Pinborg, Ed., B.D. Jackson, Trans.) The Hague: Reidel.
Bakhtin, M.M. (1986). *Speech genres and other essays* (V. W. McGee, Trans.) Austin: University of Texas Press.
Baxter, L.A. (1992). Interpersonal communication as dialogue: A

response to the "social approaches" forum. *Communication Theory, 2,* 330-336.

Beach, W.A. (Ed.) (1989). Sequential organization of conversational activities [Special Issue]. *Western Journal of Speech Communication, 53.*

Bellah, R.N., Madsen, R., Sullivan, W.M., Swidler, A., & Tipton, S.M. (1985). *Habits of the heart: Individualism and commitment in American life.* New York: Harper & Row.

Bellah, R.N., Madsen, R., Sullivan, W.M., Swidler, A., & Tipton, S.M. (1991). *The good society.* New York: Vintage Books

Bochner, A.P., & Ellis, C. (1992). Personal narrative as a social approach to interpersonal communication. *Communication Theory, 2,* 165-172.

Buber, M. (1958). *I and thou* (R.G. Smith, Trans.). New York: Charles Scribner's Sons.

Buber, M. (1964). *Daniel: Dialogues on realization* (M. Friedman, Trans.). New York: Holt, Rinehart & Winston.

Buber, M. (1965a). Afterword: The history of the dialogical principle (M. Friedman, Trans.) In *Between man and man* (R.G. Smith, Trans., pp. 202-224) New York: Macmillan.

Buber, M. (1965b). *The knowledge of man: A philosophy of the interhuman* (M. Friedman, Ed., M. Friedman and R.G. Smith, Trans.) New York: Harper.

Buber, M. (1969). *A believing humanism: Gleanings by Martin Buber* (M. Friedman, Trans.) New York: Simon and Schuster.

Buber, M. (1970). *I and Thou* (W. Kaufman, Trans.). New York: Charles Scribner's Sons.

Buber, M (1983). *Ich und Du.* Heidelberg: L. Schneider.

Carbaugh, D. (1988). *Talking American: Cultural discourses on DONAHUE.* Norwood, NJ: Ablex.

Carbaugh, D., & Hastings, S.O. (1992). A role for communication theory in ethnography and cultural analysis. *Communication Theory, 2,* 156-164.

Christensen, C.R., Garvin, D.A., & Sweet, A. (Eds.). (1991). *Education for judgment: The artistry of discussion leadership.* Cambridge, MA: Harvard Business School.

Cohen, H. (1972). *Religion of reason out of the sources of Judaism* (S. Kaplan, Trans.). New York: Ungar.

Dreyfus, H.L. (1991). *Being-in-the-world: A commentary on Heidegger's Being and Time division I.* Cambridge, MA: MIT Press.

Gabelneck, F., MacGregor, J., Matthews, R.S., & Smith, B.L. (1990). *Learning communities: Creating connections among students, faculty, and disciplines.* San Francisco: Jossey-Bass.

Gadamer, H-G. (1984). John Stewart's unpublished class notes from two courses taught by Hans-Georg Gadamer at Boston College.

Gadamer, H-G. (1989a). *Truth and method* (2nd rev. ed., J. Weinsheimer & D.G. Marshall, Trans.). New York: Crossroad.

Gadamer, H-G. (1989b). Text and interpretation. In D.P. Michelfelder & R.E. Palmer (Eds.), *Dialogue and deconstruction: The Gadamer-Derrida encounter* (pp. 21-51). Albany: State University of New York Press.

Hekman, S. (1986). *Hermeneutics and the sociology of knowledge.* Notre Dame, IN: University of Notre Dame Press.

Holquist, M. (1990). *Dialogism: Bakhtin and his world.* London: Routledge.

Jacobs, S., & Jackson, S. (1983). Strategy and structure in conversational influence attempts. *Communication Monographs, 50,* 285-304.

Jorgensen, J. (1992). Communication, rapport, and the interview: A social perspective. *Communication Theory, 2,* 148-155.

Krippendorff, K. (1993). The past of communication's hoped-for future. *Journal of Communication, 43*(3), 34-44.

Krippendorff, K. (1994). Conversation or intellectual imperialism in comparing communication (theories). *Communication Theory, 4.*

Lannamann, J.W. (1992). Deconstructing the person and changing the subject of interpersonal studies. *Communication Theory, 2,* 139-147.

Leeds-Hurwitz, W. (1992a). Forum introduction: Social approaches to interpersonal communication. *Communication Theory, 2,* 131-138.

Leeds-Hurwitz, W. (1992b). Forum continuation: Social approaches to interpersonal communication. *Communication Theory, 2,* 329-330.

Locke, J. (1894). *Essay concerning human understanding* (A. C. Fraser, Ed.). Oxford: Clarendon.

Motley, M. (1990). On whether one can(not) not communicate: An examination via traditional communication postulates. *Western Journal of Speech Communication, 54,* 1-20.

Nofsinger, R.E. (1991). *Everyday conversation.* Newbury Park, CA: Sage.

Philipsen, G.A. (1992). *Speaking culturally: Explorations in social communication.* Albany: State University of New York Press.

Prather, H. (1970). *Notes to myself.* Lafayette, CA: Real People Press.

Rorty, R. (1967). *The linguistic turn.* Chicago: University of Chicago Press.

Shotter, J. (1994). *Conversational realities.* Beverly Hills, CA: Sage.

Slavin, R.E. (1983). *Cooperative learning.* New York: Longman

Slavin, R.E. (1990). Research on cooperative learning. Consensus and controversy. *Educational Leadership, 47,* 52-54.

Stewart, J. (1978). Foundations of dialogic communication. *Quarterly Journal of Speech, 65,* 183-201.

Stewart, J. (1992). One philosophical dimension of social approaches to interpersonal communication. *Communication Theory, 2,* 337-346.

Stewart, J. (in press). *Language as articulate contact: Toward a post-semiotic philosophy of communication.* Albany: State University of New York Press.

Stewart, J., & Thomas, M. (1990). Dialogic listening: Sculpting mutual meanings. In J. Stewart (Ed.), *Bridges not walls: A book about interpersonal communication* (5th ed., pp. 192-210). New York: McGraw-Hill.

Volosinov, V.N. (1973). *Marxism and the philosophy of language* (L. Matejka & I.R. Titunik, Trans.). Cambridge, MA: Harvard University Press.

Warnke, G. (1987). *Gadamer: Hermeneutics, tradition, and reason.* Stanford, CA: Stanford University Press.

Wittgenstein, L. (1961). *Tractatus logico-philosphicus* (D.F. Pears & B.F. McGuinness, Trans.). London: Routledge & Kegan Paul.

Wold, A.H. (Ed.). (1992). *The dialogical alternative: Towards a theory of language and mind.* Oxford: Oxford University Press.

■

Preface

Human dialogue does not just happen, as if sunshine suddenly replaces a thunderstorm. But neither can dialogue be planned, pronounced, or willed. Where we find dialogue, we find people who are open to it, people who do not renounce it cynically, but no expert technicians can merchandise or guarantee this relational quality.

Therefore, dialogue thrives at the margins of human agency—those ill-defined situations in which we imagine we are somewhat in control but in which our plans surprisingly can blend into the unexpected. A teacher unexpectedly learns something profound from a beginning public speaking student, or an authoritarian supervisor is surprised to find how little actual power must be exerted in order to earn respect from subordinates. Theorists who debate whether human behavior is either determined or freely chosen might, because of their dichotomous thinking, overlook the gradual invitations and insinuations of dialogue, and therefore neglect its importance. Dialogue, which cannot be mandated, rarely happens accidentally either.

For example, only gradually did the three editors of this book discover how we could be good dialogue partners and teachers for each other. Beginning in the early 1980s, two of us (Arnett and Anderson) found ourselves disagreeing in journals and convention panels about our interpretations of philosopher Martin Buber's and psychologist Carl Rogers's concepts of dialogue. Each thought the other was missing something crucial, and that was undoubtedly true. Exploring scholarly disagreements so thoroughly, we gradually noticed our agreements and compatibilities as well. Each discovered his positions subtly changing. But more important, we discovered more about the place of respect within scholarly disagreement, a respect paving the way to friendship. Cissna, whose research focused on the impact of confirmation and disconfirmation in relational communication, entered the conversation around 1985 when he and Anderson began to specify the dialogic implications of Rogers's experiences in psychotherapy. Cissna planned a convention panel on approaches to dialogue in 1986, in which the three of us participated with Stan Deetz, John Stewart, and Maurice Friedman. Further

meetings at conferences—noodling, listening, laughing, and quibbling—
and the chance to read and respond to each other's work convinced us of
the need for this project and of our ability to complete it.

Although some disagreements undoubtedly remain, this book is
the current artifact of our dialogue. To plan it, we met for several intense
days at an old farmhouse in Illinois, stole a bunch of off-moments from
conventions and conferences, planned another convention program
together, and rang up long distance bills that our wives and administra-
tors might have regarded somewhat skeptically.

No effective dialogue develops outside a supportive environment,
and our families provided significant support and just enough tension for
us to remain creatively connected to the everyday questions raised by dialogue's demands. Each of us is grateful to Dona, Eric, and Neil Anderson;
Susan, Carolyn, and Jennifer Cissna; and Millie, Adam, and Aimee Arnett.
As with most families that pay close attention to each other, these three
mini-communities remind us of the fragility of life's expectations and
assumptions, and provide equally important reminders about the strength
of trust and love.

The university community has also helped us understand the
potentials and pitfalls of dialogue more realistically; we thank the many
student and faculty learners—too many to list—at the institutions where
we have taught, including Saint Louis University, Southern Illinois
University at Edwardsville, the University of South Florida, Marquette
University, Manchester College, and Duquesne University.

We are grateful as well for the encouragement of professional
friends and role models who through their interest, enthusiasm, research,
and critique taught us even when they did not realize they were doing so.
Although they should not be expected to shoulder the blame for our
short-sightedness and misjudgment, certainly any success we might have in
clarifying dialogic communication could be traced directly or indirectly to
these men and women. Foremost among them is Maurice Friedman of San
Diego State University, whose gracious friendship and scholarly generosity
became apparent to us even when (perhaps especially when) he occasionally disagreed with our notions. Professor Friedman will recognize his
influence as it is reflected in most of our pages. In the field of communication, too, the writings of John Stewart, Richard Johannesen, Paul Keller,
Art Bochner, and Barnett Pearce have motivated us to examine and re-
examine our assumptions about what quality communication can be.

Each of us has known many teacher-exemplars of dialogic leader-
ship who have lived dialogue inspirationally in their daily professional
lives; these people have had many more students than they realize. Rob
Anderson wants to recognize especially Robert Hawkins of Southern
Illinois University at Edwardsville; Anita Taylor of George Mason
University; and two sensitive educators who recently died unexpectedly

and too soon, Louis Banker of Fort Osage High School in Independence, Missouri, and Larry Baricevic of Saint Louis University. Ken Cissna wants to recognize especially Tom Pace, whose interest and support over the years, even from a distance, he never doubted; and Keith Jensen, who he knew only briefly and who died much too young. Ron Arnett wants to recognize especially Jean Ann Tribolet of Manchester College; Tom Hurst, Director of On Earth Peace; Ray Wagner and Paul Boase of Ohio University; and colleagues at Duquesne University for their reach of dialogue in friendship and in the caring guidance of so many students.

The Reach of Dialogue would not have been published without the enthusiastic support of Brenda Dervin of Ohio State University, who glimpsed the potential of our developing project and advocated its publication from the beginning. We are grateful not only for her expertise but also for her work in coordinating helpful feedback from several reviewers.

Finally, Barbara Bernstein of Hampton Press has helped us at every turn, in matters big and small. She models how a publisher can be concerned not only with product but with process and intellectual substance; she made it her business to respond directly to questions, shoot straight with answers, go to bat for us in helping to secure permissions, and in general listen carefully, as if our opinions mattered.

We do not intend *The Reach of Dialogue* as the last word on the subject. Rather, we offer it as the next word in an ongoing conversation that concerns itself with that deceptively simple question, wisely reiterated recently, of how we can learn just to get along together.

About the Editors

Rob Anderson, a Professor in the Department of Communication at Saint Louis University, is an award-winning classroom teacher and the author or coauthor of five books in communication theory and practice, including *Students as Real People, Before the Story,* and *Questions of Communication.* A new coauthored book, *The Conversation of Journalism,* has just been published. In teaching and writing he merges the concerns of interpersonal and mass media scholarship. His articles have appeared in various journals in speech communication, journalism, English, psychology, and education.

Kenneth N. Cissna, a Professor in the Department of Communication at the University of South Florida, has published research on interpersonal communication and communication theory in a variety of journals in communication and related fields, as well as in several edited volumes. Professor Cissna is currently editing a book on applied communication theory and practice. From 1981 to 1986, he edited the *Journal of Applied Communication Research,* and in 1990 received the Florida Communication Association's Scholar of the Year award.

Ronald C. Arnett, a Professor and Chairperson of the Department of Communication at Duquesne University, is the author of more than fifty articles and papers exploring the philosophy and ethics of communication, as well as three books, *Dialogic Education: Conversation About Ideas and Between Persons, Communication and Community: Implications of Martin Buber's Dialogue,* and *Dwell in Peace: Applying Nonviolence to Everyday Relationships.* He has chaired the Department of Communication and Rhetorical Studies at Marquette University and served as Dean/Vice-President of Academic Affairs and Professor of Communication at Manchester College. Professor Arnett received the 1988 Book Award and the 1979 Article of the Year Award from the Religious Speech Communication Association, and has edited the *Journal of Communication and Religion.*

About the Contributors

William Barrett is one of the foremost scholarly interpreters of existential philosophy in the twentieth century, and author of such classic studies as *Irrational Man*, *The Illusion of Technique*, and *Time of Need*.

Mary Field Belenky is affiliated with Listening Partners, a program of the University of Vermont. The research project she coordinated resulted in the recent nonfiction bestseller, *Women's Ways of Knowing: The Development of Self, Voice, and Mind*.

Charles T. Brown is Professor Emeritus of Communication at Western Michigan University, and the author or coauthor of a number of humanistic books in communication, including *Speech and Man* and *Monologue to Dialogue*.

Martin Buber was perhaps the world's most noted philosopher of dialogue before his death in 1965, and the author of many classic books, including *I and Thou*, *The Knowledge of Man*, and *Between Man and Man*.

Robert Cathcart is a Professor of Communication Arts and Sciences at Queens College of the City University of New York; he has written extensively on the relationships among interpersonal communication, cultural influences, and the media. Among other publications, he coedited *Inter/Media: Interpersonal Communication in a Media World*.

Blythe McVicker Clinchy is a Professor of Psychology at Wellesley College, and coauthor of *Women's Ways of Knowing*.

Charles Derber is a Professor of Sociology at Boston College and the author of *The Pursuit of Attention*, an analysis of individualism and narcissism in American conversation.

Jacques Ellul recently retired as Professor of Law and the Sociology and History of Institutions at the University of Bordeaux, France, and is the author of over thirty books, including the influential *The Technological Society*.

Caryl Emerson, a leading authority on Russian literary theorist Mikhail Bakhtin, teaches Russian literature at Cornell University. She coauthored a recent scholarly analysis of Bakhtin's work, *Mikhail Bakhtin: Creation of a Prosaics*.

Walter R. Fisher is Professor of Communication Arts and Sciences at the University of Southern California, and the author of many works in rhetoric and narrative theory, including *Human Communication as Narration: Toward a Philosophy of Reason, Value, and Action*.

Paulo Freire is a Brazilian educator and social activist whose dialogic approach to learning is most clearly articulated in *Pedagogy of the Oppressed* and his more recent conversations with Ira Shor, *A Pedagogy for Liberation: Dialogues for Transforming Education*.

Maurice Friedman is Professor Emeritus of Religious Studies, Philosophy, and Comparative Literature at San Diego State University, and the author of the definitive three volume biography *Martin Buber's Life and Work*, as well as *Touchstones of Reality* and many other books in existential philosophy and psychotherapy.

Hans-Georg Gadamer is a German scholar whose studies of hermeneutics are discussed and admired world-wide. He is the author of *Truth and Method*, the central text of contemporary philosophical hermeneutics, as well as *Reason in the Age of Science* and other important works.

Carol Gilligan is Professor of Education at Harvard University, and the author of the foremost contemporary study of the development of women's ethical experience, *In a Different Voice*.

Nancy Rule Goldberger is a faculty member at The Fielding Institute at Santa Barbara, California, and coauthor of *Women's Ways of Knowing*.

H.L. Goodall, Jr. is Professor of Communication at Clemson University, and the author of a variety of books in organizational communication and interpersonal theory, including *Casing a Promised Land: The Autobiography of an Organizational Detective as Cultural Ethnographer* and *Living in the Rock N Roll Mystery: Reading Context, Self, and Others as Clues*.

Gary Gumpert recently retired as Professor of Communication Arts and Sciences at Queens College of the City University of New York. He is the author of *Talking Tombstones and Other Tales of the Media Age*, and the co-editor of *Inter/Media: Interpersonal Communication in the Media World*.

Stanley Hauerwas is Professor of Philosophy at Duke University, a prominent Christian ethicist and pacifist, and author of *A Community of Character*, among other works.

Don Ihde is Professor of Philosophy at the State University of New York at Stony Brook, and the author of many books and articles in phenomenology, including *Listening and Voice* and *Sense and Significance*.

Abraham Kaplan is Professor Emeritus of Philosophy at the University of Haifa, Israel, and the author or coauthor of such well-known works in the human sciences as *The Conduct of Inquiry* and *Power and Society*.

Paul W. Keller is Professor Emeritus of Communication at Manchester College, and author or coauthor of numerous works exploring the ethical dimensions of interpersonal communication, including *Monologue to Dialogue*.

R.D. Laing was one of the world's most famous and controversial psychiatrists, and author of such notable books as *The Politics of Experience, Self and Others*, and *The Divided Self.*

Alasdair MacIntyre is Professor of Philosophy at Vanderbilt University; his *After Virtue* is one of the most widely cited contemporary books on ethics, and he has written or edited a variety of other scholarly works.

Thomas Merton, a theologian, poet, and Trappist monk, was one of the most important Catholic writers of the century before his death in 1968. His most famous works include *The Seven Storey Mountain* and *New Seeds of Contemplation*.

Joshua Meyrowitz is Professor of Communication at the University of New Hampshire, and author of one of the most highly praised books on media theory in recent years, *No Sense of Place: The Impact of Electronic Media on Social Behavior.*

Nel Noddings is Professor and Associate Dean in the School of Education at Stanford University, and the author of one of the most important recent contributions to ethical theory, *Caring: A Feminine Approach to Ethics and Moral Education.*

Carl R. Rogers developed "client-centered therapy" and the "person-centered approach" to interpersonal relations, and was one of the most famous and influential American psychologists before his death in 1987. He wrote such classic works as *A Way of Being* and *On Becoming a Person*.

John Stewart is Associate Professor of Communication at the University of Washington, and one of the foremost scholars of dialogue in the field of communication. His texts *Bridges Not Walls* and *Together: Communicating Interpersonally* have influenced thousands of communication students for over two decades.

Jill Mattuck Tarule is a Professor of Clinical Psychology at the Lesley College Graduate School, and coauthor of *Women's Ways of Knowing*.

■ INTRODUCTION

Dialogue probably is the most noble form of human interaction and communication scholars should be the first to appreciate its outstanding human qualities.

—*Klaus Krippendorff (1989, p. 94)*

Daily newspapers, whether reporting wars, riots, or school board meetings, indicate how consistently we miss each other as persons. We often miss the others' intentions, misjudging their identities, mishearing their words, misstating their positions. We fail to meet our neighbors and then say we miss them when they leave. The irony is that we missed them so often when they were present.

Dialogue now is offered seemingly everywhere as an antidote to impersonal forces in a complex technologized world. Whereas *communication* has until recently served as the central god-term of contemporary popular culture ("We need more communication in our company"; "Reagan was The Great Communicator"; "What we have here is a failure to communicate"), *dialogue* may be supplanting it in the faith of cultural optimists and sunny thinkers of all persuasions. When rival youth gangs are unable to stop killing each other, or when labor and management leave the table angrily, someone will suggest "more dialogue." Marriages and families in trouble may be salvaged, people hope, by workshops in "dialoguing skills."

What most people probably mean when calling for more dialogue is that they want more understanding of the side of the issue they favor. They want better listening from the other person and more acceptance of their own arguments. At the very least, they hope that dialogue can calm things down, reduce the threat, and provide a cooling-off period from verbal or physical hostilities. Most people tend to think of dialogue tactically,

1

in other words, in terms of results it can produce. Although dialogue's results are not insignificant, they are also not automatic, or even predictable. Neither will they be the prime focus of this book. Ours is not a warm fuzzy appeal for everyday communicators to be more friendly, open, humane, or sensitive; rather, it is a serious attempt to define the concept itself and to indicate some basic sources—philosophical, theoretical, and practical—that can illuminate dialogue's potential and its limitations.

Dialogue is a dimension of communication quality that keeps communicators more focused on mutuality and relationship than on self-interest, more concerned with discovering than with disclosing, more interested in access than in domination. David Bohm (1985), a professor of theoretical physics at the University of London, reflected on what he learned at an interdisciplinary conference devoted to his work:

> In the beginning, people were expressing fixed positions, which they were tending to defend, but later it became clear that to maintain the feeling of friendship in the group was much more important than to hold any position. Such friendship has an impersonal quality in the sense that its establishment does not depend on a close personal relationship between participants. A new kind of mind thus begins to come into being which is based on the development of a common meaning that is constantly transforming in the process of the dialogue. People are no longer primarily in opposition, nor can they be said to be interacting, rather they are participating in this pool of common meaning which is capable of constant development and change. In this development the group has no pre-established purpose, though at each moment a purpose that is free to change may reveal itself. The group thus begins to engage in a new dynamic relationship in which no speaker is excluded, and in which no particular content is excluded. (p. 175)

Bohm's succinct commentary provides a kind of operational definition of human dialogue in general. At once practical and theoretically suggestive, Bohm's summary of one specific meeting would serve well as an introduction to any group process text, any organizational improvement manual, or any community action tract.

Although dialogue appears to be a fundamental process-quality of understanding and immediacy, communication scholars have tended to deemphasize its study in favor of other behavioral (i.e., rules and competency) and cognitive (i.e., constructivist) approaches. This relative neglect is partly attributable, perhaps, to the fact that introductory materials designed for scholars and students are almost nonexistent, so the dialogic arena charted by such philosophers and critics as Buber, Gadamer, and Bakhtin can appear to new readers to be vast, dense, murky, and intimidating. Perhaps for others the study of dialogue has suffered from being misidentified with so-called "soft" human potential technologies of the 1960s.

The Reach of Dialogue, although scholarly in intent and scope, collects and integrates readings that presume no prior expertise in philosophical or social science concepts beyond what would be expected normally of advanced students in communication or allied fields. We have written three conceptual chapters relating dialogic concepts respectively to scholarship in interpersonal communication, to mass communication, and to ongoing communication issues of ethical and social concern. In addition, we introduce chapters with a series of brief linking essays to highlight central questions and issues.

Although a book introducing the philosophical and conceptual dimensions of dialogue must undoubtedly be ambitious, we had to limit that ambition. In order to introduce the reach of dialogue, by which we mean both its conceptual scope and its potential contribution to the human sciences, we must be focused enough, even choosy enough, not to overreach. Therefore, we chose to concentrate on defining and delineating dialogue rather than survey its myriad applications in various occupations and research areas. Our approach undoubtedly means that we will de-emphasize some people's favorite scholars or studies. For example, we purposely do not place in center stage the dialogic concerns of such influential political theorists as Habermas (1984), Fishkin (1991, 1992), or Young (1990); of such scientists as Bohm (1980, 1985) or Lynch (1985); or of such cross-cultural theorists as Tedlock (1983) or Tyler (1987). We recommend these (and other) works, but cannot cover the full territory here. Similarly, the concept of dialogue has also been influential in theology (Howe, 1963), composition (Clark 1990) and the arts (John-Steiner, 1985/1987; Richards, 1964), feminist philosophy (Benhabib, 1992); and organizational theory (Senge, 1990) in ways that cannot be fully explored in the limited space of this volume.

We have chosen instead to map the central part of the landscape of dialogic concepts especially relevant to communication theory. *The Reach of Dialogue* is divided into three major parts: "Invitation to Dialogue," which emphasizes basic definitions, limitations, and the centrality of the concept of confirmation; "The Arena of Dialogue," which stresses the concept of voice in examining—in somewhat arbitrary order—the relational, technological, and self "regions" of dialogue; and "The Trust of Dialogue," which explores the emerging concern for community. In each, the notions of such prominent theorists as Buber, Gadamer, Noddings, Rogers, Gilligan, and MacIntyre are connected by their common concern for communication and by integrative chapters written especially for this book.

Beyond defining dialogue, *The Reach of Dialogue* makes two other fundamental contributions. First, we help to extend the study of dialogue into two areas not usually associated with it: (a) the new electronic media that in many quarters are feared (often unreasonably) to be robbing humanity of a sense of presence, thus creating mass anonymity; and (b) the central role played by dialogue in the definition of self. In this latter issue, we go beyond the familiar Meadean symbolic interactionist position that selves are formed and constructed through social influences; contributions of phenomenologists and the literary theories of Bakhtin are helpful in describing how dialogue in a technologically sophisticated culture depends on different forms of self-presence.

Our second major contribution is to suggest that trust is a conceptually interesting and crucial aspect of communication, not just a feelgood term for what happens when persons experience warm and sensitive intimacy. In the final minutes of a conference on dialogue, one of the speakers was asked a simple, yet very significant, question. "If you had only one ingredient that you could give another that might invite dialogue, what would it be?" After what seemed a long pause, the response came—"the courage to trust." Maurice Friedman (1974) brought trust and courage together as companions:

> Existential trust does not mean trust *in* existence as being constituted in one particular way. It cannot be attained by "positive thinking," and it does not lead to "peace of mind" or "peace of soul." It is not inconsonant with pain, grief, anxiety, and least of all with vulnerability. Where it does not exist, one no longer goes forth to meet others. (p. 330)

Friedman's insights are revisited in Bellah, Madsen, Sullivan, Swidler, and Tipton's *The Good Society* (1991), in which trust is shown as fundamental to the health of persons, groups, and institutions.

The invitation of trust is seldom easy, but in a time of perceived limits it may be even more demanding. In addition to recognizing the natural resource limits and fiscal restrictions that plague our contemporary society, there is yet another limited resource—trust between persons. Trust is not easy to invite, maintain, or strengthen under good conditions, but in a time of increasing crime, unemployment, and stirring of generational and cultural strife, such a task is indeed demanding.

Our contention that trust is a foundation for dialogue provides a countercurrent to the narcissism encouraged by much of the material culture, and a countercurrent to the cynicism that doubts that significant social change can come from the cooperation and concerted action of common people. One of our undergraduate professors was fond of saying, "Life is great, YEA!" What made his otherwise simplistic message powerful during the divisive years of the Vietnam War was his willingness to look opposition in the eye, work against policies he abhorred, and simultaneously radiate trust that life is worth living.

The call for trust is far from an unknowing plea for naivete. There are times in which all human beings should and must distrust. The

20th century has provided too many examples that verify the legitimate basis for distrust, from the Holocaust, to the McCarthy era, to the savings-and-loan scandals, to the abuse of children by their parents, teachers, and clergy. Yet without the enabling functions of realistic existential trust, how will we ever allow sincere others the opportunity to make a difference in our lives? How, indeed, can we ever hope to make a difference ourselves?

In a profound sense, studying the dynamics of dialogue could provide the realistic alternative to the "hit-or-miss" theory of human relationships and social organization. Must we have violence, force, coercion, or threat ("hit") to maintain social order? Or, in rejecting violence, must we settle for isolation, anonymity, and weakness leading to estrangement, alienation, and mis-meeting ("miss")? Dialogue, in challenging us to refuse both hitting and missing, is an alternative through which human existence can be confirmed, voiced, and experienced in community.

REFERENCES

Bellah, R. N., Madsen, R., Sullivan, W. M., Swidler, A., & Tipton, S. M. (1991). *The good society.* New York: Alfred A. Knopf.

Benhabib, S. (1992). *Situating the self: Gender, community and postmodernism in contemporary ethics.* New York: Routledge.

Bohm, D. (1980). *Wholeness and the implicate order.* London: Routledge & Kegan Paul.

Bohm, D. (1985). *Unfolding meaning: A weekend of dialogue with David Bohm.* London: Ark.

Clark, G. (1990). *Dialogue, dialectic, and conversation: A social perspective on the function of writing.* Carbondale: Southern Illinois University Press.

Fishkin, J. S. (1991). *Democracy and deliberation: New directions for democratic reform.* New Haven, CT: Yale University Press.

Fishkin, J. S. (1992). *The dialogue of justice: Toward a self-reflective society.* New Haven, CT: Yale University Press.

Friedman, M. (1974). *Touchstones of reality: Existential trust and the community of peace.* New York: E.P. Dutton.

Habermas, J. (1984). *The theory of communicative action. Vol. 1: Reason and the rationalization of society* (T. McCarthy, Trans.). Boston: Beacon Press.

Howe, R. L. (1963). *The miracle of dialogue.* New York: The Seabury Press.

John-Steiner, V. (1987). *Notebooks of the mind: Explorations of thinking.* New York: Perennial Library. (Original work published 1985)

Krippendorff, K. (1989). On the ethics of constructing communication. In B. Dervin, L. Grossberg, B. J. O'Keefe, & E. Wartella (Eds.), *Rethinking communication. Vol. 1: Paradigm issues* (pp. 66-96). Newbury Park, CA: Sage.

Lynch, J. J. (1985). *The language of the heart: The human body in dialogue.* New York: Basic Books.

Richards, M. C. (1964). *Centering: In pottery, poetry, and the person.* Middletown, CT: Wesleyan University Press.

Senge, P. M. (1990). *The fifth discipline: The art and practice of the learning organization.* New York: Doubleday.

Tedlock, D. (1983). *The spoken word and the work of interpretation.* Philadelphia: University of Pennsylvania Press.

Tyler, S. A. (1987). *The unspeakable: Discourse, dialogue, and rhetoric in the postmodern world.* Madison: University of Wisconsin Press.

Young, I. M. (1990). *Justice and the politics of difference.* Princeton, NJ: Princeton University Press.

■ PART ONE

Invitation to Dialogue

■ 1

Communication and the Ground of Dialogue

Kenneth N. Cissna
University of South Florida

Rob Anderson
Saint Louis University

When people are in communion, when they are in this narrow sense really communicating with one another, the content of what is being communicated does not exist prior to and independently of that particular context. There is no message, except in a post-hoc reconstruction, which is fixed and complete beforehand. If I am really talking with you, I have nothing to say; what I say arises as you and I genuinely relate to one another. I do not know beforehand who I will be, because I am open to you just as you are open to me. This, I think, is what makes growth possible among human beings, and why it seems to me impossible really to teach unless you are learning; why you cannot really talk unless you are listening. You are listening not only to the other, you are listening to yourself. Indeed, in a fundamental sense—I would say in quite a literal sense—self and other are now so intertwined that we need new conceptual frameworks, new categories to describe what is happening.

—Abraham Kaplan (1969, p. 98)

On May 28th, 1975, Richard Farson served as the moderator of what the participants called a public "dialogue" between two beacons of California intellectual life, psychotherapist Carl Rogers and University of California anthropologist and regent Gregory Bateson. In introducing their conversation to the audience, Farson reported that on the way to the event he asked Bateson, "How will we know whether or not we have done our job tonight?" Bateson responded, "If either Carl or I says something that we haven't said before, we'll know that it's a success" (Kirschenbaum & Henderson, 1989, p. 185).

Dialogue implies more than a simple back-and-forthness of messages in interaction; it points to a particular process and quality of communication in which the participants "meet," which allows for changing and being changed. In dialogue, we do not know exactly what we are going to say, and we can surprise not only the other but even ourselves because we may say something, as Bateson put it, "we haven't said [or even thought] before."

TRADITIONS OF DIALOGUE

Although many different contributors to dialogue have been studied by communication scholars, most of our attention (e.g., Anderson, 1982; Arnett, 1981, 1986, 1989; Clark, 1973; Johannesen, 1971; Stewart, 1978, 1985) has focused—justifiably—on the implications of the philosophy of Martin Buber (e.g., 1965a, 1965b). For example, Johannesen (1990) acknowledged that his recent list of the characteristics of dialogue was based primarily on Buber's conceptions. Not all scholars of dialogue stress Buber's conceptual primacy. For example, when Stewart (1985) presented a paper at an international interdisciplinary conference on dialogue, he discovered that his was the only one in which Buber was a central focus.

In an effort to provide conceptual organization, we risk some oversimplification in identifying four relatively distinct but not unrelated conceptions of dialogue that co-exist in contemporary literature on this subject. One, derived from the writings of Buber and similarly minded philosophers, theologians, and psychotherapists, conceives of dialogue as a form of human meeting or relationship. A second, based on the work of conversation analysts, ethnomethodologists, and others, uses dialogue to refer to the intricacies of human conversation. A third, derived largely from the work of Mikhail Bakhtin and his contemporary interpreters, views dialogue primarily as a cultural form of human knowing. Finally, a fourth conception of dialogue can be traced to Hans-Georg Gadamer's philosophy of textual understanding and interpretation. The brief discussion that follows is intended to be more representative than comprehensive. A thorough analysis of the history of various conceptions of dialogue, their interpenetration and divergences, goes well beyond the scope and intent of either this chapter or this volume.[1]

---

[1]See Dascal (1985, pp. 1-8) and Maranhao (1990, pp. 1-22) for other discussions of the various conceptions of dialogue and Buber (1965a, pp. 209- 224) for a

First, Matson and Montagu's (1967) seminal volume, *The Human Dialogue*, is perhaps the earliest systematic attempt to represent dialogue as a form of communication or relationship. Drawing heavily on Buber, they viewed dialogue as a transactional process concerned with the development of self, the knowing of other, and the formation of human relationships, and contrasted it with a monologic representation that conceived of communication as a linear, transmission-focused process, the aim of which was largely control. "There is genuine dialogue—no matter whether spoken or silent—where each of the participants really has in mind the other or others in their present and particular beings and turns to them with the intention of establishing a living mutual relation between himself and them" (Buber, 1965a, p. 19). Dialogue, as Matson and Montagu describe it, is not so much a "phenomenological report of things as they are" but a "task to be achieved" (p. 8). In addition to the work within the communication field referred to earlier (see also Cissna & Anderson, 1990), recent authors such as Mendes-Flohr (1989) and Friedman (1955, 1985, 1986) represent this stream of thought.

Second, a number of recent volumes use the term dialogue to denote human conversation. For example, Markova and Foppa (1990) define dialogue as "face-to-face interaction between two or more persons using a system of signs" (p. 1). As they describe it, dialogue is a "result of interaction, in temporal and spatial *immediacy*, between two or more participants who face each other and who are intentionally conscious of, and orientated towards, each other in an act of communication" (p. 6). Similarly, Tannen's (1989) use of the term dialogue in the subtitle of her recent *Talking Voices: Repetition, Dialogue, and Imagery in Conversational Discourse* also connotes conversation, whether in ordinary or literary discourse. In recent years, communication scholars have devoted considerable attention to conversation (e.g., Beach, 1989; Craig & Tracy, 1983; Hopper, 1992; McLaughlin, 1984; Nofsinger, 1991). Focusing on such microscopic details of conversation as how turn-taking is arranged, how breaches in conversational etiquette are repaired, how telephone greetings are managed, and so on, those operating in this tradition do not always emphasize that these conversational intricacies are the fabric of human meeting.

---

review of the intellectual history of the dialogical principle. Dascal's anthology, explicitly described as "interdisciplinary," represents all of the conceptions of dialogue identified here. We could have identified additional conceptions to those we have mentioned. Most prominently, we might have distinguished a theological conception representing Jaspers, Howe, Tournier, Tillich, Marcel, and others. We have chosen to emphasize the similarities among Buber and others writing about human meeting or relationship and these authors, although we recognize others would choose differently. We also might have included the work of such contemporary philosophers as Jurgen Habermas and Richard Rorty, although we see dialogue as less central in their work.

A third conception of dialogue is represented by a number of contemporary interpreters of Bakhtin (see especially 1984, 1986) including, among others, Todorov (1984) and Schultz (1990). Holquist (1990) used the term *dialogism*, and Maranhao (1990) called dialogue an *antiepistemology* that will provide "a framework for rethinking knowledge" (p. 2).

Bakhtin (1984) was interested in the study of language, extending well beyond grammar and related concerns, and emphasizing "discourse," which he called "language in its concrete living totality" (p. 182). But as Schultz (1990) observed, "Once one paid attention to discourse, language-in-the-concrete, one could not avoid recognizing that such language involves using words in utterances, that is, to address other people and to respond to them in specific, unrepeatable contexts" (p. 21). Thus, as Schultz concluded, the study of human discourse becomes a study of dialogical relationships. To Bakhtin, dialogue is not exactly an attainment or communicative achievement; rather, it is a characteristic of human language itself.

Bakhtin (1986) used the term dialogue in several interrelated senses. What he called "everyday dialogue," "actual dialogue," or "real-life dialogue" refers to ordinary or everyday conversation in which two people speak with one another at whatever length, alternating speaking opportunities. He called this "the simplest and most classic form of speech communication" (p. 75). But dialogue, for Bakhtin, can also refer to less immediate encounters, as when, for example, a series of scholarly papers dealing with a particular topic published over a number of years by various authors constitutes a dialogue. So, dialogue is characterized not merely by the alternation of communication roles, but also by the way in which in dialogue the other is incorporated within one's utterance. "The utterance is addressed not only to its own object, but also to others' speech about it. . . . Even the slightest allusion to another's utterance gives the speech a dialogic turn" (Bakhtin, 1986, p. 94). What he called "dialogic reverberations" arise not only because "an utterance is a link in the chain of speech communication, and . . . cannot be broken off from the preceding links," but because "the utterance is related also . . . to subsequent links in the chain of speech communication" (p. 94).

A fourth conception of dialogue can be found in the work of Gadamer (1982) and a number of other primarily European scholars interested in hermeneutics and textual analysis (see Michelfelder & Palmer, 1989). Dialogue, for Gadamer, describes the relationship between interpreter and text and represents a mode of thinking and of questioning (Stewart, 1986). Warnke (1987) saw Gadamer's central work, *Truth and Method*, as "an attempt to resuscitate a dialogic conception of knowledge" (p. 4). Knowledge, in this view, becomes a developmental process of questioning positions, a process that presumes both an historical positioning and an immersion in a particular tradition. The analogue for this process of understanding (*verstehen*) is dialogic conversation:

Just as the conclusion of a genuine conversation is not the sole property of either one of the dialogue-partners, the outcome of *Verstehen* is neither our own property, the result of the dominance of our prejudice, or the property of the tradition, the result of its dominance. Instead, just as in conversation, the result is a unity or argument that goes beyond the original position of the various participants; indeed, the consensus that emerges in understanding represents a new view and hence a new stage of the tradition. (Warnke, 1987, p. 104; see also Gadamer, 1982; Palmer, 1969, pp. 194- 217)

These conceptions are not entirely unrelated, nor are the streams of intellectual influence pure and distinct. For example, as far as we know, Buber was not influenced by Bakhtin, although the Russian had an early introduction to Buber's writing (Clark & Holquist, 1984, p. 27) and held it in high regard (Todorov, 1984, p. 116). Still, as Matson and Montagu (1967) make clear, the theory of communication underlying a dialogic conception of relationship represents a way of understanding the world, in particular the world of other selves as well as one's self. Gadamer said he knew Buber well and was quite familiar with Buber's work (Stewart, 1986), and Stewart discussed both similarities (1985) and differences (1986) in their thought. In addition, although the literature on dialogue as conversation owes a significant debt to Bakhtin, we are convinced that significant work on conversation can be conducted within a Buberian conception of dialogue.

CHARACTERISTICS OF DIALOGUE

In this section, we briefly describe the basic characteristics of dialogue as we use the term in this volume. Although our debt to Buber and his interpreters is apparent, the conception of dialogue that we develop encompasses a broader synthesis of dialogue's basic characteristics than is often found within this tradition, merging all four of the traditions just identified with our ideas. Although not all of the authors who appear in this volume would subscribe equally to all of these characteristics, these features do point to our central phenomenon. We rely on these features of dialogue as our analysis proceeds, both in this and subsequent chapters, in our effort to provide the wider conceptual framework that we believe dialogue requires.

1. *Immediacy of presence.* To be present is simply to be available and to be relatively uninterested in orchestrating specific outcomes or consequences. Immediacy of presence suggests both the "now" and the "here" dimensions of communication. *Now* recognizes that the present is neither past nor future, whereas *here*

notes presence as a placement in space. Dialogue presumes that participants create communication that is, to a large extent, unscripted and unrehearsed. We should note, however, that in some situations, close familiarity with the discipline of a script or close rehearsal could free participants to interact more creatively. Comedy troupes such as "Second City," jazz musicians, and even basketball players typically understand this relationship between discipline and creativity.

2. *Emergent unanticipated consequences.* The condition of dialogue produces communication that cannot fully be predicted. Dialogue is fundamentally improvisational and independent of the will of any participant. Eisenberg (1990) referred to this quality as well as to the immediacy of presence in his discussion of communication as "jamming."

3. *Recognition of "strange otherness."* Dialogue results when participants refuse to assume that they already know the thoughts, feelings, intentions, or best behaviors of the other. Although the dialogue partner may be a lifelong friend, one is willing to be surprised by the fundamental strangeness—the unfamiliarity— of a position that is not one's own. Each person knows that I am not you and that you are not me. Partners in dialogue imaginatively infer realities and perspectives that are not their own and communicate such interpretations tentatively. Perspectival flexibility—ideally from both sides—characterizes dialogue.

4. *Collaborative orientation.* Dialogue is characterized by high levels of concern for self (and one's own position) as well as for the other (and for the position advanced by the other). Contrary to some popular conceptions, dialogue does not preclude heated or even agonistic exchange. It does, however, presume sincere caring about the future of the other, the relationship, and the joint project of sense-making, rather than a primary focus on just winning or losing. In dialogue, one must stand up for one's self and one must care about the other.

5. *Vulnerability.* Dialogue involves risk. Participants not only expose their ideas to the scrutiny of another, they open themselves to the other's ideas and hence to the possibility of being changed. In dialogue, we are willing to emerge from the encounter as different persons. Neither ego protection nor protected ideas are the means or goals of dialogue; persons are willing to change their minds, to be persuaded.

6. *Mutual implication.* In dialogue, each speaker anticipates a listener or respondent and incorporates him or her into one's utterances. In interpreting another's utterance, then, a partici-

pant will "find," in addition to "other" and "message," something of *self* as well. Hence, dialogue is a process in which speaker and listener interdepend, each constructing self, other, and their talk simultaneously. Even when one person seems to be the sole speaker, polyphonic "voices" of others remain interwoven with the primary voice.

7. *Temporal flow.* Dialogue, like its companion concept, conversation, presumes an historical continuity. Dialogue emerges from a past, fills the immediate present (and thus is experienced as "wide," "deep," "immersing," or "enveloping" by participants), and anticipates and prefigures an open future. Dialogue is a process, within which segments cannot be entirely isolated and separately analyzed.

8. *Genuineness and authenticity.* Within dialogue, participants assume that the other is speaking from experienced—not hypothetical, self-consciously strategic, fantasized, or deceptive—positions. The ground of dialogue is the presumption of honesty, even though psychological congruence cannot be verified. The presumption of honesty does not imply that we can or should tell all our thoughts and feelings to anyone who will listen, but that in dialogue, to use Roger's terms, significant and persistent thoughts and feelings relevant to the relationship are not deliberately hidden (see Cissna & Anderson, 1990, p. 135). Buber called it "being" rather than "seeming," which Friedman (1983) explains as follows: "The person dominated by being gives himself to the other spontaneously without thinking about the image of himself awakened in the beholder. The seeming person, in contrast, is primarily concerned with what the other thinks of him, and produces a look calculated to make himself appear 'spontaneous,' 'sincere,' or whatever he thinks will win the other's approval" (p. 7). In each dialogic situation, of course, interactants allow the other the benefit of the doubt and do not set out to discover that the other is inauthentic.

In summary, dialogue emerges as an issue concerning the quality of relationship between or among two or more people and of the communicative acts that create and sustain that relationship. It reflects the attitudes participants bring to an encounter, the ways they talk and act toward one another, the consequences of meeting, and the larger context within which dialogue occurs. Concerning, as it does, appropriate and desirable behavior toward others, discussions of dialogue inevitably involve ethical and moral concerns. Although dialogue might appear to some to be entirely either a private or a dyadic activity, in subsequent chapters we show that dialogue also operates in the public realm and at the level of community.

In the remainder of this chapter, we first introduce the concept of self, which is integral to any consideration of dialogue. Then we turn our attention to two characteristics of American culture that may preclude the emergence of dialogue. Finally, we consider the relationship between confirmation and dialogue.

DIALOGUE AND THE SELF

When we talk about communication and dialogue, we must talk about the self. Yet, no subject is more slippery, and after 2,000 years of philosophical inquiry and 150 years of social science scholarship no one has offered a conception of the self that seems altogether satisfying and coherent. We know that the self is a social construction; we are not born with a self. Our selves are talked into being through our relationships with what Mead (1934) called "significant others"—initially our parents. Just as we reject an entirely monadic and individual conception of the self, we cannot accept an entirely social model in its place. Human beings, even human infants, are not some variety of sponge, soaking up whatever self-definitions might spill our way. And, although the self is a social construction, one in which other people—and hence, our society, our culture—are completely involved, we also know that the self is unique, individual. We find ourselves closest to Friedman (1974) who described the "partnership of existence" in which "we become our selves *with* one another" (p. 304). "Paradoxically," Friedman said, "we only know ourselves when we know ourselves in responding to others" (p. 305).

But we do not, and cannot, know in advance who we will be, because who we are arises only in response to concrete situations and circumstances. As Kaplan put it in the quotation that opened this chapter, we have nothing to say, we do not know who we are, in advance of the situation in which we confront another. If self were fixed or possessed this would not be a problem: We would be who we are. And often in interpersonal relationships this is the case. We are not open to the world, and we have decided in advance who we are and how we wish to be seen. In some encounters, we set out to accomplish a strategic goal or to engage in "image control" or "impression management." In other cases, we enact the very useful social rituals and roles that characterize a society, organization, group, or relationship. Sometimes, even more simply, we seek only to get through the day unscathed. In each case, we typically respond out of routine and habit, and we know who we are and more or less what we will say. But occasionally we are more "open" or "present," and we find ourselves with a similarly open or present other. And although this is not necessarily an accident, it cannot be "willed" either. Dialogue may result—a conversation in which we may say something we never said before (or hear something we never heard said before), a conversation from which self or other may be irrevocably changed.

CULTURAL CONSTRAINTS ON DIALOGUE

At least two characteristics of the dominant American[2] culture work against the development of dialogue. We recognize that we are discussing here a white male perspective in Western culture, and we are confident that some Western women and some Western people of color have internalized these cultural dimensions less or differently—but then these do not apply universally to white males either, and concerns for dialogue are at some distance from the central concerns of our society. Other cultures, too, have their problems and deserve similar analyses with respect to their impact on interpersonal relationships and opportunities for dialogue. Still, our analysis focuses on the predominant American culture. We examine, first, the preeminent American value of individualism and its interactional extension, conversational narcissism. Then we consider our pragmatic values and our related tendency to look to techniques to manage virtually all problems, including human relationships. Both conversational narcissism and our tendency to rely on techniques constrain our opportunities to enter into dialogue.

Individualism and Conversational Narcissism

The American commitment to individualism has been well reviewed recently by Bellah and his colleagues (Bellah, Madsen, Sullivan, Swidler, & Tipton, 1985). If one believes that the individual is the greatest good and that which enhances the individual is of the greatest value, then such a person may be unable (or unwilling) to develop the respect for the other that characterizes a dialogic perspective. In dialogue, we view the other as a *person*, rather than as a thing or object. Stewart (1985) identified three distinctions in Buber's thought between being and becoming,

---

[2]We use the term *American* largely for its convenience in the adjectival form. We recognize that many nations—and societies and cultures—exist in the Americas, but also note that only the United States of America has incorporated the continental location in its name. Furthermore, although our focus is primarily on United States society, American culture has spread far beyond the national borders of the United States, and it is to the manifestations of that culture, wherever they are found, that we refer.

on the one hand, and alternatively, experiencing others as things and objective events:

1. Seeing the other as unique, rather than as an interchangeable part of an event—recognizing "some of what distinguishes *you* from all other clients, friends, or loved ones" (p. 324);
2. Encountering the unmeasurable aspects of the other, especially feelings and emotions, and contacting the other as a dynamic being who is continually in process, rather than as a finite, measurable entity; and
3. Perceiving the other as a choice-maker, who initiates action, rather than simply as a reactor, who simply participates in motion.

Still, dialogue seems to presume some form of individualism; in order to think of self and other meeting in dialogue, we must be capable of thinking in such terms as "self" and "other." Both dialogue and individualism are essentially modern phenomena. Baumeister (1987) showed that the idea of self developed in Western cultures historically from the early modern age (roughly 1500 to 1800) to the present. "A careful look at historical evidence suggests . . . that the concern with problems of selfhood is essentially a modern phenomenon. The medieval lords and serfs did not struggle with self-definition the way modern persons do" (p. 163). Buber (1965a) began his chronological review of "the history of the dialogical principle" (pp. 209-224) with a consideration of several 18th century authors, a period in Baumeister's history during which the relation of self to society emerged as an issue or problem. But more than one kind of individualism is possible. As Friedman (1974) said, "while we are unique persons, we are not so in the sense of nineteenth century American individualism" (p. 305).

Edward Sampson (1985, 1988) has considered the conception of the individual that inheres in the American culture. What Friedman referred to as 19th-century American individualism, Sampson (1988) called "self-contained individualism." Self-contained individualism sees sharp boundaries between the self and what is not-self, locates control within the person, and excludes other people from the region we call self. Although Americans tend to think of this form of individualism as natural, not only is self-contained individualism a learned, cultural product, it is not the only possible form of individualism. Sampson also identified an "ensembled individualism," a belief system (or what he calls an "indigenous psychology") that is actually more common in most of the world and that might be more conducive to dialogue. Ensembled individualism is characterized by (a) more fluid boundaries between self and other; (b) thinking of control as residing in a field of forces that includes but extends beyond the self; and (c) including other persons within the self.

To illustrate ensembled individualism further, consider Sampson's (1988) characterization of Noddings's (1984) work on caring, which is excerpted later in this volume:

> She offered a perspective on helping others based on a definition of self-in-relation . . . . Who I am is defined in and through my relations with others; I am completed through these relations and do not exist apart from them. . . . When self is defined in relation, inclusive of others in its very definition, there is no fully separate self whose interests do not of necessity include others. (p. 20)

Such a self, whose interests include others, might be more capable of engaging in dialogue than would solely self-interested representatives of American individualism.

Individualism and dialogue are not inherently oppositional. The problem we are describing concerns the particular strand of individualism that developed in the United States. Somewhere in the evolution of our society, individualism went awry and we are now faced with ample evidence that people are searching to recapture the possibilities of dialogue, relationship, and community.

The individualism of American culture influences our talk, constraining further our opportunities for dialogue. Charles Derber (1979) used the term *conversational narcissism* to describe the "ways American conversationalists act to turn the topics of ordinary conversations to themselves without showing sustained interest in others' topics" (p. 5). Christopher Lasch (1978) provided a psychodynamic and economic explanation of the emergence of narcissism in contemporary American life. Narcissism, which, Lasch said, results from "a way of life that is dying—the culture of competitive individualism" (p. xv), in its normal forms, "appears realistically to represent the best way of coping with the tensions and anxieties of modern life, and the prevailing social conditions therefore tend to bring out narcissistic traits that are present, in varying degrees, in everyone" (p. 50). The narcissist is not interested in and devalues other people and, as a consequence, tends to form short-term relationships lacking in commitment that are "bland, superficial, and deeply unsatisfying" (p. 40). This "pervasive tendency for individuals to seek predominant attention for themselves" (p. 3) constitutes what several interpersonal communication scholars called "a pattern rooted in an American culture that supports a form of individualism that, in turn, encourages self-interest and self-absorption" (Vangelisti, Knapp, & Daly, 1990, p. 251). This is a strong indictment.

Vangelisti et al. identified four ways in which narcissistic characteristics may be manifest in conversation: (a) inflated self-importance results in a self-absorption and self-admiration that others often consider arrogant and that denies a need for other people; (b) exploitation of others is sought through strategies of deceit or manipulation; (c) exhibitionism makes oneself the constant center of attention; and (d) impersonal relationships result from the tendencies to avoid intimate contact and to protect personal space. Vangelisti et al. acknowledge that the conversational narcissist may be very skillful in certain impersonal, manipulative relationships—especially work relationships—but these conversational tendencies would be detrimental, at least, to close, personal relationships and would mitigate against the possibility of dialogue.

Derber (1979) distinguished between two ways of responding to another person in conversation—what he called *shift responses* and *support responses.* Shift responses shift the attention of the conversation to oneself ("You think your job is rough? Listen to what happened to me yesterday"). Support responses keep the attention and the topic focused on the other ("Then what happened?"). As Derber describes it, conversational narcissism underutilizes support responses and overutilizes shift responses in either active or passive ways. The active shift responses are either entirely irrelevant to the other's topic or they appear to be connected to it but are not. Jurgen Ruesch (1958) calls these *tangential* responses—ones that respond to some insignificant aspect of what the other said, ignoring the main point entirely, and shifting the focus of the conversation away from the other and his or her topic and toward the self and its preferred topic ("She had a wreck in her Ford? I hate Fords. I think their ads are obnoxious.") The passive shift-response practices involve making such minimal responses to the speech of the other that the topic and attention will also shift. Cissna and Sieburg (1981) call both of these response patterns disconfirming, and more specifically, disqualifying.

We are not claiming that narcissism or its extension in conversation are uniquely American phenomena. Obviously, there are conversational bores in every society. We do believe, however, that Americans, and those influenced by our particular brand of self-contained individualism, are particularly prone to narcissism and that these conversational patterns are a significant cultural constraint on dialogue.

Furthermore, dialogue is not the only desirable form of communication in our or any society. Not all communication can or should be dialogic. Hence, conversational narcissism may be useful in limited contexts, especially in bureaucratic institutions, which "put a premium on the manipulation of interpersonal relations" and "discourage the formation of deep personal attachments" (Lasch, 1978, p. 44). Competent communication in both personal and impersonal relationships involves and requires strategic ability and an ability to negotiate satisfactory exchanges. But dialogue also satisfies human needs and is a vital level of human communication. One person acquiescing to another's narcissism (essentially, "OK, I'll agree to talk about you") is not dialogue. Nor is an exchange of narcissism—in which we might "agree," for example, to talk about me today and you tomorrow. As an ongoing pattern of conversation, narcissism essentially precludes dialogue. That it may sometimes be useful for individuals brings us to the second of the American cultural characteristics.

Pragmatism and the Emphasis on Technique

Americans are often called pragmatic—we tend to think of utility as a value, to think in terms of means and ends, and of using tools, methods, and recipes as the means to accomplish goals. We are pragmatic in our attitudes toward things (we solve traffic problems by building new roads; we deal with changing family life with microwave ovens and instant dinners), and we tend to have a pragmatic attitude toward interpersonal relationships as well. Consider two recent columnists, writing about different issues, and from very different political positions. Ellen Goodman (1991) identified our assumptions about technology in one of her columns following the 1991 war with Iraq. She called our attention to a set of then very common remarks along the lines of: "If we can win a war in the Persian Gulf, we can . . . ." Commentators and others were providing a long list of enormous and difficult problems that also could be "solved" through technology (e.g., create decent schools to educate our children, house the homeless, or reinvigorate family life).

Charles Krauthammer (1993) discussed the child custody battle between two Hollywood celebrities, Woody Allen and Mia Farrow. A reporter had noted that testimony in the trial "focused on Woody Allen's lack of parenting skills" (p. 4). The reporter noted that Allen had admitted under oath that he did not know the names of any of his children's friends, that he had never given any of them a bath, that he had never taken any of them to the barber and did not know the name of their dentist, that he had never attended a parent-teacher conference for one of his sons, and that none of the children whose custody he was seeking had ever spent a night at his apartment. Although this may sound odd, particularly out of context, Krauthammer's point, and ours, does not concern childrearing, but the identification of these issues as a technology—in this case as an absence of "parenting skills." Krauthammer said that to interpret these qualities as a lack of parenting skills "shows how far we've gone in the belief in the mechanization of ordinary human feeling" (p. 4), seeing parenting, too, as a technology.

Observers from both the political left (Goodman) and the right (Krauthammer) recognize our fixation with technology. Educators have noted the same tendency in students, particularly as it relates to interpersonal relationships. In a recent paper, Anderson (1991) described how students often use interpersonal communication courses to seek advice on how to manage their relationships and how some interpersonal communication instructors may be all too willing to provide facile advice. Plum (1981) generalized this concern to all training programs that conceive of communication as a skill. Americans tend to think all problems yield to technological solutions.

William Barrett (1979) writing about technique and our tendency to rely on technology, defined *technique* as a "standard method" that "can be taught" or "a recipe that can be fully conveyed from one person to another" (p. 19). How does this relate to dialogue? We can be prepared for dialogue, we can have certain abilities and attitudes that will predispose us in its direction (or away from it), but dialogue cannot be willed. No standard method, no recipe, can ensure dialogue. Yet, many interpersonal communication courses teach a set of techniques or skills as though dialogue will be an outcome. One of the authors of this chapter (Cissna) spent some time as a graduate student working closely with a student of Robert Carkhuff (1969) in a series of counseling courses learning what might be called a technology for helping (Carkhuff, 1971). The training was useful, but dialogue was not its outcome.

Farson (1978) criticized the tendency in humanistic psychology to make therapies and treatment modalities into technologies. Ironically, of course, humanistic psychology developed, at least in part, in reaction to a relatively inhumane, technique-dominated behavioral psychology, and proposed to provide a more holistic and humane alternative. And yet we cannot stop inventing new tools, nor using those we have. Abraham Kaplan (1964) immortalized this tendency as the "law of the instrument" (p. 28).[3]

Farson saw how, again ironically, the efforts of probably the most famous of all the humanistic and counseling psychologists, Carl Rogers, had been misunderstood as presenting or advocating a technique:

> Although he is [often] credited with having developed a therapeutic technique, I believe that he was fundamentally describing a relationship which the therapist enters without benefit of technique, meeting the client person to person. . . . For Rogers it is the therapist's ability to come to each situation with a freshness and openness that makes these situations most human and personal. He knew that in the long run that the most important factor in therapy was the therapist's fundamental and genuine respect for the client. (Farson, 1978, p. 9)

Technique is not the answer, certainly not the sole one, in counseling and

---

[3]"In addition to the social pressures from the scientific community there is also at work a very human trait of individual scientists. I call it *the law of the instrument*, and it may be formulated as follows: Give a small boy a hammer, and he will find that everything he encounters needs pounding. It comes as no particular surprise to discover that a scientist formulates problems in a way which requires for their solution just those techniques in which he himself is especially trained" (Kaplan, 1964, p. 28).

psychotherapy; nor does it assist dialogue in everyday relations. Furthermore, the use of a technique, especially a successful one, runs the risk of eroding our respect for the other on whom the technique has been used, eventually diminishing our concept of people in general. Farson (1978) calls this the "dilemma of applied technology": "we must use it, and we must not. It can enhance us, and at the same time it can undermine us" (p. 9). And, although he described Rogers as having developed a "technique to eliminate technique," we know of no meta-antitechnique for dialogue.

In the introductory chapter to his best-selling interpersonal communication text, *Bridges Not Walls,* John Stewart (1990) contrasted utilitarian and ontological ways of thinking about interpersonal communication. If we consider interpersonal communication as an instrument or a set of techniques, he suggested, we are likely to ask what we can do with it, what rules govern its use, and how we can measure our success in accomplishing certain outcomes. On the other hand, if we think about interpersonal communication ontologically, we are led to looking at the relationship between self and other that is created in and through communication. Buber and Friedman call this *the between.*

DIALOGUE AND CONFIRMATION

The *between* refers to the region of relationship—a third entity that requires both self and other, but is more than the sum of them. Loraine Halfen Zephyr (1982) called this third entity a "spiritual child" that is produced by self and other; and, like a physical child, it depends on its parents, yet is separate from them and from their efforts to control it. It is often difficult for individually oriented Americans to consider relationships—in this region of the between that belongs to neither party—very systematically. One concept that has been used to describe the between is *confirmation.*

The significance of confirmation to human life and relationships can hardly be overstated—Buber (1965b) thought, "a society may be termed human in the measure to which its members confirm one another" and "actual humanity exists only where this capacity [confirmation] unfolds" (pp. 67, 68). Watzlawick, Beavin, and Jackson (1967) call confirmation "the greatest single factor ensuring mental development and stability that has so far emerged from our study of communication" (p. 84).

Confirmation is difficult to define and has resisted efforts to operationalize it. Confirmation involves the process through which people are "endorsed" by others, implying a recognition and acknowledgment of them in their personness (Cissna & Sieburg, 1981). The specific ways of confirming vary by person, relationship, and situation, but, in general, confirmation expresses recognition of the other's existence, acknowledges a relationship of affiliation with the other, expresses awareness of the worth or significance of the other, and accepts or endorses the validity of the other's experience (Cissna & Sieburg, 1981). Especially in our earliest days in a family, confirmation is essential to becoming a self, and disconfirmation that impairs a child's basic trust can result in psychopathology (Friedman, 1983, 1985, pp. 119-140).

Because confirmation deals with self, other, and relationship, it is fundamental to a consideration of dialogue. Although Buber did not describe his concept of confirmation in great detail, Friedman (1983, 1985) did much to develop this aspect of Buber's thought.

Friedman's extension of Buber's work identified two problems that complicate the relationship of confirmation to dialogue. First, in our desire to be confirmed, almost all of us accept a confirmation that, as Friedman (1983) says, has "strings attached" (p. 42). We accept an unspoken contract that provides adequate confirmation as long as we are a good boy or girl, student or colleague, church member or soldier. Confirmation is made conditional. As a person shapes "self" to conform to the demands of the confirmation of other(s), the genuine meeting of self and other in dialogue becomes less likely.

Second, confirmation received from one's performance of a behavior or role is significantly different from confirmation that recognizes and responds to deeper levels of one's person. Friedman (1983) called this "the tension between personal calling and social role" (pp. 51-62). If, initially in our families, we find contingent confirmation, and often receive confirmation simply for engaging in an approved role, this expectation intensifies as we move into the world of work and pursue broader social relationships. In dialogue, we become most fully ourselves, we realize ourselves most deeply, as we respond to the call of the other— and in dialogue we have not "planned" what we will say or who we will be. Yet, in most relationships we have expectations for others and they for us. We "know" who we are and who the other is; we have already accepted one of the contracts to which Friedman referred. Although we appreciate the response we receive for playing our roles well, this does not necessarily satisfy our human need for confirmation.

Porter and Cissna (1990) studied the relationship between personal and social confirmation by distinguishing between confirmation-disconfirmation and acceptance-rejection. *Acceptance-rejection* referred to the positive and negative responses to self that are stimulated by a specific behavior, role performance, accomplishment, or idea. In acceptance, the artifacts or products of persons (our ideas, behaviors, etc.) are approved of or agreed with; the opposite with rejection. *Confirmation* referred to positive responses to personhood itself, involving recognition, acknowledgement, and endorsement. *Disconfirmation* involved negative responses to personhood, particularly indifferent, disqualifying, or impervious behaviors (see Cissna & Sieburg, 1981). The researchers then created lines from a play, incorporating the various combinations of confirmation or disconfirmation and acceptance or rejection. The lines were identical except for the presence of language communicating confirmation, disconfirmation, acceptance, or rejection. They then asked several hundred people to assume the role of playwright and to write the next lines in the play. Finally, two graduate students coded the lines written by the subject-playwrights as confirming or disconfirming and as accepting or rejecting.

The results indicated that respondents could distinguish between acceptance-rejection and confirmation-disconfirmation. Not only, for example, did they add different kinds of lines to the play when the previous lines had been confirming rather than disconfirming, and accepting rather than rejecting; but they wrote different lines following confirmation and acceptance (although both were "positive" appearing conditions) and following disconfirmation and rejection (both "negative" conditions). Furthermore, the respondents seemed to attach greater significance to confirmation and disconfirmation. For example, seldom did subjects write lines that extended disconfirmation, although they often communicated rejection to the other. Disconfirmation was added systematically to the conversation only in one situation: when the other had "received" confirmation and felt confirmed by it and yet had extended disconfirmation to the person. By contrast, rejection was extended to the other far more often and under far wider circumstances. As people we are attached to our ideas and roles, and we know that others are as well. This study shows that people also recognize the heightened importance of those deeper aspects of self that reach to the ontological levels of personhood.

In his discussion of confirmation, Friedman calls the duality of being and seeming the "essential problematic of the sphere of the between" (1955, p. 85; 1983, p. 7; 1985, p. 121). The realm of seeming proceeds from how one wishes to appear to the other—one produces a look, for example, calculated to win the other's approval. In being, by contrast, one gives one's self spontaneously to the other and without straining for some particular appearance. Seeming originates, Friedman says, in our need to be confirmed and in our "desire to be confirmed falsely rather than not to be confirmed at all" (1983, p. 7; 1985, p. 121). In the realm of seeming, we know in advance precisely who we are trying to be, and we desire to call out a particular image in the other. This false or pseudoconfirmation—in which we confirm or are confirmed as a fiction—cannot contribute to dialogue or to the development of self and of other as unique human beings. Although Laing (1969) is surely right that total confirmation of one person by another is an "ideal possibility seldom realized" (p. 98), the need for confirmation—as a *person*, and not overly conditional—remains essential to all of us for the emergence of a healthy self and is fundamental to any process we call dialogue.

CONCLUSION

We find serious problems with what *dialogue* and the related term *community* have come to mean in the late 20th century. Dialogue often means that both parties talked but neither really listened—and neither really expected the other to listen. Dialogue is often thought to represent an exchange of views, and perhaps the negotiation of a mutually satisfactory compromise. And community is usually used to refer to a group that has some characteristic in common, that believes or lives, presumably at least, the same way. Friedman contrasted what he called this community of affinity or likemindedness with the community of otherness. This real community begins in a common situation, involves real caring for one another despite differences, and is manifest in genuine dialogue. Much of what today is called dialogue as well as community is a mockery of those terms.

Dialogue represents a rich and, many contemporary observers would say, rare realm of human experience. Although dialogue is frequently talked about, most people find dialogue difficult to enact or even to find. Buber believed that all situations hold dialogic possibilities. Although dialogue operates differently, and with varying constrictions, in all situations, it is always present as a potential (even if sometimes an unlikely one).

Although we hope careful readers of this book would find dialogue a more likely possibility in their lives, that is not our goal. Genuine dialogue cannot be taught, and even for skillful communicators does not happen just because one wants it to.

The obligation of students, teachers, and scholars concerned with communication and dialogue is not to attempt to master a set of skills or formulae that might, if properly applied, produce a superficial approximation of dialogue. Rather, this book seeks to enlarge our understanding of the dialogic realm and to enhance our appreciation of its significance in human affairs.

REFERENCES

Anderson, R. (1982). Phenomenological dialogue, humanistic psychology, and pseudo-walls: A response and extension. *Western Journal of Speech Communication, 46,* 344-357.

Anderson, R. (1991, November). *On promising (more than) what we can deliver: A warning about the basic course in communication.* Paper presented at the annual meeting of the Speech Communication Association, Atlanta, GA.

Arnett, R. C. (1981). Toward a phenomenological dialogue. *Western Journal of Speech Communication, 45*, 201-212.

Arnett, R. C. (1986). *Communication and community: Implications of Martin Buber's dialogue.* Carbondale: Southern Illinois University Press.

Arnett, R. C. (1989). What is dialogic communication?: Friedman's contribution and clarification. *Person-Centered Review, 4*, 42-60.

Bakhtin, M. M. (1984). *Problems of Dostoevsky's poetics* (C. Emerson, Ed. and Trans.). Minneapolis: University of Minnesota Press.

Bakhtin, M. M. (1986). *Speech genres and other late essays* (V. W. McGee, Trans; C. Emerson & M. Holquist, Eds.). Austin: University of Texas Press.

Barrett, W. (1979). *The illusion of technique: A search for meaning in a technological civilization.* Garden City, NY: Anchor Books.

Baumeister, R. F. (1987). How the self became a problem: A psychological review of historical research. *Journal of Personality and Social Psychology, 52*, 163-176.

Beach, W. A. (1989). Foreword [to special issue]: Sequential organization of conversational activities. *Western Journal of Speech Communication, 53*, 85-90.

Bellah, R. N., Madsen, R., Sullivan, W. M., Swidler, A., & Tipton, S. M. (1985). *Habits of the heart: Individualism and commitment in American life.* New York: Harper & Row Perennial Library.

Buber, M. (1965a). *Between man and man* (R. G. Smith, Trans.). New York: Macmillan.

Buber, M. (1965b). *The knowledge of man: A philosophy of the interhuman* (M. Friedman, Ed.). New York: Harper & Row.

Carkhuff, R. R. (1969). *Helping and human relations* (Vols. 1 & 2). New York: Holt, Rinehart & Winston.

Carkhuff, R. R. (1971). *The development of human resources.* New York: Holt, Rinehart & Winston.

Cissna, K. N., & Anderson, R. (1990). The contributions of Carl Rogers to a philosophical praxis of dialogue. *Western Journal of Speech Communication, 54*, 125-147.

Cissna, K. N., & Sieburg, E. (1981). Patterns of interactional confirmation and disconfirmation. In C. Wilder-Mott & J. Weakland (Eds.), *Rigor and imagination: Essays from the legacy of Gregory Bateson* (pp. 253-282). New York: Praeger.

Clark, A. (1973). Martin Buber, dialogue, and the philosophy of rhetoric. In D. G. Douglas (Ed.), *Philosophers on rhetoric* (pp. 225-242). Skokie, IL: National Textbook.

Clark, K., & Holquist, M. (1984). *Mikhail Bakhtin.* Cambridge, MA: Harvard University Press.

Craig, R. T., & Tracy, K. (Eds.). (1983). *Conversational coherence: Form, structure, and strategy.* Beverly Hills, CA: Sage.

Dascal, M. (Ed.). (1985). *Dialogue: An interdisciplinary approach.* Amsterdam: John Benjamins.

Derber, C. (1979). *The pursuit of attention: Power and individualism in everyday life.* Oxford: Oxford University Press.

Eisenberg, E. M. (1990). Jamming: Transcendence through organizing. *Communication Research, 17,* 139-164.

Farson, R. (1978). The technology of humanism. *Journal of Humanistic Psychology, 18*(2), 5-35.

Friedman, M. S. (1955). *Martin Buber: The life of dialogue.* New York: Harper & Row.

Friedman, M. (1974). *Touchstones of reality: Existential trust and the community of peace.* New York: Dutton.

Friedman, M. (1983). *The confirmation of otherness: In family, community, and society.* New York: Pilgrim Press.

Friedman, M. (1985). *The healing dialogue in psychotherapy.* New York: Jason Aronson.

Friedman, M. (1986). Carl Rogers and Martin Buber: Self-actualization and dialogue. *Person-Centered Review, 1,* 409-435.

Gadamer, H-G. (1982). *Truth and method* (G. Barden & J. Cumming, Trans.). New York: Crossroad.

Goodman, E. (1991, April 8). Just who are we? *Tampa Tribune,* Nation/World-7.

Holquist, M. (1990). *Dialogism: Bakhtin and his world.* London: Routledge.

Hopper, R. (1992). *Telephone conversation.* Bloomington: Indiana University Press.

Johannesen, R. L. (1971). The emerging concept of communication as dialogue. *Quarterly Journal of Speech, 57,* 373-382.

Johannesen, R. L. (1990). *Ethics in human communication* (3rd ed.). Prospect Heights, IL: Waveland Press.

Kaplan, A. (1964). *The conduct of inquiry.* Scranton, PA: Chandler.

Kaplan, A. (1969). The life of dialogue. In J. D. Roslansky (Ed.), *Communication: A discussion at the Nobel Conference* (pp. 87-108). Amsterdam: North Holland.

Kirschenbaum, H., & Henderson, V. L. (Eds.). (1989). *Carl Rogers: Dialogues—Conversations with Martin Buber, Paul Tillich, B. F. Skinner, Gregory Bateson, Michael Polanyi, Rollo May, and others.* Boston: Houghton-Mifflin.

Krauthammer, C. (1993, April 4). The how-to approach to humanity. *The Tampa Tribune-Times,* 4-Commentary.

Laing, R. D. (1969). *Self and others* (2nd ed.). New York: Penguin.

Lasch, C. (1978). *The culture of narcissism: American life in an age of diminishing expectations.* New York: Basic Books.

Maranhao, T. (Ed.). (1990). *The interpretation of dialogue.* Chicago: University of Chicago Press.

Markova, I., & Foppa, K. (Eds.). (1990). *The dynamics of dialogue.* New York: Springer-Verlag.

Matson, F. W., & Montagu, A. (Eds.). (1967). *The human dialogue: Perspectives on communication.* New York: The Free Press.

McLaughlin, M. L. (1984). *Conversation: How talk is organized.* Beverly Hills, CA: Sage.

Mead, G. H. (1934). *Mind, self, and society: From the standpoint of a social behaviorist.* Chicago: University of Chicago Press.

Mendes-Flohr, P. R. (1989). *From mysticism to dialogue: Martin Buber's transformation of German social thought.* Detroit, MI: Wayne State University Press.

Michelfelder, D. P., & Palmer, R. E. (1989). *Dialogue and deconstruction: The Gadamer-Derrida encounter.* Albany: SUNY Press.

Noddings, N. (1984). *Caring: A feminine approach to ethics and moral education.* Berkeley: University of California Press.

Nofsinger, R. E. (1991). *Everyday conversation.* Newbury Park, CA: Sage.

Palmer, R. E. (1969). *Hermeneutics.* Evanston, IL: Northwestern University Press.

Plum, A. (1981). Communication as skill: A critique and alternative proposal. *Journal of Humanistic Psychology, 21,* 3-19.

Porter, D. T., & Cissna, K. N. (1990, June). *A cauffective model of interpersonal sequencing: An ontologically based conception of communication.* Paper presented to the annual meeting of the International Communication Association, Dublin, Ireland.

Ruesch, J. (1958). The tangential response. In P. H. Toch & J. Zubin (Eds.), *Psychopathology of communication* (pp. 37-48). New York: Grune & Stratton.

Sampson, E. E. (1985). The decentralization of identity: Toward a revised concept of personal and social order. *American Psychologist, 40,* 1203-1211.

Sampson, E. E. (1988). The debate on individualism: Indigenous psychologies of the individual and their role in personal and societal functioning. *American Psychologist, 43,* 15-22.

Schultz, E. A. (1990). *Dialogue at the margins: Whorf, Bakhtin, and linguistic relativity.* Madison: University of Wisconsin Press.

Stewart, J. (1978). Foundations of dialogic communication. *Quarterly Journal of Speech, 64,* 183-201.

Stewart, J. (1985). Martin Buber's central insight: Implications for his philosophy of dialogue. In M. Dascal (Ed.), *Dialogue: An interdisciplinary approach* (pp. 321-335). Amsterdam: John Benjamins.

Stewart, J. (1986, November). *Dimensions of dialogue in Gadamer's theory and practice.* Paper presented at the annual meeting of the Speech Communication Association, Chicago.

Stewart, J. (Ed.). (1990). *Bridges not walls: A book about interpersonal communication* (5th ed.). New York: Random House.

Tannen, D. (1989). *Talking voices: Repetition, dialogue, and imagery in conversational discourse.* Cambridge: Cambridge University Press.

Todorov, T. (1984). *Mikhail Bakhtin: The dialogical principle* (W. Godzich, Trans.). Minneapolis: University of Minnesota Press.

Vangelisti, A. L., Knapp, M. L., & Daly, J. A. (1990). Conversational narcissism. *Communication Monographs, 57,* 251-274.

Warnke, G. (1987). *Gadamer: Hermeneutics, tradition and reason.* Stanford, CA: Stanford University Press.

Watzlawick, P., Beavin, J.H., & Jackson, D.D. (1967). *Pragmatics of human communication.* New York: Norton.

Zephyr, L. H. (1982). Creating your spiritual child. In J. Stewart (Ed.), *Bridges not walls: A book about interpersonal communication* (3rd ed., pp. 33-45). Reading, MA: Addison-Wesley.

■ 2

Dialogue's Ground

Most formal models of human communication that have been proposed over the years have been basically linear, assuming that communication is the process of one person communicating something to another. Many people's informal conceptions are similar, as heard in remarks such as "I don't know what happened; I told him what to do" or "How many times do I have to tell you?" or "Just read the syllabus—it's all there." Even though more sophisticated models long ago added "feedback" to the process, relatively few of us actually think about our own communicative lives in transactional or relational ways. Furthermore, most people believe that others think and talk pretty much the way they do, and most models of communication have been developed by men. What if the communication styles of men and women differ?

Deborah Tannen (1986, 1990), a linguist, persuasively describes differences in the communication styles of men and women and the misunderstandings that arise from the failure to recognize those differences. Although men and women are concerned both with establishing satisfactory relationships and with maintaining distance from others, Tannen claims that women tend to be more oriented toward connection or involvement with others and men more focused on independence and autonomy from others.

Dialogue represents a transactional or relational conception of communication that emphasizes connection, without sacrificing autonomy. In this chapter we highlight two explorations of the ground on which dialogue may be built, one written by a man, another by a woman.

Abraham Kaplan (1964) is a scholar who is probably best known in communication and other social sciences for his now classic volume on

31

the methodology of the behavioral and social sciences, *The Conduct of Inquiry.* The book is remarkable because, among other reasons, Kaplan, a practicing philosopher, writes with exceptional clarity and insight about the research methods of behavioral science. We selected his essay, "The Life of Dialogue," for this volume because he brings that same crispness of writing and thinking to his discussion of human communication and dialogue.

In this essay, Kaplan is interpreting Martin Buber's work on dialogue, especially Buber's best known book, *I and Thou* (1923/1970). In this book, Buber contrasted two modes of human relating, I-You (or I-Thou—different translators have rendered it differently) and I-It. When we establish a relationship of I-It, we are in the realm of experiencing and using; and in this realm both self and other become objects to one another. I-Thou is the mode of real relationship, involving mutuality, presentness, and the opportunity for dialogue. In this essay, Kaplan applies these ideas to the problems of the nature of communication, the relationship between self and other, and the potential for education and learning.

Carol Gilligan is one of a number of theorists, critics, and researchers (cf. Belenky, Clinchy, Goldberger, & Tarule, 1986) who have questioned male bias in scholarship, in which the male life is presumed to be the norm. Gilligan was struck particularly by the work of psychologist Lawrence Kohlberg (e.g., 1981). Kohlberg studied how people make moral decisions, and he had proposed a highly regarded six-stage model of human moral development. Gilligan noted that his research was based *entirely on a sample of males* and that his model identified many women as deficient in moral reasoning because their judgments tend to exemplify the third stage, "where morality is conceived in interpersonal terms and goodness is equated with helping and pleasing others" (Gilligan, 1982, p. 18). In the higher stages of Kohlberg's model, relationships are subordinated to rules and universal principles of justice. In an imaginative series of studies, Gilligan showed convincingly that women's moral judgments are not less developed than men's, only that they are oriented differently.

We have selected an excerpt from the final chapter of Gilligan's highly acclaimed book, *In a Different Voice,* in which she contrasts existing conceptions of the process of developing to adulthood with the implications of her data. Instead of requiring separation from others for the actualization of the individual, Gilligan notes the fusion of identity and intimacy in the accounts of women, identity established in "the context of relationship and judged by a standard of responsibility and care" (p. 160). Gilligan found that women do speak "in a different voice" than men, using similar words to describe very different experiences of self and relationships, although women and men often assume otherwise. Gilligan closes by proposing to us an ethic of care and relationships to consider alongside one of rights and achievement.

REFERENCES

Belenky, M.F., Clinchy, B.M., Goldberger, N.R., & Tarule, J.M. (1986). *Women's ways of knowing: The development of self, voice, and mind.* New York: Basic Books.

Buber, M. (1970). *I and Thou* (W. Kaufmann, Trans.). New York: Charles Scribner. (Original work published 1923)

Gilligan, C. (1982). *In a different voice.* Cambridge, MA: Harvard University Press.

Kaplan, A. (1964). *The conduct of inquiry: Methodology for behavioral science.* Scranton, PA: Chandler Publishing Company.

Kohlberg, L. (1981). *The philosophy of moral development.* San Francisco: Harper & Row.

Tannen, D. (1986). *That's not what I meant: How conversational style makes or breaks your relations with others.* New York: Morrow.

Tannen, D. (1990). *You just don't understand: Women and men in conversation.* New York: Morrow.

■
_____

The Life of Dialogue

Abraham Kaplan

Being reminded of my youth in the world of debate very much tempts me to begin: "Mr. Chairman, Worthy Opponents, Honorable Judges, Ladies and Gentlemen." It has a sweet, old fashioned ring, does it not? The people we talk to nowadays are so seldom regarded as being worthy and honorable.

I suppose it is true after all that it is impossible to go home again. Being back here in Minnesota, and especially listening to the scientific papers, I recall that my undergraduate days were occupied with science; I took my degree in chemistry. I envy my fellow panelists their opportunity for scientific objectivity. Increasingly through the years I have moved away from the objectivity of science to what I must say is now a frankly subjective point of view. Although my topic is "Communication," and although I will be referring quite often to the ideas of Martin Buber (the philosopher and theologian who taught at the Hebrew University in Jerusalem until his death just a few years ago), in fact I will not be talking about these objective matters but about something quite subjective. The French writer Anatole France, in commenting on the inevitable subjectivity of literary criticism, said that if a critic were really honest, he would say to his audiences something like this: "Ladies and gentlemen, I am going to talk to you about myself on the subject of Shakespeare." Let me say that I am going to talk to you about myself on the subject of communication; maybe, a little more broadly, not only about myself, but also about you; about this concrete human situation at just this moment and in just this place.

Yesterday we heard about a great many fascinating people. We heard not only about the birds and the bees, frustrated tree crickets and frightened chimpanzees, but also about autistic children, abandoned children, and illegitimate children; people who were sensorially deprived and culturally deprived; pygmies and Watusis, Yankees and Red Sox. But we did not address ourselves concretely and specifically to the people that we are here and now. It seems to me that this was not an incidental feature of the scientific approach to language and communication; it is quite characteristic of the part that is played by these ideas in contemporary philosophy, at least in the English speaking world.

In philosophy there has been an interesting movement in the conceptualization of the problems of this field, a movement which—as so often is true of philosophy, alas!—is in just the reverse direction of what has been happening in linguistics and related scientific disciplines. Philosophy some three or four decades ago was extremely structural in its approach, extremely formal. It gradually moved from considerations of logical syntax to the field of semantics, and recently has been occupied with the uses and functions of language, at just a time when, as Chomsky pointed out, the linguist abstracts from the uses and functions of language to focus on structural descriptions. I believe that there is another step yet to be taken, not as an alternative, by any means, to the formal, abstract, structural approach but—as Chomsky himself emphasized—as a very much needed supplement to that approach, if we are going to interest ourselves in the human needs which communication serves. That step is to look, not at the medium of communication nor at the conditions—neurological or environmental or whatever—which make communication possible, but to look at the human beings who are communicating with one another, and to ask, what happens to people when they communicate?

I want to approach this question in terms of a basic category of Martin Buber's thinking, no doubt familiar to many of you, concerning two modalities of human relationship: the "I-Thou" modality and the "I-It" modality. Roughly speaking, in the first modality both we and the other accept ourselves as the human beings that we are; in the second modality we dehumanize, depersonalize the other and in the process also dehumanize, depersonalize ourselves.

Most philosophy today is carried on in the I-It modality. There is even a curious idiom which we have taken over from Britain—people talk of "doing" philosophy, as though there is some process to which certain impersonal materials are subjected—to what end, serving what values, expressing what human needs is very hard to say. How different this is from the approach to philosophy of a Socrates, or, for that matter, of an Isaiah: "Come, let us reason together!" Most philosophy today, Buber has said, is monologue. The philosopher is not talking to anyone, not even to his colleagues. He may be talking *for* them; he wants them to hear what he is saying. But it is not a genuine saying—there is no one at the other end, or, at any rate, no one wholly human in that kind of communication.

This style of philosophizing—as I proceed I shall suggest that it is a style found throughout our culture—is associated with certain conceptions of the nature of language and communication. The philosopher does something in his own peculiar way, then he projects his personal peculiarities onto the cosmos—he uses language in a certain way, then concludes that this is the very essence of language. The ideal language, especially for the philosophical analyst, has become more and more a language which is dehumanized and depersonalized. Many analysts look to scientific discourse, especially in its most mathematical forms. To do the scientist justice, I think we would have to say that it is not really scientific discourse the philosopher is looking at, but the philosopher's own picture, usually a distorted one, of scientific discourse. Finally, what is held up to us as a paradigm is the language we use to communicate with machines.

I would like to make something quite clear at the outset. I am a warm admirer of technology, and warmly appreciate both what has already been achieved and the great promise I see for the future, in the application of new technologies to the tasks of education. I think we have scarcely begun to exploit the potentialities of the teaching machine and of other such devices. But Chomsky was a thousand times right when he warned that there is a great danger in this development, namely, that we let the technology determine our values rather than the other way round.

I sometimes think that maybe somebody should devote some effort to the design and construction of *learning* machines; in the mass universities of the future I foresee a possibility of great lecture halls with a teaching machine at one end and a bank of learning machines at the other end, in a closed circuit, while somewhere in a small room a few human beings sit and talk, educating one another. There are two quite different processes which can go on in the schooling situation; both are types of communication, I suppose. One I call *instruction*, the transmission of information and of certain skills in the processing of that information and in the handling of other materials. There is another process for which I reserve the term *education*; it is a process of human growth, and can take place only when human beings are fully interacting with one another. I believe that instruction can be carried out by machine, probably better than it can be done by humans; and I believe that whatever can be done by machine *should* be done by machine, so as to leave the human being free to devote himself to what is most distinctively human.

There is a danger in this point of view also, and I am anxious not to be misunderstood. The danger is that the insistence on the human values which technology is to serve may become an excuse for hostility to the whole scientific enterprise, to the intellect, to reason, to the human mind. There is a danger of obscurantism here, and I want to dissociate myself from obscurantism as strongly as I can. I do not believe in the two cultures of which C.P. Snow speaks—science on one side and the humanities

on the other. Science is itself one of the greatest and the most distinctively human of man's achievements. Buber makes the point in this way, that
in differentiating the modalities of the Thou and the It he is not con-
demning the domain of the It nor the I-It modality. He says, on the contrary, "You cannot hold onto life without It, its reliability sustains you. But
should you die in It, your grave would be in nothingness." More simply,
"Without It man cannot live, but with It alone he can not live as a man."

I want to look at communication, then, not in terms of the It
alone, but in terms of the ways in which communication can bring human
beings together or hold them apart—or, at any rate, bring them together
not as human beings but as depersonalized objects to one another.

I believe that a great deal of communication in modern society is
of this second kind. There is an enormous amount of talk in our society,
an enormous amount of communication, I suppose, written as well as spoken; but in another sense there is really very little communication, very little that is actually being said. It may be, as Augenstein put it, that the
mind is the last sanctuary of individuality and integrity. I begin to wonder
if even the mind is a sanctuary, because it is increasingly being invaded by
communications which say nothing to us, which mean nothing to us, but
which nevertheless take hold of us, compel our attention, and make it
harder than it is already to see clearly ourselves, other people, and the
world around us. Apparently our society is coming increasingly to have a
horror of silence. Wherever we go nowadays someone is dinning something into our ears; whether it is in a market, an elevator, an airplane, at a
restaurant, or for that matter, in a school room. If it isn't talk we must listen to, then it is somebody's notion of music, or something else to fill the
perceptual void. Is it this same horror of being sensorially deprived of
which we were told yesterday, I wonder?

At the same time there is in our society the most exaggerated
conception of what can be accomplished by talk, both for good and for
ill. We think that if only the right things are said, somehow all will be well.
We are probably the greatest masters of euphemism the world has ever
known. We also fear that if the wrong things are said, the foundations of
society will totter. I have never been able to understand why in so many
communities there is so much anxiety about the kinds of speakers who
are invited to a campus. The man comes, and however outrageous his
views are, he talks for an hour or two and goes his way; but I talk to the
students day after day, week after week, and month after month, and
when at the end of the semester I read the final exams I see I've had no
effect whatever. Charlie Brown once called Lucy a name, and she said to
him, "Sticks and stones may break my bones, but names will never hurt
me—you blockhead!" We worry about violence on television screens, but
we are not so much worried, apparently, about the violence in the real
world around us—in our own cities, in Vietnam, in the Middle East. We

want to protect our children from the symbol rather than from the reality; the symbol comes to be more real to us than the reality itself. I suppose that there is a whole generation now for whom the cosmos and space have taken on reality only because we've seen it on TV. In our time, that is the final authentication.

We pay an enormous price for this belief in magic. Magic always exacts an enormous price; more accurately, it is reality that takes its revenge on us for closing our eyes to it. Part of the price we pay, I believe, is what is variously called alienation, the crisis of identity, and such like. I believe that one reason—one only but a significant reason—for the rise of the demonstration as a social phenomenon, whether on campuses or on city streets, is connected with this alienation. The demonstrator is saying, "Look at me as a human being, listen to me, and talk *to* me, not at me. Let us establish communication; this is what I am demanding above all else."

In so many institutions, not just educational institutions but pervasively in our society, this human need which we all know and feel deeply is more and more being denied. Aristotle wrote a treatise on ethics in which two whole chapters were devoted to the subject of friendship. He says, "Even if a man had all other goods, if he had no friends life would not be worth living." I doubt if a single book on ethics written in English in the twentieth century so much as contains the word "friendship" in the index, except possibly as an example of an abstract noun. So far as our general social patterns are concerned, we do not have friends; we have contacts, connections, clients, customers, or constituents. (Why these words all begin with "C" Chomsky might explain!)

We even formulate some of our technological aims in just this perspective. Augenstein spoke of "human engineering." There are some real and important problems dealt with under that rubric; I do not want to derogate their importance. But I also want to call attention to how easy—I almost said "natural" but I think it is quite unnatural—how easy it is for us to see a person as material to be shaped or as an instrumentality to be used, rather than as a human being. Real life, Martin Buber once said, is meeting. It is a certain kind of relationship in which the humanity of those relating is absolutely central.

What bearing does this have on the communication process? Let me put it this way. There is a certain kind of communication which we all know, very precious to us, very different from the kinds of communication which are most common and which are most commonly analyzed. I would like to propose a distinctive label for it. Let me call it "communion" instead of communication.

The model that has been built up for the usual kind of communication is a very valuable model for many purposes; let me insist upon that. It is roughly as follows. There is a source of possible messages, each of which can be conceived as the result of certain choices from among the set of alternatives that can be selected for transmission. The choices are made with linked probabilities, not altogether independent of one another; the materials are suitably encoded and fed into a channel where they are transmitted to a receiver, having been distorted in certain respects by the noise in the channel; they are then decoded, more or less accurately; finally, someone takes the decoded message and goes his way. Notice that in this process the human beings appear only at the termini; everything else of interest takes place in between.

In what I am calling communion the relationship between the human beings is a direct one. It is unmediated; it is as though the human beings are put directly into contact with one another. (In fact, we use such idioms as "Keep in touch with me.") Although in a strict sense there are, of course, many mediating processes, somehow they do not have the significance in communion which they have in communication. Consider what happens when you are experiencing grief, and a friend puts his arm around you. (Charlie Brown asks somewhere whatever happened to the good, old-fashioned, arms-around-the-shoulder sympathy which he never gets.) No words are exchanged and they aren't needed, but there is something important which relates the two people in that situation. Or, you look at someone whom you know, or whom you would like to know, and your eyes meet. The eyes are the window of the soul, as are the hands, the lips - everything with which we can communicate. When the eyes meet, it is not that something which lies between the two people connects them, but as though two human beings, for those brief moments, have become just one. Eye contact is a very intimate relationship; were you to catch the eye of a stranger and hold it, in our culture at least, either the contact would be broken very quickly or the relationship would move to a new plane—whether of hostility or of something quite other, I do not know. But it would not remain where it was; you are not the same again after what has passed between you. Yet it is not so much that something has passed between you, but that in that moment you were truly *with* one another as human beings.

There are many human relationships which manifest *reciprocity*—I do something for you, you do something for me. Quite often it would be more accurate to say, "I do something *to* you, and in return I allow *you* to do something to me." This is a very different kind of relationship than a *mutual* one, in which we do something together which neither of us can do separately. Mutuality does not involve our depersonalizing each other, but exactly the contrary; it allows each to become even more fully human. There is a difference after all, is there not, between talking *with* someone and talking *to* them or, in that suggestive idiom, talking *at* them.

There is a kind of communication distinct from both monologue and dialogue for which I propose the term *duologue*. In duologue there are two people talking, but they are not talking with one another. Duologue is not communion in the present sense; it is a kind of communication. Information is being transmitted, but not to human beings; at any rate, there are not two human beings at the same time. The mark of duologue is that the two people are not really together in mutuality; they are at best only in a reciprocal relationship. While one person is talking, the other one is not listening; he is only thinking of what he will say when it is his turn to talk. The cocktail party is the institutionalization of duologue, and so, I am afraid, is the classroom. First the professor talks and the students don't listen; then the students talk or write and the professor doesn't listen or read; at any rate, they are not human beings talking *with* one another. Each is doing something *to* the other, while he claims that he is doing something *for* the other, although it is never quite clear who is doing what for whom.

What is most characteristic of communion is that feature of language which Marler called "openness," and which Chomsky described as creative, or as governed by a transformational generative grammar. I would put it in layman's terms in this way. When people are in communion, when they are in this narrow sense really communicating with one another, the content of what is being communicated does not exist prior to and independently of that particular context. There is no message, except in a *post-hoc* reconstruction, which is fixed and complete beforehand. If I am really talking with you, I *have* nothing to say; what I say arises as you and I genuinely relate to one another. I do not know beforehand *who* I will be, because I am open to you just as you are open to me. This, I think, is what makes growth possible among human beings, and why it seems to me impossible really to teach unless you are learning; why you cannot really talk unless you are listening. You are listening not only to the other, you are listening to yourself. Indeed, in a fundamental sense—I would even say in quite a literal sense—self and other are now so intertwined that we need new conceptual frameworks, new categories to describe what is happening.

Chomsky said that in his view the study of language is a branch of theoretical psychology. That seems to me to be very much in the right direction. I should want also to insist that it must be a social psychology. Perhaps we should say that the study of language is really a branch of theoretical sociology, as Marler put it. A certain kind of social structure or a certain pattern of involvement of several organisms is essential to communication. Buber says that we become human beings only insofar as we enter into this special relationship with other human beings; through the *Thou* a man becomes an *I*. I caught something very like this in the invocation which Dr. Carlson delivered: "We need each other to become ourselves." We need talk, not merely to fill a sensory vacuum, but to fill what would otherwise be a far more intolerable void within ourselves, where we seek an identity.

Just as there is a difference between communion and communication, between I-Thou and I-It, there is a corresponding difference between a self which is truly human and a self which is only an object among other objects—an It in the domain of the It. This is the difference between an *identity* and an *identification*. We all have plenty of identifications. They are not only easy to come by, they are impossible to avoid. Everywhere you turn, you are given another identification, another number. The identity is something quite different. It is not what allows us to be located in the domain of the It. Our identity is what makes us the particular persons that we are.

I do not know if we can speak of a "breakdown" of communication. Perhaps it would be more accurate to speak of the failure to achieve communication—I do not know whether we have ever had it; I do not believe in the myth of a Golden Age. This failure, then, truly to communicate with one another is very much bound up with the search for identity. That search has been a task for the young ever since there were young. But the failure of communication, I believe, is also bound up with great social problems both on the domestic and the foreign scene. More and more people seem to be coping with their problems by adopting negative identities, thinking to find themselves by differentiating themselves from the other, to become selves not by being *with* the other, but by being against the other. Racism, both black and white, has, I think, this psychodynamic. "I can't talk with you; indeed, I won't talk with you. Only in that refusal can I be myself." In the Rabbinic tradition there is a beautiful aphorism which runs, 'If I am I only because you are you, and you are you only because I am I, then I am not I and you are not you." For then we face one another only as two mirrors endlessly reflecting their emptiness into one another.

I am sure that if you heard it yesterday, the line of Augenstein's is still with you—the deeply moving line, "Little George, it's important to me that you are who you are." That is perhaps the greatest thing which any human being can say to any other human being. It is important to me that you are who you are, and that I am who I am; you and I together can communicate with each other, and thereby more fully realize all the potentialities for the human which lie within us.

Such ideas have quite a history in modern times. The sociologist and philosopher, George Herbert Mead, is especially associated with the theory of an intimate relationship between the development of the self and the use of what he calls "significant symbols." In Mead this fundamental dialogue with the "generalized other" takes place within the self. Moreover, the self is analyzed in Mead as though it comes to be once for all. We pay a lot of attention to the infant at just the stage when he is learning to talk, and we imagine that once he has learned how to talk he has acquired a self; the rest is no longer of any particular concern to us. We leave off, it seems to me, at precisely the point where we should begin. The self comes to be in every dialogue; it is generated in every act of communication. I am other than I was because of what I am now saying to you. If I am really saying it to you, if you are *with* me in this act of communication, you also are now other than you previously were.

People can be together, in various senses of that term, without really being *with* one another, just as they can talk without really communicating. Buber calls this kind of togetherness a *collectivity* and he contrasts it with a *community*. A community is an aggregation in which there is a binding of human beings to one another; in a collectivity, he says, there is no binding together, only a bundling together. We *use* one another in the collectivity. We may say "we," but this is a kind of group egotism. It has no genuine content, any more than the word "I" has a genuine content when the man who speaks it has no identity and truly does not know who he is; it may be he has not yet become an "I." So also in our social aggregations we too often have not yet become a community.

The question may be asked whether it is possible to establish communion between two people with absolutely opposing ideas.

It seems to me that unless we can establish communion in these cases, we will not have communion at all. It is easy to talk with people we love; the trick is to be able to talk with people we do not love. Alas, we must even learn to live in a world of hate. Only, I should like to say that ideas can differ from one another without opposing one another. I am a relativist; I do believe that values are objective, but I also believe that they can be objective and at the same time plural. I think there is too great a tendency for us to suppose that all values can be linearly ordered. We too often assume that there is a single dimension of values, so that if you consider any two different values, one must be better and the other worse. We recognize that this is not so in the arts; it makes no sense to ask whether Keats was a better poet than Chopin was a composer. That's just idle talk; what we want to do is to appreciate the poetry and also appreciate the music. There are many kinds of poetry even, and for that matter, many different kinds of sonnets, and so on. In the house of our Lord there are indeed many mansions. We can absolutely oppose another only when we close ourselves off from the other. My thesis has been that when we do that, we are closing ourselves off from ourselves as well. I think I would have to say that if two people are absolute in their opposition to one another, they have both abandoned their humanity; it is not possible for human beings absolutely to oppose one another. The same point could be put in this way, that loving is intrinsic to our human nature. As soon as we begin to see *them* as no longer human, we ourselves become increasingly involved in inhumanities. I would say, therefore, that it *is* possible to establish communion between people with opposing ideas. It can be done just insofar as we abandon our absolute stance, and are prepared really to talk with the other. I think of a concrete political case which is very meaningful to me. The problems today in the Middle East can be regarded as being in a significant degree problems of instituting dialogue. There is an apocryphal story that an American Undersecretary recently exclaimed in the United Nations, "Why can't Israel and her Arab neighbors settle their differences like Christian gentlemen?" It is said that a Buddhist who overheard him remarked, "The trouble is, that's just what they're doing!"

Many people who talk about the problems of our cities are victims again of a myth of the Golden Age. They speak of the "breakdown of the community," as though somewhere, in the past, people really were together, and now we have lost it all; usually the loss is blamed on technology or science or numbers or something modern. All that, I think, is a myth; but I do think it is true that a great deal of our lives with other people is spent in collectivities and not in communities. Recently someone proposed what I think is a brilliant numerical measure of the degree of civilization of any society: the number of strangers whom you can trust, or, as I would prefer to say in this context, the number of strangers whom you can talk to, whom you can talk with, whom you can understand and know that they understand you. This, of course, is another way of saying that you enter into community with them.

It is one of the features of our time, I am afraid, that we can talk with strangers only in times of disaster. Last night when we were snowbound or thought we might be—I confess, I *hoped* we might be—there was a little electricity in the air, so it seemed to me, a little movement away from the I-It to the I-Thou, a little softening, a little humanizing of one another. This effect was observed in the power black-out in New York, and earlier during the Blitz in London. What a pass we have come to, if we can allow ourselves our humanity only when there is some chance that we will pay for it with our lives! Instead, we pay with our lives the rest of the time, with the kind of lives we lead—what Thoreau called lives of quiet desperation. Perhaps in our time they are not so quiet, but they are just as desperate. Unless we talk with one another, we deny ourselves our humanity in the very moment when we turn aside from the humanity of the other.

To what can we attribute the withholding of self? Is it a lack of mutual trust? If I had to answer in brief, I probably could not do better than with the one word "fear." Fear of mutuality operates on several different levels. There is fear of rejection; there is fear of acceptance, which may betray my inadequacy; there is fear of being accepted and proving adequate, but then finding myself committed. There may also be fear for the very integrity of the self. If I open myself to you, I may be swallowed; if I give myself to you, there may be nothing left of me. There is, I think, a basic dilemma of identity: I need the other for my identity, but the other is at the same time a threat to my identity. The dilemma might be put in this way: How can I be what I am without fear of being different from you, and how can I be *with* you without fear of losing my identity? I do not think that such dilemmas have solutions: we only learn to cope with them, and go on to the next.

There are some profoundly moral and religious implications in all this, which Buber made explicit. No doubt many of you have already been drawing out these implications. One might distinguish between two kinds of evil in human experience. One is that in which the It predominates in our lives—not that the It itself is evil, but the domination of the It is evil. This is the kind of evil in which we do not communicate with others; we only manipulate others. We keep them in the domain of the It. This violates a principle of Kantian morality to be found in many versions in Christianity, in Judaism, and in other world religions. It is the evil which consists in treating other human beings only as means to ends, and not experiencing them as ends in themselves. There is a second kind of evil, much harder to see, intimately bound up with the first. That is the evil in which we talk, but only to ourselves. It is the evil, not of living in the domain of the It, but of mistaking I for Thou. We worship, but we worship only idols of our own making, and become, as the Psalmist rightly pointed out, like the idols we ourselves have made.

A central problem of religious thought can be formulated as a problem in communication. It is expressed in the cry, "Why art Thou silent? Why does not God give me a sign? How shall I reach Him? Why does He turn away from me?" Quite extraordinary, is it not, how these same locutions might be used to express our sense of alienation from other human beings. If only we can establish communication! Every Thou, in Martin Buber's idiom, is a glimpse of the eternal Thou. The religious experience is an intensification of the experience which we have in every encounter in which we are truly with the other and experience the other as Thou.

In that case, Buber concludes—and I think quite rightly—God talks to man all the time. He talks to man in all the things and all the beings which He sends to man; man answers in all his dealings with these things and beings. We can answer in two different ways—it is the same contrast which I have been drawing on all along. Buber finds these two responses symbolized in the two Scriptural characters of Adam and Abraham. God called to Adam, "Where art thou?" and Adam ran and hid. But God said, "Abraham, Abraham," and he answered, "Here I am!", thereby instituting the dialogue which established the Biblical religion.

There are some very popular words today—cliches, in fact: "encounter," "confrontation," and (I will be the first to admit it) "dialogue." These three words have a very interesting property—you can combine them in any order and sound as though you are really "with it." "We have entered upon this confrontation so as to make possible a dialogue which will lead to a genuinely human encounter." Or, "We have entered upon this dialogue so that the encounter . . ." You can work out the variations. I believe that these words have become cliches because what they are pointing to, in however vague and confused a way, is something universal, and universally important to us.

I want to conclude by injecting one other element into an already complicated situation. The aim of all communication, it seems to me, is to arrive at communion. To put it more boldly, the aim of all talk is to pave the way for silence. In all talk we move from silence to silence. Only, there are two very different kinds of silence. There is the silence of hostility, of ignorance, of bewilderment; the silence which means that I have nothing to say to you nor you to me. There is the very different silence of understanding, of love, of knowledge, where the situation is not that we have nothing to say to each other, but that nothing more needs to be said. What we really need, I think—I invite my scientific colleagues to look at this problem—is a syntax of silence. We might do well to focus on the ways in which human beings communicate when they are not using language, or its conventional equivalents in gesture and the like.

A psychiatrist friend in Los Angeles told me once of the following experience. Late one night he was at the Los Angeles General Hospital and had occasion to go to the surgical waiting room. There was only one person there, a woman who was sobbing as though her heart would break. He asked the nurse on duty who it was. She said, "That is Mrs. Gonzales; her husband has just died on the operating table." He said, "Oh, I know the case." He went over and sat down by her, and said, "Mrs. Gonzales, I am Dr. Ingham. It happens that I knew about your husband's case. He had the best of care; I know the surgeon. He would have died very shortly in any case . . ." and he went on. As he talked, her crying subsided, and was replaced by a few whimpers; then she quieted down and was even able to smile a little through her tears, as she held his hand. He sat and talked with her for some time, then looked at his watch and realized he had to leave. As he was walking out the nurse on duty called him over and said, "Dr. Ingham, I didn't know that you spoke Spanish." "Spanish! I don't know any Spanish." She said, "Well, then, what were you talking about with Mrs. Gonzales? She doesn't know a word of English." That really was talk, real communication, was it not?

There is a need to become aware of and develop the use of nonverbal expressions for more meaningful intra- and interpersonal relationships. But man has an unlimited capacity for perversion. We can turn everything to an evil purpose, misuse every instrumentality. It is quite true that in many of the examples I gave of real communication or communion, I turned to the nonverbal. But the nonverbal also can become a device for not being with others, but on the contrary, for holding people apart. Consider, for instance, the falsely hearty handshake, or my favorite example, what I call the "stewardess syndrome." (I recently lectured on "Loneliness" and discussed the stewardess syndrome at some length. After the lecture, among the people who came up to talk with me was one very attractive young woman who looked vaguely familiar; she said, "I was the stewardess on your flight to. . .!") I do think that nonverbal methods of communication can be used very much more, but this use would only shift the problem. Let me also make clear, in the other direction, that I did not mean to imply that words always keep people apart; words can also serve to bring people together.

I think that in our schools, at any rate, there is altogether too little silence. Everybody in the school situation seems to panic at the thought that maybe someone will be sitting without talking or listening to talk, and without even reading or writing. We have our students carefully read Walt Whitman, and perhaps even parse his lines about loafing and inviting the soul, but we do not allow them to do it. If you are on the faculty, you cannot invite your soul because you have a committee meeting; if you are a student it is because you have an assignment to read, a paper to write. It may be that, not only in our schools but throughout our society, if we talked less, we might say more; if we did not try so hard to communicate, we might be able to commune. If we did not search so hard for our own identities, but occupied ourselves with the other, we might find what we were not seeking. If we listen, it may be that we will be able at last to respond, "Here I am!"

The impulse to escape is always present. This is the impulse in all of us to turn away from the real world which presents problems that sometimes seem overwhelming, and to turn instead to a fantasy world of our own making, where we can solve problems without effort. "The mind is its own place, and in itself can make a hell of heaven and a heaven of hell." I see a good deal of this turning away from reality. I think that is the significance of the use of drugs in our time; and there are other escape mechanisms operative. But I don't think anything is gained by closing the door for escape, or by putting heavier shackles on our prisoners. Men try to escape from reality when they find the reality painful and feel powerless to do anything about it. What we need to do is to address ourselves to what is producing the pain, and to the fact as well as the feeling of powerlessness. This seems to me to be as true with regard to the problems of the ghetto as it is with regard to the problems of student unrest—as it is, indeed, with regard to the problems of war and peace on the world scene. Of course, the reality is painful, and, of course, our powers are limited, and of course, the problems are almost insoluble. But there is a world of salvation in the word "almost." At any rate, there is a world of hope in that "almost," and perhaps that is all—or almost all—that a man can ask for.

■

Visions of Maturity

Carol Gilligan

Like the stories that delineate women's fantasies of power, women's descriptions of adulthood convey a different sense of its social reality. In their portrayal of relationships, women replace the bias of men toward separation with a representation of the interdependence of self and other, both in love and in work. By changing the lens of developmental observation from individual achievement to relationships of care, women depict ongoing attachment as the path that leads to maturity. Thus the parameters of development shift toward marking the progress of affiliative relationship.

The implications of this shift are evident in considering the situation of women at mid-life. Given the tendency to chart the unfamiliar waters of adult development with the familiar markers of adolescent separation and growth, the middle years of women's lives readily appear as a time of return to the unfinished business of adolescence. This interpretation has been particularly compelling since life-cycle descriptions, derived primarily from studies of men, have generated a perspective from which women, insofar as they differ, appear deficient in their development. The deviance of female development has been especially marked in the adolescent years when girls appear to confuse identity with intimacy by defining themselves through relationships with others. The legacy left from this mode of identity definition is considered to be a self that is vulnerable to the issues of separation that arise at mid-life.

But this construction reveals the limitation in an account which measures women's development against a male standard and ignores the

From In a Different Voice: Psychological Theory and Women's Development (pp. 170-174) by Carol Gilligan, copyright © 1982, Carol Gilligan. Reprinted with the permission of Harvard University Press.

possibility of a different truth. In this light, the observation that women's embeddedness in lives of relationship, their orientation to interdependence, their subordination of achievement to care, and their conflicts over competitive success leave them personally at risk in mid-life seems more a commentary on the society than a problem in women's development.

The construction of mid-life in adolescent terms, as a similar crisis of identity and separation, ignores the reality of what has happened in the years between and tears up the history of love and of work. For generativity to begin at mid-life, as Vaillant's data on men suggest, seems from a woman's perspective too late for both sexes, given that the bearing and raising of children take place primarily in the preceding years. Similarly, the image of women arriving at mid-life childlike and dependent on others is belied by the activity of their care in nurturing and sustaining family relationships. Thus the problem appears to be one of construction, an issue of judgment rather than truth.

In view of the evidence that women perceive and construe social reality differently from men and that these differences center around experiences of attachment and separation, life transitions that invariably engage these experiences can be expected to involve women in a distinctive way. And because women's sense of integrity appears to be entwined with an ethic of care, so that to see themselves as women is to see themselves in a relationship of connection, the major transitions in women's lives would seem to involve changes in the understanding and activities of care. Certainly the shift from childhood to adulthood witnesses a major redefinition of care. When the distinction between helping and pleasing frees the activity of taking care from the wish for approval by others, the ethic of responsibility can become a self-chosen anchor of personal integrity and strength.

In the same vein, however, the events of mid-life—the menopause and changes in family and work—can alter a woman's activities of care in ways that affect her sense of herself. If mid-life brings an end to relationships, to the sense of connection on which she relies, as well as to the activities of care through which she judges her worth, then the mourning that accompanies all life transitions can give way to the melancholia of self-deprecation and despair. The meaning of mid-life events for a woman thus reflects the interaction between the structures of her thought and the realities of her life.

When a distinction between neurotic and real conflict is made and the reluctance to choose is differentiated from the reality of having no choice, then it becomes possible to see more clearly how women's experience provides a key to understanding central truths of adult life. Rather than viewing her anatomy as destined to leave her with a scar of inferiority (Freud, 1931), one can see instead how it gives rise to experiences which illuminate a reality common to both of the sexes: the fact that in life you never see it all, that things unseen undergo change through time, that there is more than one path to gratification, and that the boundaries between self and other are less clear than they sometimes seem. Thus women not only reach mid-life with a psychological history different from men's and face at that time a different social reality having different possibilities for love and for work, but they also make a different sense of experience, based on their knowledge of human relationships. Since the reality of connection is experienced by women as given rather than as freely contracted, they arrive at an understanding of life that reflects the limits of autonomy and control. As a result, women's development delineates the path not only to a less violent life but also to a maturity realized through interdependence and taking care.

In his studies of children's moral judgment, Piaget (1932/1965) describes a three-stage progression through which constraint turns into cooperation and cooperation into generosity. In doing so, he points out how long it takes before children in the same class at school, playing with each other every day, come to agree in their understanding of the rules of their games. This agreement, however, signals the completion of a major reorientation of action and thought through which the morality of constraint turns into the morality of cooperation. But he also notes how children's recognition of differences between others and themselves leads to a relativizing of equality in the direction of equity, signifying a fusion of justice and love.

There seems at present to be only partial agreement between men and women about the adulthood they commonly share. In the absence of mutual understanding, relationships between the sexes continue in varying degrees of constraint, manifesting the "paradox of egocentrism" which Piaget describes, a mystical respect for rules combined with everyone playing more or less as he pleases and paying no attention to his neighbor (p. 61). For a life-cycle understanding to address the development in adulthood of relationships characterized by cooperation, generosity, and care, that understanding must include the lives of women as well as of men.

Among the most pressing items on the agenda for research on adult development is the need to delineate *in women's own terms* the experience of their adult life. My own work in that direction indicates that the inclusion of women's experience brings to developmental understanding a new perspective on relationships that changes the basic constructs of interpretation. The concept of identity expands to include the experience of interconnection. The moral domain is similarly enlarged by the inclusion of responsibility and care in relationships. And the underlying epistemology correspondingly shifts from the Greek ideal of knowledge as a correspondence between mind and form to the Biblical conception of knowing as a process of human relationship.

Given the evidence of different perspectives in the representation of adulthood by women and men, there is a need for research that elucidates the effects of these differences in marriage, family, and work relationships. My research suggests that men and women may speak different languages that they assume are the same, using similar words to encode disparate experiences of self and social relationships. Because these languages share an overlapping moral vocabulary, they contain a propensity for systematic mistranslation, creating misunderstandings which impede communication and limit the potential for cooperation and care in relationships. At the same time, however, these languages articulate with one another in critical ways. Just as the language of responsibilities provides a weblike imagery of relationships to replace a hierarchical ordering that dissolves with the coming of equality, so the language of rights underlines the importance of including in the network of care not only the other but also the self.

As we have listened for centuries to the voices of men and the theories of development that their experience informs, so we have come more recently to notice not only the silence of women but the difficulty in hearing what they say when they speak. Yet in the different voice of women lies the truth of an ethic of care, the tie between relationship and responsibility, and the origins of aggression in the failure of connection. The failure to see the different reality of women's lives and to hear the differences in their voices stems in part from the assumption that there is a single mode of social experience and interpretation. By positing instead two different modes, we arrive at a more complex rendition of human experience which sees the truth of separation and attachment in the lives of women and men and recognizes how these truths are carried by different modes of language and thought.

To understand how the tension between responsibilities and rights sustains the dialectic of human development is to see the integrity of two disparate modes of experience that are in the end connected. While an ethic of justice proceeds from the premise of equality—that everyone should be treated the same—an ethic of care rests on the premise of nonviolence—that no one should be hurt. In the representation of maturity, both perspectives converge in the realization that just as inequality adversely affects both parties in an unequal relationship, so too violence is destructive for everyone involved. This dialogue between fairness and care not only provides a better understanding of relations between the sexes but also gives rise to a more comprehensive portrayal of adult work and family relationships.

As Freud and Piaget call our attention to the differences in children's feelings and thought, enabling us to respond to children with greater care and respect, so a recognition of the differences in women's experience and understanding expands our vision of maturity and points to the contextual nature of developmental truths. Through this expansion in perspective, we can begin to envision how a marriage between adult development as it is currently portrayed and women's development as it begins to be seen could lead to a changed understanding of human development and a more generative view of human life.

REFERENCES

Freud, Sigmund. "Female sexuality." (1931). Vol. XXI. In *The Standard Edition of the Complete Psychological Works of Sigmund Freud*, trans. and ed. James Strachey. London: The Hogarth Press, 1961.

Piaget, Jean. *The moral judgment of the child.* (1932). New York: The Free Press, 1965.

■ 3

Dialogue's Limits

A small but intriguing literature describes a 20th-century North American tribe known as the Nacirema (e.g., Spradley & Rynkiewich, 1975). Although Miner's (1956) study of their body rituals was published several decades ago, relatively few studies have been completed even today (e.g., Thompson, 1972; Walker, 1970).

Although the Nacirema live in a rich land and devote considerable time to economic pursuits, much of their day is spent in various ritual activities. In fact, their belief in magic might seem extraordinary to us. Their health practices are illustrative (see Miner, 1956). Their fundamental belief seems to be that the human body is ugly and that its natural development is toward debility and disease. In order to avoid these problems, the people rely on powerful rituals and ceremonies. For example, each dwelling has at least one ritual center containing a small box or chest built into the wall in which are stored the many "charms and magical potions" without which the natives do not believe they could live. The preparations are obtained from powerful medicine men, whose assistance is obtained in exchange for substantial gifts. The medicine men, however, do not provide the healing potions, but decide on the proper ingredients, which they write in a language understood only by the medicine men and the herbalists, who, for another gift, provide the necessary potion.

The sickest people are taken to an imposing temple called a *latipso*, which can be found in all but the smallest communities. No matter how serious the illness, the guardians of many temples will not admit someone who cannot make an even larger gift. After admission, attendants first remove the person's clothes, even though in everyday life the Nacirema generally avoid allowing others to see their bodies or observe their natural functions. In the *latipso*, bathing and excretory acts, ordinarily performed only in the privacy of the household shrine, are ritualized and are overseen by special attendants. Another part of the healing process involves inserting magic wands into the sick person's mouth at regular intervals and jabbing magically treated needles into their flesh. So great, however, is the people's faith, that, as Miner observed, "the fact that these temple ceremonies may not cure, and may even kill the neophyte, in no way decreases the people's faith in the medicine man" (p. 506).

Over the years, anthropologists have studied a great many societies, some of which have appeared "exotic" to Western anthropologists, Miner, in his essay in *American Anthropologist*, from which the Nacerima material was derived, was attempting simultaneously to call attention to the cultural basis of one aspect of American life ("Nacirema" is simply American spelled backward), and to highlight the tendency of anthropologists at that time to accept the familiar uncritically while making the unknown seem strange, tendencies not unknown to the rest of us. The communication field in recent years has embraced the study of our culture under the rubric of "cultural studies" (e.g., Grossberg, Nelson, & Treichler, 1992).

Culture, to borrow Kluckhohn's (1949) classic statement, refers to "the total way of life of a people, the social legacy the individual acquires from his group" (p. 24). Culture refers to a shared perspective, or organized view of the world. It designates the conventional understandings, what a people take for granted about things, events, and persons. Those understandings guide action and become "manifest in act and artifact" (Shibutani, 1962, p. 131). Culture is learned through human communication and becomes "an outline scheme which, running ahead of experience, defines and guides it" (p. 130).

For our purposes, culture constitutes one of the constraints or limits of dialogue. We do not and cannot simply choose at any moment how to communicate from among all the human communication possibilities; we have available to us a much smaller subset of communicative options that we have learned are appropriate, acceptable, even desirable. These are constituted in significant part by our culture. We have selected two readings to illustrate aspects of American culture that function as limits to dialogue.

William Barrett (1979) is a contemporary philosopher concerned about the modern world's fascination with technologies and techniques. Barrett is concerned that we may become the unintentional victims of our own technologies, the products of our own products. His biggest concern is probably that this reduction in human freedom will not even be noticed because the way of life embodied in science and technology has become part of the "presuppositions [that] are so much the invisible medium of our actual life that we have become unconscious of them" (p. 223). Like the Nacirema described by Miner, who continue to be ill without noticing the linkage of illness to their cultural technologies, contemporary American society may become communicatively toxic as a direct result of our most "advanced" efforts to improve it.

Our selection by Charles Derber illustrates one implication of the American penchant for individualism and how it is manifest in conversation. In *The Pursuit of Attention: Power and Individualism in Everyday Life*, Derber explores the social nature of attention. According to Derber, the process and outcome of any encounter depends on how communicators seek and give attention. Two people each seeking to focus attention primarily on the self would lead to a very competitive interaction; two people able to give attention to the other would result in a more cooperative mode. In the chapter included here, Derber discusses an extreme form of self-absorption in which people consistently turn the topics of conversation to themselves, without showing any serious interest in topics introduced by the other. Following Freud (1957) and Lasch (1978), he calls this "conversational narcissism."

REFERENCES

Barrett, W. (1979). *The illusion of technique.* Garden City, NY: Anchor Books.
Freud, D. (1957). *On narcissism.* London: Hogarth.
Grossberg, L., Nelson, C., & Treichler, P.A. (Eds.). (1992). *Cultural studies.* New York: Routledge.
Kluckhohn, C. (1949). *Mirror for man.* New York: Whittlesey House.
Lasch, C. (1978). *The culture of narcissism.* New York: Basic Books.
Miner, H.M. (1956). Body ritual among the nacirema. *American Anthropologist, 8,* 503-507.
Shibutani, T. (1962). Reference groups and social control. In A.M. Rose (Ed.), *Human behavior and social processes* (pp. 128-147). Boston: Houghton-Mifflin.
Spradley, J.P., & Rynkiewich, M.A. (Eds.). (1975). *The nacirema: Readings on American culture.* Boston: Little, Brown.
Thompson, N.B. (1972). The mysterious fall of the Nacirema. *Natural History Magazine,*
Walker, W. (1970). The retention of folk linguistic concepts and the ti'ycir caste in contemporary Nacireman culture. *American Anthropologist, 72,* 102-105.

■
_____

Technique, Technicians, and Philosophy

William Barrett

WHAT IS A TECHNIQUE?

The Yurok Indians are a tribe living on our Pacific Coast who subsist very largely on the salmon that swim out of the ocean into their rivers. Before the season the salmon begin running, the Yurok build a dam to trap the fish in order to ensure a good catch for the winter. The building of this dam is preceded and accompanied by much ceremony and ritual. There are mass enactments of the tribal myths, purification baths, fasting from certain foods, sexual abstinence, and a taboo against certain kinds of incontinent talk. When the fishing has been done, and the catch is in, there follows a corresponding short period of détente, a kind of bacchanalia in which sexual freedom and verbal license are tolerantly allowed to run their course.

The dam itself is a fairly complex technological achievement; but for the Yurok the rituals that accompany it are as much part of the whole technique of hunting the salmon as the act of building or the preparing of nets and other gear. To the civilized mind this represents a failure to separate subjective and objective components in the business of the hunt. The primitive does not understand this separation, and if he could be made to understand, would rebel against it. All his inherited ways teach him the wisdom of not separating man from the nature within which he moves. Thus he comes to think of the fish that are caught as a gift of nature, and even the skill of the fisherman as another such gift. Consequently, the whole hunt is not a sheer self-assertion of the human will against nature. Belatedly, we have come to recognize that these rituals may have a "psychological" efficacy. But this acknowledgment itself shows that we cannot return to his condition, for the terms in which we would honor it are also altogether alien to it.

In the broad anthropological sense, all rituals may be considered as techniques; and a culture is the sum of its rituals. Some rituals still attend our own technology. When a hydroelectric dam is completed, there may be various ceremonies in celebration: a crowd gathers, politicians speak, a band plays; and if the occasion warrants, there may even be a prayer delivered by a clergyman. But such pomp is halfhearted, if we compare it with the Yurok. The detached anthropologist would note that, in the whole spectrum of human cultures, ours is one in which ritual becomes more perfunctory and external in relation to its technology.

The imposing structure of technology, as the dominating presence in modern society, tends to assimilate the meaning of "technique" to itself. This assimilation shows itself more plainly in other languages than English: in German, for example, *Technik* signifies technology, and in intellectual discussion is likely to be used more often than its cognate, *Technologie*, and similarly for *technique* and *technologie* in French. The assimilation of these two terms to each other is the great fact of modern history. What we are dealing with here, and what we shall be dealing with throughout, is the single phenomenon indicated by the hyphenated form *technique-technology*.

The two, in fact, have become inseparable. The majority of us have only minimal techniques in relation to the machines we use. We know how to press buttons, and most of us drive our automobiles without knowing what a carburetor is. But if our civilization were to lose its techniques, all our machines and apparatus would become one vast pile of junk. We would not know how to produce the power that keeps the machines running, and we would not know how to replace those machines that wore out. We would roam amid a landscape of dynamos, factories, and laboratories, and with all this equipment still intact as so much sheer physical matter, we would nevertheless be a civilization without a technology. Modern science and technology are the offspring of *method* and they persist only so long as we command this method. *Technology is embodied technique.*

We do, of course, still use the word in other areas, as in the arts, which appear alien to technology. We commonly speak, for example, of a painter's or a writer's technique. We even give studio courses in these subjects. And if we enroll as students, we seek to learn to paint or to write, as the case may be. But even here, and perhaps most of all here, if we watch how the various meanings grade off, we get a glimpse of the more precise and limited sense of technique. The teacher may give us certain quite simple and mechanical rules to get started. But if the pupil persists and develops, he eventually reaches a point where the teacher has to tell him he is on his own, and there is no prescribed technique that will paint his picture for him. Then other words have to be invoked—a special knack, a gift, flair, talent, or, most remote of all, genius. Indeed, it was a simple consideration like this that led Kant to define genius as the ability to produce something over and above any rules. Genuine creation is precisely that for which we can give no prescribed technique or recipe; and technique reaches its limits precisely at that point beyond which real creativity is called for—in the sciences as well as the arts.

But it is just at this point in the arts, where technique ceases to be sufficient, that we catch a glimpse of the meaning that is central to technique-technology. A technique is a standard method that can be taught. It is a recipe that can be fully conveyed from one person to another. A recipe always lays down a certain number of steps which, if followed to the letter, ought to lead invariably to the end desired. The logicians call this a *decision procedure.*

As children we became familiar with such procedures in our elementary arithmetic. Adding, subtracting, and multiplying were perfectly automatic procedures, even if they sometimes strained our attention. Problems in long division were a little more vexing because, for the sake of speed, they sometimes involved a certain amount of shrewd guessing. But if you went slowly, they were no different from the other operations. All you had to do was follow a routine method carefully, and you came out with the correct answer. Quite early too, in school mathematics, we encountered other kinds of problems that could not be solved in such mechanical fashion. In high school geometry, for example, you can prove some theorems only by devising a certain *construction*. You have to draw a line or figure that is not there in the original data. For this you had to be inventive; and if you weren't clever enough for that, you were forced simply to memorize the proof in the text—which had originally been the creation of genius by some ancient Greek. These two procedures—free construction and the rigorous application of a rule or rules—are antithetical but complementary. Together, they define the substance of mathematics.

Thus, even though we cannot formulate it, we come very early to know what the logical essence of the machine is, and consequently the meaning of technique that is central to technology. A machine is, logically speaking, an embodied decision procedure. By going through a finite and unvarying number of steps it arrives invariably, so long as it is not defective, at a definite result. When your car starts up in the morning, it is solving a problem by going through a number of prescribed steps. It is performing the same kind of operation, logically speaking, that you did as a child when you had to perform simple long division, though it is to be hoped more quickly. All that we desire from a machine of this kind is that it go through the routines written into it. The last thing we want from it is that it be creative or inventive in any way. When your automobile starts to sound in the morning as if its starting up were a matter of improvisation or invention, it is usually time to trade it in.

I.

Stripped down thus to its logical essence, the machine would hardly seem to be a threatening thing. It merely performs routine actions in our service; it does our long division for us, so to speak. It is when the machine becomes more clever that we begin to fear it. It may become cleverer than ourselves, and something we cannot control. There is also the fact that clever people can sometimes become quite thoughtless in pursuing their goals; thus the more complex and subtle the technology the more likely sometimes it is to carry with it damaging side effects that were never expected.

But whatever its source, there is no doubt that the suspicion of technology has become so widespread that the dominant myth of our time may very well become that of Frankenstein's monster. And, as should be the case with myths, this one has begun to have a strong grip not only on the intelligentsia but on the popular mind as well. The horror movies, for example, are mostly a re-creation of this myth in one form or another, and their audience has grown steadily. Most of science fiction, as a prophecy of the future, is one prolonged horror story. For the student of our culture, this situation has a very curious and striking ambiguity about it. While our writers, and some of the best of them, were seeking to recreate myths in literature for the sake of an age that seemed to have lost the capacity for myth, all this time technology was bringing in one very big myth through the back door. And there is the further irony about this: While technology is something essentially pointed toward the future, it has nevertheless been able to stir in the unconscious of the modern audience the primeval fears and horrors of monsters and ogres with which the old legends and fairy tales abound.

It would be pointless here to repeat the legitimate complaints that have made us fear technology. The cause of the environment has now found its champions and, it is hoped, will find more as time goes on. What is to the point, and particularly on a philosophical level, is to try to call attention to the very mixed and intricate nature of the matter of technology, especially when there is a tendency to drastic oversimplification on one side or the other. The real depth of the problem begins when we see how difficult it may be to separate out the beneficial and detrimental effects of technology. Chemical fertilizers, for example, have enabled our agriculture to become enormously productive, and so feed millions of people who might otherwise go hungry; yet these same fertilizers leach off into streams, pollute our waters, kill fish, and turn lakes into stagnant ponds. Medical technology has reduced those age old enemies of mankind, plagues and pestilence, all over the world; and as a result we now face the threat of overpopulation, which may become the most serious problem humankind will have to deal with in the next century. In cases like this, technology does not seem like the alien monster of a horror story, but very human indeed—ourselves writ large. We seem to carry over into technology that deepest and most vexing trait of the human condition itself: that our efforts are always ineradicably a mixture of good and evil.

We seem thus at once to have both too much technology and hardly enough. We do not as yet, for example, have enough technology actually operant to feed all the people on this planet.

Our ambivalence is further compounded by the fact that, complain as much as we do about all the hardware of technology, we secretly nourish a fascination with technique itself. The publishing market is regularly flooded with "how to" manuals of all kinds. We turn to books to learn how to make love, and in consequence sex comes to be thought of as mainly a technique. Treatises on mental health appear that carry with them their own built-in little self-help kit of psychotherapy. All of this would be comic if it weren't also so pathetic—and ultimately dangerous. This worship of technique is in fact more childish than the worship of machines. You have only to find the right method, the definite procedure, and all problems in life must inevitably yield before it. Our ambivalence here toward the whole phenomenon of technique-technology could scarcely be more complete. I do not know that there are any statistics on the matter, but I suspect that a good many persons who put their trust in manuals of sex may be the very same persons who take up the cause of the environment and rail against technology.

Philosophy has a very special relation to this muddled state of affairs, if the philosopher would only stop to think about it. Philosophy is, in fact, the historical source of technology in its modern sense. This claim may seem surprising at first sight, but we have only to recall our earlier discussion to see that it is in no way exaggerated. We pointed out then that technique, in its strictly technological sense, involved two factors. (1) There must be a clear and distinct separation of the subjective and objective components in any situation in order for us to take rational hold of the problem. (2) The objective problem, thus isolated, is to be dealt with by a logical procedure that seeks to resolve it into a finite number of steps or operations. Both these conditions were the creation of philosophy. Descartes ushered in the modern age by establishing the primacy of *method*, in the course of which he fixed the distinction between subject and object as sharply as could possibly be done. And as for logic itself, that was originally the creation of philosophers in the ancient days of the Greeks.

Thus the whole of technology, as we now know it, is the late, and maybe the final offspring of philosophy. There is not the least exaggeration in this judgment. It merely reports the simple historical course of things.

But being a parent does not now confer any special privileges upon the philosopher. He is absorbed into the technical scheme of things with everybody else. One of the chief characteristics of the technical society is the specialization of labor. This follows from the logical nature of technique itself. Since technology is merely the embodiment of a logical procedure, and this procedure divides the problem into a number of partial and successive steps, therefore the social accomplishment of the task will be divided into the accomplishment of these component parts. Consequently, we are each assigned our particular slot in the society.

The philosopher has to feel a little uncertain here. He is still secretly committed to a discipline that is uneasy before such specialization. Voltaire described his Dr. Pangloss, the ridiculous metaphysician in *Candide*, as "professor of things in general." The irony was meant to be devastating. Talk about everything in general fails to be specific about anything, and is therefore empty of sense. Ever since, philosophers in the modern period have labored under the shadow of Voltaire's censure. Moreover, unlike their ancient brethren, they now have to contend with modern science, which did speak—and triumphantly so—about very definite and specific things. Yet the philosopher, uneasy as he may be, is still condemned to the tag of his calling. So far as he is still assigned to the profession of philosophy, he must seek to frame some general scheme of ideas, however tentative, about the way things are. He is condemned to be a "professor of things in general." The ghost of Dr. Pangloss still haunts him.

An escape seems to beckon by way of social imitation. Simply as a social being, the philosopher will feel this push anyway. In any society the individual has to establish his social status by demonstrating competency in the ways that are normally approved by that society. In a technical society this means that the individual establishes his technical proficiency at some kind of task. Since there are no privileged exceptions, the philosopher is dragged into the net like everyone else. He seeks therefore to justify himself and his existence as a peculiar kind of technician. There are even "technical" journals in philosophy, as in mathematics and physics. The philosopher thus adopts a protective coloration that helps him escape notice in his society. But if he stops to think for a moment, he will realize he is playing a game: The so-called technical publications of philosophy do not resemble those in mathematics and physics. If he thinks a little longer, he will conclude that philosophy is the kind of subject in which there cannot be technical journals of that kind. But these considerations easily get lost in the heat of the battle. Prestige and personal vanity involve one in controversy; the technique of the philosopher has to do with words, and arguments about words; and the more he immerses himself in hair-splitting debates the more he can feed his illusion that he is a genuine technician. He becomes absorbed into what was at first his protective coloration. The philosopher disappears into the technician. From a larger historical perspective, there is an amusing but very somber irony here: Philosophy, which was the original sire of technique, is now about to be devoured by its own offspring.

Pulled by these opposing forces—on the one hand, to become a specialist and lose himself in technical details, and on the other hand still to maintain contact with the larger questions of his ancient calling—the philosopher experiences a great sense of relief if he should happen upon a technique that seems to satisfy both requirements at once. Such was the response when *Principia Mathematica* appeared on the scene. It was a technique, and a sufficiently intricate one, such that the ability to understand and handle it gave one the credentials of technical competence. On the other hand, it was not a narrow technique; it seemed to have the most universal implications, and so far from shutting one off in a narrow technical cubbyhole, it seemed to open a broad highway into other disciplines. Thus one could be a "professor of things in general" without having to hang one's head in embarrassment.

But technique also has the characteristic that it sometimes breeds its own obsolescence. Just as the material products of technology become worn out and obsolete, so too the technique that begot them has to be replaced by another. In philosophy this usually means a total change in style and language.

The turnover in philosophic styles has been very rapid in this century. Perhaps that is fitting in a technical civilization, which seems to accelerate history in its every aspect. If one persists long enough as an academic philosopher one sees these styles in philosophy come and go, and one strives to attain some normal human balance between enthusiasm and disillusion. If the rapid succession of reigning orthodoxies does not seem to serve philosophy, which is supposed to aspire after perennial truth, still there are some advantages to be gained from the turnover. At least one narrow technique will yield to another, and one error is driven out by the next. Whether truth is ever attained thereby, we cannot be sure; but at least one hopes that it may hover somewhere over the whole process. And if one does not become disillusioned altogether, there can also be certain moments of illumination in the very shock of change, as in the following story:

My colleagues and I were met to revise the course of studies for students majoring in philosophy. The particular bone of contention in this case was the requirement of mathematical logic, which some students felt was not really relevant to their particular interests. Most of my col-leagues, and I myself, felt that some minimal exposure to the subject was a necessary discipline to go through. The vigorous dissenter in this case was an active young colleague, who made his position very plain: He had never had training in the subject, had never felt the need of it, and did not see why students should have to spend their time in going through with it. Had he been a humanist in his general tendencies, the dissent would have been understandable, though it would probably have been offered much more diffidently. But in fact he was a technician of sorts, and altogether convinced of the value of his own chosen technique. He was now immersed in linguistics, and was convinced that this discipline would provide the definite and final key to philosophy.

There are certain moments when the passage of time strikes us with its brutal illumination, and this was one. I felt that this young man and I could be interchangeable across the gap of a generation. Twenty-five years ago this young philosopher would have been urging that mathe-matical logic was central and indispensable to philosophy. And were I twenty-five years younger I might very well be exhibiting his total passion for the new technique. *Autre temps autres moeurs.* This young philosopher believes that the whole of what we traditionally know as philosophy will disappear without a trace into linguistics. The particular technique has changed, but what persists unchanged is an underlying conviction of our era, that technique of some sort is decisive for philosophy.

So the case of Russell, Whitehead, and Wittgenstein is worth returning to. Its lesson, apparently, has not yet been learned; and that les-son, one of the really significant legacies from an earlier generation, might help to deliver the present generation from some of the illusions about the omnipotence of its current techniques.

Monopolizing the Conversation: On Being Civilly Egocentric

Charles Derber

"Conversation indeed" said the Rocket. "You have talked the whole time yourself. That is not conversation." "Somebody must listen" answered the Frog, "and I like to do all the talking myself."

"You are a very irritating person" said the Rocket, "and very ill bred. I hate people who talk about themselves, as you do, when one wants to talk about oneself, as I do . . . "

OSCAR WILDE, from "The Remarkable Rocket"

Individualism has a counterpart in American psychology. People tend to seek attention for themselves in face-to-face interactions. This attention-getting psychology reflects an underlying character structure of "self-orientation" that emerges in highly individualistic societies.[1] Erich Fromm has theorized that a shared character structure develops in each society, a "social character" that is a response to the requirements of the social order and best suited for survival and success within it. The self-oriented character type develops a highly egocentric view of the world and is motivated primarily by self-interest. To cope with social and economic insecurity bred by individualism, he becomes preoccupied with himself. His "attention-getting" psychology is thus rooted in a broad self-absorption engendered by social conditions highly developed in contemporary America.[2]

In informal conversation, the self-oriented person repeatedly seeks to turn attention to himself. This "conversational narcissism" is closely related to the individualistic norms already discussed. As shown in the first chapter, attention is allocated according to norms in which each individual is responsible for himself, and is free, within limits of civility, to take as much as he can. These norms legitimate focusing on one's own needs in informal talk and are consistent with the effort by self-oriented conversationalists to gain predominant attention for themselves.

The Forms of Conversational Narcissism

Conversational narcissism is the key manifestation of the dominant attention-getting psychology in America. It occurs in informal conversations among friends, family and coworkers. The profusion of popular literature about listening and the etiquette of managing those who talk constantly about themselves suggests its pervasiveness in everyday life; its contemporary importance is indicated by the early appearance of these problems in the most recent edition of Emily Post's etiquette manual.[3]

In observations of ordinary conversations, I have found a set of extremely common conversational practices which show an unresponsiveness to others' topics and involve turning them into one's own.[4] Because of norms prohibiting blatantly egocentric behavior, these practices are often exquisitely subtle; ritual forms of civility and face-saving have evolved to limit the overt expression of egoism in social life.[5] Although conversationalists are free to introduce topics about themselves, they are expected to maintain an appearance of genuine interest in those about others in the conversation. A delicate face-saving system requires that people refrain from openly disregarding others' concerns and keep expressions of disinterest from becoming visible. Practices of conversational narcissism are normally, then, driven underground and expressed in disguised forms where they are not readily discerned by any member of the conversation.[6]

To explore the narcissistic practices that occur most often, we must distinguish between two kinds of attention-response: the *shift-response* and the *support-response*. The shift- and support responses are alternative ways one can react to others' conversational initiatives. The differences between the two can be seen in the following examples:[7]

John: I'm feeling really starved.
Mary: Oh, I just ate. (shift-response)

John: I'm feeling really starved.
Mary: When was the last time you ate? (support-response)

John: God, I'm feeling so angry at Bob.

Mary: Yeah, I've been feeling the same way toward him. (shift-response)

John: God, I'm feeling so angry at Bob.

Mary: Why, what's been going on between the two of you? (support-response)

John: My mother would pack me melted cheese sandwiches every day.

Mary: My mom never made me a lunch I could stand to eat. (shift-response)

John: My mother would pack me melted cheese sandwiches every day.

Mary: Hey, your mother was all right. (support-response)

John: I saw Jane today on the street.

Mary: I haven't seen her in a week. (shift-response)

John: I saw Jane today on the street.

Mary: Oh, how's she doing? (support-response)

John: I just love Brahms.

Mary: Chopin's my favorite. (shift-response)

John: I just love Brahms.

Mary: Which is your favorite piece? (support-response)

The shift-response and support-response are both commonly used. They are superficially so little different that few conversationalists notice the distinction. Yet they affect the flow of attention and the development of topics in markedly different ways. When Mary uses the shift-response, she temporarily shifts the attention to herself and creates the potential for a change in topic. When using the support-response, she keeps the attention and topic securely focused on John.

Of the two responses, only the shift-response changes who is the subject of the conversation. For example, if Mary says to John, "I'm going to the movies tonight," John can temporarily make himself the subject with any of the following replies:

That reminds me, I've got to go home tonight.

I'm sick of movies these days.

Gee, I wonder what I'm going to do tonight.

With each of these shift-responses, John introduces the dilemma of whether the conversation will continue with Mary as the subject or will turn to him. Alternatively, he could offer the following kinds of support responses:

What movie?

Great, you deserve a break.

Are you feeling good enough to go?

These support-responses are attention-giving ones not in competition with Mary's initial assertion. They keep the conversation clearly focused on her and give her license to continue as the subject. Support-responses, unlike shift-responses, cannot normally be introduced to transfer attention to the self.[8]

Conversational narcissism involves preferential use of the shift-response and underutilization of the support-response. We can distinguish between active and passive narcissistic practices. The active practices involve repeated use of the shift-response to subtly turn the topics of others into topics about oneself. The passive practices involve minimal use of support-responses so that others' topics are not sufficiently reinforced and so are terminated prematurely.

NOTES

1. In contrast, an "attention-giving" psychology is based on the tendency for the individual to focus attention on the needs and concerns of others as well as himself in social life. While the attention-getting psychology is more consistent with the individualistic norms of the dominant culture and is more pervasive in the society, the attention-giving psychology is expected of members of subordinate groups, especially women, and tends to characterize their behavior in face-to-face interactions with those more powerful.

While a dominant psychology of attention develops in every culture, there is thus significant variation by sex and social status. I am concerned in this chapter only with the dominant form in American culture. In the second part of the book I examine the variations among groups who occupy different positions in the social structure.

2. In his classic work, *Escape from Freedom*, Fromm discussed the concept of social character and emphasized the primacy of individualism in shaping character structure in modern capitalist cultures. The theme of egoism has been central in many analyses of the psychology bred by individualism. In his work on suicide, Durkheim treated egoism as a response to the weakening of social bonds and traditional collectivities. The disaffiliated individual is centrally self-oriented as his isolation breeds self-absorption and his individualized social and economic position erodes collective purposes and engenders preoccupation with his own needs.

Several American social theorists have recently pointed to the emergence of self-orientation as a central element in American social character. Philip Reiff has discussed "psychological man"—a character type bred by modern individualism and concerned primarily with his own personal growth and gratification. Richard Sennett has discussed the fall of "public man" and the rise of the more self-oriented and private man of contemporary culture. Christopher Lasch has spoken of the growth of the narcissistic character as a response to the survival pressures of contemporary individualism. The breakdown of family life and other community supports and the burdening of each individual with economic and social responsibilities formerly shared with others necessarily generates a focus on oneself and preoccupation with one's own needs. These themes are elaborated in the last chapter. See Emile Durkheim, *Suicide*, Philip Reiff, *The Triumph of the Therapeutic*, Richard Sennett, *The Fall of Public Man*, Christopher Lasch, *The Culture of Narcissism.*

3. See Emily Post, *Etiquette*, Chapter 1.

4. These studies are described in the Introduction, pp. 7-8.

5. The ritual order has been richly described by Erving Goffman, "Face-Work," in *Interaction Ritual.*

6. This unawareness may extend to the self-oriented individual himself. Conversational narcissism is typically not conscious behavior but reflects rather a habitual focus on or absorption with oneself that is non-self-consciously expressed in conversational patterns. Use of terminology such as conversational initiatives or strategies should thus not be understood as always referring to willful or manipulative behavior but to unreflective behavior that has the effect of creating shifts in topic and attention.

7. The illustrations of shift-responses here are drawn from the transcriptions of the dinner conversations (see p. 8). The support-responses here are hypothetical, presented in this format to highlight the contrast with shift-responses. Unless otherwise indicated, all examples presented in the text in this chapter are drawn from the transcripts. For purposes of readability, the presentation of the transcripts is nontechnical and does not include special markings denoting pauses or interruptions.

8. Under special circumstances, a support-response can be used as an attention-getting initiative by subtly redirecting the conversation. By asking a certain form of question about the other, for example, the respondent may steer the talk toward new ideas, leading eventually toward a focus on himself. However, it cannot lead to a shift in the next turn in the conversation, and normally sustains the talk on the other's topic for at least several successive turns.

REFERENCES

Durkheim, Emile. *Suicide.* New York: Free Press, 1951.

Fromm, Erich. *Escape From Freedom.* New York: Avon, 1941.

Goffman, Erving. *Interaction Ritual.* New York: Anchor, 1967.

Lasch, Christopher. *The Culture of Narcissism.* New York: Basic Books, 1978.

Post, Emily. *Etiquette.* New York: Funk & Wagnalls, 1973.

Reiff, Philip. *Fellow Teachers.* New York: Harper, 1973.

Sennett, Richard. *The Fall of Public Man.* New York: Knopf, 1977.

Wilde, Oscar. *The Fairy Tales of Oscar Wilde.* New York: Hart, 1975.

■ 4
Dialogue's Confirmation

What are our responsibilities to our children? What do children need from their parents and other adults? Food and nourishment, physical safety and shelter, education and health care? All of these are important, but none of them are sufficient for an infant (literally, "without speech") to grow up to be a person. The primary *human* need is for confirmation. To be confirmed as the person that one is is what each of us most needs. Confirmation, Friedman (1983, 1985) showed, is essential to becoming a self. Confirmation does not mean that one is simply treated nicely, or that one is always agreed with, or that anything one does if OK and that one is never corrected or punished. Confirmation means, simply yet profoundly, being recognized as a person in the world. Confirmation and its opposite, disconfirmation, are associated in the writing of R.D. Laing (1967) with love and violence:

> Love and violence, properly speaking, are polar opposites. Love lets the other be, but with affection and concern. Violence attempts to constrain the other's freedom, to force him to act in the way we desire, but with ultimate lack of concern, with indifference to the other's own existence or destiny. (p. 58)

Laing is a British psychiatrist who conducted intensive investigation of the family lives of patients who came to him diagnosed as schizophrenic. Over a period of years, he and his colleagues conducted interviews, not only with the patients themselves, but with as many family members and combinations of family members as possible, with and without the patient present. In *Sanity, Madness, and the Family*, Laing and Esterson (1970) described in detail their studies of 11 of these families. They reported that in every case they studied, not only in those 11, but in more than 200, the behavior of the patient that seemed to be so bizarre when considered in isolation, seemed much more sensible when considered in the context of the interaction in their family. The patterns of communica-

71

tion in these families were themselves rather bizarre. The patients had been trying to cope with families who had been subjecting at least that patient to a pervasive pattern of disconfirmation.

In our selection from Laing's *Self and Others*, the author illustrates both confirmation and disconfirmation, using fascinating examples from both ordinary and clinical data. As with most authors who have written about confirmation, Laing acknowledges the contribution of Martin Buber to his understanding of these processes.

No one has written more about the thought and life of Buber than has Maurice Friedman. One of Buber's most intriguing ideas concerned the significance of confirmation in human relationships and human society. Although Buber did not develop his thought about confirmation in detail, Friedman (1983, 1985) has explored its implications far more fully (Friedman's own metaphor was that Buber left the idea of confirmation mostly in seed and that his own role has been in bringing the seed to flower).

We have selected a chapter from one of Friedman's earlier books, *Touchstones of Reality* (one of the best and most inspiring books we have ever read). In this chapter on the "partnership of existence," Friedman asserts that all real human living is in partnership with others, in which each of us becomes a person through going out to meet the other. Although he used the term *confirmation* only occasionally in this chapter, it is through recognizing and responding to the other, as Friedman discusses it, that confirmation occurs.

REFERENCES

Friedman, M. (1983). *The confirmation of otherness: In family, community, and society.* New York: Pilgrim Press.
Friedman, M. (1985). *The healing dialogue in psychotherapy.* New York: Jason Aronson.
Laing, R.D. (1967). *The politics of experience.* New York: Ballantine.
Laing, R.D., & Esterson, A. (1970). *Sanity, madness, and the family: Families of schizophrenics* (2nd ed.). Middlesex, England: Penguin Books.

■

Confirmation and Disconfirmation

R.D. Laing

In human society, at all its levels, persons confirm one another in a practical way, to some extent or other, in their personal qualities and capacities, and a society may be termed human in the measure to which its members confirm one another.

The basis of man's life with man is twofold, and it is one—the wish of every man to be confirmed as what he is, even as what he can become, by men; and the innate capacity in man to confirm his fellow-men in this way. That this capacity lies so immeasurably fallow constitutes the real weakness and questionableness of the human race: actual humanity exists only where this capacity unfolds. On the other hand, of course, an empty claim for confirmation, without devotion for being and becoming, again and again mars the truth of the life between man and man.

Men need, and it is granted to them, to confirm one another in their individual being by means of genuine meanings: but beyond this they need, and it is granted to them, to see the truth, which the soul gains by its struggle, light up to the others, the brothers, in a different way, and even so be confirmed.

Martin Buber (1957)

Total confirmation of one man by another is an ideal possibility seldom realized. For practical purposes, as Buber states, confirmation is always "to some extent or other." Any human interaction implies some measure of confirmation, at any rate of the physical bodies of the participants, even when one person is shooting another. The slightest sign of recognition from another at least confirms one's presence in *his* world. "No more fiendish punishment could be devised," William James once wrote, "even were such a thing physically possible, than that one should be turned loose in society and remain absolutely unnoticed by all the members thereof."

Thus, we can think of confirmation as partial and varying in manner, as well as global and absolute. One can think of action and interaction sequences as more or less, and in different ways, *confirmatory* or *disconfirmatory*. Confirmation can vary in intensity and extensity, quality and quantity. By reacting "lukewarmly," imperviously, tangentially, and so on, one fails to endorse some aspects of the other, while endorsing other aspects.

Modes of confirmation or disconfirmation vary. Confirmation could be through a responsive smile (visual), a handshake (tactile), an expression of sympathy (auditory). A confirmatory response is *relevant* to the evocative action, it accords recognition to the evocatory act, and accepts its significance for the evoker, if not for the respondent. A confirmatory reaction is a direct response, it is "to the point," or "on the same wavelength" as the initiatory or evocatory action. A partially confirmatory response need not be in agreement, or gratifying, or satisfying. Rejection can be confirmatory if it is direct, not tangential, and recognizes the evoking action and grants it significance and validity.

There are different levels of confirmation or disconfirmation. An action may be confirmed at one level and disconfirmed at another. Some forms of "rejection" imply limited recognition—the perception of and responsiveness to what is rejected. An action "rejected" is perceived and this perception shows that it is accepted as a fact. Direct "rejection" is not tangential; it is not mocking or in other ways invalidating. It need neither depreciate nor exaggerate the original action. It is not synonymous with indifference or imperviousness.

Some areas of a person's being may cry out for confirmation more than others. Some forms of disconfirmation may be more destructive of self-development than others. One may call these schizogenic. The ontogenesis of confirmation and disconfirmation has barely begun to be explored. Responsiveness adequate to the infant will be inappropriate to an older child or an adult. There may be periods in one's life when one has experienced more confirmation or disconfirmation than at other periods. The qualities and capacities confirmed or disconfirmed by mother or father, brothers, sisters, friends, may differ widely. An aspect of oneself negated by one person may be endorsed by another. A part or aspect of oneself which is "false," or which one regards as false, may be confirmed actively and persistently by one or both parents, or even by all the significant others at the same time. At different periods of life, the practical or felt need for, and modes of, confirmation or disconfirmation vary, both as to the aspects of the person's being in question and as to the modes of confirming or disconfirming particular aspects.

Many families have now been studied (not only those in which one person has come to be regarded as psychotic) where there is little genuine confirmation of the parents by each other and of the child by each parent, separately or together, but this may not be obvious, though it can be studied objectively. One finds interactions marked by pseudo-confirmation, by acts which masquerade as confirming but are counterfeit.[1] Pretences at confirmation go through the appearances of confirmation. The absence of genuine confirmation, or pseudo-confirmation, may take the form of confirming a fiction the child is taken to be, without the actual child receiving recognition. The characteristic family pattern that has emerged from the studies of the families of schizophrenics does not so much involve a child who is subject to outright neglect or even to obvious trauma, but a child who has been subjected to subtle but persistent disconfirmation, usually unwittingly. For many years lack of genuine confirmation takes the form of actively confirming a false self, so that the person whose false self is confirmed and real self disconfirmed is placed in a false position. Someone in a false position *feels guilt, shame, or anxiety at not being false.* Confirmation of a false self goes on without anyone in the family being aware that this is the state of affairs. The schizogenic potential of the situation seems to reside largely in the fact that it is not recognized by anyone; or if the mother or father or some other member or friend of the family is aware of this state of affairs, it is not brought into the open and no effort is made to intervene— if such intervention were only to state the truth of the matter.

Here we shall look at some acts of confirmation or disconfirmation, without prejudgments as to whether or to what extent they are schizogenic.

There may be a failure to recognize a person as agent. The attribution of agency to human beings is one way we distinguish people from things set in motion by agents external to themselves. In some childhoods this quality of being human, whereby one can come to feel that one is an agent in one's own right, is not confirmed by the original significant others. It is illuminating to match observations on the way a child is treated by his parents with the "delusions" the psychotic child or adult expresses.

Julie said she was a "tolled bell" (told belle), that she was "tailored bread" (bred). When it was possible to observe the interaction between her mother and her, one could see that her mother could not or did not confirm agency on Julie's part. Her mother could not respond to spontaneity and *inter*acted with her only if she, mother, could initiate the interaction. Her mother visited the hospital daily. One saw Julie daily sitting passively while her mother combed her hair, put ribbons and hairpins in it, powdered her face, applied lipstick to her lips and mascara to her eyes, so that the final appearance resembled nothing so much as that of a beautiful, lifesize, lifeless doll which her mother "told" (tolled). Julie seemed to have been her mother's "transitional object," to use Winnicott's term. One might say: "What could her mother do but this, if her daughter was catatonic?" It is significant and remarkable that it was *this passive listless "thing" which her mother regarded as normal.* She reacted to spontaneity on Julie's part with anxiety and attributions of badness or madness. To be good was to do what she was told (Laing, 1960, pp. 196-224).

FURTHER EXAMPLES OF CONFIRMATION AND DISCONFIRMATION

. . . 3. I began a session with a schizophrenic woman of twenty-five, who sat down in a chair some distance away from me while I sat half facing her in another chair. After about ten minutes during which she had not moved or spoken, my mind began to drift away on preoccupations of my own. In the midst of these, I heard her say in a very small voice, "Oh please don't go so far away from me."

Psychotherapy with real card-carrying schizophrenics is a separate subject, but the following are a few remarks on the issue of confirmation or disconfirmation in psychotherapy.

When she made this remark I could have responded in many ways. A comment some psychotherapists might make is, "You feel I am away from you." By this, one would neither confirm nor disconfirm the validity of her "feeling" that I was no longer "with" her, but would confirm the fact that she experienced me as away. The endorsement of the "feeling" is noncommittal about the validity of the feeling, namely, whether or not *I* was actually going away from her. One could "interpret" why she should be frightened at me not staying "with" her, e.g. a need to have me "with" her as a defence against her own anger if I am not. One might construe her plea as an expression of her need to fill her emptiness by my presence, or to treat me as a "transitional object," and so on.

In my view the most important thing for me to do at that moment was to confirm the fact that she had correctly registered *my* actual withdrawal of my "presence." There are many patients who are very sensitive to desertion, but are not sure of the reliability, much less validity, of their own sensitivity. They do not trust other people, and they cannot trust their own mistrust either. Jill is tormented, for instance, by not knowing whether she just "feels" that Jack is preoccupied and uninterested, while Jack is pretending to be intensely attentive; or whether she can "trust" her feelings to register the real state of the relationship. One of the most important questions, therefore, is whether such mistrust of her "feelings" and the testimony of others arises from persistent inconsistencies within an original nexus—between the evidence of empathic attributions about others, her experience of herself, the testimony of others about their feelings, and the constructions they place on her experience of, and intentions towards, them, etc.—so that she has never been able to arrive at any trust in herself in any respect.

The only thing, therefore, I could say to my patient was, "I am sorry."

4. A nurse was engaged to look after a somewhat catatonic, hebephrenic schizophrenic patient. Shortly after they had met, the nurse gave the patient a cup of tea. This chronically psychotic patient, on taking the tea, said, "This is the first time in my life that anyone has ever given me a cup of tea." Subsequent experience with this patient tended to substantiate the simple truth of this statement.[2]

It is not so easy for one person to give another a cup of tea. If a lady gives me a cup of tea, she might be showing off her teapot, or her tea-set; she might be trying to put me in a good mood in order to get something out of me; she may be trying to get me to like her; she may be wanting me as an ally for her own purposes against others. She might pour tea from a teapot into a cup and shove out her hand with cup and saucer in it, whereupon I am expected to grab them within the two seconds before they will become a dead weight. The action could be a mechanical one in which there is no recognition of *me* in it. A cup of tea could be handed me without *me* being *given* a *cup of tea*.

In our tea ceremonial, it is the simplest and most difficult thing in the world for *one person,* genuinely being his or her self, *to give,* in fact and not just in appearance, *another person,* realized in his or her own being by the giver, *a cup of tea,* really, and not in appearance. This patient is saying that many cups of tea have passed from other hands to hers in the course of her life, but this notwithstanding, she has never in her life had a cup of tea really given her.

Some people are more sensitive than others to not being recognized as human beings. If someone is *very* sensitive in this respect, they stand a good chance of being diagnosed as schizophrenic. Freud said of hysterics, as Fromm-Reichmann was later to say of schizophrenics, that they needed both to give and receive more love than most people. One could put this the other way round. If you need to give and receive *too much* "love,"[3] you will be a high risk for the diagnosis of schizophrenia. This diagnosis attributes to you the incapacity, by and large, to give or receive "love" in an adult manner. When you smile at such a thought, this may confirm the diagnosis since you are suffering from "inappropriate affect."

NOTES

1. Cf. Wynne *et al.* (1958).
2. This anecdote was told me by Dr. Charles Rycroft.
3. Whatever "love" is.

REFERENCES

Buber, M. (1957). "Elements of the inter-human contact." *Psychiatry* 20.
Laing, R.D. (1960). *The Divided Self.* London: Tavistock Publications; (Penguin Book, 1965) New York: Pantheon.
Wynne, L.C., Ryckoft, I.M., Day, J., & Hirsch, S. (1958). "Pseudo-mutuality in the family relations of schizophrenics." *Psychiatry* 21, 205.

The Partnership of Existence

Maurice Friedman

Man is given freedom. Man exists as freedom, and with that freedom is possibility undreamt of in the realm of the animals. This includes destructive possibilities quite as much as constructive ones. Aggression does not need to mean destructiveness. It is possible to direct one's aggression into positive channels. But when wedded to existential mistrust, aggression inevitably becomes destructive. Existential mistrust quickly becomes reciprocal. If you reflect suspicion on someone else, it is reflected back on you until you find the very evidence you are looking for: the other also mistrusts you and acts in ways to confirm your worst fears about him. The typical behavior of large groups and societies in relation to one another is exactly what we would call paranoid if we encountered it in individuals. Each group has a shut-in, closed world, sealed off from seeing in the way that the other sees. Each interprets the motives of the other in terms of its own world of defenses, fears, and suspicions.

Objective clear analysis—psychological, social, economic, political, and/or international—will never by itself overcome man's destructive tendencies; for it does not get at what is essentially at issue: existential mistrust. Perspective alone will not do it. What we need is a direction, and direction has to do with our existence as persons in relationship to one another.

Aristotle told us a long time ago that man is a *zoon politikon*. But to say that man is a political or social animal does not tell us *per se* of any partnership of existence. It might only be a social contract, a *modus vivendi*, a *mariage de convenance*. In order that we not bash in one another's heads all the time, we act *as if* we believed in not doing to the other what we would not want done to ourselves—as long as we cannot get away with treating him as we would like to! Aristotle's teacher Plato faced this question as honestly as he could in his great dialogue *The Republic*. But the only thing he could come up with as an alternative to Thrasymachus' "Justice is the interest of the stronger" and Glaucon and Adeimantus' justice as a social contract based on mutual fear was the good of the individual soul. As the Hindu conceived the destiny of the individual as bound up with cosmic and social *dharma*, so Plato saw the harmony of the soul as connected with the harmony of a society divided into classes of guardians, merchants, and workers very similar to the Hindu caste system. But this too has nothing to do with the partnership of existence. There is no room in Plato's *Republic* for a direct, unmediated relationship between man and man; there is no room for genuine community, for real fellowship. There is only the totalitarian state run by the aid of the "royal lie" which has been imposed upon the people by the one man who knows "the Good, the True, the Beautiful"—the Philosopher King—in order to get them to behave the way they ought according to his theories.

If we speak of the "partnership of existence," we are suggesting, in contrast, not that people can live by some altruistic ideal but that our very existence is only properly understood as a partnership. We become selves *with* one another and live our lives with one another in the most real sense of the term. Put in the language of "touchstones of reality," we cannot find reality simply by remaining with ourselves or making ourselves the goal. Paradoxically, we only know ourselves when we know ourselves in responding to others.

To say I become a self with others does not mean I ever reach symbiotic unity with them or that I can always be in relationship with them. On the contrary, the ground on which we stand is not only the ground of our uniqueness but of our singleness. We are like that marvelous myth that Plato puts into the mouth of Aristophanes in his great dialogue *The Symposium*. In this myth people are pictured as originally having four arms and four legs and rolling around the world and challenging the gods themselves to combat. Then Zeus cuts them in half. Immediately each half throws its arms around the other, and they cling together until Zeus intervenes once again and makes them separate. From that moment they go around the world, each looking for his other half. They are not self-sufficient as halves, but neither can they ever become whole again even if they should find their other halves. This is a wonderful paradigm of human existence as such. While we are unique persons, we are not so in the sense of nineteenth-century American individualism.

There is a paradox here and a hardly comprehensible one. I cannot regard my "I" merely as a product of social forces and influences, for then it is no longer an "I." There has to be that in me which can respond if I am going to talk about any sort of personal uniqueness. Therefore, I cannot say with George Herbert Mead, "The self is an eddy in the social current." I cannot turn the self into a mere confluence of social and psychological streams. On the other hand, if I speak of our having an "essence," that is misleading because it suggests something substantive that is within us as a vein of gold runs through a mountain waiting to be mined. What can we really say more than that we have in us the potentiality of response which can be awakened? But we must do the responding. No one can handle our side of the dialogue even from the beginning. There is an irreducible uniqueness that has to do with the fact that each person, even identical twins, has a very personal way of responding that can be discerned at six months and even earlier.

This does not mean that we are born already a self, or an "I." If we did not grow up with human parents, we would never become a person—not just in the sense that we would not take on the conventional social adaptations but that we would not be called into existence as an "I." Eric Erickson remarks in *Childhood and Society* that if the parent smiles at a child and the child does not smile back at the parent, there comes a time when the parent no longer has the resources to smile at the child. It is a two-way street. This does not imply that we do not exist as a self when we are not with some other person, any more than that in being with another we are automatically in mutual relationship. There is a distinction between our awareness of our self as some sort of continuity and our becoming ourselves in the meeting with others—with everything that meets us and calls us out.

We must respond to this call from where we are, and where we are is never merely social or merely individual but uniquely personal. We need to be confirmed by others. Our very sense of ourselves only comes in this meeting with others. We do not begin as isolated consciousness. Yet through this confirmation we can grow to the strength of Socrates, who said, "I respect you, Athenians. But I will obey the god and not you." Socrates would have been willing to drink the cup of hemlock even if not a single Athenian had voted for him. Not that Socrates saw himself as responsible only to the god. He expressed his responsibility to his fellow Athenians precisely in opposing them.

Responsibility means to respond. I cannot respond until I am in the situation, until I am face to face with you. I must really respond to you before I can love you. If I can then deal lovingly with you, that means that something real has taken place in our actual relationship. I have not simply manifested or expressed an intellectual or emotional attitude which I possessed before entering the relationship. Genuine response is response of the whole person. Yet we ought not think of the question of how to be a whole person but only of how, in any given situation, to respond more wholly rather than less so. A more whole response in one situation may help us to a still more whole response in a succeeding one. But we never become "whole persons" as a state of being, attained once for all. In every situation we are asked to respond in a unique way. Therefore, our wholeness in that situation is unique too. Although I am an Eagle Scout, I cannot accept the Scout motto, "Be prepared," if it means being prepared with the answer before one reaches the situation in which one has to answer. The only real preparation we can have is our preparation to respond in so far as our resources allow in the situation.

The deceptive aura that clings to the phrase "integration of the person" is the notion that you can become a perfect sphere in abstraction from and in advance of your relations to what is not yourself. In fact, you always integrate yourself in terms of a particular moment, in terms of a particular situation. If the situation calls you, you do not have the choice of not responding at all; for even a failure to respond is a decision, and even a halfway response is some sort of response. But you may bring yourself into wholeness in responding or you may fail to do so. Each moment of personal wholeness is unique even though you become more and more "yourself" through such response—hence more and more recognizable by others in a personal uniqueness that extends beyond the moment.

The "integration of the person" does not take place before the response, as a goal in itself. It only takes place in the act of responding. There are many people who hold that one must first be a "real person" and only then will one be able to enter into real dialogue, make real decisions. But the fact is that we do not become whole for our own sakes or in terms of ourselves. That is because we *touch* on reality at the moment when we touch on what is not ourselves, on what calls us, and we bring ourselves into wholeness from the depths of our being in response to this call. This is what the Hasidim mean by "serving God with the evil urge." Serving God with the "evil" urge does not mean actually doing or taking part in evil. Nor does it mean, in the manner of Jung, the integration of the evil and good in yourself. It means, rather, integrating yourself in responding—in making a real decision. Decision here is not a conscious matter but the movement of the whole person. Real guilt, by the same token, arises because you have failed to respond, have responded with less wholeness and awareness than you might have.

When we are called out in a fundamental way, we discover that we have resources of which we would not have dreamed. Our ordinary, casual responses are put aside, and we bring ourselves together in a rare act of whole decision. Or, if we do not, we know the genuine remorse that comes from not having been able to collect ourselves in the face of what we recognize as a call to our inmost depths. Abraham Lincoln responded with greatness to a unique historical situation and became the unique person that he was. You only really exist when you exist in a situation, and you become yourself in responding to that situation.

Our resources in each situation are limited, of course, but we do not know what that factual limitation will be before and apart from the situation. Our freedom is a "finite freedom," as Paul Tillich says, and that finite freedom varies from moment to moment. Insofar as we have freedom within the situation, we have the possibility of responding more wholly. But to respond more wholly we must be more fully aware. Full awareness here is the awareness of dialogue itself, the awareness of what addresses you. In talking with another person, for example, you may pick up only the intellectual level of what he says while, consciously or not, he is addressing you on many levels at the same time. It may make you anxious to recognize and respond to that address; so you block off your awareness of it. Later on though, the anxiety will probably come into the circle of your awareness—through dreams, fantasies, memories, twinges of pain or embarrassment. When that happens, it might become possible in a new situation to enter into relationship with a greater awareness and a wholer response than before. Much of our guilt is not deliberate commission or omission but simply that fuzzy awareness—"If only I'd really known!" We are responsible even for our lack of awareness, for that failure to hear which eventually turns into an inability to hear.

What is true of our awareness is also true of our response. We can be guilty even when we do and say all the right things if we do not respond with our whole being. One of the most terrible responsibilities in the world is that of really being present, of being a presence for the other. We cannot achieve dialogue by an act of will, for dialogue is a genuinely two-sided affair. We cannot know in advance that there can *not* be dialogue in a particular situation, but neither can we know that there *will* be dialogue. We cannot will that the other respond, nor can we even will our own presence and presentness. We are, nonetheless, responsible for what we are, for our presentness or lack of it. To know that it is you that the other is demanding and nothing that you can hand out, whether it be prescriptions or wise sayings, to know that what is really demanded is that you be present for and to him is terrifying. The demand is total and uncompromising, and we are often not able to be fully present even when we really want to. Our lack of awareness is the limitation of the *given* situation. But in the long run our degree of awareness is not necessity but possibility, something for which we can be responsible.

When we become aware and do respond, we respond not to the way the other is regarding and treating *us* but to *him*—to that in him which calls out to us even when *he* does not speak to us. Even though he is not conscious of our answering his call, in some way he will feel our response. He may be asking us for help without knowing that he is doing so. If we refer his existence only back to ourselves and how he regards us, we will fail to hear the question that he puts, we will fail to answer the real need that he has. Because we repress our awareness of our own negative characteristics, we dislike those people in whom they are manifest. Yet even then, it is possible to ask ourselves whether, over and above what upsets us in them and we find so threatening, there is something they are trying to tell us, something to which we are called to respond. This applies even to those who are unjust to us. If someone upbraids and accuses us falsely and with great passion, that very excess and unfairness suggests that there is some hurt in this person that is expressing itself in this distorted way. In the depths he may be asking for understanding and reassurance from us. Listening and responding at a greater depth is the direction away from a specious individualism to the reality of the partnership of existence.

Those people who relate to the world only as a function of their own becoming will not change no matter how concerned they are about changing. But those people whose trust is grounded in the partnership of existence are changed every time they go out to meet another. They become anew and are reborn in each new situation. We can help allow this, and in this sense we can will it. But there is another will that easily falls into despair because it sees everything as depending on it alone. If we change, it is because someone or something comes to meet us as we go to meet it—not because we decide to change. Our will may be necessary to break the inertia, to overcome the obstacles, but then we have to allow ourselves to be taken up into the flowing interaction.

We are all persons to a certain extent by courtesy of one another. We call each other back into being persons when sleepiness, sickness, or malaise have divested us of our personhood. What makes us persons is the stamp of uniqueness, of personal wholeness, and this is not anything that can ever be looked at or grasped as an object. This stamp of uniqueness is not something we can know directly in ourselves. We know it of each other as we enter into relationship, but we know it of ourselves only in that dim awareness that has to do with becoming more and more uniquely ourselves in responding to what is not ourselves.

The whole self is not what I am aware of when I am simply self-conscious. For then I am turning myself into an object and lose my intuitive grasp of the person that I am. That intuitive awareness that comes in responding is not incompatible with objectivity, analysis, or psychoanalysis. But it *is* incompatible with making these latter the final court of appeal as to what is real. It is ultimately an interhuman awareness that is in question here. Our awareness has to guard itself against becoming completely reflective self-consciousness or completely objective analysis. Our intuitive awareness of ourselves grows in listening and responding if we use ourselves as a radar screen: hearing not just how the other responds but also how we ourselves respond to him. We can do this without turning our self into an object.

Our wholeness is most there when we have forgotten ourselves in responding fully to what is not ourselves. It is not just *ekstasis*, mystic ecstasy, that occasionally lifts us out of the burden of self-consciousness. Any genuine wholehearted response—"When the music is heard so deeply that you are the music while the music lasts"—can bring us to this immediacy. Our self-consciousness returns when we go back, as we must, from immediacy to mediacy. Yet even it need not get in the way as much as we usually suppose. The fact that we are reflective can be handled lightly instead of heavily, especially if we do not make the mistake of identifying our "I" with that reflective consciousness and regarding the rest as just the objects that the "I" looks at. The more we do that, the more we become Dostoievsky's Underground Man, "twiddling our thumbs" and totally unable to act. One of the forms of lack of personal wholeness, correspondingly, is that endless self-preoccupation which splits us into two parts, one of which is the observer and the other the actor who is being observed. This bifurcation of consciousness prevents us from having any sort of spontaneous response, from ever really going outside of ourselves.

An equally important and frequent form of lack of personal wholeness is that which comes because we do not have the courage to stand our ground in a situation and to make our unique personal witness in response to it. Afraid of what other people think, we fear the consequences of real decision. The antidote to this is not to set our self-becoming as our end. Our becoming whole is merely the corollary of the reality that we find again and again in meeting others. To meet others and to hold our ground when we meet them is one of the most difficult tasks in the world. We tend, as a result, to alternate between two opposite forms of not meeting: "meeting" others through leaving our ground—taking on other people's thoughts and feelings while losing our own—and "protecting," our own ground through closing ourselves off and holding others at arm's length. But we have to discover in the wisdom of our own daily living the right movement between the two and not make openness, going out to others, meeting the "Thou," or loving others a principle. If we do, we shall lose what would make it a real going out, namely, the renewal of our resources that comes in this swinging movement. It will become a theory—something imposed on ourselves—and we shall more and more lose the genuine resources, the spontaneity, necessary for real outgoing. That part of our lives which we cannot live joyfully is that part to which we do not bring our real resources. We have, instead, imposed upon ourselves an idea of what we *ought* to do. That includes the image that we have of ourselves and that we keep up at the expense of spontaneous interaction with others.

We do not help another if we bring anything but our self. Our seeming compliance with his demands is really a deception which makes us as guilty as he may be. We allow the other to believe that we are going along with him, and we suppress from our awareness as well as his that part of us which does not go along with him—until, sooner or later, the time comes when we throw off the suppression and him with it. When the person who has repressed himself breaks out, he usually lays *all* the blame on the person whom he has allowed to dominate him, not admitting to himself what in some part of his being he knows very well: that submission is also a form of domination and manipulation.

How are we so sure that what the other is *really* asking of us is that we comply with his demands, that we distort ourselves for his benefit? We rationalize, "He wants my help. Why should I not give it to him? Why should I not put myself aside for his sake?" What he really needs from us is ourselves, even if that means that we oppose him. He may seem to be asking us to be nothing but "the good mother" or "the good father" to him, but in fact his deepest need and his real question to us is, "Are you going to meet me as the person that you are so that through you I may come up against real otherness and find a touchstone of reality?" The more he appears to be asking us to distort reality, to enter into compliance with him, the more insistently is he asking us that question. Family studies of the National Institute of Mental Health have shown that children in homes where no conflict is allowed to become manifest tend, when they go out into the world, to become schizophrenic. They have not been able to become persons through coming up against real opposition. They have always been smothered in the miasma of pseudo-harmony.

Central to holding our ground is the problem of firmness and anxiety. Do we have the courage to hold our ground—not as a Stoic stance but simply as trust? It is only by holding our ground that we can experience the other's side of the relationship. We are inclined to think that we have to choose between being ourselves and shutting him out, on the one hand, and being "unselfish" and going over to his side, on the other. Actually we cannot know *his* side of the relationship without standing our ground because we can only know him *as a person* in a relationship in which his uniqueness becomes manifest in coming up against our uniqueness. Otherwise, what we see is a distortion of him—the way he is when he has no real person to come up against. Some people would be halfway decent if we gave them a chance by demanding that they start with us. Our notion that they are totally evil may be because we have let them be and have not asked of them what we have not only a right but a duty to demand: that they turn toward us as the person or persons encountering them at this moment, the persons the meeting with whom is, *in this moment*, their access to reality and meaning.

One reason people do not have the courage to show themselves to others as they are is that they wish to avoid conflict. They propitiate and conciliate the other, not wishing the wrathful parent to make his appearance in the form of the friend, the beloved, or the teacher. The truth is the exact opposite. Instead of being afraid that we shall come into conflict with the other if we stand our ground, we should recognize that the only way we can *avoid* coming into conflict with him is standing our ground. We must hold our ground, imagining the other's side of the relationship but also letting him see our side. Otherwise, we are moment by moment making a false, deceitful contract in which we are letting the other think that we are going along with him freely and gladly while, in fact, underneath the resentment builds up. Then it is inevitable that conflict will come; for we are not affirming and responding as a whole person, and one day that part of us which is denying him will be revealed—in small ways and in big.

Each successive meeting gives us a little more strength and trust for the next one, especially when we discover that we can allow conflict to be expressed and the relationship is not destroyed. This does not mean that it is possible to express conflict and hostility in every relationship. It depends very much upon the amount and kind of hostility that is expressed and the strength of the relationship. There are some relationships that have so little resources that as soon as the volcano of hostility erupts, the relationship bursts asunder with no possibility of reconciliation. But to assume that we cannot express conflict without automatically destroying every relationship that we value means *either* that we are suffered only under the intolerable condition of never allowing the porcupine quills to show or, still worse, that what is in us is so murderous that were it to come out, it would necessarily destroy the other. The more we have repressed, the greater the fear is that what is underneath will be murderous if released. There are people who become more and more fixed in their own benevolent image and can never show any other face because of their terror of what lies beneath. The more they suppress, the greater the malignancy that accumulates under cover of their benevolence.

We discover the real limits of our resources in the relationship itself. We cannot be present simultaneously for everyone, and we often have to choose in a particular situation between our responsibility to one person and to another. If we stand in relationship to more than one person—and who does not?—we frequently find ourselves caught in genuine dilemmas of responsibility that are not easy to resolve. We learn we can only give so much. We do not shut other people out, but neither do we have the illusion that we can be there for everybody. Part of our holding our ground, moreover, is the realization that we can never *wholly* take responsibility for anyone, even though we were the one person on earth to whom he could turn. We can only really help others if we recognize what is essential in the situation: the limits of the grace of each hour. There are no formulae that can help us in these sometimes tragic situations. There is only the growing sureness about what we can give and what we cannot, the sense of our own limits and of our resources, and our willingness to risk ourselves and make mistakes.

The word "person" bridges over and unites three separate realities of personal existence. On the one hand when one speaks of person and personality, one speaks of the mysterious imprint of uniqueness on an incessantly changing, varying process which could have no essential unity as an "I" were it not for this imprint. Secondly, however, the person finds his full reality in the present, and personality exists in an actualized form only in the present. When we speak, as we must, of personality extending over time, it is the alternation between actual and potential personality that we really mean. The existence of the person in time is not a smooth process but an alternation between moments of real presentness and other moments—of sleep, of semiconsciousness, of distraction, inner division, illness—when a person falls from actualized presentness into mere subsistence, or potentiality.

A person finds himself as person, thirdly, through going out to meet the other, through responding to the address of the other. He does not lose his center, his personal core, in an amorphous meeting with the other. If he sees through the eyes of the other and experiences the other's side, he does not cease to see through his own eyes and experience the relationship from his own side. We do not experience the other through empathy or analogy. We do not know his anger because of our anger; for he may be angry in an entirely different way from us. But we can glimpse something of his side of the relationship. That too is what it means to be a real person. A real person does not remain shut within himself or use his relations with others as a means to his own self-realization. He realizes himself as an "I," a person, through going out again and again to meet the "Thou." To do this, however, he must have the courage to address and the courage to respond—the existential trust that will enable him to live in the valley of the shadow.

■ PART TWO

The Arena of Dialogue

■ 5

Anonymity, Presence, and the Dialogic Self in a Technological Culture

Rob Anderson
Saint Louis University

And these tend inward to me, and I tend outward to them,
And such as it is to be of these more or less I am,
And of these one and all I weave the song of myself.

—Walt Whitman, "Song of Myself"

The possibility of dialogue has been a persistent criterion by which communication is judged in the social arena. Jacques Ellul's (1985) critique of technology and mediated communication is only one of many that bemoan what appears to some to be our modern renunciation of dialogue. When language "uses a loudspeaker and crushes others with its powerful equipment, when the television set speaks," he wrote, "the word is no longer involved, since no dialogue is possible. What we have . . . is machines that use language as a way of asserting themselves" (p. 23).

If Ellul is right, media "machinery" has engineered a subtle but hostile takeover; a uniquely human-to-human presence has been sacrificed in our zeal for information. But is he right?

Central questions arise for contemporary mediated culture, then. How fragile is human dialogue? How might technology, especially so-called "mass media," diminish or enhance the possibilities for dialogue in everyday life? Is dialogue perhaps a hinge concept between two regions of mod-

91

ern life not traditionally associated with it: the technology of our outer existence and the complexity of our inner existence? What can an enlarged conception of dialogue contribute to different senses of self in an age of MTV, teenagers with "beepers" in high school hallways, computer "bulletin boards" that can substitute for face-to-face interaction, electronic newspapers, telecommuting for jobs, teleconferencing, and "virtual reality?"

To provide tentative answers, I first explore the current status of our scholarly communication interest in dialogue by supporting a new synthesis of the concept in which four regions of dialogical inquiry are identified—the philosophical/theoretical, the interpersonal, the technological, and the self. Only the first two of these have received significant attention from communication scholars.

Second, I examine the work of several critics of media culture and evaluate their pessimism about what I term the *technological region* of dialogue. I want to open for discussion their fears that dialogue and personalization may have been dealt a severe blow by technology. In this regard, I highlight the incisive but sometimes neglected work of Berger, Berger, and Kellner (1974) on the *anonymity* ascribed to what they term a *homeless* modern consciousness, and I also highlight a counterbalancing concept, expanded *presence*, a potential contribution of the new electronic media that invites, rather than renounces, dialogical possibility.

Finally, I explore in some detail the conceptually inviting territories of the third region, technology, and the fourth, self. If dialogue has been *dismissed* in the technological region by some critics, it tends to be *neglected* as even a factor in the self region. Evidently, analysts assume that because *dialogue* is usually defined as an interpersonal phenomenon, and *self* is usually defined as an inner experience, dialogue is not expected. Symbolic interactionists (McCall & Becker, 1990; Mead, 1934) offer one partial counterargument to this conclusion by claiming that the genesis of self is social, of course, and I agree with the suggestion of Bakhtin and his circle (Clark & Holquist, 1984) that self is actually a "boundary phenomenon" between inner and outer, and inherently dialogical. The contribution of technology to a modern dialogic consciousness is examined in the chapter's last section through Bakhtin's work and that of anthropologist Vincent Crapanzano. My central claim is that the two relatively neglected but interdependent regions of technological media and inner experience, far from inhibiting dialogue and its possibilities, both offer fresh perspectives for dialogic scholarship.

DIALOGUE: FOUR REGIONS FOR INQUIRY

Dialogue implies more than a simple back-and-forthness of messages in interaction; it points to a particular relationally based process/quality of communication in which the participants not only meet to exchange messages but to allow fully for changing and being changed. Although many different contributors to dialogue have been studied by communication scholars, most of our attention appears to have been focused—with justification—on the philosophy of theologian Martin Buber (1965), or of thinkers presumably influenced by him (e.g., Anderson, 1982; Arnett, 1981, 1986; Clark, 1973; Friedman, 1974; Johannesen, 1971; Stewart, 1978, 1985).

Cissna and I (Chapter 1, this volume) have offered a somewhat broader eight-part synthesis of dialogue's basic characteristics. These notions are applied throughout this chapter to show how an expanded dialogue need not depend on the limited context of unmediated face-to-face interaction and how self—often discussed as if it were agentic or even monadic (Bellah, Madsen, Sullivan, Swidler, & Tipton, 1985, 1991), or simply socially formed—can be considered a fully dialogical concept. Although a fuller discussion of these points is beyond the scope of this chapter, a brief notation of each, suggesting their essential interdependence, may be helpful:

- *Immediacy of presence.* A condition of dialogue suggests that communicators are available to and for each other in a "here-and-now" sense similar to that described by Berger and Luckmann (1966, pp. 22 ff.). Spontaneity, rather than rehearsal, is more associated with dialogical meeting, although this need not suggest that dialogue precludes personal or interpersonal discipline.
- *Emergent unanticipated consequences.* As dialogue develops, the future opens. Predictability diminishes, and outcomes seem more a function of transactions than of individuals. Efficiency experts, bureaucrats, and authors of accountability reports sometimes become annoyed with dialogue.
- *Recognition of strange otherness.* The very strangeness or unfamiliarity of the other provides the ground for new learning; thus, dialogic communicators welcome surprise.
- *Collaborative orientation.* In dialogue, communicators do not do things to each other. Rather, they coparticipate in developing a fresh relation for and with each other. At times, this relation may be argumentative struggle; at times quiet acceptance. Both conditions may be characterized by mutuality.
- *Vulnerability.* Dialogue's participants are willing to be changed. They seek less to protect positions and egos than to discover what emerges for them within the encounter with the other.
- *Mutual implication.* Speakers and listeners define each other dialectically through language; self conceptions, therefore, become embedded in relationships. Dialogue partners find that the listening process is not merely directed toward the other's messages, but also reflects a self. In a sense, messages

and selves cease to belong to people and begin to belong to the relational situation.

- *Temporal flow.* Dialogue is sustained by an historical continuity. Partners in dialogue find that it is necessarily ongoing, emerging from a past that is simultaneously developing and thus disappearing. Dialogue is process, not event.
- *Genuineness/authenticity.* Dialogic quality appears to depend on the participants assuming that others speak from actual lived experience, not fantasies. Although the possibility of deceit is always present, dialogue cannot be sustained by inauthenticity or mistrust.

Obviously, a condition of dialogue stretches our culture's normal transmission or transportation assumptions that communication involves separate persons simply alternating their messages in order to cause effects in others (Carey, 1989).

Identifying four regions of dialogical inquiry might guide us in charting this territory: the philosophical/theoretical, the interpersonal, the technological, and the self. The most well-developed of these currently is the first, through the narrative and conceptual work in philosophy and philosophical anthropology (e.g., Bakhtin, 1981; Buber, 1965; Friedman, 1974; Gadamer, 1982; Hagege, 1990; Schrag, 1986), and in communication (e.g., Arnett, 1986; Johannesen, 1990; Keller & Brown, 1968; Krippendorf, 1989; Pilotta & Mickunas, 1990; Poulakos, 1974; Stewart, 1978; Thomlison, 1982). Several other significant works examine practical implications of the first region for second region, face-to-face interaction. Prominent among these have been Rogers (1980; Cissna & Anderson, 1990), Freire (1970; De Lima & Christians, 1979; Shor & Freire, 1987), the "dialectical" or "interactional" psychologists (Pervin & Lewis, 1978; Riegel, 1979), and the dialogical anthropologists (Crapanzano, 1992; Maranhao, 1990; Tedlock, 1983; Tyler, 1987).

Yet, the third and fourth regions, technology and self, are often neglected and need charting. These are the next places to explore in our attempt to understand the dynamics of dialogue. And to go there seems to change some of our intellectual ground rules.

THE REGION OF TECHNOLOGY: ANONYMITY OR (AND?) PRESENCE?

Anonymity

Although theories and systems in the philosophical and interpersonal regions are obviously relevant to dialogue, I largely set them aside here because their relevance has for so long been recognized. Although much work remains to be done in these regions, I synthesize other linkages to expand our sensitivity for dialogue. For example, although new "super media" (Real, 1989) technology clearly promises an expanded reach for communication, this promise has for many critics a dark side as well. These social commentators, often representing such academic fields as sociology and political science, tend to portray the media system as an ongoing threat to dialogue in Western culture.

Ellul (1964, 1981, 1985) is perhaps the most persistent scholarly critic of the technological enterprise. Technology—by which he does not refer merely to machinery or electronics but to the complex techniques by which persons believe they must manipulate reality—carries with it certain values. Actually, for Ellul (1981), technology demands allegiance to these values—utility, happiness, consumption, knowledge, bureaucracy, objectification, and others—in order to perpetuate itself (pp. 43-50). In fact, the technological universe becomes "an extraordinarily icy, extraordinarily alien universe" in which people cannot live spontaneously (p. 48). Within the technological milieu, "the suppression of the subject is transforming traditional human relations, which require the voice, which require seeing, or which require a physical relationship between one human being and the next. The result is the distant relationship" (p. 49). Note how many of his presumed technological values and tendencies could be considered antidialogical; Ellul sees persons immersed in a technological culture becoming mere consumers of products, alienated from others, willing to barter authenticity within narrow roles, and ready to handle other persons as they would handle objects.

Other critics of modern social systems share his concern. Italian sociologist Franco Ferrarotti (1988) describes "the end of conversation" as the disturbing result of media technology. He asserts that, ironically, "the mass media do not mediate. They restrict themselves to telling about themselves" (p. 13). Thus, they provide a "vocation for narcissism" (p. 13). In a similar vein, Bellah and his colleagues (1985) suggest that media, especially television, are partly responsible for two tendencies of modern American individualism (or "pseudo-integration"). Neither trend supports dialogue. First, they show, the "dream of personal success"—which may be similar to the outcomes of Ellul's technique orientation—motivates persons to try to define themselves as winners in a society that must also create losers. Although we become isolated, we ultimately admire in a shadowy way people who seem to want to win as much as we do. Second, we see an unnatural and expressivist tendency to focus, as television dramas often do, on the free expression of how a person feels (p. 281). This expression obviously can be a contribution to dialogue, but I agree with Fulkerson (1990) that it is misleading to associate "expressivism" (ventilating feelings from a self-oriented perspective) with dialogue (see Hart & Burks, 1972).

Television takes some heavy hits from critics of electronic culture—and not just because it encourages selfishness and alienation. Other aspects of the public dialogue, we are told, also have been diminished. The "super media can bolster the 'hegemony' of the dominant over the subordinate" (Real, 1989, p. 256). Beyond the power dimension, some critics have made much of the observation (McLuhan, 1964; Ong, 1967, 1982) that media can reshape our perceptual habits. Perhaps no recent attack on television has been as pointed as Postman's (1985): "We have reached . . . a critical mass in that electronic media have decisively and irreversibly changed the character of our symbolic environment" (p. 28). "A television-based epistemology pollutes public communication and its surrounding landscape," he claims (p. 28), partly because television has three basic commandments: "Thou shalt have no prerequisites"; "Thou shalt induce no perplexity"; "Thou shalt avoid exposition like the ten plagues visited upon Egypt" (pp. 147-148). In a television-based culture, in other words, the historical perspective needed for genuine dialogue and the possibility for unanticipated consequences become impossible, according to Postman. Communicators who have adopted television's implicit dramatic epistemology expect clean starts to their encounters with others, clear-cut alternatives, tidy conclusions, and no ambiguities. Postman fears that communicators have learned to favor the visual over the linguistic and experiential immersion over careful consideration.

Noelle-Neumann (1984), writing from her experience as a German researcher of public opinion, warns of other insidious effects of mass media. In her theory of "the spiral of silence," people who perceive themselves in a minority on any issue begin to inhibit the ways in which they voice their concerns. Conversely, people who believe their views are part of the popular or majority sentiment become more likely to speak. Mass media interact with this interpersonal tendency (which is similar to Bellah's observation of the kinds of personal success modern people chart for themselves) to create the "spiral": If the majority speaks more, their voices will be more frequently and prominently reported in media, and majority speakers will become increasingly encouraged to believe they are more representative of the society than they "really" are. The minority, responding to media emphases on majority concerns, become even more silent; they believe they are in an even smaller minority that seems to be vanishing rapidly. What is the use of speaking? The different groups and their concerns swirl in opposite directions with technological media as catalysts, and the possibility for dialogue becomes more and more distant.

A prototypical and persuasive analysis of how media have changed cultural communication patterns is Berger, Berger, and Kellner's (1974) important but somewhat neglected study, *The Homeless Mind.* This book gathers in one synthesis many of the themes and threads of other critics, and the authors' discussion of how persons can become distanced from each other is sensible and realistic, if a bit dated. Without denying that personalized communication is possible and desirable, they claim technology encourages broad-based social conditions of interchangeability that could also be called anonymity. That is, people still speak, but to roles and bureaucracies and not to uniquely considered others, and thus do not speak with the genuine possibility of being changed by the discourse.

Although Berger et al. do not draw this allusion, in a sense, the technologized people they describe do not (to echo Brel's song) "have their own names." Because people sense they and their functions are "components," within bureaucracies they could have any "name" (identity) at all, and thus they will tend toward "self-anonymization" (p. 33). A "double consciousness" develops in which one can experience another simultaneously "in terms of his concrete individuality and in terms of the highly abstract complexes of action in which he functions. . . . The other must be anonymized" (p. 32). Experiences, jobs, feelings, persons, turn into "packages." Although my description is an obvious oversimplification of a book that itself claims to be a simplification, the authors have expressed effectively a fear that how we communicate in a technologized environment affects us at deep levels in our relationships, in our senses of self, and even in our expectations for relationships. If anonymous, we can easily become "homeless."

Anonymity, then, is a term that condenses a number of threats to interpersonal communication in a technological culture. Anonymity means we can lose our motivation to speak and our motivation to listen at the same time. To be anonymous, even partially to self, and amid anonymous others, is to remove the very ground for dialogue.

Most such accounts of how media have diminished dialogue and heightened our sense of personal alienation, although not new—Mills (1956) set much of the tone in the 1950s—at least share one feature; they tend to be written by scholars in sociology, not communication studies. This observation is not made to invalidate their concerns, but to indicate that when an observer assumes a certain stance, he or she is likely not only to see certain things but to develop certain worries. "What are the effects on society?" is a very different question than "What are the effects on communication?", even if the same phenomena are observed. I suspect communication scholars, with perhaps more focus on processes than on structural outcomes, might be more likely to see another side of the issue. That is, they might see that media potentially both inhibit and enhance dialogical encounters.

Presence

Not all scholars and critics who survey the technological landscape are pessimistic. Some see technology as a new set of possibilities for dialogue, a new terrain in which persons can create responsible dialogue. Far from robbing humanity of dialogical potential, technologies, especially in the electronic media, can be understood as providing a new playing field, a fresh region, in which to imagine and implement dialogue (Ball-Rokeach & Reardon, 1988). As Ong (1967) wrote, "Nowhere in pretechnological society can one find instances of human cooperation so massive and intense as that required for countless technological projects today. . . . Technological society is team society. Its major achievements are communal . . ." (p. 307).

Obviously, face-to-face interaction remains the "ideal type," the standard by which all other forms of human interaction are implicitly compared (Berger & Luckmann, 1966; Rafaeli, 1988, p. 128). In some ways that is natural, but in some ways, too, it becomes an unnecessary restraint on our conceptualizing. Are there ways that technologically mediated messages can function within a dialogical relationship? We should not dismiss the possibility too readily.

Perhaps the central characteristic of the so-called "new media" is the trend toward greater and greater *interactivity* (Brand, 1988; Kaplan, 1990; Rice & Williams, 1984). Thus, our technology may have created an interpersonal distance for a time that placed communication efficiency as a prior goal to intimacy; the same technology now appears to be increasingly applied toward reduction of the perceived interpersonal distance that technology itself originally fostered. This, I suspect, is the reason we are recently getting more analyses that blur our previously clean-cut distinctions between interpersonal communication and mass communication (Armstrong & Rubin, 1989; Bierig & Dimmick, 1979; Carbaugh, 1989; Carey, 1989; Gumpert & Cathcart, 1986; Gumpert & Fish, 1990; Hawkins, Wiemann, & Pingree, 1988; Meyrowitz, 1985; Newcomb, 1984; Ong, 1982; Rice & Williams, 1984).

The theories of Paul Levinson (see Meyrowitz, 1985, pp. 121-122) are helpful in this regard. He argues that the history of media is a history of sacrificing presence systematically for a time in order to reclaim a fuller presence. After a certain point in their development, media tend to evolve "toward fuller replication of the means of communication that existed before media and technology" (p. 121). Thus, "the addition of voice to the telegraph, or sound to silent movies, or color to television . . . is perceived as an 'improvement' simply because the medium becomes less like a medium and more like life" (p. 121). Are anonymity and alienation necessary consequences of technological media, as the social critics assumed? Or, instead, is anonymity only a temporary toll that media must extract from society so that we might get on with the journey of dialogue? Levinson and Meyrowitz would seem to argue that human dialogue will ultimately become more possible, more varied, and perhaps more fruitful within interactive media systems. The face-to-face encounter may remain our "ideal type." But do we want to say that dialogue resides only there?

An early step in this journey toward an expanded dialogue was Horton and Wohl's (1956) concept of "para-social interaction" in which audiences establish psychologically intimate and experientially knowledgeable relationships with media figures. Although the electronically mediated and one-way environment is commonly assumed to be an impediment to dialogue, television and radio audiences seek to transcend such limits through a psychological move (leap?) of identification. Celebrities may be experienced not simply as performers, but as acquaintances or even friends who the audience "knows." What may be happening in such cases is that the media respondent uses the message, however unidirectional in literal reality, as a site of psychological meeting or dialogue—both the distant/near performer and the auditor have a say in what develops in this experientially near, inferred relation. The audience seeks and finds, that is to say, "creates," presence out of a previously anonymous relation. Ong (1967) defined presence not so much as a physical state as a relational one: "It is a call of one interior through an exterior to another interior" (p. 309).

The concept of *presence* is a useful theoretical counterweight to *anonymity*. The potential for each is inherent within a media environment; but the potential for both dialogue and monologue is inherent within any face-to-face encounter, as well. If you and I face each other interpersonally, both I-Thou choices and I-It choices are available to us. We can meet, in Buber's sense, or we can miss and objectify each other. Similarly, some media theorists show that mediated culture can make relationships more mutual and dialogical. Ball-Rokeach and Reardon (1988), for example, offer the term *telelogic communication* as an analogue to *dialogic communication* to refer to:

> alternating dialogue between people at a distance who use both conventional and unconventional language and electronic optical channels. Telelogic communication is often geographically and temporally unbounded. . . . Participants in telelogic communication may range from a few to millions of people who share a common focus of attention that precipitates and maintains their mutual participation in communication. (pp. 137-138)

As with the face-to-face interpersonal environment, the context is "open" and potentially mutual, awaiting our assumptions and our acts. Hyde (1982, p. 12), therefore, encourages us to be neither too much a critic nor too much a cheerleader for technology—but instead to approach it as open-mindedly as possible.

Philosopher Don Ihde (1982) suggests that our experience of media is an "aesthetic stance" in which we are neither detached and distanced observers nor direct participants. If it is true that the media we support and use inform us about ourselves, as he suggests, then we may be in the process of teaching ourselves how to be present in a "quasi-near, quasi-far" world—a world in which commitments are still made and adhered to, but are less binding and more temporary (pp. 78-79). This is a world in which engagements are real but relatively interchangeable. The implications of Ihde's position are intriguing. It is not that dialogue is impossible in such a world; rather, we may have to divorce dialogue from some of its connotations of warm intimacy. And we may need to redefine what kind of privacy facilitates community with the new interpersonalized media. For example, is a late night radio talk show caller who does not identify him- or herself, but who does discuss intimate feelings, talking in a public sphere or a private one? The answer again is that media's aesthetic stance demands the new context of a "quasi-public, quasi-private" blend. Our media experience does not automatically fit the old categories.

Increased presence can evolve from a variety of new media phenomena. Interactive television systems can now permit viewers not only to provide immediate evaluative feedback to broadcasters, but to dictate which camera angle they would like to see on a down-and-in pass play, or which conclusion they would prefer in a dramatic presentation. The connection of effects is becoming more mutual; viewers and "authors" of the televised "text" are both in charge, and as in dialogue, the emergent results cannot be reliably foretold. A new generation of "authorless" (or, alternatively, "authorfilled") creative texts may be confronting us with interactive media. "The Aspen Movie Map," a videodisk that is now over a decade old, sufficiently demonstrated this phenomenon and is probably primitive in its genre by now. Viewers could explore the town at their own pace, making personal choices of where and when to go. Many buildings could be entered. Visitors could see different seasons if they desired and, in some cases, different eras. Stewart Brand (1988) recalls:

> "Aspen" shook people. Scales fell from eyes at conferences where it was demoed about what computers could do, about what videodisk could be, about how *un-authored* a creative work could become. For the first time the viewer could be thought of as an animal instead of a vegetable, active and curious instead of passive and critical. (p. 141)

Increasingly, we are merging sensory media to construct new worlds for experience ("virtual reality"), not just to "receive" old ones or previously packaged ones (Biocca, 1992). Perhaps Berger, Berger, and Kellner never considered that their analysis of media-transmitted "packages" and media-induced "homelessness" might be made obsolete by new media realities that are essentially "receiver"-*constructed*.

Any media watcher could proliferate examples. No need; two other prominent illustrations of the trend toward dialogical presence will suffice. First, computer bulletin board systems (BBS) involve people with others at significant, even sometimes intimate levels of interaction, although sensory involvement is certainly restricted (Chesebro & Bonsall, 1989, pp. 100-103; Williams, Phillips, & Lum, 1985, pp. 249-252). Even though anonymity (in one sense) is a feature of such exchanges, BBSs offer (with talk radio call-in shows) an anonymity that retains essential features of personal identity, a public forum that is also paradoxically private. Again, our traditional distinctions blur. Through this medium the person can express in a genuine and spontaneous way thoughts that might not have been shared otherwise—and, most important, receive nearly immediate, if sensorily limited, feedback. As with face-to-face presence, messages are virtually simultaneously present for both parties; texts are available for both communicators precisely as they are created. Communicators can be accessible to and with others in this one message mode in a way that is dialogically comparable to face-to-face interaction. Indeed, the increased interactivity of such systems may provide at the same time an increased "personalness" and a democratization of message dissemination.

My second example is multisensory and important in blurring distinctions between electronically mediated and face-to-face interpersonal communication. We assume these to be distinct types of interaction, with face-to-face communication characterized by the physical presence of the interactants. Telephones, after all, can now connect us immediately with visual screens, but that is not equated with "face-to-face" impact or presence. But what if we can establish through media a physical presence along with face-to-face interaction? This is now feasible through technologies developed and tested by an MIT research group some years ago, but never implemented. The head of MIT's Media Laboratory was intrigued by the possibility of what he called "the transmission of presence."

Stimulated by the needs of a national defense agency that was looking for ways to disperse officials and military planners during a nuclear attack, yet still have them fully communicating as if they were together, Media Lab technicians experimented with what they called the "Talking Heads" teleconference system. If perfected, does this become the ultimate in media interactivity and presence? Nicholas Negroponte, director of the Lab, explained:

> We came up with the idea of projecting onto video screens sculpted like people's faces and also having the screens swivel a bit—so they could nod, shake their head, turn to each other. At each site the order of sitting of the five people would be the same. At my site I'm real and you're plastic and on my right, and at your site you're real and I'm plastic and on your left. If we're talking and looking at each other, and one of the faces across the table interrupts, we would stop and turn toward him. (Brand, 1988, p. 92)

Head-tracking devices and fixed video cameras at each site would transmit images, and the rear-projection receiving screens could be "molded like life masks to the shape of anyone's face" (p. 92). Because color is possible, the nuances of individual facial appearance such as eyes, hair color, and skin tone can also be captured. Thus, dialogical nuance—surprise, doubt, identification with the other's feelings, spontaneous feedback, and so forth—become physically "present," although mediated.

Such technologies, of course, raise questions about the locus of self. If the traditional boundaries are blurred between public and private, between impersonal and personal, between mass and interpersonal communication, between anonymity and presence, then we should not be surprised that people's grasp of what a self is seems to loosen. Self cannot be tied to a physical location, say the symbolic interactionists after Mead, but instead is formed by the interior dialogue of persons who learn to internalize society's voices. This makes sense and is increasingly true in a media world of multiplying relationships—but does such a self provide solid ground from which modern persons can engage in further dialogue? The link between technological ecology and self must be explored in the context of dialogue; these two regions are connected.

Excellent clues for such exploration come from the work of Russian literary theorist Mikhail Bakhtin. Although Bakhtin's thought focuses on an earlier mass medium, the novel, he also earns the thorough attention of communication theorists interested in electronically based mass communication; he explains how the supposedly "inner" phenomenon of self interdepends dialogically through language on the supposedly "outer" phenomenon of technology.

THE REGION OF SELF: BAKHTIN, LANGUAGE, AND DIALOGUE

The past 15 years or so have seen the emergence of a "new" intellectual figure whose work explores nearly the entire terrain of the study of dialogue. Of course, Bakhtin's (1981, 1986) scholarly contribution is hardly recent; most of it was originally published decades ago. Rather, what is new is the Western world's discovery of him and the rapid assimilation of his concepts within wide-ranging intellectual fields—philosophy, literary criticism, anthropology, history, linguistics, and others (see Clark & Holquist, 1984; Morson, 1986; Todorov, 1984). Bakhtin's own work, about which some scholarly controversy swirls (some critics assert that other authors published some of Bakhtin's scholarship under their own names, for political reasons), expands our definition of which human activities can appropriately be termed *dialogical.* In this section, Bakhtin's work illuminates the relationship between the technological region and the region of self in the study of dialogue. Bakhtin points to a self that negotiates dialogic reality at the boundary between inner and outer human existence. Before examining the self proper, however, some context for Bakhtin's approach to technology is helpful.

Ong (1982) reminds us that Plato argued against the technology of writing, claiming that it depersonalized human contact. Sound familiar? Ong proposed:

> Because we have by today so deeply interiorized writing, made it so much a part of ourselves, as Plato's age had not yet made it fully a part of itself, . . . we find it difficult to consider writing to be a technology as we commonly assume printing and the computer to be. Yet writing (and especially alphabetic writing) is a technology, calling for the use of tools and other equipment. . . . (pp. 81-81)
>
> By contrast with natural, oral speech, writing is completely artificial. . . . (p. 82)
>
> To say writing is artificial is not to condemn it but to praise it. (p. 82)

Ong, therefore, suggested that technology can be understood as a continuum of artifices designed to help humans extend themselves communicatively. McLuhan (1964), of course, made essentially the same point when he referred to media as "extensions of man."

Although Bakhtin did not focus on electronic media, he showed through his analysis of fiction that the technology of writing is yet another avenue to dialogue. The immediate presence or absence of an author of a text does not mean that dialogue is therefore present or absent. Rather, dialogue is a persistent feature of texts, even ones from dead or unknown authors. The basis of meaning is itself dialogical, he claimed. Within each "utterance" is the voice of a speaker and the voice of an implied correspondent, as well as the social and psychological artifacts of the dialogue that has been developed within the communicators' culture. As Bakhtin wrote, "The word is a two-sided act. It is determined equally by whose word it is and for whom it was meant. . . . A word is territory *shared* by both addresser and addressee, by the speaker *and* his interlocutor" (Voloshinov, 1973, pp. 85-86).

Todorov, one of Bakhtin's interpreters, put it in a slightly different way:

> Concretely, one always addresses someone, and that someone does not assume a purely passive role (as the term "recipient" could lead one to infer): the interlocutor participates in the formation of the meaning of the utterance, just as the other elements—similarly social—of the context of uttering do. (Todorov, 1984, p. 30)

If a conduit sense of communication simplistically implies that one person speaks to another, Bakhtin's model conversely would demonstrate that, in part, a speaker speaks from the other. An "addressee is thus involved throughout the process of encoding,. . ." said Rommetveit (1987, p. 93) in his synthesis of new approaches to communication and cognition. A human "author" cannot be aware of all the meaning available within even his or her "own" text; other voices already are speaking there. As Ihde (1976) claimed, "the voices of language have already penetrated all my experience, and this experience is already always 'intersubjective'" (pp. 120-121).

This "shared territory" nature of language creates a view of society as itself dialogical. Bakhtin considered society to be constituted by the "already said" (Stewart, 1986), in the sense that society is spoken into existence by a vast array of different voices inhabiting each word, asking to be heard. He used the term *polyphony* to refer to the coexistence of such voices within a single text. To Bakhtin, dialogue is not dependent on special conditions of face-to-face interactional quality; instead, dialogue can be in many ways inherent even in mediated, seemingly unidirectional message contexts such as the novel. Or, we might say, such as in a television show, a film, or a computer program. As Newcomb (1984) noted, ". . . viewers absorb television into other forms of dialogue, respond with parallel stories and comments, [and they] block, mold, and shape the 'words' of television in a range of ways" (p. 47). Bakhtin's concept of *heteroglossia*, the coexistence of multiple dialogic styles within a language, suggests that context far transcends text, and listeners not only engage single messages dialogically, but the so-called "single" messages are already laced with the "dialogism" of the society that created them. Presence is multiple.

Humans learn these things through increased contact with and sensitivity to differences—different voices, different opinions, and different characters speaking from "zones" of meaning other than our own. This was the dialogical function the novel of Bakhtin's day could fulfill as well as any medium.

Bakhtin showed that physical presence is not necessary for dialogic experience. Crapanzano (1990) argued that his fellow anthropologists in field interviews should similarly account for a fuller sense of dialogue. Specifically, during a "primary dialogue" of an interview, for example, an interlocutor may maintain a secondary or "shadow" dialogue internally with real or imagined dialogue partners. His is clearly a more complex and interactive concept than the "reference group" or the "significant other." For members of a particular culture or community, Crapanzano maintains, this inner speech can have as much force as the primary dialogue. Unless the interviewer somehow can understand these shadow conversation partners and the nature of a respondent's (and his or her own) implicit interaction with them, much that is authoritative in this other life will be missed. Crapanzano (1992) believes that the typical symbolic interactionist conception of a self dialectically formed through interaction between self and other does not fully account for the "cultural production" of self (p. 82). Beyond Mead's philosophy, he believes, is the territory of the shadow dialogue, the presence of an imagined third party for each person human conversation. "The function of the Third," in fact,

> may be conceived as the (absent) interlocutor in those silent but forceful secondary, or shadow, dialogues that accompany any primary dialogue (for example the dialogue between the student of anthropology who engages silently with his mentors back home and all they symbolize as he converses with his friends in the field). (p. 93)

Merging Crapanzano's notion of "shadow dialogue" with Bakhtin's approach to language—and with the new media interactivity and presence—yields a fuller understanding of how a media system enhances a dialogic self at the margin of inner/outer experience.

Bakhtin and other theorists of dialogic inner speech such as Ihde and Crapanzano in essence redefine presence in human experience. Linguistic connection is the social presence through which humans develop a self—experiencing ourselves as both shaped and shapers. To Bakhtin, a self is neither interiorized nor externally imposed. Instead, self to him is "a boundary phenomenon" (Clark & Holquist, 1984, p. 230) mediating inner and outer experience. And "inner speech," involved in the maintenance of self, is itself dialogical (Emerson, 1986). As Todorov (1984, p. 116) pointed out, Bakhtin at the time he wrote could not have been influenced by Mead's as-yet-unpublished American work, but was familiar with and valued the work of Buber.

Anyone seeking to understand the notion of self must eventually come to grips with dialogue and go beyond analyzing face-to-face interpersonal talk. Conversely, anyone wanting to understand the process of dialogue cannot afford to ignore the region of the human self. Several vectors of dialogue converge at the self—interpersonal interaction, social and technological heteroglossia, and the interior utterance. To study "self" is to study the region of dialogue that integrates, to some extent, the other three regions—the philosophical/theoretical, the interpersonal, and the technological.

CONCLUSION

Our usual modern sense of dialogue, that of face-to-face interaction with certain assumptions of quality discourse, is still viable. Yet the concept of dialogue is rich enough to apply to other regions of human experience as well. In addition to the philosophical and interpersonal regions, we should add the paradoxically interdependent influences of technology and self. That is, modern society has made technology and media interdependent with self; we have begun to define our selves through our contexts. And it is with media as context that we establish daily existence. As McLuhan was reported to have said, we don't know who discovered water, but we're pretty sure it wasn't a fish.

Although some critics of media systems are justifiably concerned about the effects of anonymity, the overall tendency of the new electronic environment is toward increased presence and rejuvenated possibilities for dialogue. The result of dialogue is far from guaranteed, however. As Carey (1989) warned, the new media revolution ". . . has within it the same seeds of miscarriage that have historically attended innovations in communications," most notably a preoccupation with "a ritual of control" (p. 195).

This new media environment has framed self as a merged issue, not a separate one to be puzzled out independently from dialogue or technology. Therefore, in this chapter I have suggested that new work in the field of dialogue might focus more on the interdependent regions of technology and self.

REFERENCES

Anderson, R. (1982). Phenomenological dialogue, humanistic psychology, and pseudo-walls: A response and extension. *Western Journal of Speech Communication, 46,* 344-357.

Armstrong, C.B., & Rubin, A.M. (1989). Talk radio as interpersonal communication. *Journal of Communication, 39,* 84-94.

Arnett, R.C. (1981). Toward a phenomenological dialogue. *Western Journal of Speech Communication, 45,* 201-212.

Arnett, R.C. (1986). *Communication and community: Implications of Martin Buber's dialogue.* Carbondale: Southern Illinois University Press.

Bakhtin, M.M. (1981). *The dialogic imagination* (C. Emerson & M. Holquist, Trans.). Austin: University of Texas Press.

Bakhtin, M.M. (1986). *Speech genres and other essays* (V. McGee, Trans.). Austin: University of Texas Press.

Ball-Rokeach, S.J., & Reardon, K. (1988). Monologue, dialogue, and telelog: Comparing an emergent form of communication with traditional forms. In R. P. Hawkins, J. M. Wiemann, & S. Pingree (Eds.), *Advancing communication science: Merging mass and interpersonal processes* (pp. 135-161). Newbury Park, CA: Sage.

Bellah, R.N., Madson, R., Sullivan, W.M., Swidler, A., & Tipton, S.M. (1985). *Habits of the heart: Individualism and commitment in American life.* New York: Harper & Row.

Bellah, R.N., Madsen, R., Sullivan, W.M., Swidler, A., & Tipton, S.M. (1991). *The good society.* New York: Vintage Books.

Berger, P., Berger, B., & Kellner, H. (1974). *The homeless mind: Modernization and consciousness.* New York: Vintage Books.

Berger, P. L., & Luckmann, T. (1966). *The social construction of reality.* New York: Doubleday.

Bierig, J., & Dimmick, J. (1979). The late night radio talk show as inter-personal communication. *Journalism Quarterly, 56,* 92-96.

Biocca, F. (1992). Communication within virtual reality: Creating a space for research. *Journal of Communication, 42,* 5-22.

Brand, S. (1988). *The media lab: Inventing the future at M. I. T.* New York: Penguin Books.

Buber, M. (1965). *Between man and man* (R. G. Smith, Trans.). New York: Macmillan.

Carbaugh, D. (1989). *Talking American: Cultural discourses on Donahue.* Norwood, NJ: Ablex.

Carey, J.W. (1989). *Communication as culture: Essays on media and society.* Boston: Unwin Hyman.

Chesebro, J.W., & Bonsall, D.G. (1989). *Computer-mediated communication: Human relationships in a computerized world.* Tuscaloosa, AL: The University of Alabama Press.

Cissna, K.N., & Anderson, R. (1990). The contributions of Carl R. Rogers to a philosophical praxis of dialogue. *Western Journal of Speech Communication, 54,* 125-147.

Clark, A. (1973). Martin Buber, dialogue, and the philosophy of rhetoric. In D. G. Douglas (Ed.), *Philosophers on rhetoric* (pp. 225-242). Skokie, IL: National Textbook Company.

Clark, K., & Holquist, M. (1984). *Mikhail Bakhtin.* Cambridge, MA: Harvard University Press.

Crapanzano, V. (1990). On dialogue. In T. Maranhao (Ed.), *The interpretation of dialogue* (pp. 269-291). Chicago: University of Chicago Press.

Crapanzano, V. (1992). *Hermes' dilemma & Hamlet's desire: On the epistemology of interpretation.* Cambridge, MA: Harvard University Press.

De Lima, V.A., & Christians, C. G. (1979). Paulo Freire: The political dimension of dialogic communication. *Communication, 4,* 133-155.

Ellul, J. (1964). *The technological society* (J. Wilkinson, Trans.). New York: Vintage Books.

Ellul, J. (1981). *Perspectives on our age: Jacques Ellul speaks on his life and work* (J. Neugroschel, Trans.; W. H. Vandenburg, Ed.). New York: The Seabury Press.

Ellul, J. (1985). *The humiliation of the word* (J. M. Hanks, Trans.). Grand Rapids, MI: William B. Eerdmans.

Emerson, C. (1986). The outer word and inner speech: Bakhtin, Vygotsky, and the internalization of language. In G. S. Morson

108   THE REACH OF DIALOGUE

(Ed.), *Bakhtin: Essays and dialogues on his work* (pp. 21-40). Chicago: University of Chicago Press.

Ferrarotti, F. (1988). *The end of conversation: The impact of mass media on modern society.* New York: Greenwood.

Freire, P. (1970). *Pedagogy of the oppressed* (M. B. Ramos, Trans.). New York: The Seabury Press.

Friedman, M. (1974). *Touchstones of reality: Existential trust and the community of peace.* New York: E. P. Dutton.

Fulkerson, G. (1990). The ethics of interpersonal influence: A critique of the rhetorical sensitivity construct. *The Journal of Communication and Religion, 13,* 1-14.

Gadamer, H.-G. (1982). *Truth and method* (G. Barden & J. Cumming, Trans.). New York: Crossroad Publishing.

Gumpert, G., & Cathcart, R. (Eds.). (1986). *Inter/media: Interpersonal communication in a media world* (3rd ed.). New York: Oxford University Press.

Gumpert, G., & Fish, S. L. (Eds.). (1990). *Talking to strangers: Mediated therapeutic communication.* Norwood, NJ: Ablex.

Hagege, C. (1990). *The dialogic species: A linguistic contribution to the social sciences* (S. L. Shelly, Trans.). New York: Columbia University Press.

Hart, R. P., & Burks, D. M. (1972). Rhetorical sensitivity and social interaction. *Speech Monographs, 39,* 75-91.

Hawkins, R. P., Wiemann, J. M., & Pingree, S. (Eds.). (1988). *Advancing communication science: Merging mass and interpersonal processes.* Newbury Park, CA: Sage.

Horton, D., & Wohl, R. R. (1956). Mass communication and para-social interaction: Observations on intimacy at a distance. *Psychiatry, 19,* 215-229.

Hyde, M. J. (1982). Introduction: The debate concerning technology. In M. J. Hyde (Ed.), *Communication philosophy and the technological age* (pp. 1-12). Tuscaloosa, AL: University of Alabama Press.

Ihde, D. (1976). *Listening and voice: A phenomenology of sound.* Athens: Ohio University Press.

Ihde, D. (1982). The experience of media. In J. J. Pilotta (Ed.), *Interpersonal communication: Essays in phenomenology and hermeneutics* (pp. 69-80). Washington, DC: University Press of America.

Johannesen, R. L. (1971). The emerging concept of communication as dialogue. *Quarterly Journal of Speech, 57,* 373-382.

Johannesen, R. L. (1990). *Ethics in human communication* (3rd ed.). Prospect Heights, IL: Waveland Press.

Kaplan, S. J. (1990). Communication technology and society. In G. M. Phillips & J. T. Wood (Eds.), *Speech communication: Essays to commemorate the 75th Anniversary of The Speech Communication Association* (pp. 205-234). Carbondale: Southern Illinois University Press.

Keller, P. W., & Brown, C. T. (1968). An interpersonal ethic for communi-
cation. *Journal of Communication, 18,* 73-81.
Krippendorf, K. (1989). On the ethics of constructing communication. In
B. Dervin, L. Grossberg, B. J. O'Keefe, & E. Wartella (Eds.),
Rethinking communication: Vol. 1. Paradigm issues (pp. 66-96).
Newbury Park, CA: Sage.
Maranhao, T. (Ed.). (1990). *The interpretation of dialogue.* Chicago:
University of Chicago Press.
McCall, M. M., & Becker, H. S. (1990). Introduction. In H. S. Becker & M.
M. McCall (Eds.), *Symbolic interaction and cultural studies* (pp. 1-15).
Chicago: University of Chicago Press.
McLuhan, M. (1964). *Understanding media: The extensions of man.* New
York: McGraw-Hill.
Mead, G. H. (1934). *Mind, self and society.* Chicago: University of Chicago
Press.
Meyrowitz, J. (1985). *No sense of place: The impact of electronic media on social
behavior.* New York: Oxford University Press.
Mills, C. W. (1956). *The power elite.* New York: Oxford University Press.
Morson, G. S. (Ed.). (1986). *Bakhtin: Essays and dialogues on his work.*
Chicago: University of Chicago Press.
Newcomb, H. M. (1984). On the dialogic aspects of mass communication.
Critical Studies in Mass Communication, 1, 34-50.
Noelle-Neumann, E. (1984). *The spiral of silence: Public opinion—our social
skin.* Chicago: University of Chicago Press.
Ong, W. J. (1967). *The presence of the word: Some prolegomena for cultural and
religious history.* New York: Simon & Schuster.
Ong, W. J. (1982). *Orality and literacy: The technologizing of the word.*
London: Methuen.
Pervin, L. A., & Lewis, M. (Eds.). (1978). *Perspectives in interactional psychol-
ogy.* New York: Plenum Press.
Pilotta, J. J., & Mickunas, A. (1990). *Science of communication: Its phenomeno-
logical foundation.* Hillsdale, NJ: Lawrence Erlbaum Associates.
Postman, N. (1985). *Amusing ourselves to death.* New York: Penguin Books.
Poulakos, J. (1974). The components of dialogue. *Western Speech, 38,* 199-
212.
Rafaeli, S. (1988). Interactivity: From new media to communication. In R.
P. Hawkins, J. M. Wiemann, & S. Pingree (Eds.), *Advancing communi-
cation science: Merging mass and interpersonal processes* (pp. 110-134).
Newbury Park, CA: Sage.
Real, M. R. (1989). *Super media.* Newbury Park, CA: Sage.
Rice, R. E., & Williams, F. (1984). Theories old and new: The study of new
media. In R. E. Rice & Associates (Eds.), *The new media:
Communication, research and technology* (pp. 55-80). Beverly Hills, CA:
Sage.

Riegel, K. (1979). *Foundations of dialectical psychology*. New York: Academic Press.

Rommetveit, R. (1987). Meaning, context, and control: Convergent trends and controversial issues in current social-scientific research on human cognition and communication. *Inquiry, 30*, 77-99.

Rogers, C. R. (1980). *A way of being*. Boston: Houghton Mifflin.

Schrag, C. O. (1986). *Communicative praxis and the space of subjectivity*. Bloomington: Indiana University Press.

Shor, I., & Freire, P. (1987). *A pedagogy for liberation: Dialogues on transforming education*. Granby, MA: Bergin & Garvey.

Stewart, J. (1978). Foundations of dialogic communication. *Quarterly Journal of Speech, 64*, 183-201.

Stewart, J. (1985). Martin Buber's central insight: Implications for his philosophy of dialogue. In M. Dascal (Ed.), *Dialogue: An interdisciplinary approach* (pp. 321-335). Amsterdam: John Benjamins.

Stewart, S. (1986). Shouts on the street: Bakhtin's anti-linguistics. In G. S. Morson (Ed.), *Bakhtin: Essays and dialogues on his work* (pp. 41-58). Chicago: University of Chicago Press.

Tedlock, D. (1983). *The spoken word and the work of interpretation*. Philadelphia: University of Pennsylvania Press.

Thomlison, T. D. (1982). *Toward interpersonal dialogue*. New York: Longman.

Todorov, T. (1984). *Mikhail Bakhtin: The dialogical principle* (W. Godzich, Trans.). Minneapolis: University of Minnesota Press.

Tyler, S. A. (1987). *The unspeakable: Discourse, dialogue, and rhetoric in the postmodern world*. Madison: University of Wisconsin Press.

Voloshinov, V. N. (1973). *Marxism and the philosophy of language* (L. Matejka & I. R. Titunik, Trans.). New York: Seminar Press.

Williams, F., Phillips, A. F., & Lum, P. (1985). Gratifications associated with new communication technologies. In K. E. Rosengren, L. A. Wenner, & P. Palmgreen (Eds.), *Media gratifications research: Current perspectives* (pp. 241-252). Beverly Hills, CA: Sage

■ 6

The Relational Region: The Language of Mutuality

Walter Lippmann (1922) observed that modern people "live in grooves" (p. 31), and communication scholars are no different. The most deeply grooved approach to communication study, especially in the United States, is individualistic—it focuses on messages seemingly created by individual actors and aimed at other individuals. Although this habit has yielded some important insights, it has just as surely obscured others.

James Carey (1989) showed how American studies of communication are "grounded in a transmission or transportation view of communication. We see communication basically as a process of transmitting messages at a distance for the purpose of control. The archetypal case of communication, then, is persuasion . . ." (p. 42). This perspective is most appropriate, in other words, to either a cybernetic systems philosophy wherein messages serve feedback functions or an agonistic rhetorical philosophy in which rhetors seek to express persuasively their already developed positions in order to sway others. Unfortunately, an individualistic lens is not particularly useful for envisioning the often mysterious development of understanding in the first place or in explaining how people work together to coordinate different goals into collaborative effort.

These foundational human activities must be understood through a more basic sense of communication that recalls its own etymological roots. What characterizes communication is its *commonness*, its process character of existing only when shared, when concocted between persons by and through their relation to each other, each as an other. Communication is common, too, in the sense of omnipresence; each way we turn we find something new to study, some new way to image lives symbolically and behaviorally relative to other lives. Although its force can be sharpened or leveled, dialogic communication defines what can be considered an ideal case for communication study. By examining the practical consequences of dialogue, we glimpse the practical potential of communication itself.

111

We could consider the philosophical approach to dialogue, introduced in Part I, as dialogue's first "region": Philosophers and theologians have speculated eloquently about the ideal dimensions of human dialogue. If the *philosophical region* defines dialogue and moves beyond an individualistic paradigm for the human sciences, in this chapter we introduce a somewhat more pragmatic extension of the philosophical region that we are calling the *relational region*. Here our concern remains philosophically informed, yet dialogue has practical everyday implications that, although they could be considered within the philosophical region, transcend it also. Persons cooperatively create worlds of small talk, social support, media immersion, and even solitary confrontations with self-doubt, future plans, and social satisfaction. We sample the thought of three theorists whose prime concern in these essays is with the relational implications of everyday dialogue.

First, we consider the 20th-century German philosopher Hans-Georg Gadamer, who has become perhaps the most influential voice of contemporary hermeneutics. Hermeneutics, the study of the problems of textual interpretation, is clearly linked to communication through Gadamer's claim that a positivist scientific method has failed us, and a subjective and idiosyncratic constructivist approach to reality is equally a dead end. Instead, says Gadamer, hermeneutics is a "practical philosophy" in which the model for human interpretation, learning, and communication is found in conversation. Conversation with person or text is a relational and linguistic engagement in which each side openly questions the other from the standpoint of historical context or "situatedness."

French sociologist and social commentator Jacques Ellul, most famous for his critique of modern technology in *The Technological Society* (1964), emphasizes in our excerpt from a later work the issue of uncertainty, which is central to understanding the continuous flow of interpretation in dialogic situations. Considered dialogically, effective communication is not the conveyance of certainty, but the productive experience of uncertainty and ambiguity in a context in which new testing of meaning can occur. Surprise, astonishment, difference, and even confusion form the ground of human creativity from which we can become new. Genuine human practicality and effective communication, Ellul asserts, is not in the accurate transportation of "what I have to say" to "what you've heard," but instead is in the encounter leading to what neither of us could have predicted. This synergy is very much in keeping with Gadamer's critique of fidelity criteria in textual studies. Some philosophers, in other words, argue that communication is not necessarily "better" if a listener develops a textual interpretation essentially similar to that intended by a speaker.

The third probe into the relational region is that of American psychologist Carl R. Rogers. Rogers's work, most accessible in *On Becoming* a *Person* (1961) and *A Way of Being* (1980), developed a praxis of dialogue supported less by philosophical rigor than by his own experience as a psychotherapist, counselor, and group leader. Rogers observed that the most effective professionals in various "helping fields" focused more on their immediate relationship with a client than on prescriptions, methods, techniques, or theoretical models. In other words, personal growth appeared to be facilitated when persons did not focus on themselves as objects, but as "processes" in constant relational change. Facilitators who were "client-centered" and "person-centered" could more easily enter into dialogue with others when they exhibited three experiential conditions: "congruence" (a generalized matching of inner experience and outer behavior); "empathy" (the experience of imaginatively taking the perspective of the other without sacrificing one's own perspective); and "unconditional positive regard" (the experience of accepting the other as a person—but not necessarily all of his or her behavior—without attaching conditions for such acceptance). Given these conditions and their perceptions, Rogers believed the relationship itself is freed to grow, thus freeing persons as well.

REFERENCES

Carey, J. W. (1989). *Communication as culture: Essays on media and society.* Boston: Unwin Hyman.

Ellul, J. (1964). *The technological society* (J. Wilkinson, Trans.). New York: Vintage Books.

Lippmann, W. (1922). *Public opinion.* New York: The Free Press.

Rogers, C. R. (1961). *On becoming a person.* Boston: Houghton Mifflin.

Rogers, C. R. (1980). *A way of being.* Boston: Houghton Mifflin.

Language as the Medium of Hermeneutical Experience

Hans-Georg Gadamer

We say that we "conduct" a conversation, but the more fundamental a conversation is, the less its conduct lies within the will of either partner. Thus a fundamental conversation is never one that we want to conduct. Rather, it is generally more correct to say that we fall into conversation, or even that we become involved in it. The way in which one word follows another, with the conversation taking its own turnings and reaching its own conclusion, may well be conducted in some way, but the people conversing are far less the leaders of it than the led. No one knows what will "come out" in a conversation. Understanding or its failure is like a process which happens to us. Thus we can say that something was a good conversation or that it was a poor one. All this shows that a conversation has a spirit of its own, and that the language used in it bears its own truth within it, ie that it reveals something which henceforth exists.

We have already seen in the analysis of romantic hermeneutics that understanding is not based on "getting inside" another person, on the immediate fusing of one person in another. To understand what a person says is, as we saw, to agree about the object, not to get inside another person and relive his experiences. We emphasised that the experience of meaning which takes place in understanding always includes application. Now we are to note that this whole process is linguistic. It is not for nothing that the actual problems of understanding and the attempt to master it as an art—the concern of hermeneutics—belongs tra-

From Truth and Method (pp. 345-351, 528) by Hans-Georg Gadamer, English translation copyright © 1975, by Sheed & Ward Ltd. Reprinted with the permission of The Continuum Publishing Company.

ditionally to the sphere of grammar and rhetoric. Language is the middle ground in which understanding and agreement concerning the object takes place between two people.

In situations in which understanding is disrupted or made difficult, the conditions of all understanding emerge with the greatest clarity. Thus the linguistic process by means of which a conversation in two different languages is made possible through translation is especially informative. Here the translator must translate the meaning to be understood into the context in which the other speaker lives. This does not, of course, mean that he is at liberty to falsify the meaning of what the other person says. Rather, the meaning must be preserved, but since it must be understood within a new linguistic world, it must be expressed within it in a new way. Thus every translation is at the same time an interpretation. We can even say that it is the completion of the interpretation that the translator has made of the words given him.

The example of translation, then, shows that language as the medium of understanding must be consciously created by an explicit mediation. This kind of conscious process is undoubtedly not the norm in a conversation. Nor is translation the norm in our attitude to a foreign language. Rather, having to rely on translation is tantamount to two people giving up their independent authority. Where a translation is necessary, the gap between the spirit of the original words and that of their reproduction must be accepted. It is a gap that can never be completely closed. But in these cases understanding does not really take place between the partners of the conversation, but between the interpreters, who are able to have a real encounter in a common world of understanding. (It is well-known that there is nothing more difficult than a dialogue in two different languages in which one person speaks one and the other person the other, each understanding the other's language, but not speaking it. As if impelled by a higher force, one of the languages always tries to establish itself over the other as the medium of understanding.)

Where understanding takes place, we have not translation but speech. To understand a foreign language means that we do not need to translate it into our own. If we really master a language, then no translation is necessary—in fact, any translation seems impossible. The understanding of a language is not yet of itself a real understanding and does not include an interpretative process but it is an accomplishment of life. For you understand a language by living in it—a statement that is true, as we know, not only of living, but also of dead languages. Thus the hermeneutical problem is not one of the correct mastery of language, but of the proper understanding of that which takes place through the medium of language. Every language can be learned in such a way that its perfect use means that a person is no longer translating from or into his native tongue, but thinks in the foreign language. For two people to be able to understand each other in conversation this mastery of the language is a necessary pre-condition. Every conversation automatically presupposes that the two speakers speak the same language. Only when it is possible for two people to make themselves understood through language by talking together can the problem of understanding and agreement be even raised. Dependence on the translation of an interpreter is an extreme case that duplicates the hermeneutical process of the conversation: there is that between the interpreter and the other as well as that between oneself and the interpreter.

A conversation is a process of two people understanding each other. Thus is characteristic of every true conversation that each opens himself to the other person, truly accepts his point of view as worthy of consideration and gets inside the other to such an extent that he understands not a particular individual, but what he says. The thing that has to be grasped is the objective rightness or otherwise of his opinion, so that they can agree with each other on the subject. Thus one does not relate the other's opinion to him, but to one's own views. Where a person is concerned with the other as individuality, eg in a therapeutical conversation or the examination of a man accused of a crime, this is not really a situation in which two people are trying to understand one another.[1]

All this, which characterises the situation of two people understanding each other in conversation, has its hermeneutical application where we are concerned with the understanding of texts. Let us again start by considering the extreme case of translation from a foreign language. Here no one can doubt that the translation of a text, however much the translator may have felt himself into his author, cannot be simply a reawakening of the original event in the mind of the writer, but a recreation of the text that is guided by the way the translator understands what is said in it. No one can doubt that we are dealing here with interpretation, and not simply with reproduction. A new light falls on the text from the other language and for the reader of it. The requirement that a translation should be faithful cannot remove the fundamental gulf between the two languages. However faithful we try to be, we have to make difficult decisions. If we want to emphasise in our translation a feature of the original that is important to us, then we can do it only by playing down or entirely suppressing other features. But this is precisely the attitude that we call interpretation. Translation, like all interpretation, is a highlighting. A translator must understand that highlighting is part of his task. Obviously he must not leave open whatever is not clear to him, but must declare himself. Yet there are border-line cases in which, in the original (and for the "original reader"), something is, in fact, unclear. But precisely these hermeneutical border-line cases show the straits in which the translator constantly finds himself. Here he must resign himself. He must state clearly how he understands. But inasmuch as he is always in the position of not really being able to give expression to all the dimensions of his text, this means for him a constant renunciation. Every translation that takes its task seriously is at once clearer and flatter than the original. Even if it is a masterly re-creation, it must lack some of the overtones of the original. (In rare cases of really fine translation the loss can be made good or even lead to gain—think, for example, of how Baudelaire's *Les fleurs du mal* seems to have acquired an odd new vigour in Stefan George's version).

The translator is often painfully aware of his inevitable distance from the original. His dealing with the text has something of the effort to understand another person in conversation. Only that the situation here is one of an extremely wearisome process of understanding, in which one sees the gap between one's own meaning and that of the other person as ultimately unbridgeable. And, as in conversation, when there are such unbridgeable differences, a compromise can sometimes be achieved in the to and fro of dialogue, so the translator will seek the best solution in the toing and froing of weighing up and considering possibilities—a solution which can never be more than a compromise. As in conversation one tries to get inside the other person in order to understand his point of view, so the translator also tries to get right inside his author. But this does not automatically mean that understanding is achieved in a conversation, nor for the translator does this kind of empathy mean that there is a successful recreation. The structures are clearly analogous. Reaching an understanding in conversation presupposes that both partners are ready for it and are trying to recognise the full value of what is alien and opposed to them. If this happens mutually, and each of the partners, while simultaneously holding on to his own arguments, weighs the counter-arguments, it is finally possible to achieve, in an imperceptible but not arbitrary reciprocal translation of the other's position (we call this an exchange of views), a common language and a common statement. Similarly, the translator must respect the character of his own language, into which he is translating, while still recognizing the value of the alien, even antagonistic character of the text and its expression. Perhaps, however, this description of the translator's activity is too abbreviated. Even in these extreme situations, in which it is necessary to translate from one language into another, the subject-matter can scarcely be separated from language. Only that translator can succeed who brings into language the object that the text points to; but this means finding a language which is not only his, but is also proportionate to the original.[2] The situation of the translator and that of the interpreter are fundamentally the same.

The example of the translator, who has to bridge the gulf between languages, shows clearly the reciprocal relationship that exists between interpreter and text, corresponding to the mutuality of understanding in conversation. For every translator is an interpreter. The fact that it is a foreign language that is being translated means that it is simply an extreme case of hermeneutical difficulty, ie of alienness and its con-quest. All "objects" with which traditional hermeneutics are concerned are, in fact, alien in the same sense. The translator's task of re-creation differs only in degree, not qualitatively, from the general hermeneutical task presented by any text.

This is not, of course, to say that the hermeneutic situation in regard to texts is exactly the same as that between two people in conversa-tion. Texts are "permanently fixed expressions of life"[3] which have to be understood, and that means that one partner in the hermeneutical con-versation, the text, is expressed only through the other partner, the inter-preter. Only through him are the written marks changed back into mean-ing. Nevertheless, by being changed back into intelligible terms, the object of which the text speaks itself finds expression. It is like a real con-versation, in that it is the common object that unites the two partners, the text and the interpreter. Just as the translator makes mutual understand-ing in the conversation he is interpreting possible only by becoming involved in the subject under discussion, so in relation to a text it is indis-pensable that the interpreter involve himself with its meaning.

Thus it is quite correct to speak of a hermeneutical conversation. But from this it follows that hermeneutical conversation, like real conver-sation, finds a common language, and that this finding of a common lan-guage is not, any more than in real conversation, the preparation of a tool for the purpose of understanding but, rather, coincides with the very act of understanding and reaching agreement. Even between the partners of this "conversation" a communication takes place, as between two people, that is more than a mere adaptation. The text brings an object into lan-guage, but that it achieves this is ultimately the work of the interpreter. Both have a share in it.

Hence the meaning of a text is not to be compared with an immovably and obstinately fixed point of view which suggests only one question to the person who is trying to understand it, namely how the other person could have embraced such an absurd opinion. In this sense understanding is certainly not concerned with understanding historically, ie reconstructing the way in which the text has come into being. Rather, one is understanding the text itself. But this means that the interpreter's own thoughts have also gone into the re-awakening of the meaning of the text. In this the interpreter's own horizon is decisive, yet not as a personal standpoint that one holds on to or enforces, but more as a meaning and a possibility that one brings into play and puts at risk, and that helps one truly to make one's own what is said in the text. I have described this above as a "fusion of horizons." We can now see that this is the full realiza-tion of conversation, in which something is expressed that is not only mine or my author's, but common.

The basis of the systematic significance which the linguistic nature of conversation has for all understanding we owe to German romanticism. It has taught us that understanding and interpretation are ultimately the same thing. This insight, as we have seen, advances the idea of interpretation from the merely occasional pedagogical significance that it had in the eighteenth century to the systematic position indicated by the key importance that the problem of language has acquired in philosophy.

Since the romantic period we can no longer hold the view that, should there be no direct understanding, interpretative ideas are drawn on, as needed, out of a linguistic store-room in which they are lying ready. Rather, language is the universal medium in which understanding itself is realised. The mode of realisation of understanding is interpretation. This statement does not mean that there is no special problem of expression. The difference between the language of a text and the language of the interpreter, or the gulf that separates the translator from the original, is not a merely secondary question. On the contrary, the fact is that the problems of linguistic expression are already problems of understanding. All understanding is interpretation, and all interpretation takes place in the medium of a language which would allow the object to come into words and yet is at the same time the interpreter's own language.

Thus the hermeneutical phenomenon proves to be a special case of the general relationship between thinking and speaking, the mysterious intimacy of which is bound up with the way in which speech is contained, in a hidden way, in thinking. Interpretation, like conversation, is a closed circle within the dialectic of question and answer. It is a genuine historical life-situation that takes place in the medium of language and that, also in the case of the interpretation of texts, we can call a conversation. The linguistic quality of understanding is the concretion of effective-historical consciousness.

The relation between language and understanding is seen primarily in the fact that it is the nature of tradition to exist in the medium of language, so that the preferred object of interpretation is a linguistic one.

NOTES

1. The process of getting inside another person, when it is concerned with him and not with whether he is objectively correct, is marked by the insincerity, described above (p 326f) of the questions asked in such a conversation

2. We have here the problem of 'alienation', on which Schadewaldt has important things to say in the appendix of his translation of *Odyssey* (RoRoRo-Klassiker, 1958, p 324)

3. Droysen, *Historik*, ed Hübner, 1937, p. 63

■

Seeing and Hearing: Prolegomena

Jacques Ellul

The word is, of necessity, spoken to someone. If no one is present, it is spoken to oneself or to God. It presupposes an ear; the Great Ear, if necessary. It calls for a response. Every word, even a swearword, an insult, an exclamation, or a soliloquy, begins a dialogue. The monologue is a dialogue in the future or the past, or else it is a dialogue incorporated into a monologue. Here again, time is involved. Dialogue develops according to a variable timetable, but dialogue cannot exist unless those engaging in it are inserted into time.

Language is a call, an exchange. I avoid using the threadbare term "communication." It is not true that language exists only to communicate information. This concept is superficial and holds little interest for us. Obviously, language is *also* communication. It communicates information *also*. But if we spoke only to convey information our relationships would be greatly impoverished. To verify this you have only to listen to the "information" given on television, in spite of the speakers' talent and the surprising and varied way things are presented.

Language is uncertain, communicating information but also a whole universe that is fluid, without content or framework, unpretentious, and filled with the rich complexity of things left unexpressed in a relationship. What is not said also plays a role in language. More accurately, what is said sometimes hides what could be said, and on the other hand sometimes it reveals what is not said. Language never belongs to the

120

order of evident things. It is a continuous movement between hiding and revealing. It makes of the play in human relationships something even more fine and complex than it would be without language. Language exists only for, in, and by virtue of this relationship. Dialogue involves the astonishing discovery of the other person who is like me, and the person like me who is different. We need both similarity and difference at the same time. I speak the same language that you do; we use the same code. But what I have to say is different from what you have to say. Without this difference there would be neither language nor dialogue.

Do we have something to say? In spite of the condemnation of this concept by linguists and modern artists, I insist that I speak because I have something to say. If this pressure were absent, I would not speak. Speech is not born of nothing. It does not itself give birth to the signified that it points to. In spite of the extravagant modern ideas we will examine later, it is still true that when I speak to another person, it is because I have a desire to convey to him something I have that he does not have— or that I think he does not have. And based on this situation, I find the words and phrases that correspond to what I indeed have to say. There is something that precedes speech.

Speech does not take its pattern directly from what there is "to say;" it creates in addition a sphere of unexpectedness, a wonderful flowering which adorns, enriches, and ennobles what I have to say, instead of expressing it directly, flatly, and exactly. I have an idea in mind—or a fact, an outline. I begin to write, and if I reread what I have written a few days later, I am amazed by what I have written. It tallies, to be sure, with what I had to say, up to a point, but it overflows this, and I realize that I have written a different text. What I have written conjures up ideas, images, and shapes which I did not expect, which I have forgotten.

Dialogue involves a certain distance. We must be separated as well as different. I do not speak to a person identical to me. I must have something to say which the other lacks, but he must also be different from me. Yet similarity is required as well. When Adam sees Eve he bursts into speech. He speaks because of her and for her. She was flesh of his flesh, bone of his bone; and yet different: a dissimilar similar person.

Speech fills the infinite gap that separates us. But the difference is never removed. Discourse begins again and again because the distance between us remains. I find I must repeatedly begin speaking again to restate what I have said. The result is an inevitable, yet rich and blessed, redundancy. The word is resumed and repeated because it is never fully explicit or an exact translation of what I have to say. It is never precisely received, never precisely understood. Language is Word. The Word contains fuzziness, a halo that is richer and less precise than information.

Even the simplest word—*bread*, for instance—involves all sorts of connotations. In a mysterious way, it calls up many images which form a dazzling rainbow, a multitude of echoes. When the word *bread* is pronounced, I cannot help but think of the millions of people who have none. I cannot avoid the image of a certain baker friend of mine, and of the time during the Nazi occupation when bread was so scarce and of such poor quality. The communion service comes to me: the breaking of bread at the Last Supper and the image of Jesus, both present and unknown.

I pass quickly to the moral lessons I learned as a child: that it is crime to throw away a piece of bread, since it is a sacred substance. And from there, of course, I arrive at the enormous, incredible amount of wastefulness in our society. We waste many things besides bread, but it remains the negative symbol of our squandering ways. Memories come back to me: the warm, crusty bread of my childhood. The promised bread of life that will satisfy all hunger. And not living by bread alone. What ever happened to this Word of the Father which is proclaimed without being understood?

Not all of these memories are conjured up every time I hear the word, and they do not all come at once, but it is a rarity when none of them follows the oft-repeated request: "pass me the bread." Language deals with connotations and overtones. It takes its place in the center of an infinitely delicate spider's web, whose central structure is fine, rigorous, and dense. As you move away from the center, the web becomes larger and distended, until it reaches incoherence, at its edge, where it sends off threads in every direction. Some of these threads go a great distance, until they arrive at the invisible spots where the web is anchored. This complex web is a marvel which is never the same, not for me at different points in time nor for another person.

The spoken Word puts the web in motion so that waves sweep through it and cause lights to flicker. The waves induce vibrations that are different for the other person and for me. The word is uncertain. Discourse is ambiguous and often ambivalent. Some foolishly try to reduce language to something like algebra, in which each word would have a mathematically precise meaning, and only one meaning. Each word would be put in a straitjacket, having only one meaning, so that we would know with scientific precision what we were saying. And the receiver of our message would always know exactly what we meant.

But the blessed uncertainty of language is the source of all its richness. I do not know exactly how much of my message the other person hears, how he interprets it, or what he will retain of it. I know that a kind of electric current is established between us; words penetrate him, and I have the feeling that he either reacts positively or else rejects what I have said. I can interpret his reaction, and then the relationship will rebound, accompanied by a rich halo of overtones. He does not understand, and I see that. So I speak again, weaving another piece of cloth, but this time with a different design. I come up with what I think will reach him and be perceived by him. The uncertainty of meaning and the ambiguity of language inspire creativity. It is a matter of poetics, but not just the esthetics of poetry. There is a poetics of language and of relationships also. We must not limit this poetics to language, which must be constantly rewoven, but remember that the relationship is *also* involved. Language requires that we recommence this relationship, which is always uncertain. I must disavow it over and over again, through sharp questioning, explanation, and verbal interchange.

Discourse is ambiguous; it is never clear. It arrives from one person's unconscious aggregate of experiences, desires skills, and knowledge, only to fall into another person's, thus producing a different meaning. Because of these continual misunderstandings, new life is breathed into the relationship. We must constantly begin all over again, and as a result the relationship becomes a rich, complex landscape, with unexpected mountain passes and inaccessible peaks. By all means let's not turn language into something mathematical, nor reduce the rich complexity of human relationships to identical formulas.

Meaning is uncertain; therefore I must constantly fine-tune my language and work at reinterpreting the words I hear. I try to understand what the other person says to me. All language is more or less a riddle to be figured out; it is like interpreting a text that has many possible meanings. In my effort at understanding and interpretation, I establish definitions, and finally, a meaning. The thick haze of discourse produces meaning.

All of intellectual life (and I use the word "all" advisedly), even that of specialists in the most exact sciences, is based on these instabilities, failures to understand, and errors in interpretation which we must find a way to go beyond and overcome. Mistaking a person's language keeps me from "taking" the person—from taking him prisoner.

We are in the presence of an infinitely and unexpectedly rich tool, so that the tiniest phrase unleashes an entire polyphonic gamut of meaning. The ambiguity of language, and even its ambivalence and its contradiction, between the moment it is spoken and the moment it is received produce extremely intense activities. Without such activities, we would be ants or bees, and our drama and tragedy would quickly be dried up and empty. Between the moment of speech and the moment of reception are born symbol, metaphor, and analogy.

Through language I lay hold of two completely different objects. I bring them together, establishing between them a relationship of similarity or even identity. In this manner I come to know this distant, unknown object, through its resemblance. It becomes intelligible to me, because through language I have brought it near this other one that I know well. This is an astonishing process, and logically a foolish one. It is obviously an indefensible operation, yet there it is, utterly successful, utterly enlightening. The uncertainty and the ambiguity of language have permitted it to function. I have access to the unknown through verbal identification, as well as through symbolic language that allows me to express the inexpressible.

As a result of this alchemy, after many efforts, the nugget of pure gold appears: we are in agreement. This is completely unexpected, and always a miracle. Through metaphors and syllogisms, analogies and myths, in the tangles of uncertainties and misunderstandings, agreement crops up. In the middle of so much "noise" (in the sense of interference), word and meaning come to the surface and permit an unclouded agreement, a conformity, in which heart meets heart. The innermost being of one person has reached the innermost of another through the mediation and ambassadorship of this language go-between. Overloaded with meaning, it has now been stripped of all excess and reduced to its essence. Now we can engage in common action without fear of error. Our life together can continue on the basis of a renewed authenticity.

But we must be careful: this happy result is achieved only to the degree that—exactly to the degree that—we have experienced all the "interference" of meaning: the rich connotations, the polyphony, and the overtones produced. In the middle of all this, and because of it, a common understanding springs forth and is formulated. It is not exactly what I said (fortunately!). Rather, it is more than that. Nor is it exactly what a tape recorder could have taken down. Instead, it is a symphony of echoes that have reverberated in me. Our agreement commits us to a renewed relationship that will be more profound and genuine. We will be continually reinventing this relationship, just as our speaking must continually recommence.

The word reduced to the value of an algebraic formula with only one possible meaning would be useful for us in carrying out an identical superficial activity. But such language could never create meaning, and would never produce agreement and communication with another person. "Algebraic" language could never produce or suggest a story. Bees communicate pieces of information to each other, but do not produce anything like history.

History is produced by the tangle of our misunderstandings and interpretations. Something unexpected is continually cropping up even in the simplest of our relationships. This unexpected element involves us in some action, explanation, or procedure that will constitute the history of our relationship. History is a product of language and the word. This applies not only to something memorized so that we can tell it later. The historian, even if his field is the history of science, is always limited to telling stories—sometimes his own. This is not only true of the history that is distant from us, which only language can evoke and make new again, since it is told in the present. It is also true of the history we are making, which has yet to be invented: history in process, whether mine or the story of my society or of humanity in general. In every case, language alone sets history in motion, defines it, and makes it possible or necessary. This can be a word from the politician or from the masses. The word can also obstruct and impede history, when mythical language immerses us in an ahistorical time that is repetitive and continually reduced to myth. Language is either historical or ahistorical, either a discourse on action to be undertaken or of myth to listen to. According to the sort of language used, human history either arises and becomes a significant aspect of humanity's existence, or else it remains on the level of everyday incoherence.

As in the case of human agreement, history is born and organized, continues, and takes on meaning as a result of the innumerable sounds arising from the Word. Finally the moment comes when understanding takes place, when language is understood after so many setbacks. From the level of being and of the heart, language proceeds to the level of intelligence, and finally it is understood, beyond and because of the repeated misunderstandings which have been progressively eliminated. All this takes place without losing any part of the symphony of meaning.

The instant when language is understood seems like a genuine illumination. It is not the sum of the understood fragments, not the slow and tortuous march of a gradual and complicated unfolding, nor is it the triumphant QED of a solved algebra problem. Instead, this moment of insight is an inspiration which reveals in an instant the meaning of the entire message the other person was trying to give me. Everything is reduced to this sparkling moment which makes order out of the rest of the imbroglio and finds the way out of the maze. In a single instant the entire idea becomes clear: the other person's argument ceases being mere rhetoric, and his symbols and metaphors are no longer pointless. In a flash that some have compared to a kind of vision, communication between two intelligent beings has taken place.

Have I really "seen" what the other person said? Sudden insight has nothing in common with sight but its instantaneousness. Insight is not a kind of vision, but rather a light. The difference between the two will become clear in a later section. With insight, meaning becomes perfectly transparent. The other person's words become mine; I receive them in my own mind. I experience utter intellectual delight, but a delight in my whole being as well, when I understand and am understood.

■

The Necessary and Sufficient Conditions of Therapeutic Personality Change

Carl R. Rogers

For many years I have been engaged in psychotherapy with individuals in distress. In recent years I have found myself increasingly concerned with the process of abstracting from that experience the general principles which appear to be involved in it. I have endeavored to discover any orderliness, any unity which seems to inhere in the subtle, complex tissue of interpersonal relationship in which I have so constantly been immersed in therapeutic work. One of the current products of this concern is an attempt to state, in formal terms, a theory of psychotherapy, of personality, and of interpersonal relationships which will encompass and contain the phenomena of my experience.[1] What I wish to do in this paper is to take one very small segment of that theory, spell it out more completely, and explore its meaning and usefulness.

THE PROBLEM

The question to which I wish to address myself is this: Is it possible to state, in terms which are clearly definable and measurable, the psychological conditions which are both necessary and sufficient to bring about constructive personality change? Do we, in other words, know with any precision those elements which are essential if psychotherapeutic change is to ensue?

Before proceeding to the major task let me dispose very briefly of the second portion of the question. What is meant by such phrases as "psychotherapeutic change," "constructive personality change?" This problem also deserves deep and serious consideration, but for the moment let me suggest a commonsense type of meaning upon which we can perhaps agree for purposes of this paper. By these phrases is meant: change in the personality structure of the individual, at both surface and deeper levels, in a direction which clinicians would agree means greater integration, less internal conflict, more energy utilizable for effective living; change in behaviors away from behaviors generally regarded as immature and toward behaviors regarded as mature. This brief description may suffice to indicate the kind of change for which we are considering the preconditions. It may also suggest the ways in which this criterion of change may be determined.[2]

THE CONDITIONS

As I have considered my own clinical experience and that of my colleagues, together with the pertinent research which is available, I have drawn out several conditions which seem to me to be *necessary* to initiate constructive personality change, and which, taken together, appear to be *sufficient* to inaugurate that process. As I have worked on this problem I have found myself surprised at the simplicity of what has emerged. The statement which follows is not offered with any assurance as to its correctness, but with the expectation that it will have the value of any theory, namely that it states or implies a series of hypotheses which are open to proof or disproof, thereby clarifying and extending our knowledge of the field.

Since I am not, in this paper, trying to achieve suspense, I will state at once, in several rigorous and summarized terms, the six conditions which I have come to feel are basic to the process of personality change. The meaning of a number of the terms is not immediately evident, but will be clarified in the explanatory sections which follow. It is hoped that this brief statement will have much more significance to the reader when he has completed the paper. Without further introduction let me state the basic theoretical position.

For constructive personality change to occur, it is necessary that these conditions exist and continue over a period of time:

1. Two persons are in psychological contact.
2. The first, whom we shall term the client, is in a state of incongruence, being vulnerable or anxious.
3. The second person, whom we shall term the therapist, is congruent or integrated in the relationship.

4. The therapist experiences unconditional positive regard for the client.
5. The therapist experiences an empathic understanding of the client's internal frame of reference and endeavors to communicate this experience to the client.
6. The communication to the client of the therapist's empathic understanding and unconditional positive regard is to a minimal degree achieved.

No other conditions are necessary. If these six conditions exist, and continue over a period of time, this is sufficient. The process of constructive personality change will follow.

A Relationship

The first condition specifies that a minimal relationship, a psychological contact, must exist. I am hypothesizing that significant positive personality change does not occur except in a relationship. This is of course a hypothesis, and it may be disproved.

Conditions 2 through 6 define the characteristics of the relationship which are regarded as essential by defining the necessary characteristics of each person in the relationship. All that is intended by this first condition is to specify that the two people are to some degree in contact, that each makes some perceived difference in the experiential field of the other. Probably it is sufficient if each makes some "subceived" difference, even though the individual may not be consciously aware of this impact. Thus it might be difficult to know whether a catatonic patient perceives a therapist's presence as making a difference to him—a difference of any kind—but it is almost certain that at some organic level he does sense this difference.

Except in such a difficult borderline situation as that just mentioned, it would be relatively easy to define this condition in operational terms and thus determine, from a hard-boiled research point of view, whether the condition does, or does not, exist. The simplest method of determination involves simply the awareness of both client and therapist. If each is aware of being in personal or psychological contact with the other, then this condition is met.

The first condition of therapeutic change is such a simple one that perhaps it should be labeled an assumption or a precondition in order to set it apart from those that follow. Without it, however, the remaining items would have no meaning, and that is the reason for including it.

The State of the Client

It was specified that it is necessary that the client be "in a state of incongru-ence, being vulnerable or anxious." What is the meaning of these terms?

Incongruence is a basic construct in the theory we have been developing. It refers to a discrepancy between the actual experience of the organism and the self picture of the individual insofar as it represents that experience. Thus a student may experience, at a total or organismic level, a fear of the university and of examinations which are given on the third floor of a certain building, since these may demonstrate a funda-mental inadequacy in him. Since such a fear of his inadequacy is decided-ly at odds with his concept of himself, this experience is represented (dis-tortedly) in his awareness as an unreasonable fear of climbing stairs in this building, or any building, and soon an unreasonable fear of crossing the open campus. Thus there is a fundamental discrepancy between the experienced meaning of the situation as it registers in his organism and the symbolic representation of that experience in awareness in such a way that it does not conflict with the picture he has of himself. In this case to admit a fear of inadequacy would contradict the picture he holds of him-self; to admit incomprehensible fears does not contradict his self-concept.

Another instance would be the mother who develops vague ill-nesses whenever her only son makes plans to leave home. The actual desire is to hold on to her only source of satisfaction. To perceive this in awareness would be inconsistent with the picture she holds of herself as a good mother. Illness, however, is consistent with her self-concept, and the experience is symbolized in this distorted fashion. Thus again there is a basic incongruence between the self as perceived (in this case as an ill mother needing attention) and the actual experience (in this case the desire to hold on to her son).

When the individual has no awareness of such incongruence in himself, then he is merely vulnerable to the possibility of anxiety and dis-organization. Some experience might occur so suddenly or so obviously that the incongruence could not be denied. Therefore, the person is vul-nerable to such a possibility.

If the individual dimly perceives such an incongruence in him-self, then a tension state occurs which is known as anxiety. The incongru-ence need not be sharply perceived. It is enough that it is subceived—that is, discriminated as threatening to the self without any awareness of the content of that threat. Such anxiety is often seen in therapy as the individ-ual approaches awareness of some element of his experience which is in sharp contradiction to his self-concept.

It is not easy to give precise operational definition to this second of the six conditions, yet to some degree this has been achieved. Several research workers have defined the self-concept by means of a Q sort by the individual of a list of self-referent items. This gives us an operational picture of the self. The total experiencing of the individual is more difficult to capture. Chodorkoff (2) has defined it as a Q sort made by a clinician who sorts the same self-referent items independently, basing his sorting on the picture he has obtained of the individual from projective tests. His sort thus includes unconscious as well as conscious elements of the individual's experience, thus representing (in an admittedly imperfect way) the totality of the client's experience. The correlation between these two sorting[3] gives a crude operational measure of incongruence between self and experience, low or negative correlation representing of course a high degree of incongruence.

The Therapist's Genuineness in the Relationship

The third condition is that the therapist should be, within the confines of this relationship, a congruent, genuine, integrated person. It means that within the relationship he is freely and deeply himself, with his actual experience accurately represented by his awareness of himself. It is the opposite of presenting a facade, either knowingly or unknowingly.

It is not necessary (nor is it possible) that the therapist be a paragon who exhibits this degree of integration, of wholeness, in every aspect of his life. It is sufficient that he is accurately himself in this hour of this relationship, that in this basic sense he is what he actually is, in this moment of time.

It should be clear that this includes being himself even in ways which are not regarded as ideal for psychotherapy. His experience may be "I am afraid of this client" or "My attention is so focused on my own problems that I can scarcely listen to him." If the therapist is not denying these feelings to awareness, but is able freely to be them (as well as being his other feelings), then the condition we have stated is met.

It would take us too far afield to consider the puzzling matter as to the degree to which the therapist overtly communicates this reality in himself to the client. Certainly the aim is not for the therapist to express or talk out his own feelings, but primarily that he should not be deceiving the client as to himself. At times he may need to talk out some of his own feelings (either to the client, or to a colleague or supervisor) if they are standing in the way of the two following conditions.

It is not too difficult to suggest an operational definition for this third condition. We resort again to Q technique. If the therapist sorts a series of items relevant to the relationship (using a list similar to the ones developed by Fiedler [3, 4] and Brown [1]), this will give his perception of his experience in the relationship. If several judges who have observed the interview or listened to a recording of it (or observed a sound movie of it) now sort the same items to represent *their* perception of the relation-ship, this second sorting should catch those elements of the therapist's behavior and inferred attitudes of which he is unaware, as well as those of which he is aware. Thus a high correlation between the therapist's sort and the observer's sort would represent in crude form an operational def-inition of the therapist's congruence or integration in the relationship; and a low correlation, the opposite.

Unconditional Positive Regard

To the extent that the therapist finds himself experiencing a warm accep-tance of each aspect of the client's experience as being a part of that client, he is experiencing unconditional positive regard. This concept has been developed by Standal (8). It means that there are no *conditions* of acceptance, no feeling of "I like you only *if* you are thus and so." It means a "prizing" of the person, as Dewey has used that term. It is at the oppo-site pole from a selective evaluating attitude—"You are bad in these ways, good in those." It involves as much feeling of acceptance for the client's expression of negative, "bad," painful, fearful, defensive, abnormal feel-ings as for his expression of "good," positive, mature, confident, social feelings, as much acceptance of ways in which he is inconsistent as of ways in which he is consistent. It means a caring for the client, but not in a pos-sessive way or in such a way as simply to satisfy the therapist's own needs. It means a caring for the client as a *separate* person, with permission to have his own feelings, his own experiences. One client describes the ther-apist as "fostering my possession of my own experience . . . that [this] is *my* experience and that I am actually having it: thinking what I think, feel-ing what I feel, wanting what I want, fearing what I fear: no 'ifs,' 'buts,' or 'not reallys.'" This is the type of acceptance which is hypothesized as being necessary if personality change is to occur.

Like the two previous conditions, this fourth condition is a matter of degree,[4] as immediately becomes apparent if we attempt to define it in terms of specific research operations. One such method of giving it defin-ition would be to consider the Q sort for the relationship as described under Condition 3. To the extent that items expressive of unconditional positive regard are sorted as characteristic of the relationship by both the therapist and the observers, unconditional positive regard might be said to exist. Such items might include statements of this order: "I feel no revulsion at anything the client says"; "I feel neither approval nor disap-proval of the client and his statements—simply acceptance;" "I feel warm-ly toward the client—toward his weaknesses and problems as well as his potentialities;" "I am not inclined to pass judgment on what the client tells me;" "I like the client." To the extent that both therapist and observers perceive these items as characteristic, or their opposites as uncharacteristic, Condition 4 might be said to be met.

Empathy

The fifth condition is that the therapist is experiencing an accurate, empathic understanding of the client's awareness of his own experience. To sense the client's private world as if it were your own, but without ever losing the "as if" quality—this is empathy, and this seems essential to therapy. To sense the client's anger, fear, or confusion as if it were your own, yet without your own anger, fear, or confusion getting bound up in it, is the condition we are endeavoring to describe. When the client's world is this clear to the therapist, and he moves about in it freely, then he can both communicate his understanding of what is clearly known to the client and can also voice meanings in the client's experience of which the client is scarcely aware. As one client described this second aspect: "Every now and again, with me in a tangle of thought and feeling, screwed up in a web of mutually divergent lines of movement, with impulses from different parts of me, and me feeling the feeling of its being all too much and suchlike— then whomp, just like a sunbeam thrusting its way through cloudbanks and tangles of foliage to spread a circle of light on a tangle of forest paths, came some comment from you. [It was] clarity, even disentanglement, an additional twist to the picture, a putting in place. Then the consequence— the sense of moving on, the relaxation. These were sunbeams." That such penetrating empathy is important for therapy is indicated by Fiedler's research (3) in which items such as the following placed high in the description of relationships created by experienced therapists:

> The therapist is well able to understand the patient's feelings.
>
> The therapist is never in any doubt about what the patient means.
>
> The therapist's remarks fit in just right with the patient's mood and content.
>
> The therapist's tone of voice conveys the complete ability to share the patient's feelings.

An operational definition of the therapist's empathy could be provided in different ways. Use might be made of the Q sort described under Condition 3. To the degree that items descriptive of accurate empathy were sorted as characteristic by both the therapist and the observers, this condition would be regarded as existing.

Another way of defining this condition would be for both client and therapist to sort a list of items descriptive of client feelings. Each would sort independently, the task being to represent the feelings which the client had experienced during a just completed interview. If the correlation between client and therapist sorting were high, accurate empathy would be said to exist, a low correlation indicating the opposite conclusion.

Still another way of measuring empathy would be for trained judges to rate the depth and accuracy of the therapist's empathy on the basis of listening to recorded interviews.

The Client's Perception of the Therapist

The final condition as stated is that the client perceives, to a minimal degree, the acceptance and empathy which the therapist experiences for him. Unless some communication of these attitudes has been achieved, then such attitudes do not exist in the relationship as far as the client is concerned, and the therapeutic process could not, by our hypothesis, be initiated.

Since attitudes cannot be directly perceived, it might be somewhat more accurate to state that therapist behaviors and words are perceived by the client as meaning that to some degree the therapist accepts and understands him.

An operational definition of this condition would not be difficult. The client might, after an interview, sort a Q sort list of items referring to qualities representing the relationship between himself and the therapist. (The same list could be used as for condition 3.) If several items descriptive of acceptance and empathy are sorted by the client as characteristic of the relationship, then this condition could be regarded as met. In the present state of our knowledge the meaning of "to a minimal degree" would have to be arbitrary.

Some Comments

Up to this point the effort has been made to present, briefly and factually, the conditions which I have come to regard as essential for psychotherapeutic change. I have not tried to give the theoretical context of these conditions nor to explain what seem to me to be the dynamics of their effectiveness. Such explanatory material will be available, to the reader who is interested, in the document already mentioned (see footnote 1).

I have, however, given at least one means of defining, in operational terms, each of the conditions mentioned. I have done this in order to stress the fact that I am not speaking of vague qualities which ideally should be present if some other vague result is to occur. I am presenting conditions which are crudely measurable even in the present state of our technology, and have suggested specific operations in each instance even though I am sure that more adequate methods of measurement could be devised by a serious investigator.

My purpose has been to stress the notion that in my opinion we are dealing with an if-then phenomenon in which knowledge of the dynamics is not essential to testing the hypotheses. Thus, to illustrate from another field: if one substance, shown by a series of operations to be the substance known as hydrochloric acid, is mixed with another substance, shown by another series of operations to be sodium hydroxide, then salt and water will be products of this mixture. This is true whether one regards the results as due to magic, or whether one explains it in the most adequate terms of modern chemical theory. In the same way it is being postulated here that certain definable conditions precede certain definable changes and that this fact exists independently of our efforts to account for it.

THE RESULTING HYPOTHESES

The major value of stating any theory in unequivocal terms is that specific hypotheses may be drawn from it which are capable of proof or disproof. Thus, even if the conditions which have been postulated as necessary and sufficient conditions are more incorrect than correct (which I hope they are not), they could still advance science in this field by providing a base of operations from which fact could be winnowed out from error.

The hypotheses which would follow from the theory given would be of this order:

If these six conditions (as operationally defined) exist, then constructive personality change (as defined) will occur in the client.

If one or more of these conditions is not present, constructive personality change will not occur.

These hypotheses hold in any situation whether it is or is not labeled "psychotherapy."

Only Condition 1 is dichotomous (it either is present or is not), and the remaining five occur in varying degree, each on its continuum. Since this is true, another hypothesis follows, and it is likely that this would be the simplest to test:

If all six conditions are present, then the greater the degree to which Conditions 2 to 6 exist, the more marked will be the constructive personality change in the client.

At the present time the above hypothesis can only be stated in this general form—which implies that all of the conditions have equal possible weight. Empirical studies will no doubt make possible much more refinement of this hypothesis. It may be, for example, that if anxiety is high in the client, then the other conditions are less important. Or if unconditional positive regard is high (as in a mother's love for her child), then perhaps a modest degree of empathy is sufficient. But at the moment we can only speculate on such possibilities.

SOME IMPLICATIONS

Significant Omissions

If there is any startling feature in the formulation which has been given as to the necessary conditions for therapy, it probably lies in the elements which are omitted. In present-day clinical practice, therapists operate as though there were many other conditions in addition to those described, which are essential for psychotherapy. To point this up it may be well to mention a few of the conditions which, after thoughtful consideration of our research and our experience, are not included.

For example, it is *not* stated that these conditions apply to one type of client, and that other conditions are necessary to bring about psychotherapeutic change with other types of client. Probably no idea is so prevalent in clinical work today as that one works with neurotics in one way, with psychotics in another; that certain therapeutic conditions must be provided for compulsives, others for homosexuals, etc. Because of this heavy weight of clinical opinion to the contrary, it is with some "fear and trembling" that I advance the concept that the essential conditions of psychotherapy exist in a single configuration, even though the client or patient may use them very differently.[5]

It is *not* stated that these six conditions are the essential conditions for client-centered therapy, and that other conditions are essential for other types of psychotherapy. I certainly am heavily influenced by my own experience, and that experience had led me to a viewpoint which is termed "client centered." Nevertheless my aim is stating this theory is to state the conditions which apply to *any* situation in which constructive personality change occurs, whether we are thinking of classical psychoanalysis, or any of its modern offshoots, or Adlerian psychotherapy, or any other. It will be obvious then that in my judgment much of what is considered to be essential would not be found, empirically, to be essential. Testing of some of the stated hypotheses would throw light on this perplexing issue. We may of course find that various therapies produce various types of personality change, and that for each psychotherapy a separate set of conditions is necessary. Until and unless this is demonstrated, I am hypothesizing that effective psychotherapy of any sort produces similar changes in personality and behavior, and that a single set of preconditions is necessary.

It is *not* stated that psychotherapy is a special kind of relationship, different in kind from all others which occur in everyday life. It will be evident instead that for brief moments, at least, many good friendships fulfill the six conditions. Usually this is only momentarily, however, and then empathy falters, the positive regard becomes conditional, or the congruence of the "therapist" friend becomes overlaid by some degree of facade or defensiveness. Thus the therapeutic relationship is seen as a heightening of the constructive qualities which often exist in part in other relationships, and an extension through time of qualities which in other relationships tend at best to be momentary.

It is *not* stated that special intellectual professional knowledge—psychological, psychiatric, medical, or religious—is required of the therapist. Conditions 3, 4, and 5, which apply especially to the therapist, are qualities of experience, not intellectual information. If they are to be acquired, they must, in my opinion, be acquired through an experiential training—which may be, but usually is not, a part of professional training. It troubles me to hold such a radical point of view, but I can draw no other conclusion from my experience. Intellectual training and the acquiring of information has, I believe, many valuable results—but becoming a therapist is not one of those results.

It is *not* stated that it is necessary for psychotherapy that the therapist have an accurate psychological diagnosis of the client. Here too it troubles me to hold a viewpoint so at variance with my clinical colleagues. When one thinks of the vast proportion of time spent in any psychological, psychiatric, or mental hygiene center on the exhaustive psychological evaluation of the client or patient, it seems as though this *must* serve a useful purpose insofar as psychotherapy is concerned. Yet the more I have observed therapists, and the more closely I have studied research such as that done by Fiedler and others (4), the more I am forced to the conclusion that such diagnostic knowledge is not essential to psychotherapy.[6] It may even be that its defense as a necessary prelude to psychotherapy is simply a protective alternative to the admission that it is, for the most part, a colossal waste of time. There is only one useful purpose I have been able to observe which relates to psychotherapy. Some therapists cannot feel secure in the relationship with the client unless they possess such diagnostic knowledge. Without it they feel fearful of him, unable to be empathic, unable to experience unconditional regard, finding it necessary to put up a pretense in the relationship. If they know in *advance* of suicidal impulses they can somehow be more acceptant of them. Thus, for some therapists, the security they perceive in diagnostic information may be a basis for permitting themselves to be integrated in the relationship, and to experience empathy and full acceptance. In these instances a psychological diagnosis would certainly be justified as adding to the comfort and hence the effectiveness of the therapist. But even here it does not appear to be a basic precondition for psychotherapy.[7]

Perhaps I have given enough illustrations to indicate that the conditions I have hypothesized as necessary and sufficient for psychotherapy are striking and unusual primarily be virtue of what they omit. If we were to determine, by a survey of the behaviors of therapists, those hypotheses which they appear to regard as necessary to psychotherapy, the list would be a great deal longer and more complex.

Is This Theoretical Formulation Useful?

Aside from the personal satisfaction it gives as a venture in abstraction and generalization, what is the value of a theoretical statement such as has been offered in this paper? I should like to spell out more fully the usefulness which I believe it may have.

In the field of research it may given both direction and impetus to investigation. Since it sees the conditions of constructive personality change as general, it greatly broadens the opportunities for study. Psychotherapy is not the only situation aimed at constructive personality change. Programs of training for leadership in industry and programs of training for military leadership often aim at such change. Educational institutions or programs frequently aim at development of character and personality as well as at intellectual skills. Community agencies aim at personality and behavioral change in delinquents and criminals. Such programs would provide an opportunity for the broad testing of the hypotheses offered. If it is found that constructive personality change occurs in such programs when the hypothesized conditions are not fulfilled, then the theory would have to be revised. If however the hypotheses are upheld, then the results, both for the planning of such programs and for our knowledge of human dynamics, would be significant. In the field of psychotherapy itself, the application of consistent hypotheses to the work of various schools of therapists may prove highly profitable. Again the disproof of the hypotheses offered would be as important as their confirmation, either result adding significantly to our knowledge.

For the practice of psychotherapy the theory also offers significant problems for consideration. One of its implications is that the techniques of the various therapies are relatively unimportant except to the extent that they serve as channels for fulfilling one of the conditions. In client-centered therapy, for example, the technique of "reflecting feelings" has been described and commented on (6, pp. 26-36). In terms of the theory here being presented, this technique is by no means an essential condition of therapy. To the extent, however, that it provides a channel by which the therapist communicates a sensitive empathy and an unconditional positive regard, then it may serve as a technical channel by which the essential conditions of therapy are fulfilled. In the same way, the theory I have presented would see no essential value to therapy of such techniques as interpretation of personality dynamics, free association, analysis of dreams, analysis of the transference, hypnosis, interpretation of life style, suggestion, and the like. Each of these techniques may, however, become a channel for communicating the essential conditions which have been formulated. An interpretation may be given in a way which communicates the unconditional positive regard of the therapist. A stream of free association may be listened to in a way which communicates an empathy which the therapist is experiencing. In the handling of the transference an effective therapist often communicates his own wholeness and congruence in the relationship. Similarly for the other techniques. But just as these techniques *may* communicate the elements which are essential for therapy, so any of them may communicate attitudes and experiences sharply contradictory to the hypothesized conditions of therapy. Feeling may be "reflected" in a way which communicates the therapist's lack of empathy. Interpretations may be rendered in a way which indicates the highly conditional regard of the therapist. Any of the techniques may communicate the fact that the therapist is expressing one attitude at a surface level, and another contradictory attitude which is denied to his own awareness. Thus one value of such a theoretical formulation as we have offered is that it may assist therapists to think more critically about those elements of their experience, attitudes, and behaviors which are essential to psychotherapy, and those which are nonessential or even deleterious to psychotherapy.

Finally, in those programs—educational, correctional, military, or industrial—which aim toward constructive changes in the personality structure and behavior of the individual, this formulation may serve as a very tentative criterion against which to measure the program. Until it is much further tested by research, it cannot be thought of as a valid criterion, but, as in the field of psychotherapy, it may help to stimulate critical analysis and the formulation of alternative conditions and alternative hypothesis.

SUMMARY

Drawing from a larger theoretical context, six conditions are postulated as necessary and sufficient conditions for the initiation of a process of constructive personality change. A brief explanation is given of each condition, and suggestions are made as to how each may be operationally defined for research purposes. The implications of this theory for research, for psychotherapy, and for educational and training programs aimed at constructive personality change, are indicated. It is pointed out that many of the conditions which are commonly regarded as necessary to psychotherapy are, in terms of this theory, nonessential.

NOTES

1. This formal statement is entitled "A theory of therapy, personality and interpersonal relationships, as developed in the client-centered framework," by Carl R. Rogers. The manuscript was prepared at the request of the Committee of the American Psychological Association for the Study of the Status and Development of Psychology in the United States. It will be published by McGraw-Hill in one of several volumes being prepared by this committee. Copies of the unpublished manuscript are available from the author to those with special interest in this field.

2. That this is a measurable and determinable criterion has been shown in research already completed. See (7), especially chapters 8, 13, and 17.

3. There is no intent here to maintain that diagnostic evaluation is useless. We have ourselves made heavy use of such methods in our research studies of change in personality. It is its usefulness as a precondition to psychotherapy which is questioned.

4. The phrase "unconditional positive regard" may be an unfortunate one, since it sounds like an absolute, an all or nothing dispositional concept. It is probably evident from the description that completely unconditional positive regard would never exist except in theory. From a clinical and experiential point of view I believe the most accurate statement is that the effective therapist experiences unconditional positive regard for the client during many moments of his contact with him, yet from time to time he experiences only a conditional positive regard—and perhaps at times a negative regard, though this is not likely in effective therapy. It is in this sense that unconditional positive regard exists as a manner of degree in any relationship.

5. I cling to this statement of my hypothesis even though it is challenged by a just completed study by Kirtner (5). Kirtner has found, in a group of 26 cases from the Counseling Center at the University of Chicago, that there are sharp differences in the client's mode of approach to the resolution of life difficulties, and that these differences are related to success in psychotherapy. Briefly, the client who sees his problem as involving his relationships, and who feels that he contributes to this problem and wants to change it, is likely to be successful. The client who externalize his problem, feeling little self-responsibility, is much more likely to be a failure.

Thus the implication is that some other conditions need to be provided for psychotherapy with this group. For the present, however, I will stand by my hypothesis as given, until Kirtner's study is confirmed, and until we know an alternative hypothesis to take its place.

6. In a facetious moment I have suggested that such therapists might be made equally comfortable by being given the diagnosis of some other individual, not of this patient or client. The fact that the diagnosis proved inaccurate as psychotherapy continued would not be particularly disturbing, because one always expects to find inaccuracies in the diagnosis as one works with the individual.

REFERENCES

Brown, O.H. An investigation of therapeutic relationship in client-centered therapy. Unpublished doctor's dissertation, Univer. of Chicago, 1954.

Chodorkoff, B. Self-perception, perceptual defense, and adjustment. *J. abnorm. soc. Psychol.*, 1954, 49, 508-512.

Fiedler, F.E. A comparison of therapeutic relationships in psychoanalytic, non-directive and Adlerian therapy. *J. consult. Psychol.*, 1950, 14, 436-445.

Fiedler, F.E. Quantitative studies on the role of therapists' feelings toward their patients. In O.H. Mowrer (Ed.), *Psychotherapy: theory and research.* New York: Ronald, 1953.

Kirtner, W.L. Success and failure in client-centered therapy as a function of personality variables. Unpublished master's thesis, Univer. of Chicago, 1955.

Rogers, C.R. *Client-centered therapy.* Boston: Houghton Mifflin, 1951.

Rogers, C.R., & Dymond, Rosalind F. (Eds). *Psychotherapy and personality change.* Chicago: Univer. of Chicago Press, 1954.

Standal, S. The need for positive regard: a contribution to client-centered theory. Unpublished doctor's dissertation, Univer. of Chicago, 1954.

■ 7

The Technological Region: Contexts of Mediation

Annie Dillard (1989), in her essay on the writer's life, muses on the biological experiment in which a male butterfly is presented a choice between a live female butterfly and an oversized painted cardboard representation of a female. Invariably, "over and over again, he jumps the piece of cardboard" (p. 18), even when the actual female nearby moves her wings desperately. "Films and television stimulate the body's senses, too, in big ways," observes Dillard, and "even knowing you are manipulated, you are still as helpless as the male butterfly drawn to painted cardboard" (p. 18).

Are persons helpless before the representations of media? As discussed in the chapter introducing Part II, many commentators have been skeptical about the human effects of highly technologized media. Mass media in the 19th and 20th centuries were considered both hallmarks of modernity and, at least potentially, usurpers of personhood. As they expanded the available store of common cultural information, the argument goes, they atomized, manipulated, and trivialized their audiences. The so-called "new media" of personalized electronic connection (computer bulletin board systems and databases, videotex, etc.), may not be mass-audience phenomena in the same sense as such earlier channels as print, radio, film, and television, and they stress interactivity much more than earlier media. However, many critics fear that such technological additions may become emotional and cultural subtractions.

The basic question may be stated in various ways. Do technologies increase efficiency and a reliance on contrivance at the expense of the interpersonal face-to-face connection traditionally assumed to be the paradigm case of human communication? Is society becoming less humane as it becomes dependent on media that may seem more capable of informing than of educating or caring? Must a society forego its potential for community, or, in larger political terms, a public, as its members gain the expanded information resources made possible by science?

Rather than choose sides and slug it out on such issues as scientific versus artistic approaches to society, or technology versus humanity, our approach in this volume is in a sense to deny the necessary sidedness of such debates. Furthermore, rather than assume that technology increasingly precludes dialogue or increasingly guarantees it, we choose to suggest only that *technology increasingly recharacterizes dialogue*. Three scholarly sources excerpted in this chapter support this point.

First, Joshua Meyrowitz has ably charted the theoretically altered region of technology. His award-winning book *No Sense of Place* is one of our richest and most rewarding recent explorations of media environment. Cultural ground rules for communication have changed; Meyrowitz demonstrates how previous human confinements or requirements of place and direct physical presence need not define the experience of human dialogue. Although we may not like or enjoy all the changes effected or facilitated by electronic media, Meyrowitz senses an increased potential for dialogue. We need to develop a theory of mediated place to complement a theory of physical space.

Media communication can therefore be intensely interpersonal, as Robert Cathcart and Gary Gumpert demonstrate in their useful typology. To them, the traditional division of the communication field into such areas as interpersonal, group and public, and mass communication is inadequate because these categories ignore how omnipresent media have become in all spheres of human existence. Read alongside Meyrowitz's work, this typology suggests new dimensions and directions in dialogic research.

In our third excerpt, rhetorical scholar Walter Fisher examines a specific problem in the emerging media drama: If mediated contexts are in many ways interpersonal, what are the effects of this fact on our social mechanisms of argumentation and decision-making? To whom do we address ourselves when many may be listening simultaneously and often in quite different experiential contexts? And, to whom do we listen when many voices compete for our attention? Perhaps, implies Fisher, distinguishing public argumentation from private may be useful after all. In the excerpt we have selected, Fisher applies his well known *narrative paradigm* to the specific issue of expert testimony in public controversies, testimony that often contradicts private self-concepts of social actors, counterposes "rival stories," and creates an impasse for decision-making. The relation of public and self is therefore of significant concern in our understanding of the potential of dialogue.

REFERENCE

Dillard, A. (1989). *The writing life.* New York: HarperPerrenial.

■

The Separation of Social Place From Physical Place

Joshua Meyrowitz

The book of Genesis tells of God's visit to Abraham and Sarah when they are old and childless. God tells Abraham that within a year Sarah will give birth to a son. Sarah overhears this promise from inside her tent, and she laughs to herself because she is already well past menopause. Since Sarah is alone in her tent, she assumes that her laughter will go unnoticed. But God quickly asks Abraham: "Wherefore did Sarah laugh? . . . Is anything too hard for the Lord?" So surprised is Sarah by the exposure of her private behavior that she denies that she laughed.[1]

Our awe and surprise over such eavesdropping feats has diminished greatly in an age of electronic media. Being "alone" in a given place once meant that one was out of range of others' scrutiny. For people to experience each other directly, they had to travel through space, stay through time, and be admitted through the entrances of rooms and buildings. And these rules of physical place pertained to tents and palaces alike.

Although oral and print cultures differ greatly, the bond between physical place and social place was common to both of them. Print, like all new media, changed the patterns of information flow *to* and *from* places. As a result, it also changed the relative status and power of those in different places. Changes in media in the past have always affected the relationship *among* places. They have affected the information that people *bring* to places and the information that people have in given places. But the relationship between place and social situation was still quite strong.

Electronic media go one step further: They lead to a nearly total dissociation of physical place and social "place." When we communicate through telephone, radio, television, or computer, where we are physically no longer determines where and who we are socially.

PHYSICAL PASSAGE AND SOCIAL PASSAGE

The relationship between physical place and social situation still seems so natural that we continue to confuse physical places with the behaviors that go on in them. The words "school" and "home," for example, are used to refer both to physical buildings and to certain types of social interaction and behavior.

Before electronic media, there was ample reason to overlook the difference between physical places and social situations. Places defined most social information-systems. A given place-situation was spatially and temporally removed from other place-situations. It took time to travel from situation to situation, and distance was a measure of social insulation and isolation. Since rooms and buildings can be entered only through set doorways, people once could be included in and excluded from situations in clearly observable and predictable ways. Electronic media, however, make significant inroads into the situations once defined by physical location.

Communication and travel were once synonymous. Our country's communication channels were once roads, waterways, and railroads. Communication speed was limited to the speed of human travel. Even the legendary Pony Express took ten and a half days to communicate a message from Missouri to California.[2] The invention of the telegraph caused the first break between information movement and physical movement. For the first time, complex messages could move more quickly than a messenger could carry them.[3] With the invention and use of the telegraph, the informational differences between different places began to erode.

Just as students today are less anxious about attending a faraway college when home is only a phone call away, so did the telegraph greatly aid in the settlement of the Western frontier. The telegraph brought East and West closer together informationally. Physical distance as a social barrier began to be bypassed through the shortening of communication "distance." The mutual monitoring of East and West made the country seem smaller and other places and people closer.

Movement from situation to situation and from social status to social status once involved movement from place to place. A place defined a distinct situation because its boundaries limited perception and interaction. Like all electronic media, the telegraph not only defies limits formerly set by distance, but also bypasses the social rite of "passage," that is, the act of moving both physically and socially from one "position" to another.

If people are to behave very differently in different social situations, some clear form of movement from one situation to the next is needed. If a celebration and a memorial service take place in the same place and time, there can be no distinct behaviors for each situation. Entrances and the rites associated with them, whether formal (carrying a bride over the threshold) or informal ("Please knock before you enter my room"), have traditionally allowed for orderly transitions from situation to situation and from behavior pattern to behavior pattern.

The boundaries marked by walls, doors, and barbed wire, and enforced by laws, guards, and trained dogs, continue to define situations by including and excluding participants. But today such boundaries function to define social situations only to the extent that information can still be restricted by restricting physical access. And while much social information is still accessible only by going to a certain place or by meeting people face-to-face, the once consonant relationship between access to information and access to places has been greatly weakened by recent changes in communication media.

The messages in all early media—stone, clay, papyrus, parchment, and paper—have physical volume and weight. When they are heavy or unmovable, people have to go to a specific place to experience them. Even when they are portable, however, they still have to be physically transported from place to place, and they move with the people who possess them. They have to be carried into places, stored in places, and carried out of places. These media, like the people who carry them, are subject to the restraints of social and physical passage.

Electronic messages, however, do not make social entrances; they steal into places like thieves in the night. The "guests" received by a child through electronic media no longer can be stopped at the door to be approved of by the masters of the house. Once a telephone, radio, or television is in the home, spatial isolation and guarding of entrances have no effect on information flow. Electronic messages seep through walls and leap across great distances. Indeed, were we not so accustomed to television and radio and telephone messages invading our homes, they might be the recurring subjects of nightmares and horror films. Whether the effects of such media on our society are good, bad, or neutral, the reprocessing of our physical and social environment is revolutionary.

As a result of electronically mediated interactions, the definition of situations and of behaviors is no longer determined by physical location. To be physically alone with someone is no longer necessarily to be socially alone with them. When there are other people "there" on the telephone, or radio, or television, intimate encounters are changed

By altering the informational characteristics of place, electronic media reshape social situations and social identities. The social meaning of a "prison," for example, has been changed as a result of electronic media of communication. Prisons were once more than places of physical incarceration; they were places of informational isolation as well. A prisoner was not only limited in movement but also "ex-communicated" from society. The placement of prisoners in a secure, isolated *location* once led to both physical and informational separation from society. Today, however, many prisoners share with the larger society the privileges of radio, television, and telephone.[4] Whether this is good or bad is difficult to say, but it is different.

Prisoners' access to the world changes the social environment of both those inside and outside prison. Those outside prison cannot use television as a "private" forum in which to discuss problems of crime and crime prevention, and prisoners can "enter" society through the wires of the telephone. One survey of 208 inmates indicated that nine out of ten prisoners had "learned new tricks and improved their criminal expertise by watching crime programs."[5] Special publications such as *The Prisoner's Yellow Pages* have been prepared to help prisoners contact law libraries, counseling services, and employment agencies.[6]

For better or worse, those prisoners with access to electronic media are no longer completely segregated from society. The use of electronic media has led to a redefinition of the nature of "imprisonment" and to a de facto revision of the prison classification system: The communication variables of "high information" prisons versus "low information" prisons now have been added to the physical variables of "high security" and "low security."

The example of prisons may be extreme, but the impact of electronic media on prisoners is paralleled by the effects of electronic media on children, women, the poor, the disabled, and other groups whose social place was once shaped, at least in part, by physical isolation from the larger world.

Electronic media bring information and experience to everyplace from everyplace. State funerals, wars, hostage crises, and space flights are dramas that can be played on the stage of anyone's living room. And the characters in these dramas are experienced almost as if they were sitting on the living room sofa.

Communicating through electronic media is certainly not equivalent to traveling from place to place and interacting with others in live encounters, but the information transmitted by electronic media is much more similar to face-to-face interaction than is the information conveyed by books or letters. And "relationships" with others through electronic media are accessible to virtually everyone without regard to physical location and social "position."

Media "Friends"

Electronic media's encroachment on place is suggested in one of the clichés of the broadcasting industry: "This show is brought to you *live* from . . ." Once, physical presence was necessary for the experience of a "live," ongoing event. You "had to be there" to experience an informal and intimate interaction. Place once defined a very special category of communication. Electronic media, however, have changed the relative significance of live and mediated encounters. Through electronic media of communication, social performers now "go" where they would not or could not travel, and audiences are now "present" at distant events.

What sort of relationship is formed between people who experience each other only through electronic media? In a perceptive article on media written in the 1950s, Donald Horton and R. Richard Wohl suggest that even when the communication is unidirectional, such as in radio and television, a special relationship develops that did not and could not exist in print media. What is unusual about the new mass media, they suggest, is that they offer the illusion of face-to-face interaction with performers and political figures. "The conditions of response to the performer are analogous to those in a primary group. The most remote and illustrious men are met *as if* they were in the circle of one's peers."[7]

Horton and Wohl suggest that the new media lead to a new type of relationship which they call "para-social interaction." They argue that although the relationship is mediated, it psychologically resembles face-to-face interaction. Viewers come to feel they "know" the people they "meet" on television in the same way they know their friends and associates. In fact, many viewers begin to believe that they know and understand a performer better than all the other viewers do. Paradoxically, the para-social performer is able to establish "intimacy with millions."

Horton and Wohl's framework explains the popularity of talk show hosts such as Jack Paar, Johnny Carson, and Dick Cavett. These are people, according to Horton and Wohl, who have no traditional performance skill; they are not singers, musicians, actors, or even professional-quality comedians. The content of their "performance" is mostly small talk and running gags. Yet they are likeable and interesting in the same way that a close friend is likeable and interesting. The viewer can rely on them to be "themselves." As Horton and Wohl suggest, the pure para-social performer is simply "known for being known." Within this framework, it makes sense that stories about Johnny Carson's threats to resign from the "Tonight" show, his arrest for suspicion of drunk driving, and his divorce settlement have been reported on the network news and in front page headlines.

Even performers with traditional skills often exploit the intimacy of the new media (or find that they cannot avoid it). As a result of close personal observation, many athletes, musicians, journalists, and politicians are now judged not only on the basis of their "talent" but also on the basis of their personalities. The para-social framework may explain why many singing stars turn to more and more personal lyrics and themes as their careers develop and why public officials often add more private information to their public speeches as they become more widely known. The theory can also be extended to actors playing fictional roles. For many viewers, soap opera and other television characters are real people to whom they can turn for inspiration and advice. During his first five years on network television, the fictional "Dr. Marcus Welby" received a quarter of a million letters, most requesting medical advice.[8]

Horton and Wohl do not link their framework to an analysis of the impact of electronic media on physical place, but they do offer observations that support such an analysis. They note, for example, that the para-social relationship has its greatest impact on the "socially isolated, the socially inept, the aged and invalid, the timid and rejected."[9] Because electronic media provide the types of interaction and experience which were once restricted to intimate live encounters, it makes sense that they would have their greatest effect on those who are physically or psychologically removed from everyday social interaction. (One researcher has found that the strength of the para-social relationship increases with the viewer's age, that many elderly people think of newscasters as their friends, and that some older viewers "interact" with newscasters by responding to them verbally.[10]) Even among "average" people, the para-social relationship takes its place among daily live interactions with friends, family, and associates. Indeed, "real" friends often discuss the antics of their para-social friends.

The para-social framework is extremely useful in analyzing many phenomena not specifically discussed by Horton and Wohl. The framework explains, for example, why it is that when a "media friend" such as Elvis Presley, John Kennedy, or John Lennon dies or is killed, millions of people may experience a sense of loss as great as (and sometimes greater than) the feelings of loss accompanying the death of a relative or friend. Even an awareness of the para-social mechanism is not enough to permit escape from its "magic"; the death of John Lennon, for example, was strangely painful to me and my university colleagues who had "known" him and grown up "with" him. Sociologist Candice Leonard has suggested that such mediated relationships lead to a "new genre of human grief."[11]

Unlike the loss of a real friend or relative, the death of a media friend does not provide traditional rituals or clear ways to comfort the bereaved. Indeed, the mourning for a para-social friend is filled with paradox and helplessness. Attempts to comfort the dead person's family with words or flowers are intrusions by strangers. And intensely felt personal grief is simultaneously strengthened and weakened by the extent to which it is shared with the crowd. In order to banish the demons of grief and helplessness, therefore, thousands of people take to the streets or hold vigils near the para-social friend's home or place of death.

Ironically, but appropriately, the media provide the most ritualized channels of mourning. Radio and television present specials and retrospectives. And many people use the telephone to contact real friends who shared the intimacy with the para-social friend. But the final irony is that, in some ways, the para-social performer does not die. For the *only* means through which most people came to know him or her—records, films, and videotape—are still available. The relationship is frozen, rather than destroyed. In part, it is the potential and hope for increased intimacy that dies, and the never to be face-to-face consummation of the relationship that is mourned.

The para-social relationship has also led to a new form of murder and a new type of murder motive. Police generally distinguish between two types of murders: those committed by a person who knows the victim, and those committed by a stranger. Yet, there is now a third category: the para-social murder. While the media and police noted that John Lennon's murderer was a "complete stranger"—meaning that the two had never physically met—they overlooked the powerful para-social ties between them. Mark David Chapman knew John Lennon so well that for a time he thought he *was* John Lennon.[12] A similarly bizarre relationship existed between would-be presidential assassin John Hinckley and actress Jodie Foster. Hinckley committed his "historic act" in order to cement a "personal" relationship with Foster.[13]

In both love and hate, normal and bizarre, the para-social relationship is a new form of interaction. It has some of the traditional characteristics of both live encounters and communication through books, but it is, in fact, neither.

In formulating the notion of para-social interaction, Horton and Wohl point to the differences between "old" and "new" media. But they overlook the overall evolutionary trend, even within each type of medium, toward a shrinking of the differences between live and mediated encounters. Writing systems have evolved toward greater replication of spoken sounds (from hieroglyphs to the phonetic alphabet) and photography and electronic media have evolved toward fuller representations of face-to-face sensory experiences.

Media theorist Paul Levinson has detailed the long-term evolutionary course of media.[14] He argues that the trend is toward fuller replication of the means of communication that existed *before* media and technology. Levinson's theory gives substance to our intuitive sense that one form of a medium is "better" than another. The addition of voice to the telegraph, or sound to silent movies, or color to television, he suggests, is perceived as an "improvement" simply because the medium becomes less like a medium and more like life.

Levinson uses his theoretical framework to reject the criticism of many social theorists who suggest that media are distorting the human condition by taking us further and further away from "reality." Levinson argues, in contrast, that human beings use media to recreate as "natural" and as "human" a means of communicating as possible, while at the same time overcoming pre-technological limitations to communication (lack of permanent records, impossibility of speaking or seeing across vast distances, impossibility of being in two places at once, and so on).

Levinson's fascinating description of media history shows how an early form of a medium first gives up aspects of the "real world" in order to overcome a spatial or temporal limitation and how later forms of the medium then recapture aspects of natural communication. The telegraph, for example, gave up speech in order to travel quickly across the continent and globe; but then the telegraph evolved into the telephone which regained the human voice.

A major problem with Levinson's framework, however, is that he completely overlooks the ways in which the original spatial and temporal "limits" help to define the nature of social interaction. In suggesting that media recreate reality, Levinson defines "reality" in terms of sensory functions of communication—seeing, hearing, speaking. He ignores the ways in which the substance of human interaction changes when the barriers among situations are removed.

The theories of Levinson and of Horton and Wohl are helpful here because they suggest that face-to-face interaction is no longer the only determinant of personal and intimate interaction. The evolution of media has begun to cloud the differences between stranger and friend and to weaken the distinction between people who are "here" and people who are "somewhere else." These frameworks suggest that electronic media are unique in that they mask the differences between direct and indirect communication. What is missing from these theories, however, is an appreciation of how much social behavior changes when people are able to communicate "as if" they were in the same place when they are, in fact, in different places.

The Binding of Message to Context

The discussion thus far has suggested that electronic media weaken the significance of physical place as a determinant of social situations. Interestingly, many electronic media also strengthen one aspect of the relationship between messages and physical locations. For just as expressive and presentational messages are always about the emitting person, so are they tied to the physical location of the sender. Quotes in a newspaper may have nothing to do with the place in which the words were spoken, but a recording of a speech also captures aspects of the physical environment in which the speech was made.

Teddy Roosevelt's meetings with the press often took place while he was being shaved in the White House.[15] If he desired, Roosevelt could formulate a formal, impersonal "statement" for public release. Such a statement would be discursive and devoid of personal expression. It could be completely context-free (that is, have nothing to do with shaving). But electronic messages are usually context-bound. A President can lie in bed and write a formal statement to send to a newspaper, but a President would probably choose to get up, wash, and dress to deliver a similar statement for television. Further, for television, some background must be chosen—an office, or a fireplace, or a national monument. Even radio and telephone transmit background sounds from the sender's environment. Communication over electronic media, therefore, is similar to live interaction to the extent that it binds both people and their messages to the originating environment. And just as viewers may sense that they have "met" a person they see on television, so may they feel that they have "visited" the places they see. (Indeed, the millions of unrecalled "experiences" each of us has with things, places, and people through television may be the source of many feelings of déjà vu if we eventually experience them in real life.)

Another way to describe the difference between a printed "statement" and a television message is that television combines the situation of production of the message with the situation of presentation of the message (and often with the situation of reception of the message as well). In a print interview, for example, the interviewer and interviewee are in one place and the resulting interview is presented and received in another "place." In an interview designed to be printed, the interviewee can distinguish between "on" and "off" the record; he or she can establish one type of interaction with the interviewer and another type of interaction with the readers of the interview. A good example of this comes from a magazine interview of Barbra Streisand. Describing the process, the interviewer, Lawrence Grobel, writes:

> The interview sessions became, at times, a battle. When I touched on subjects that weren't comfortable for her, she would answer evasively or glibly and I would tell her what I thought of her answers—and get on her nerves. . . . Things often got emotional.
>
> For the next few weeks [after the interview sessions ended], she would call regularly to add another thought she'd had. I would fumble for my tape recorder, attach it to the telephone and we'd be off again.
>
> . . . She clearly regarded this interview as something special. It was going to be her definitive statement, she said, in which she would talk about subjects that had been rumored but neither confirmed nor denied.[16]

This description suggests that, during the long preparation for an interview to be printed, the private relationship with the interviewer ("a battle," "answer evasively") is clearly separated from the public relationship with readers ("her definitive statement").

The "place" inhabited by the interviewer and interviewee on television, however, is often the same one experienced by the television viewer. The interview subject must speak to the interviewer and the audience at the same time, and a new situation and behavior style arise. The strange mixture of formality and informality, of intimacy and distance in television interviews is the result of the merging of formerly distinct social situations.

Print allows for segregation of situations. The experience one has and the experience one writes about are different. Print media preserve the sanctity of place and the clear separation of different strains of behavior. Electronic media, however, play with place in a strange way. They violate its boundaries and change its social significance, yet they also use place as a backdrop for social events. Electronic media bind expression to physical settings but also merge many formerly distinct behavioral settings.

Time and Space "Saturation"

With its natural insulation, physical place was once the prime determinant of the definition of a situation. The spatial and temporal isolation of a physical location allowed for one definition of the situation to "saturate" the time/space frame. Goffman discusses "saturation" as a characteristic of Anglo-American societies where social performances tend to be given indoors and where "the impression and understanding fostered by the performance will tend to saturate the region and time span, so that any individual located in this space-time manifold will be in a position to observe the performance and be guided by the definition of the situation which the performance fosters."[17]

Any medium can pull a person out of the definition of the situation. Print media and electronic media, however, differ in their impact on the definitions of situations and on the relationship between situations and places.

Print media tend to create new, totally absorbing definitions. Reading is best done alone, in a quiet place, and to the exclusion of other activities. Indeed, special places are designated for reading. These places are designed to separate people, often into single-person cubicles. A reader, of course, is "connected" with other people by reading what they have written or what has been written about them, but the reader tends to be removed from those physically present. (Indeed, even when someone hands you a greeting card, you must ignore them for a moment in order to read it.) In this sense, reading is "anti-social"; it isolates the reader from live interactions. Reading is linear and absorbing. It is difficult to walk, talk, eat, exercise, make love, or drive an automobile while reading. Yet most of these activities are possible while watching television, and all are possible while listening to the radio.

In these ways, electronic media invade places, yet do not "occupy" them in the way that other media such as books do. Television not only changes the definition of the situation in places, but it does so in an unstable and inconsistent manner.

The funeral of Senator Hubert Humphrey, for example, was "brought" to the American home on January 14, 1978. Not only was this situation ("funeral of popular politician") combined with whatever situation existed previously in the home ("eating Sunday dinner," for example), but the new situation could also be lost and regained simply by changing channels. In the New York City area, the Humphrey funeral was broadcast live on ABC and NBC; Channel 9 carried a monster movie with hundreds of people being killed; Channel 5 broadcast a music and dancing program, "Soul Train"; Channel 11 provided a dubbed Japanese monster movie; Channel 2 showed a Tarzan cartoon; and Channel 13 broadcast "Zoom," showing at one point a boy helping his father to catch fish. Not only was the average viewer not required to travel to any specific place to see the Humphrey funeral (and all the types of accompanying expressions that were once accessible only to those present at such events), but the experience of the funeral was not allowed to saturate the time/space frame. Further, the nature of the combined situation (eating dinner during funeral) was itself unstable. The viewers could easily change their "place" by flipping channels.*

The "disrespect" for place and occasion inherent in the use of electronic media was even more dramatically demonstrated when one network stopped covering the Humphrey funeral in the middle of the service to broadcast an important golf match. Similarly, one network's offering during Anwar Sadat's dramatic peace mission to Israel involved alternating "live" coverage of Lod Airport in Israel with "live" coverage of the Ohio State-Michigan football game.

Electronic media destroy the specialness of place and time. Television, radio, and telephone turn once private places into more public ones by making them more accessible to the outside world. And car stereos, wristwatch televisions, and personal sound systems such as the Sony "Walkman" make public spaces private. Through such media, what is happening almost anywhere can be happening wherever we are. Yet when we are everywhere, we are also no place in particular.

"Home is wherever there's a telephone," says one telephone company ad. This analysis suggests, as well, that "anywhere there's a telephone is no longer the same home." Those entering many places no longer find them informationally special. Places visited for the first time now look familiar if they (or places like them) have already been seen on television. And places that were once very different are now more similar because nearly every place has a television set, radio, and telephone. With elec-

---

*One recent study of television habits found that more than a third of the viewers of a typical hour-long television program do not watch the program to the end, that about 40% of viewers in cable households "always" or "often" search for another program during commercial breaks, and that 40-50% of television viewers are eating, washing the dishes, talking on the telephone, or reading while "watching television."[18]

tronic media, most places—from the child's room to the priest's home to the prisoner's cell—now have a strong common denominator. Those aspects of group identity, socialization, and hierarchy that were once dependent on particular physical locations and the special experiences available in them have been altered by electronic media.

NOTES

1. Genesis, Chapter 18, Verses 10-15.

2. Settel, 1967, p. 17.

3. One exception to this was the system of semaphore tower stations designed by Claude Chappe about fifty years before Morse's telegraph. The "arms" were set in different positions to signify different letters. The system was adopted by the French government. But the semaphore was only a crude forerunner of the telegraph. The transmission of semaphore messages still depended on "ordinary" sensory perception (the arms were large enough to be visible five miles away at the next relay station). No messages could be sent during bad weather or at night. And such a system must have been relatively difficult to construct and operate and impossible to duplicate in as many locations as the telegraph and other electronic media would later service. See Settel, 1967, p. 15 for a brief discussion of semaphores.

4. Access to media in prisons varies from state to state and from prison to prison, and, apparently, there have been no comprehensive surveys of media access in correctional institutions. Available sources of information, however, indicate that there has been substantial access to media among most prisoners since the late 1960s. Charlotte A. Nesbitt, of the American Correctional Association notes that "in most jails and prisons, prisoners do have access to telephones, radios, and television" (personal correspondence, June 1983). A survey conducted in 1979 by the Criminal Justice Information Service (operated by the Contact organization) indicates that all states except Ohio allow prisoners to make telephone calls and that approximately fifty percent of the states allow inmates to receive calls ("Your Number, Please," 1979). The Director of the Federal Prison System, Norman A. Carlson, reports that federal prisons do not allow personal television sets, but that each housing unit within each prison generally has at least one television set and that a majority vote among prisoners determines program selection (personal correspondence, June 1983). Many state prisons do allow personal television sets, radios, tape players, and stereos in prisoners cells (Donna Hunzeker, Director, Information Services, Contact Inc., personal correspondence, June 1983).

5. Hendrick, 1977, p. 5.

6. Board of Institutional Ministry, 1978.

7. Horton and Wohl, 1956, p. 215.

8. Gross and Jeffries-Fox, 1978, p. 247.

9. Horton and Wohl, 1956, p. 223.

10. Levy, 1979.

11. Candice Leonard, personal communication, December 1980.

12. Mathews et al., 1980. Like Lennon, Chapman played the guitar and married a Japanese woman. Chapman had also taped Lennon's name over his own on his workplace identification tag.

13. "Hinckley's Last Love Letter," 1981.

14. Levinson, 1979.

15. Cornwell, 1965, p. 18.

16. "Playboy Interview: Barbra Streisand," 1977, p. 81.

17. Goffman, 1959, p. 106.

18. Television Audience Assessment, 1983, p. 1.

BIBLIOGRAPHY

Board of Institutional Ministry. *The Prisoner's Yellow Pages.* 2nd ed. Los Angeles: Universal Press, 1978.

Goffman, Erving. *The Presentation of Self in Everyday Life.* New York: Anchor, 1959.

Gross, Larry, and Suzanne Jeffries-Fox. "'What Do You Want to Be When You Grow Up, Little Girl?'" In *Hearth and Home: Images of Women in the Mass Media.* Ed. Gaye Tuchman, Arlene Kaplan Daniels, and James Benét. New York: Oxford Univ. Press, 1978, pp. 240-265.

Hendrick, Grant H. "When Television is a School for Criminals." *TV Guide,* 29 Jan. 1977, pp. 4-10.

"Hinckley's Last Love Letter," *Newsweek,* 13 April 1981, p. 35.

Horton, Donald, and R. Richard Wohl. "Mass Communication and Para-Social Interaction: Observations on Intimacy at a Distance." *Psychiatry,* 19 (1956), 215-229.

Levinson, Paul. "Human Replay: A Theory of the Evolution of Media."

Diss. New York Univ. 1979.

Levy, Mark R. "Watching TV News as Para-Social Interaction." *Journal of Broadcasting,* 23 (1979), 69-80.

Mathews, Tom, et al. "Lennon's Alter Ego." *Newsweek,* 22 Dec. 1980, pp. 34-35.

"Playboy Interview: Barbra Streisand." *Playboy,* October 1977, pp. 79-82; 87-92; 95-98; 100; 102; 104; 106-107; 193-194, 197-200.

Settel, Irving. *A Pictorial History of Radio.* New York: Grosset & Dunlap, 1967.

Television Audience Assessment, Inc. *Executive Summary: The Audience Rates Television.* Cambridge, MA: Television Audience Assessment, 1983.

■
_____

Mediated Interpersonal Communication: Toward a New Typology*

Robert Cathcart
Gary Gumpert

In 1962, Franklin Fearing offered four generalizations about situations in which human communication takes place:

1. They are situations in which human beings enter into certain strategic relationships with each other or with their environment.
2. They are situations the central characteristic of which is the production and utilization of signs, symbols, and symbolic acts.
3. They are situations which provide a maximal opportunity through the use of signs and symbols for the sharing of experience, achievement of goals, gaining of insights and, in general, mastering one's environment.
4. The sign or symbols material used in these situations is subject to the perceptual process of the individuals involved.[1]

We cite this not as the preferred way of looking at communication, but rather as descriptive of the research interests of communication scholars. It is interesting and provocative that nowhere in this situational map can "media" be located as an important component of human communication. The same is true for accepted definitions of communication. For exam-

From Mediated Interpersonal Communication: Toward a New Typology (pp. 267-277, *Quarterly Journal of Speech,* 69) by Robert Cathcart and Gary Gumpert, copyright © 1983, Speech Communication Association. Reprinted by permission of the publisher.

ple, communication is "the process by which an individual (the communicator) transmits stimuli (usually verbal) to modify the behavior of other individuals (the audience)."[2] Or, "Communication: the transmission of information, ideas, emotions, skills, etc. by the use of symbols—words, figures, graphs, etc."[3] Definitions, particularly those used in the study of speech communication, have minimized the role of media and channel in the communication process. The focus has been on the number of participants, source and receiver relationships, and forms and functions of messages. The media of communication have been accepted, more or less, as fixed or neutral channels for the transmission of messages among participants.[4] It is difficult to find an interpersonal communication text or resource book that treats the subject of media as a significant factor.[5] The role of media in personal communication has, by and large, been overlooked.

Mass communication scholars have exhibited a concern with the individual's interaction with the mass media. Robert K. Merton, Joseph Klapper, and Wilbur Schramm have analyzed the effects of mass media on the individual. In 1962 Elihu Katz and Paul Lazarsfeld wrote *Personal Influence: The Part Played by People in the Flow of Mass Communication.*[6] The subtitle is significant for it indicated the authors' emphasis on the role of the individual in the mass communication process rather than on the role media plays in shaping interpersonal behavior. Despite this orientation, most definitions of "mass communication" fail to take into account the influential role of media in interpersonal communication. A definition which holds that mass communication connotes all mass media of communication in which a mechanism of interpersonal reproduction intervenes between the speaker and the audience makes "medium" synonymous with "mass communication." Such a definition does not suffice because it overlooks the role of the media in interpersonal interaction. *All media are not mass media.* Any so called mass medium can be used for point-to-point transmission, e.g., "ham radio," and any point-to-point medium can be used to reach a mass audience, e.g., "junk mail." Mass communication refers to a specific utilization of medium—a circumstance of communication in which a medium replicates, duplicates, and disseminates identical content to a geographically wide spread population. Therefore, the term "media" does not characterize a distinct type of communication because it does not account for or suggest its use. In the typology of human communication, "media" should not be relegated solely to the category "mass communication," nor should it be excluded from the other categories: interpersonal communication, group communication, and public communication.

To bridge the definitional gaps and reconcile the role of media in human communication, the following should be added to Fearing's generalizations:

1. There are interpersonal situations which require media for the purpose of communication.
2. The media are a part of a complex of variables that influence behaviors and attitudes.
3. The content of media is both a reflection and a projection of interpersonal behaviors.
4. An individual's self image and its development is media-dependent.

If these claims accurately reflect the realities of media and human interaction then we would argue that what is needed is a new typology which will include media technology. The new typology should incorporate the traditional concepts of communication with the role of technological media.

I

Any typology which overlooks pervasive, potent media functions and connections ignores an increasingly significant and complex aspect of human communication. It must be recognized that even intrapersonal communication is media involved. Intrapersonal communication refers to the internal dialogue that occurs between the "I" and the "me"—the dual processing system where information received from outside is processed through the ego to form a self-image.[7] It is generally accepted that there can be no sense of self without interaction with others, i.e., without role taking and feedback which corrects or verifies the outcomes of internal dialogues.[8] Obviously, television, radio, and film provide feedback which reinforce, negate and/or verify an individual's self-image.[9] Portraits developed in novels, magazines, and newspapers have long served in the formulation and reinforcement of socially acceptable and unacceptable self-images.[10]

Of increasing importance are photographs and recordings in the intrapersonal dialogue. The photograph creates and reflects socially desirable images. Voice and video recordings are being utilized to check self-image as well as improve one's projected image.[11] What makes this significant is the complete credulity with which persons accept photographs and recordings as unimpeachable portrayals of reality, often overriding interpersonal responses.[12]

Intrapersonal communication has traditionally been referred to as nonobservable internalized dialogue which occurs in all humans. The medium of recording materializes that dialogue bringing the internal more in line with the external, thereby altering the way the individual processes information during intrapersonal communication. There is a growing reliance upon media technology for self-assessment and image formation. This alone would call for research to determine the role media play in creating the "significant other."

II

Interpersonal communication refers to dyadic interaction which takes the form of verbal and nonverbal exchanges between two or more individuals, consciously aware of each other, usually interacting in the same time and space, performing interchangeable sender-receiver roles.[13] Through the interpersonal communication process people maintain and adjust their self-image, relate to others, cooperate in decision making, accomplish tasks, and make order of their environment. All acts of communication emerge from the need of two humans to connect symbolically. The dyad serves as the paradigm of human communication. Michael Schudson, in an examination of the dyadic model, claims that "we have developed a notion that all communication *should* be like a certain model of conversation, whether that model really exists or not,"[14] and "the ideal is not one concocted by social scientists. Rather it is a widely shared ideal in contemporary American culture which social science has uncritically adopted."[15]

Humans have always sought mechanical means of extending and enhancing face to face communication to efficiently serve needs for security, socialization, collectivization, and fantasy. The result has been the permanentizing and electrifying of the channels of communication which make possible the reproduction of human communication over time and space. Each new technology not only extended the reach of human communication, it also altered the ways in which humans related to information and to each other.[16] If, however, it is maintained that mediated communication is synonymous with interpersonal communication, i.e., adds only neutral channels of transmission, it will not be understood how media have altered interpersonal connections. It is time, therefore, to expand the traditional typology to include *"mediated interpersonal communication."* A number of scholars have recognized the need. Gerald R. Miller states:

> I will argue . . . that mass communication messages potentially affect interpersonal relationships in even more fundamental, pervasive ways which at this writing have received relatively little research attention. Specifically, I will propose that the media often: (1) exert a powerful impact on people's initial perceptions of other interpersonal transactions; (2) influence the manner in which information about other transactions is processed and interpreted; and in many cases (3) distract persons from gathering the kind of information they need to relate effectively in interpersonal settings.[17]

Robert K. Avery and Thomas A. McCain point out that "the placement of intrapersonal communication and mass communication at opposite ends of a single continuum has resulted in masking the multifaceted nature of the differences among types of communicative encounters."[18] They state that radio phone-in talk shows are a form of interpersonal communication with unique characteristics. They conclude that, "the examination of interpersonal and media encounters must continue. Research on personal junctures with media and other needs careful description and understanding." [19]

The term "mediated interpersonal communication" is a general category referring to any situation where a technological medium is introduced into face to face interaction. It includes:

1) *interpersonal mediated communication:* telephone conversations, letters, CB radio, electronic mail, audio and video cassettes.

2) *media-simulated interpersonal communication:* para-social interactions, broadcast-teleparticipatory communication, etc.

3) *person-computer interpersonal communication:* computers utilized as interpersonal proxies.

4) *unicommunication:* the utilization of such artifacts as T-shirts and bumper stickers for interpersonal interaction.[20]

Interpersonal mediated communication refers to any person-to-person interaction where a medium has been interposed to transcend the limitations of time and space. A technology is interposed between and is integral to the communicating parties. The interposed medium determines the quantity and quality of information and also shapes the relationships of the participants.[21] For example, a handwritten or typed letter can facilitate a personal relationship over distance, but the time it takes to transport the message along with the lack of immediate feedback alters the quality and quantity of information shared. The time factor also alters the relationship between the two participants. More significantly, interpersonal written communication differs from face-to-face communication because it requires mastery of a secondary coding system—written language—and a knowledge of the conventions of that medium. The fact that written communication can be stored and retrieved makes the exchange context-free and permanent. Consequently, there are things that can be said face-to-face that could never be put into writing.

Communication mediated by the personal letter is but one of several forms of interpersonal mediated communication. The telephone also transcends space—it allows us to carry on conversations in an essentially private and intimate manner far beyond the reach of the unmediated human voice.[22] Telephoning, however, utilizes only one sensory channel, and this limits the amount and quality of information transmitted. One has to compensate for the lack of nonverbal signals, which in turn, lowers predictability and makes for less control.

The widespread use of interposed interpersonal communication such as letter writing and telephoning has altered face-to-face relationships. For example, we do not have to leave the confines of our dwellings to maintain relationships over distance.[23] Face-to-face contact with the people in the street and marketplace can be avoided. The eyes, nose, and tongue can be protected from unwanted stimuli. Physical contact is eliminated even though telephone company ads suggest that we "reach out and touch someone." In addition, the telephone is altering proxemic norms. Edward Hall established that Americans maintain carefully proscribed interpersonal distances and that violation of spacial norms is risky.[24] The telephone alters interpersonal spacial relationships. Telephonic conversation always takes place at a socially "intimate" distance. The other person's voice is literally next to our ear—the distance at which, according to Hall, the sense of sight is not nearly as important as touch, smell, and the feel of bodily warmth. Perhaps this is why, at times, the telephone can be so threatening. It invades intimate space, but denies us most of the sensory means of communication control and verification present in intimate situations.

Other interposed media such as "CB" and "ham radio," audio and video cassettes (utilized for one-to-one communication), computers (used to connect two or more people) can be categorized as interpersonal mediated communication.[25] They share with face-to-face communication the characteristics of interchangeability of sender-receiver roles, immediacy of feedback, and use of unrestricted codes. They differ from interpersonal communication in the lack of privacy and communication control—whatever message is sent is available to all receivers—making the information more *public* than private. This tends to transform the sender of a message into a *performer*, placing emphasis on messages which entertain or carry general public information. The association of audio and video tape with radio and television broadcasting further suggests public performance, de-emphasizing verbal content, and, at the same time, limiting intimacy.

III

The ambiguity of private and public communication suggests another variation of mediated interpersonal communication: *media-simulated interpersonal communication*. This phenomenon was first explored by Horton and Wohl in their analysis of "para-social interaction."[26]

> In television, especially, the image which is presented makes available nuances of appearance and gesture to which ordinary social perception is attentive and to which interaction is cued. Sometimes the "actor"— whether he is playing himself or performing in a fictional role—is seen engaged with others; but often he faces the spectator, uses the mode of direct address, talks as if he were conversing person-

ally and privately. The audience, for its part, responds with something more than mere running observation; it is, as it were, subtly insinuated into the program's action and internal social relationships and, by dint of this kind of staging, is ambiguously transformed into a group which observes and participates in the show by turns. The more the performer seems to adjust his performance to the supposed response of the audience, the more the audience tends to make the response anticipated. This simulacrum of conversational give and take may be called *para-social interaction.* (p. 215)[27]

Para-social interaction is a staple of mass media "personality" shows. The main ingredient is the illusion of intimacy created by the media personality through imitation of the gestures, conversational style, and the informal milieu of the face-to-face interaction. The audience members know the performer in the same way they know their friends; by observation and interpretation of gestures, voice, conversations, and actions. The celebrity program is designed to coach the audience into making personal judgments. Audience members report that they know these personalities better than their friends and neighbors. Though designed and controlled by media programmers and broadcast to a relatively undifferentiated audience, the para-social interaction is not one-sided. The audience members are not passive observers of a skilled performance. Rather, they make appropriate responses to the personality's performance; they join into the joking, teasing, praising, admiring, gossiping and telling of anecdotes. When they play this answering role, they are doing exactly the things that lead to friendship and intimacy. As Horton and Wohl point out, "the relationship of the devotee to the persona is . . . of the same order as, and related to, the network of actual social relations. . . . As a matter of fact, it seems profitable to consider the interaction with the persona as a phase of the role-enactments of the spectator's daily life."[28] The broadcast audience's need for intimacy and the ability of performers to simulate face-to-face interaction explains in part the success of such personalities as Don MacNeil, Arthur Godfrey, Jack Paar, Phil Donahue, and Johnny Carson.

In the case of para-social interaction, though, there can be only the illusion of intimacy and friendship. The sender and receiver roles are sharply separated and *never* interchange. This form of communication is highly institutionalized and control is not in the hands of either the sender or the receiver but is pre-planned by media specialists who design and orchestrate the interaction. Though the audience member is aware that several million others are watching and interacting at the same time, the interaction seems intimate because the performer discloses personal information which is associated with intimacy. It seems private because the listener/viewer agrees to react as though the disclosure was made by a close friend in a face-to-face situation.[29]

The importance of simulated mediated interpersonal communication is two-fold. One, it functions as a substitute for face-to-face relationships. It is less demanding for some people to work out a close relationship with Johnny Carson than with their next-door neighbor. The "parasocial friend" is always predictable, never unpleasant, always sympathetic, never threatening. In other words, there are no challenges to the audience member's self-esteem, nor limits on his or her ability to respond appropriately. Two, media producers of para-social interaction set up unreal expectations which lead many people to feel that their own interpersonal relationships are inadequate because the para-social relationship is based upon an ideal of face-to-face communication which is seldom achieved in practice. This leads to increased feelings of alienation and a greater reliance upon mass media for interpersonal satisfaction.

Closely related to para-social interaction and an important part of media simulated interpersonal communication is the radio talk show or what we call "broadcast teleparticipatory media." In a study of the talk radio phenomenon, Robert K. Avery and Donald G. Ellis point out that the exchange of messages between a call-in listener and talk radio host "creates a pattern of talk which defines a symbol system for the interactants. That is, social reality is uniquely defined by the interactants, and hence becomes significant to the communication process."[30] A later study by Avery and McCain states:

> After reviewing the results of several talk radio shows, one might easily come to the conclusion that although the communication patterns between a call-in listener and a talk radio host reveal numerous similarities to the face to face encounter the unique characteristics imposed by this communication setting afford a special context that needs to be considered in order to develop a complete understanding of this particular media-person transaction.[31]

It is significant that radio talk show conversation is more a public performance than a private and interrelational act. Despite its public aspect, the phone-in part of talk radio is carried on as though it were a private telephone conversation. The radio host is quite aware that the conversation is part of a public performance and one that must be handled and manipulated well if it is to be commercially viable. At the same time, the majority of the audience never call the talk show host but vicariously participate in the host-caller interaction much like neighbors who listen in on the telephone party line to learn what is going on and identify with one of the parties. For the non-caller the interaction serves an important non-threatening function; coaching the listener for future media-person and face-to-face conversations. The listener-caller selects a favorite radio host and interacts on a daily basis in much the same way that all of us select friends to interact with face-to-face. For the phone-in audience the radio talk show provides a relatively safe environment in which members can contact important public personalities, giving them status and a feeling of connection. The willingness of the "personality" to come into the home as a companion, listening to the caller and providing assurance that beliefs and values are shared, simulates interpersonal interaction.

Similar to para-social interaction, broadcast teleparticipatory interaction represents a form of simulated interpersonal communication. Unlike telephone talk, sender-receiver roles are relatively fixed, there is little or no relational development, and the communicative code is restricted-implicit rather than unrestricted-implicit. Even on phone-in shows featuring psychologist hosts where callers often disclose intimate sexual information, both interactants follow carefully proscribed restricted language codes more suitable for public forums than the more unrestricted intimate codes of personal telephoning. Avery and Ellis report that callers never forget who is in control of the interaction.[32] Callers know they can be cut off if they are boring, too bizarre, too emotional, too aggressive, etc. If they do not please the host, who acts as interpreter and gatekeeper of what is interesting and acceptable to the audience, they will be stopped by disconnection.

Broadcast teleparticipatory media are viewed as entertainment by those in control of the program. They shape the public perception of an ideal interpersonal performance. The seven second tape delay technology makes source control absolute. Programmers can bleep out anything they think should not be heard, making the conversation "safe" for all participants. The exercise of this control teaches the audience the restricted code of "public" interpersonal communication; rewarding those who can perform the "ideal" intimate communication with the host. It is this public aspect, along with the placing of control in the hands of an unseen, unknown source, that establishes broadcast teleparticipatory interaction as a distinct type of mediated interpersonal communication. Research by Avery, Ellis, McCain and others verifies that this is a firmly established and growing mode of interaction, one which many Americans are dependent upon for supplementing and/or substituting for daily face-to-face interaction.

IV

The *person-computer interpersonal encounter* represents another facet of "mediated interpersonal communication." It includes any situation in which one party activates a computer which in turn responds appropriately in a graphic, alphanumeric, or vocal mode (or combinations thereof) thereby establishing a sender/receiver relationship.[33] In the computer-person interaction the computer is programmed by a person, but that person is not the sender or receiver of the message. The human partner interacts not with the computer programmer, but with the computer program. Ithiel de Sola Pool points out that prior to the introduction of the computer every communication device "took a message that had been composed by a human being and (with some occasional loss) delivered it unchanged to another human being. The computer for the first time provides a communication device by which a person may receive a message quite different from what any human sent. Indeed, machines may talk to each other."[34]

Although person-computer transactions simulate dyadic communication, the process and the alternatives are predetermined. The human partner activates the computer, but once the encounter has begun the computer program controls the communication. To compensate for the loss of control we anthropomorphize the computer; i.e., give it human qualities. The human partner can then "role-play" a face-to-face interaction because all the components of dyadic communication exist, except that one of the partners is a machine.

Not all human-computer contacts, however, are characterized by this particular interactive quality. The person-computer mediated encounter should be contrasted with the situation in which one communicates *through* a computer rather than *with* a computer. "Electronic mail," for example, represents a change of medium (paper to display screen) in which the computer is interposed. In this case the computer is a high-speed transmitter of what is essentially a written message. The person-computer mediated encounter, on the other hand, always involves direct dialogue between individual and computer.

V

In 1975, Gumpert described "communication from one to many of values prescribed by associations in the environment through various non-electronic media. Uni-communication is a type of mediated interpersonal behavior."[35]

Uni-communication is that communication mediated by objects of clothing, adornment, and personal possessions—houses, automobiles, furniture, etc.—which people select and display to communicate to others their status, affiliation, and self-esteem. It includes, also, more explicit messages like imprinted T-shirts, jackets, and caps, as well as bumper stickers, armbands, and buttons.

Communicating something about one's status and role through clothing and personal possessions is, of course, an ancient and well established mode of communication.[36] Personal possessions— everything from the exterior and interior design of homes to a pair of Gucci loafers—can and do take on symbolic functions which impart implicit information to others and reinforce one's self-image. What has received little attention is how this attenuated, symbolic interaction operates as a form of mediated interpersonal communication. What makes it interpersonal is that it is self-disclosing and it produces sender-receiver relationships. The item displayed can serve one or more purposes and establish one or more relationships. For example, it can reveal group affiliation (wearing a Masonic ring), mark one's status (driving a white Mercedes Benz 450SL), identify a role (carrying a brief case), and express support for or rejection of established values and institutions (wearing a Star of David, displaying orange colored, spikey hair). The fact that a single item of attire can have multiple meanings makes it useful in establishing a variety of relationships. A studded black leather vest with "Hells Angels" inscribed can serve to identify, reject, boast, etc., depending upon the context and the receiver's response. Uni-communication is extremely helpful for informing people of status, role, and affiliation in situations where face-to-face interaction is difficult and possibly risky.

What makes uni-communication important in an updated communication typology is an expanded function brought on by the mass media of communication and the mass distribution of "pop" symbols. Increasingly, individuals in all levels of society are making explicit messages out of these symbols and transmitting them to mass audiences. Wearing a T-shirt imprinted with "No Nukes" makes use of a utilitarian item of clothing to "broadcast" a message to any and all who come close enough to read the words and view the person displaying them. The bumper sticker, "Jesus Saves," makes use of an automobile, which is both a means of transportation and a symbol, to carry an additional and more explicit message to fellow drivers.

Such messages ordinarily do not originate with the person displaying them. Rather, they are mass produced and distributed by groups who are campaigning for certain causes. The persons displaying these messages become part of the campaign as well as part of the transmission system. This makes uni-communication different from other forms of interpersonal interaction. It communicates affiliation with a group or suggests a social role rather than making an individual statement. Uni-communication facilitates stimulus generalization rather than stimulus discrimination.[37] Receivers respond to the attached symbols and the individual as one entity; deriving different messages depending on the receiver's perceptions of the affiliate group or social role. Uni-communication discloses how the displayer views her or himself in affiliation with others rather than in relationship to an individual receiver.

Receivers of uni-communication are confronted by the message in situations where face-to-face interaction is neither expected or desired. There is, however, a response and an interaction. The response is like the reaction to a billboard or a poster. We may not want to see it or read it, but the fact that it comes into our view draws our attention, makes us read, and we are forced to respond. The response is to the person as part of the message— with hostility, or anger, or admiration, or identification. It is an interpersonal interaction. Seldom is there any immediate, verbal feedback. Similar to the para-social and other mediated interactions, communication is carried on at a distance even though each person may be within social speaking range. The receiver decides what the message means and works out an appropriate verbal scenario. The sender has in mind a message, or maybe several messages, which may or may not coincide with the messages being formulated by receivers. Each is satisfied that something has been communicated. Each has been involved in a personal communicative interaction. Senders have made a statement—one which says something about who they are and how they feel. Receivers respond as though the message was directed at them as individuals. The fact that this same interaction is replicated thousand of times all over the nation (made possible by both mass distribution and mass media) creates a kind of national interpersonal dialogue about values, roles, and status.

We believe that uni-communication serves important interpersonal functions in our society. A study of it would tell us something about how we communicate and with whom in an increasingly impersonal environment where long established institutions of social interaction are undergoing change. For example, we have created public places like "discos" and "singles" bars to serve courtship and match-pairing functions once exclusively the domain of the home and the church. These places exist to promote interpersonal relationships. In such places, the communication process is aided by the kind of clothing and jewelry worn which become explicit messages to others concerning one's status, one's availability, and one's feeling about the kinds of interactions one desires. We point this out as only one area of potential research into a type of mediated communication which has been ignored.

In summary, there may be other types of mediated interpersonal communication which we have not recognized. There are, of course, other forms of communication which need to be placed in an updated communication typology. The mediated political campaign is one example. The printed magazine or journal distributed to a select audience which is part of a specialized network, what Gumpert has called "mini-communication,"[38] is another example. We could go on, but the point is that a typology which compartmentalizes thought and research and prevents investigations of important types and forms of human communication cannot be tolerated. We are quite convinced that the traditional division of communication study into interpersonal, group and public, and mass communication is inadequate because it ignores the pervasiveness of media. We propose that media be incorporated in definitions of communication and that we begin to realign our research to account for the significant impact of media.

NOTES

1. Franklin Fearing, "Human Communication," in Lewis Anthony Dexter and David Manning White, eds., *People, Society and Mass Communications* (New York: The Free Press, 1953), p. 42.

2. C.I. Hovland, I.L. Janis, and H.H. Kelly, *Communication and Persuasion* (New Haven: Yale University Press, 1953), p. 12.

3. B. Berelson and G. Steiner, *Human Behavior* (New York: Harcourt Brace, and Jovanovich, 1964), p. 527.

4. See, for example, David K. Berlo, *The Process of Communication* (New York: Holt, Rinehart and Winston, 1960), p. 31, who states that, "Channel is a medium, a carrier of messages." Also, Frank E.X. Dance and Carl E. Larson, *The Functions of Human Communication* (New York: Holt, Rinehart and Winston, 1976), which makes no mention of media as channel or medium as a variable.

5. In developing the first edition of *Inter/Media:Interpersonal Communication in the Media World* (New York: Oxford University Press, 1979), we were unable to find textbooks which treated media as a significant variable in interpersonal communication. See, for example, Dean C. Barnlund, *Interpersonal Communication: Survey and Studies* (New York: Houghton Mifflin Co., 1968); Joseph A. DeVito, *The Interpersonal Communication Book* (New York: Harper and Row, 1977); Gerald M. Phillips and Nancy Metzger, *Intimate Communication* (Boston: Allyn and Bacon, 1976); and John Stewart and Gary D'Angelo, *Together: Communicating Interpersonally* (Reading: Addison Wesley, 1975).

6. See Wilbur Schramm, *The Process and Effects of Mass Communication* (Urbana: University of Illinois Press, 1954); Joseph T. Klapper, *The Effects of Mass Communication* (New York: Free Press, 1960); and Robert K. Merton, "Patterns of Influence: A Study of Interpersonal Influence and Communication Behavior," in P.F. Lazarsfeld and F.N. Stanton, *Communication Research* (New York: Harper, 1949); Elihu Katz and Paul F. Lazarsfeld, *Personal Influence: The Part Played by People in the Flow of Mass Communication* (New York: The Free Press, 1955).

7. For a discussion of the sense of self as the individual "I" and the "Me" as social attitudes, see George Herbert Mead, *Mind, Self and Society* (Chicago: University of Chicago Press, 1934).

8. Duncan claims that, "The self and society originates and develops *in* communication," H.D. Duncan, *Communication and Social Order* (New York:

Bedminster Press, 1962), p. 76. B. Aubrey Fisher explains, "Dialogue implies the expression of self and the development of mutual understanding (that is, congruence) along with the development of self through social interaction. . . . And the concept of role taking allows for the individual to discover and develop self through social interaction." *Perspectives on Human Communication* (New York: Macmillan Publishing Co., 1978), p. 179.

9. See Michael Novack, "Television Shapes the Soul" in L.L. Sellars and W.C. Rivers, eds., *Mass Media Issues* (New York: Prentice Hall, 1977).

10. See Virginia Kidd, "Happily Ever After and other Relationship Styles: Advice on Interpersonal Relations in Popular Magazines," *Quarterly Journal of Speech*, 61 (1975); and James Lull, "The Social Uses of Television," *Human Communication Research*, 6 (1980).

11. The widespread use of audio and video recordings to improve the image of politicians, beauty contestants, salespersons, etc., is documented in newspaper and magazine articles. See, for example, "Rose Queen Prepares for the Pageant," *Los Angeles Times*, December 27, 1981, B-3; and "Cops Go High Tech for Fiesta, Plan Second Year of Taping," *Santa Barbara Journal*, March 15, 1981, p. 14.

12. For a discussion of the effects of photographs on perceptions of reality see, Susan Sontag, *On Photography* (New York: Farrar, Straus and Giroux, 1973).

13. We are using the term "interpersonal communication" in its generic sense, emphasizing function rather than relationship. Our approach is similar to that of Donald P. Cushman and Robert T. Craig: "Interpersonal communication systems are distinguished from other general levels in terms of function, structure, and process, but primarily in terms of function. . . . A well-defined interpersonal system is necessarily a *small* system—paradigmatically a dyad. . . . Relationship issues like affection and openness, and processes of development, presentation, and validation of self-conceptions seems necessary in view of the basic function of interpersonal systems." See Donald P. Cushman and Robert T. Craig, "Communication Systems: Interpersonal Implications" in Gerald R. Miller, ed., *Explorations in Interpersonal Communication* (Beverly Hills: Sage Publications, 1976), p. 46.

14. Michael Schudson, "The Ideal of Conversation in the Study of Mass Media," *Communication Research*, 5 (1978), 323.

15. Schudson, p. 323.

16. For a discussion of the symbiotic relationship between technology and communication from a historical perspective, see Walter Ong, *Interfaces of*

the Word: Studies in the Evolution of Consciousness and Culture (Ithaca: Cornell University Press, 1977); and Marshall McLuhan, *The Gutenberg Galaxy* (Toronto: University of Toronto Press, 1962).

17. Gerald R. Miller, "A Neglected Connection: Mass Media Exposure and Interpersonal Communicative Competency," in G. Gumpert and R. Cathcart, eds., *Inter/Media: Interpersonal Communication in a Media World*, 2nd ed., (New York: Oxford University Press, 1982), p. 50.

18. Robert K. Avery and Thomas A. McCain, "Interpersonal and Mediated Encounters: A Reorientation to the Mass Communication Process," in G. Gumpert and R. Cathcart, eds., *Inter/Media: Interpersonal Communication in a Media World*, 2nd ed., p. 30.

19. Gumpert and Cathcart, p. 39.

20. While the categories listed under the concept of "mediated interpersonal communication" can be demonstrated, the classification labels should be considered "in progress."

21. In comparing mediated interpersonal communication and interpersonal communication we will utilize the following basic characteristics of interpersonal communication: (1) It is transmitted through multiple channels. Sight, smell, touch, and taste operate as receiving channels. (2) It is spontaneous and evanescent. It cannot be recreated. (3) Feedback is immediate and continuous. (4) Interchangeable sender-receiver roles provide maximum control of content. (5) There is unlimited channel capacity and no production costs. (6) It utilizes implicit and restricted audio-verbal and audio-visual codes which make for privacy and intimacy. (7) Psychological as well as sociological and anthropological information is generated and processed. (8) Basic skills and conventions are learned informally at an early age, usually in non-institutional settings.

22. For an extensive analysis of the influence of the telephone, see Ithiel de Sola Pool, ed., *The Social Impact of the Telephone* (Cambridge: M.I.T. Press, 1977). For a discussion of the significance of letter writing as verbal expression, see Walter J. Ong, *The Presence of the Word* (New Haven: Yale University Press, 1967).

23. The electronic relationship and its implications for the future is one of the primary issues examined by Alvin Toffler, *The Third Wave* (New York: William Morrow and Company, Inc., 1980). Melvin M. Webber examines a related notion when he proposed "non-place communities." See *Explorations into Urban Structure*, edited by Melvin M. Webber et al. (Philadelphia: University of Pennsylvania Press, 1971).

24. Edward T. Hall, *The Hidden Dimension* (New York: Doubleday & Co., 1966), pp. 113-130.

25. See Bert Cowlan, "A Revolution in Personal Communications: The Explosive Growth of Citizens Band Radio," in G. Gumpert and R. Cathcart, *Inter/Media: Interpersonal Communication in a Media World* (New York: Oxford University Press, 1979), pp. 116-21. See Sherry Turkle, "Computer as Rorschach," *Society,* 17 (1980).

26. Donald Horton and R. Richard Wohl, "Mass Communication and Para-Social Interaction: Observations on Intimacy at a Distance," *Psychiatry,* 19 (1956), 215-29.

27. Horton and Wohl, p. 215.

28. Horton and Wohl, p. 228.

29. Horton and Wohl, p. 219.

30. Robert K. Avery and Donald G. Ellis, "Talk Radio as an Interpersonal Phenomenon," in G. Gumpert and R. Cathcart, p. 112.

31. Avery and McCain, p. 37.

32. Avery and Ellis, p. 113.

33. For an overview of person-computer interactions, see Hollis Vail, "The Home Computer Terminal: Transforming the Households of Tomorrow," *The Futurist,* December 1980. For more general discussion of microcomputers, see Christopher Evans, *The Micro Millennium* (New York: The Viking Press, 1979).

34. Ithiel de Sola Pool, "Forward" to *The Coming Information Age: An Overview of Technology, Economics, and Politics* by Wilson P. Dizard, Jr. (New York: Longman, 1982), pp. xi-xii.

35. Gary Gumpert, "The Rise of Uni-Comm," *Today's Speech,* 23 (1975), 34.

36. For an historical analysis of the symbolic nature of clothes, see Anne Hollander, *Seeing Through Clothes* (New York: The Viking Press, 1976).

37. See Gerald R. Miller, "A Neglected Connection: Mass Media Exposure and Interpersonal Communication Competency," pp. 51-53, for a discussion of generalization and discrimination responses in interpersonal communication.

38. Gary Gumpert, "The Rise of Mini-Comm," *Journal of Communication,* 20 (1970), 280-90.

A Case: Public Moral Argument

Walter R. Fisher

Public moral argument needs to be distinguished from reasoned discourse in interpersonal interactions and from arguments occurring in specialized communities, such as theological disputes, academic debates, and arguments before the Supreme Court. The features differentiating *public* moral argument from such encounters are: (1) it is publicized, made available for wide consumption and persuasion of the polity at large; and (2) it is aimed at what Aristotle called "untrained thinkers," or, to be effective, it should be.[79] Most important *public* moral argument is a form of controversy that inherently crosses professional fields. It is not contained, in the way that legal, scientific, or theological arguments are, by their subject matter, particular conceptions of argumentative competence, and well-recognized rules of advocacy. Because this is so and because its realm is public-social knowledge, *public* moral argument naturally invites participation by field experts and tends to become dominated by the rational superiority of their arguments. *Public* moral argument, which is oriented toward what ought to be, is often undermined by the "truth" that prevails at the moment. The presence of "experts" in *public* moral arguments makes it difficult, if not impossible, for the public of "untrained thinkers" to win an argument or even to judge arguments well—given, again, the rational-world paradigm.

Public *moral* argument is moral in the sense that it is founded on ultimate questions—of life and death, of how persons should be defined and treated, of preferred patterns of living. Joseph Gusfield designates such questions as "status issues." Their resolution, he writes, indicates "the group, culture, or style of life to which the government and society are publicly com-

From Human Communication as Narration (pp. 71-75, 83-84) by Walter Fisher, copyright © University of South Carolina Press. Reprinted with the permission of the publisher.

173

mitted."[80] In addition to nuclear warfare, desegregation would be included in this category, as would disputes about abortion and school prayer.

Public moral *argument* refers to clear-cut inferential structures, according to the rational-world paradigm, and to "good reasons," according to the narrative paradigm. Public moral *argument* may also refer to public controversies—disputes and debates—about moral issues. The nuclear warfare controversy is an obvious case in point, but so are others mentioned above. One could add disputes over pornography, the Equal Rights Amendment (ERA), and crime and punishment. This characterization of public moral *argument* is attentive to argument as product and as process.

The problem posed by the presence of experts in public moral argument is illustrated by the dispute between Hans Bethe and Edward Teller over the 1982 nuclear-freeze proposition in California. Their positions were published in the *Los Angeles Times,* so they were public.[81] They obviously concerned a moral issue and they were reasoned statements. Both men were credible. Which one was to be believed and followed? Who in the general public could contend with them? Teller answered the second question in unequivocal terms: "The American public is ignorant, even of the general ideas on which they [nuclear weapons] are based." Here was revealed the fate of nonexperts who would argue about nuclear warfare. Only experts can argue with experts, and their arguments— although public—cannot be rationally questioned by nonexperts. As Perelman noted, rationality of the traditional sort forecloses discussion and debate if it becomes full and final as an ideal.[82] In the presence of experts—those best qualified to argue, according to the rational-world paradigm—the public has no compelling reason to believe one expert over the other. Nonexperts cannot be judges; they become spectators whose choice becomes only a nonrational choice between actors on a stage. Within the narrative paradigm's perspective, however, the experts' stories are not at all beyond analysis by the layperson. The lay audience can test the stories for coherence and fidelity. The lay audience is not perceived as a group of observers, but as active, irrepressible participants in the meaning-formation of the stories that any and all storytellers tell in discourses about nuclear weapons or any other issue that impinges on how people are to be conceived and treated in their ordinary lives.

It may be asked at this point: How is it that freeze referendums were approved in eight out of nine states and in twenty-eight cities and counties in 1982? One answer is "fear," the "most intelligent feeling of our time." Another answer is "distrust," distrust of those responsible for the development, deployment, and use of nuclear weapons. The second answer is, I believe, more accurate. It does not deny the existence of fear. It insists on the "rationality" of fear *among other things,* as reasons for those who voted for and against the referendum. Those who opposed the referendum did so because of a basic distrust of Soviet leaders and a fundamental trust of our own. What I am saying is that there were good reasons for trust and distrust, that the response of voters was rational, given the narrative paradigm. A most important point is that the good reasons that are expressed in public moral argument relate to issues not accounted for in the rational-world paradigm. These issues include motivations and values of the characters involved in the ongoing narrative of nuclear warfare, the way in which they conceive and behave in respect to the conflict, and the narrative probability and narrative fidelity of the particular stories they tell, which may well take the form of "reasoned argument." When the *full* range of good reasons for responses is taken into consideration, experts and laypersons meet on the common ground of their shared, human interests. And it is fair to judge arguers on those broad terms, for, as Toulmin observed, "a scientist off duty is as much an 'ordinary' man as a tinker or a bus-conductor off duty."[83]

From the narrative perspective, the proper role of an expert in public moral argument is that of a counselor, which is, as Walter Benjamin notes, the true function of the storyteller.[84] His or her contribution to public dialogue is to impart knowledge, like a teacher, or wisdom, like a sage. It is not to pronounce a story that ends all storytelling. An expert assumes the role of public counselor whenever she or he crosses the boundary of technical knowledge into the territory of life as it ought to be lived. Once this invasion is made, the public, which then includes the expert, has its own criteria for determining whose story is most coherent and reliable as a guide to belief and action. The expert, in other words, then becomes subject to the demands of narrative rationality. Technical communities have their own conceptions and criteria for judging the rationality of communication. But, as G. Holton has demonstrated, the work even of scientists is inspired by stories; hence their discourse can be interpreted usefully from the narrative perspective. Holton writes tellingly of the "nascent movement" in science, the impulse to do science in a particular or in a new way, and how science is informed by "themes"—thematic concepts, methods, and hypotheses inherited from Parmenides, Heraclitus, Pythagoras, Thales, and others.[85]

Viewed from the perspective of the rational-world paradigm, Schell's case, his argument and its reception, evokes despair. If one looks to MacIntyre's *After Virtue* for relief, one will be disappointed and disheartened further, for he provides the historical and philosophical reasons for the fate of *The Fate of the Earth* and similar such arguments. His own argument is that "we still, in spite of the efforts of three centuries of moral philosophy and one of sociology, lack any coherent, rationally defensible statement of a liberal individualist point of view."[86] He offers some hope with the idea that "the Aristotelian tradition can be restated in a way that restores intelligibility and rationality to our moral and social attitudes and commitments." He observes, however, "the new dark ages" are "already upon us." The "barbarians are not waiting beyond the frontiers; they have already been governing us for quite some time. And it is our lack of consciousness of this that constitutes part of our predicament. We are waiting not for Godot, but for another—doubtless very different—St. Benedict."[87]

The reasons for this state of affairs are: (1) the rejection of a teleological view of human nature and the classical conception of reason as embodied in Aristotelian logic and rhetoric; (2) the separation of morality from theological, legal, and aesthetic concerns; and (3) the evolution of the individualistic sense of self and the rise of emotivism. The consequence of these movements is a situation in which ethical arguments in public are rendered ineffectual because of "conceptual incommensurability."

A case in point is protest—where advocates of reform argue from a position of "rights" and those who oppose them reason from the stance of "utility." MacIntyre observes:

> the facts of incommensurability ensure that protestors can never win an *argument*; the indignant self-righteousness of protestors arises because the facts of incommensurability ensure equally that the protestors can never lose an argument either. Hence, the *utterance* of protest is characteristically addressed to those who already *share* the protestors' premises. . . . This is not to say that protest cannot be effective; it is to say that protest cannot be rationally effective.[88]

Thus, when arguers appealing to justice and equality contend with adversaries who base their cases on success, survival, and liberty, they talk past each other.

From the perspective of the narrative paradigm, the dynamic of this situation is that rival stories are being told. Any story, any form of rhetorical communication, not only says something about the world, it also implies an audience, persons who conceive of themselves in very specific ways. If a story denies a person's self-conception, it does not matter what it says about the world. In the instance of protest, rival factions' stories deny each other in respect to self-conceptions and the world. The only way to bridge this gap, if it can be bridged through discourse, is by telling stories that do not negate the self-conceptions that people hold of themselves.

There is hope in the fact that narrative as a *mode of discourse* is more universal and probably more efficacious than argument for nontechnical forms of communication. There are several reasons why this should be true. First, narration comes closer to capturing the experience of the world, simultaneously appealing to the various senses, to reason and emotion, to intellect and imagination, and to fact and value. It does not presume intellectual contact only. Second, one does not have to be taught narrative probability and narrative fidelity; one culturally acquires them through a universal faculty and experience. Obviously one can, through education, become sophisticated in one's understanding and application of these principles. But, as Gadamer observes, "I am convinced of the fact that there are no people who do not 'think' sometime and somewhere. That means there is no one who does not form general views about life and death, about freedom and living together, about the good and about happiness."[89] In other words, people are reflective and from such reflection they make the stories of their lives and have the basis for judging narratives for and about them. On the other hand, appreciation of argument requires not only reflection, but also specialized knowledge of issues, reasoning, rules of rationality, and so on. Third, narration works by suggestion and identification; argument operates by inferential moves and deliberation. Both forms are modes of expressing good reasons, so the differences between them are structural rather than substantive.

NOTES

79. Aristotle, *Rhetoric*, 1.2.1257 10.

80. Joseph R. Gusfield, *Symbolic Crusade: Status Politics and the American Temperance Movement* (Urbana: University of Illinois Press, 1976), p. 173.

81. *Los Angeles Times*, October 17, 1982, pt. 4, pp. 102.

82. Chaim Perelman, "The Rational and the Reasonable," in The New Rhetoric and the Humanities: *Essays on Rhetoric and Its Applications* (Dordrecht Holland: D. Reidel, 1979), pp. 117-23.

83. Stephen Toulmin, *The Return to Cosmology: Postmodern Science and Theology of Nature* (Berkeley: University of California Press, 1982), p. 81.

84. Walter Benjamin, "The Storyteller," in Hannah Arendt, ed., *Illuminations* (New York: Schocken Books, 1969), pp. 108-9.

85. G. Holton, *Thematic Origins of Modern Science* (Cambridge, Mass.: Harvard University Press, 1973), pp. 28-29. See also Walter Ong, *Orality and Literacy: The Technologizing of the Word* (London: Methuen, 1982), p. 140.

86. Alasdair MacIntyre, *After Virtue: A Study in Moral Theory* (Notre Dame, Ind.: Notre Dame University Press, 1981), p. 241.

87. Ibid., p. 245.

88. Ibid., p. 69.

89. Hans-Georg Gadamer, *Reason in the Age of Science* (Cambridge, Mass.: MIT Press, 1981), p. 58. See also S.M. Ogden, "Myth and Truth," in *The Reality of God* (University Park: The Pennsylvania State University Press, 1977), p. 114; Bernard J.F. Lonergan, *Insight: A Study of Human Understanding* (New York: Harper & Row, 1958), p. xiv, xxii, xxx.

■ 8

The Self Region: Voices at the Boundary

Perhaps one of the major impediments to a dialogical perspective in communication is that it is just not very intuitively satisfying. Experience itself is too easily experienced as individual. To each person, experience and therefore self feels like *mine*, contained *in here*, somehow produced by consciousness. When voiced, the self can be experienced as even more palpable, as a possession would.

The "answer merchants," instant experts who try to commodify any human relations insight, therefore set out to package and market stronger selves, happier selves, nicer selves, more sensitive selves, and more efficient selves through workshops, books, infomercials, and even religions. Just practicing a few simple techniques, we are promised, will rejuvenate our lives, making us better persons. What a relief—someone, somewhere, knows the answers and can transfer them to us.

Presuming the separation of selves fits neatly with both an acquisitive consumerist social milieu ("I'll get mine and you get yours") and modernism's reliance on objective technique (how-to knowledge can be packaged scientifically for achieving individualistic goals). Assuming the atomized self, however, fits less comfortably with a pluralistic and postmodern social ethic. A complex society hears a multitude of social voices. Considered from an atomistic self-model, the pluralization of voices makes sense only if they can be heard in harmony—that is, if they represent consensus or can be brought into concerted cooperation. From the perspective of a dialogic self, the voices, however different, are fundamentally interdependent in their genesis. They emerge from the dynamic and changeable potential of social relationships, "the between" to Buber, not the isolated experiences of different people. Differing voices need not be brought to consensus in order to make sense; instead, sensemaking comes from, first, recognizing that each different voice emerges from dialogue, and, second, recognizing that each different voice energizes dialogue. We need to listen more alertly and to coordinate the access of voices to each other, assuming neither a normative consensus nor the desirability of encouraging voices merely to echo each other. Although Habermas (1979, 1992), among other critical theorists, clearly advocated a dialogue privileging dissent, it is on this issue of implied consensus that feminist dialogical scholars (Benhabib, 1992; Young, 1990) have critiqued political philosophers of rationality such as Habermas. To these critics, the distinctiveness of voices, rather than their normative social "fit," is what is primarily important.

H. L. Goodall emphasizes the mystery of autobiography as well as its distinctiveness, affirming the mystery surrounding the multiple voices of selves. Goodall as author alternates between personal and professional voices, and in our excerpt advocates that the traditional rhetorical concept of *ethos* be disengaged from the atomistic self-model and re-engaged within the perspective of dialogic narrative. To illustrate, he constructs a three-voiced "kitchen conversation" on the nature of autobiography. The first position—drawing on atomistic self assumptions—focuses on a narrator displaying a story that is, in effect, authored and self-possessed. The second position taken in his conversation represents the postmodern challenge to the modern, in that the self's ability to represent itself is made problematic. Within this position, the illusory and contradictory nature of language is upheld to demonstrate how selves are not so easily located. Autobiography thus seems impossible, at least in its traditional senses. The third position is Goodall's attempt to reconcile self and other within the mysteries—the unspecifiabilities—of context.

In his description of polyphonic qualities of texts and the nature of dialogic engagement, Goodall implicitly justifies Don Ihde's elaboration of the phenomenological primacy of listening. To Ihde (1976), the self is a boundary phenomenon persons learn to recognize as it is both constituted by and becomes pivotal in human conversation: "The 'innermost' is *not* distant from the 'outermost,'" he shows in one place (p. 119), and in another, "the voices of language have already penetrated all my experience" (p. 120).

In his concern for inner speech, Ihde reinforces the insights developed by two Russian scholars of this century—the literary criticism of Mikhail Bakhtin and the psychological research of Lev Vygotsky. Because of inner speech, Caryl Emerson shows in her ambitious synthesis of their work, a singular and packaged consciousness is impossible. The inner language of experience is not like the outer language of discourse, but the two are, in Emerson's words, in "permanent dialogue." This dialogue becomes not just the nature of the self, but the nature of the language in which selves live. Embedded in Emerson's synthesis is a communicology of dialogue based on the central role of difference in interpretation. Understanding anything is not a matter of apprehension, appropriation, or projection, but of engagement—encountering the other (whether person, text, or object) by negotiating its terms together with our own essentially *different* terms.

REFERENCES

Benhabib, S. (1992). *Situating the self: Gender, community and postmodernism in contemporary ethics.* New York: Routledge.

Habermas, J. (1979). *Communication and the evolution of society* (T. McCarthy, Trans.). Boston: Beacon Press. (Original work published 1976)

Habermas, J. (1992). *Autonomy and solidarity: Interviews with Jurgen Habermas* (rev. ed., P. Dews, Ed.). London: Verso.

Ihde, D. (1976). *Listening and voice: A phenomenology of sound.* Athens: Ohio University Press.

Young, I. M. (1990). *Justice and the politics of difference.* Princeton, NJ: Princeton University Press.

■

Autobiography, Style, and Dialogic Authenticity: The Detective's Mystery as Mystery of Self

H.L. Goodall

Instead of being merely an organism that responds to the play of factors on or through it, the human being is seen as an organism that has to deal with what it notes. It meets what it so notes by engaging in a process of self-indication in which it makes an object of what it notes, gives it meaning, and uses the meaning as the basis for directing its action. Its behavior with regard to what it notes is not a response called forth by the presentation of what it notes but instead is an action that arises out of the interpretation made through the process of self-indication.

—Herbert Blumer

Self-consciousness, as the artistic dominant in the structure of a character's image, presupposes a radically new authorial position with regard to the represented person. . . . A man never coincides with himself. One cannot apply to him the formula of identity A = A. . . the genuine life of the personality takes place at the point of non-coincidence between a man and himself, at his point of departure beyond the limits of all that he is as a material being, a being that can be spied on, defined, predicted apart from its own will, "at second hand." The genuine life of the personality is made available only through a dialogic penetration of that personality, during which it freely and reciprocally reveals itself.

—Mikhail Bakhtin

Man is the symbol-using (symbol-making, symbol-misusing) animal inventor of the negative (or moralized by the negative) separated from his natural condition by instruments of his own making goaded by a spirit of hierarchy (or moved by the sense of order) and rotten with perfection.

—Kenneth Burke

In this essay I want to explore the writing of autobiography as a natural theme in texts devoted to the practice of interpretive ethnography. This chapter, then, will serve as a transition from studies of contexts to studies of self within contexts. It is a setup, if you will, in which the detective does the setting prior to the commission of what will at first appear to be a crime. In this case we are concerned with investigations of self, an act of writing often thought to be a crime among the social sciences, a crime of supreme self-indulgence or worse—irrelevant to the pursuit of scholarly inquiry. But the detective's task is to establish grounds for a serious questioning of that assumption, and to show, in fact, that what at first appears to be mere self-indulgence is actually—well . . . you'll see.

To make this work, I must use the familiar "professional" voice again. I do so because the contexts in which we must immerse ourselves involve current literary discussions about the descriptive and analytical adequacies of traditional rhetorics of cultural display (Clifford 1988; Geertz 1988; Goodall 1989a; Rosaldo 1989; Rose 1989; Tyler 1987; Van Maanen 1988) as well as the role of self and Other in autobiographical writing (Anderson 1987; Eakin 1985; Egan 1984; Gunn 1982; Olney 1972; Siebenschuh 1983; Stoller and Olkes 1987; G. O. Taylor 1983).

I do this also because the place for the use of this voice, indeed this genre of writing, seems most appropriate for investigations of what William James termed "knowledge about" (theoretical arguments *about* the world) rather than "acquaintance with" (immersion *in* the world). For me then, this voice is appropriate for "knowledge about" arguments that exist primarily in the professional discourse of the field.

To begin this exploration requires locating ethnography within the larger framework of writing cultural critique. Cultural critique, in turn, relies on an appreciation of the relationship between the various sites of cultural production and institutionalized forms of knowledge used to represent them (see Connor 1989; Fish 1980; McHale 1987). First, I will provide a reading of the texts involved in both the production and representation of ethnographic and literary knowledge. This reading will show how these texts and their rhetorics have induced my own particular response. Then I will offer an argument for restructuring the rhetorical nature of *ethos* from a concern with the ethical character of the

speaker/author to a narrative display of the dialogic character of relationship between the speaker/author and the reader/other. I offer this argument because, as I will attempt to show, such a move is inherent to judgments concerning the textual authenticity of descriptive rhetorics.

READING AT THE BORDERS OF INTERPENETRATING TEXTS: THE CRITICAL SITE FOR THEORIES OF AUTOBIOGRAPHY AND STYLE

Ethnography is a form of cultural critique (see Marcus and Fischer 1986).
Viewed this way, ethnography has been shifting its theoretical interests
from understanding—through intensive fieldwork—the various symbolic
dimensions of the everyday life exhibited by exotic peoples and their environments, to a mediating concern for how such an acquired understanding can or should be written and for how various rhetorical strategies may
be employed toward that end. As Clifford Geertz phrases it:

> "Being There" authorially, palpably on the page, is in any case as diffi-
> cult a trick to bring off as "being there" personally, which after all
> demands at the minimum hardly more than a travel booking and per-
> mission to land; a willingness to endure a certain amount of loneli-
> ness, invasion of privacy, and physical discomfort; a relaxed way with
> odd growths and unexplained fevers; a capacity to stand still for artistic
> insults, and the sort of patience that can support an endless search for
> invisible needles in infinite haystacks. And the authorial sort of being
> there is getting more difficult all the time. The advantage of shifting at
> least part of our attention from the fascinations of field work, which
> have held us so long in thrall, to those of writing is not only that this
> difficulty will become more clearly understood, but also that we shall
> learn to read with a more percipient eye. A hundred and fifteen years
> (if we date our profession, as conventionally, from Tylor) of assevera-
> tional prose and literary innocence is long enough. (1988, 23-24)

Given Geertz's long list of ills that befall the ethnographer, his
sense of a shift of interest from fieldwork to deskwork, from acting *in situ*
to recreating said *in situ* as text, from scientific validity to literary quality—
all this, like his insistence that writing is "getting more difficult all the
time," should be read at least as much as a challenge as an invitation.
However, as soon as that sentiment is aired it quickly becomes problematic: Certainly his rhetorical stance should be read as a challenge, but as a
challenge to what?

In this section of the essay I forward the argument that the challenge here has at least as much to do with issues of style and autobiogra-

phy as it has to do with the available means of representing situations and Others. To do this, I think, requires invoking a metaphor, because this particular argument requires simultaneous travel to distant destinations that always correspond but have not yet been shaped that way. The metaphor, then, is one of a visit to an everyday place—a neighbor's house—that will change, unexpectedly and perhaps forever, our views on the nature of the work we do in our own homes.

Let us, then, leave the comfortable disarray of our own house, within the convenient context of this sentence, and simply walk across the lawn to visit the next-door neighbor, to go there perhaps to derive (borrow) something or better yet to recover (in the sense that means to get something back). We go there unaware that something is happening in that house, for our arrival has not been preceded by a phone call. This is why when we arrive we enter what is obviously a very busy kitchen where we suddenly realize that we are in the presence of a lively conversation in literary studies concerning how style functions as argument in contemporary nonfiction.

Is that Jimi Hendrix in the background?

STYLE AND AUTOBIOGRAPHY AS ETHNOGRAPHIC TERRITORIES

Why should autobiography, much less the style through which it is committed as text, be of concern to the practice of ethnography? After all, ethnographers have always been "in the texts" they have created, whether their presence has been relatively active (e.g., Levi-Strauss 1955; Malinowski 1922, 1935; Conquergood 1985, 1987; or Goodall 1989a, 1989c) or relatively passive (e.g., Ardrey 1967; Carbaugh 1988; Katriel and Philipsen 1981; Van Maanen 1981), and whether the texts they perform are dedicated to understanding Others (Bateson 1936; Mead 1928; Rosaldo 1989; Trujillo and Dionisopoulos 1987) or devoted to furthering understanding of the concerns of the field (Clifford 1988; Clifford and Marcus 1986; Goodall 1989b; Pacanowsky 1988; Philipsen 1977) or the nature of doing fieldwork (Fetterman 1989; Van Maanen 1988).

The issue here is not, however, whether authors are present, but *how their presence is manifested in prose* and what the nature of those manifestations should suggest to us about the scope and limitations of their arguments. As Geertz has it, "Getting themselves into their text [that is, representationally into their text] may be as difficult for ethnographers as getting themselves into the culture [that is, imaginatively into the culture]" (1988, 17).

This problem is easy enough to state and relatively straightforward in its implications: the issue here is one first of the explicit symbolic capacities of language to induce understanding (Burke 1969; Gregg 1984) through the proverbial "shedding of light on a subject," and second of the implicit symbolic baggage carried by any use of language that casts into the shadows everything not directly in the path of the light. So it would seem that language is not merely an issue and not only the nature of the problem; language is also the only way to approach the issue and the only code available to cipher some solution to the problem (if a solution is the necessary outcome, which I will show later is hardly the case).

Furthermore, language is itself too broad a category to be very useful as a map or territory for this linguistic dilemma, for language holds all of the known world as its domain, all of the universes of discourse and deportment as its legitimate work, and all known metaphors as its cosmic (used here in the Latin sense of "universal") vehicle for the doing of that work. No, language *qua* language won't help because it won't do, and yet we can't do anything here without it.

However, one of the uses of language, if not its principle [sic] use, is to make rhetoric. One of the slier characteristics of rhetoric is its ability—within the body of the appropriate magician and much to the dismay of philosophers since Socrates—to cast spells, to work magic on a subject. When the issue is language, this trick is very much like the strategy of chasing one's tail with one's head in the vain hope of wearing the tail out before the head gives out, and being able at some point to sneak up on the tail and observe it firsthand while it is napping and unaware.[1] As incredible as it seems this strategy often works, at least in sentences that say it works, which is what this sentence now does. What we have done here, courtesy of the rhetoric employed to make the previous sentence, is to wear out the wagging *tail* of language, for once examining it not as a tail that holds us hostage to its wagging, but as a *tale* that is told in the voice of some actor.

We are, therefore, reclaiming for the head its rightful place before the tale. When we do so we come back to the voice of the actor who lives in and through the tale, and we get there by recovering, through and for rhetoric, the interdependence of self and style as the naturally occurring, evocative, metaphorical comet that, in its spin across any given universe of discourse, leaves behind, in the telling evidence of the tail (tale) of its passage, traces of brilliance and magic and stardust that induce all of those who may read the stars to find in their meanings a renewed human intensity, a renewed appreciation for the value of the individual experience as the shaper of all that is, or that can be, known and made known to others.

We are concerned, suddenly, for the *how* of the human voice that makes the tale through intricate weavings of words, that has lived the life that finds itself in the midst of the weaving process, and that must make sense out of—as well as make sensible—both the experience of the words and the words of the experience. We find ourselves embarked on a journey into the deeper reaches of self, Other, and context that form the inner and outer borders of an exotic and uncharted territory, a territory that coexists within us in the everyday as well as in one of the mythical dimensions of a forgotten chapter in the histories of rhetoric and knowing. We find ourselves, then, present at a site, a critical site known in literary and cultural studies as the intersection of autobiography and style.

THREE APPROACHES TO THIS CONVERSATION

There seem to be three general positions, three approaches to this conversation about style and autobiography, that suggest three ways to work out the experience and role of style in the writing of autobiography (see Eakin 1985, 181-278). My use of these three positions is *not* meant to imply that there are only three ways of working out this relationship, merely that this is the way the conversation in literary studies is, from my reading, currently being constituted.

First Position: Autobiography as Metaphor for Self

The first position is a historically informed tradition for seeing autobiography as a *metaphor of self* (see especially Olney 1972). Viewed from this perspective, the ontological status of autobiography reveals a text as the site of individual identity and the making of a text as an exercise in translating one's life experiences, personality, and character into a narrative form.

James Clifford's observations about the narrative problems inherent to ethnobiography seem equally applicable here, particularly his two formulaic but eerily prescient questions: "Where, in short, does a person begin? Where does he or she end?" (see Clifford, quoted in Aaron 1978, 41-42). Between those questions, and the prose decisions the author commits to print in an effort to resolve them, lies an even stranger series of inner penetrations that, as Olney observes, "shift[s] attention from *bios* to *autos*—from the life to the self" (Olney 1980, 19).

Viewing autobiography as a metaphor for self, then, carries with it a necessary rhetorical bifurcation—what Louis Renza calls "writing's law of gravity" (1980, 279)—that forces the author to choose between third and first-person carriers of the metaphor.[2] Each choice brings with it an array of possible assembly tactics, uses of language, and images of self, but the most important characteristic of this dilemma is the way in which it governs how the author positions him or herself in the text as either the *object* or *subject* of his or her own life. To become an "author," when authorship itself is viewed as the position one takes towards one's own experiences and the voice one uses to re-create it, is to reserve (or perhaps, *preserve*) for the self a poetics of space in which the poet becomes the poem. Viewed this way, one's life is experienced either as an ordered composition in which the "Name" stands out as the performer in the there-and-then of experience, or as a composition ordered from elsewhere, usually the narrow perspectival moment and motives of the language of here-and-now as rendered in the first person, in which the performance appears fated or destined or shaped by forces outside of the immediate arena of the self.

This position, the one historically represented by autobiographical voices from Augustine to Rousseau on the one hand to Henry Adams and Norman Mailer on the other, provides more than information about available rhetorical strategies and tactics of representation. This position speaks directly to the way in which the self is viewed by the self, which has obvious effects on issues greater than style.

Imagine, if you will, how each of these positions influences the writing of an ethnography. The question "Who are you?" usually directed at the Other in the ethnographer's quest comes back around to be asked this way: "Who am I when I study You?" Do I see myself as an actor engaging the scenes I encounter, the signifier of the signified, or am I merely the recipient of these performances, a person enmeshed in the webs of signification that are happening in this curious surround that I call "culture" when I run out of rhetorical room or when all else that helps me make sense either does not work or breaks down?

But these are merely the broad strokes of a much finer set of implications to be drawn from this initial question on positioning in the text. Consider, beyond the voice of "I am" that is and that acts upon, the mind-set of its owner. Here we encounter a tension that is very real and very difficult to resolve. I am speaking of the tension between "owning" the voice and the experiences of that voice as one's own (and therefore taking full responsibility for it) and avoiding the neocolonialism that tends to affect an individual who encounters a "Them" and tries to make sense of the experience by remaining an "Us." The experience may be my own, but it is also the Other's, and we have not yet reached a stage of linguistic evolution where these two opposing forces can comfortably rest in the same text without some conflict.

Or consider the finer weave of a text written from the voice of the participant fated by hegemonic forces beyond her or his control to be in this scene and to have to give it a reading of some sort. Here we confront a tension not of Buberian "I-Thou" proportions, but of trying to name those forces that you bring to this reading and at the same time trying desperately to avoid their influences on what you see and experience.

This tension may be easier to work out because our discipline's history is one shaped by texts that increasingly absent the author and embed all real and potential insights, arguments, and meanings within extant literatures. Hence, "the literature" speaks only the language that "the literature" has been taught to speak, and those doing the teaching are forced to acquire their vocabulary and grammar from "the literature" (see Connor 1989; Goodall 1989b). It is a Catch-22 of immense proportions.

Either way you turn, the first position that defines autobiography as a metaphor for self includes strategies of textual representation that bear further scrutiny. Hayden White, for example, in his discussions of narrative, argues that "even in the simplest prose discourse, and even in one in which the object of representation is intended to be nothing but fact, the use of language itself projects a level of secondary meaning below or behind the phenomena being "described." This secondary meaning exists quite apart from the "facts" themselves and any explicit argument that might be offered in the extradescriptive, more purely analytical or interpretive, level of the text" (quoted in Siebenschuh 1983, 105).

The narrative itself reveals a subconscious, poetic level that is both the product of the author's own subconscious, poetic, symbolic environment and the subconscious, poetic, symbolic environment of the reader (Goodall 1983). Here again is White:

> This figurative level is produced by a constructive reader of the text more or less subconsciously to receive both the description of the facts and their explanation as plausible, on the one side, and as adequate to one another, on the other.
>
> As thus envisaged, the historical discourse can be broken down into two levels of meaning. The facts and their formal explanation appear as the manifest or literal surface of the discourse, while the figurative language used to characterize the facts points to a deeper structural meaning. (Quoted in Siebenschuh 1983, 106).

Style, then, however plain or ornate, is not mere ornament but is a co-conspirator to the metaphors of self. Just as there can be no neutral language, no purely "objective" observation, neither can there be such a thing as a "neutral style." For behind the style is always the person, behind the narrative the author's self. And in standing just over there, in front of them and across the street at this particular intersection, is the reader, and the reader's self, also never neutral or objective.

Viewed as a metaphor for self, the voice of the narrator in autobiography is always "the *displayed* self . . . who speaks, who lives in time" (Gunn 1982, 8, 9). Curiously, then, the language of self that is part author's deep reach into the life of experience and part reader's deep reach into the experience of the text, is a language of display, not distortion (see Gunn 1982 for further explication).[3] It is through the metaphors of language that the metaphors of self are manifested, and it is through this manifestation that the self exists. Therefore, it is through the act of writing (and reading) autobiography, through the displays of language and metaphors, through the dialectical tensions of voices that create and experience the text, that the self is actually discovered. As Olney nicely sums up this position, "We do not see or touch the self, but we do see and touch its metaphors: and thus we 'know' the self, activity, or agent, represented in the metaphor and the metaphorizing" (1972, 31).

This first position makes a compelling case if and only if we accept the premise that a self exists and therefore may be discovered and experienced through the mediating presence of a text, a text authored by some sense of self. However, as Michael Sprinker argues, "The self is constituted in a discourse it never fully masters," because "the self can no more be the author of its own discourse than any producer of a text can be called the author—that is the originator—of his [sic] writing" (quoted in Olney 1980, 342, 325). This brings us, then, into contact with a different way of seeing this intersection, a new contributor to this kitchen conversation, a voice representing the literary, mostly French, left.

Second Position: Autobiography as Language of Privation and Death

The challenge to the idea that autobiography represents something other than metaphors of self is derived from poststructuralist, postmodern interpretations of the positioning of language in culture that call into question the positioning of the author in the text. Viewed from this perspective, language and culture are not resources for freedoms of expression and creation, but sources of institutional constraint, instruments of hegemonic distortion, that seriously call into question the possibility of an individualized self much less its representation (see Derrida 1976; de Man 1979).

There is a strong economic, neo-Marxist, critical theory flavor to this conversation. The voices involved in it see a text as a "production" and its writer not as a writer, but as a "producer." The overarching principle here is one of production and consumption, and what is produced is determined by what is demanded, needed, or co-opted for the engines of consumption. Hence, autobiography can be read as a demand made by a postmodern "panic" culture (Kroker, Kroker, and Cook 1989) that, suspended between the hyperemotional realities of public anxiety and private dread, privileges the possibility of unity over the fragmentation of personal experience.[4] This "fact" of postmodern life is reminiscent of this note from Albert Camus: "Nostalgia for other people's lives. This is because, seen from the outside, they form a whole. While our life, seen from the inside, is all bits and pieces. Once again, we run after an illusion of unity" (1964, 17). When autobiography is thus reduced to a source of capitalistic critique, the self revealed in it does indeed die. Formal argument for this position is often found in Paul de Man's (1979) critique of William Wordworth's *Essays on Epitaphs*, in which de Man deconstructs the poet's attitude toward autobiography as self-restoration as revealing, paradoxically, "a language of deprivation" (Eakin 1985, 186). De Man argues:

> To the extent that language is figure (or metaphor, or prosopopeia) it is indeed not the thing itself but the representation, the picture of the thing and, as such, it is silent, mute as pictures are mute. . . . To the extent that, in writing, we are dependent on this language we all are, like the Dalesman in the *Excursion*, deaf and mute—not silent, which implies the possible manifestation of sound at our own will, but silent as a picture, that is to say eternally deprived of voice and condemned to muteness. (1979, 922-23)

All references to life, to knowing a life, outside the "pictures" of language are hereby—and ironically within sentences claiming their own muteness—reduced to mere illusions. As Eakin reads this text, "The deconstruction of autobiographical discourse is now complete; stripped of the illusion of reference, autobiography is reinscribed once more in the prisonhouse of language: 'Death is a displaced name for a linguistic predicament, and the restoration of mortality by autobiography (the prosopopeia of the voice and the name) deprives and disfigures to the precise extent that it restores'" (Eakin 1985, 186-87).

Autobiography, then, is not an experience of self but the production of a convenient fiction. It is a commodity produced in an illusion of self by a victim of language and culture, and it is produced for consumers who are themselves victimized through consumption by the very act of its production. Autobiography serves as a cultural sedative, not a powerful metaphor for self but merely a metaphorical Valium that depresses consciousness by insisting that life, any life, is but an illusion of self, that writing is an illusion of creation and discovery, and that any pretense that autobiography may have to the capture, experience, or understanding of self, context, and Other is just that—pretense. There is no self, no subject, no use to the first-person "I." The world is a fated, overdetermined, lost paradise of language in which third-person estrangement and distance must pass for the experience of life.

Admittedly, this is a political reading of a political tract; but de Man's was a political life. In de Man's critique are the residues of a history he lived that, as events have shown, he would rather have not had chronicled. It is possible, therefore, to read into his sentences the desire to "forget" by way of justifying, insisting, that all attempts to recapture a past and to use such a vehicle for self-exploration are futile, distorted, controlled. Within his critique, then, lies quite another text, an autobiographical text, that reveals a desire to deny that figures of language, or pictures, *can* speak (for explication of this perspective, see especially Neumann 1988a). What de Man finds in muteness can be read as a desire for forgetting, for who among us can so easily agree with a position that denies voice(s), historical accuracy, or representational truth to the death-camp pictures of Auschwitz, or that would deny to autobiography the testimony to personal discovery found in a text such as Paul Frielander's *When Memory Comes?*

This is not to suggest that de Man, or for that matter other critics of culture and language who draw premises from the political left, should be discounted. Their awareness of the limitations of language to represent perceived reality—and their contribution to understanding, with Lacan for instance, that our construction of self is a tap into the linguistic unconscious structures that are deeply embedded in mind and culture (1966)— provides complementary evidence, albeit "left-handed," as well as complementary testimony, albeit ironic, for the weave of the argument being constructed here.

Nor would I suggest that de Man's views of language are to be discarded wholesale, merely that their retail price is too high. He effectively deconstructs the "how" of autobiographical metaphors and places the whole notion of language in sync with a postmodern questioning of the possibility of representational truth. In so doing, he contributes to a position that is in accord with another set of voices in the autobiographical dialogue, voices that trace their own heritage to a profound concern for the impossibility of any one-to-one equation between language and reality. It is to these voices that the kitchen crowd now turns.

Third Position: Autobiography as Mysterious Reality, Self as Mystery

Robert Elbaz, in his essay "Autobiography, Ideology, and Genre Theory" (1987), suggests an entry point for a third position in our ongoing conversation: "Behind this preoccupation with referentiality is the problem of differentiation between fiction and nonfiction" (8). He goes on to argue that in the tensions found between and among the arguments of Emile Benveniste and Philippe Lejeune there is an opening in the discourse on autobiography for recovering the self through manifestations of the first-person singular. This view, however—founded as it is on an existential phenomenology of experience and a dramatistic view of how an interplay of language and voice constructs texts of self and identity—seeks to collapse the traditionally regarded, canonized, modernist categories of "genre" into a postmodern crisis of interpretation.

To review the history of this discussion requires more space than I have in this essay, but to summarize through Elbaz: Benveniste's thesis is that "a speaker's being depends upon the audience and the nature of the discourse he [sic] directs at it, his performance, his role within the social whole. And it is precisely this role that defines the I" (Elbaz 1987, 6). Lejeune, then, applies this thesis to the name inscribed on the autobiographical text and suggests that "the declaration by the author on the first page of his [sic] autobiography that indeed this is the 'true' story of his life, and his signature to that effect, sends the reader back to the existence of a 'real person' . . . on which the reader can check" (Elbaz 1987, 7).

The tension here, according to Elbaz, is in the misreading that Philip Lejeune provides of Emile Benveniste's intention, and the opening is there precisely because of it. Referentiality is a futile pursuit, both for the "extratextual . . . social and material conditions that make for the possibility of discourse [as well as for] the individual author who generates it" (Elbaz 1987, 8). The text, any text, does not try to mediate the "true conditions" of history, science, or one's own life; instead, it is a positioned performance that connects an author and a reader through a dynamic, communicative encounter. Elbaz concludes: "History, science, or for that matter any meaningful statement, in no way duplicate reality; they construct it. For language is functional to the ideological position of the speaking subject, and 'reality' is the creation of this same subject. One does not report, duplicate, or verify the truth: one makes it" (8-9).

Chris Anderson's study of style as argument in the work of Tom Wolfe, Joan Didion, Truman Capote, and Norman Mailer deepens the value of this perspective by situating "the principal theme of contemporary nonfiction [in] its own rhetorical dilemma" (1987, 5). Anderson then suggests that the writing, always autobiographical, of these authors is "profoundly metadiscursive, concerned with the problems of style and expression and language in America, and in this way it provides all the terms we need for understanding its internal workings and its cultural value" (5).

Viewing the work of these authors as emblematic of similar endeavors at the borders of rapidly disappearing genres, Anderson reveals a countercultural stance emerging in the rhetorical performance of the words themselves. Anderson's notion of style becomes at one with the ways the words themselves weave self into context, context into Other and even other back into the self, a rhetorical feast in which serious display and serious self-indulgence come to grips with issues that go beyond representation of experience to the experience of representation.

Within the realms of this experience, each author in his or her own way confronts a situation, a story, that is essentially "wordless," and each author, in her or his own way, must find a way *not* out of the problem, but *into* its mystery, and through that quest "circumvent the inevitable limits of language" (Anderson 1987, 180). Summing up his accomplishment,

Anderson finds a powerful counterargument to the politics of language that rely on the death of a subject and the impossibility of self:

> Contemporary American prose is not finally about wordlessness, not about failure, but about the rhetorical power of words at a time when language is constantly being threatened. For every impulse toward silence there is a linguistic impulse, a rhetorical impulse, underneath. For every acknowledgment of failure there is a new form which gains strength and cogency from that failure. The story of contemporary American prose . . . is not about the rupturing or the collapsing of the envelope of language, the death of the membrane. It is about the expansion of the membrane to accommodate new realms of experience. . . . This is what makes it important for American culture. (180)

What are these new realms of experience? To get at this is to get at the core of the interpenetrations of culture and writing, which is to suggest that it is to get at the heart of autobiography, style, and interpretive ethnography. The way in, however, lies not in finding a new method or countering an ideology but in the ways in which language allows us to define what it is that we are seeing and doing with words, and equally important, what the words we use are doing to us.

I briefly introduced the work of Gabriel Marcel in the Preface. To recap: Marcel (1949a, 1949b, 1950) suggests that there is a profound difference between defining a situation as a "problem" and defining it as a "mystery." As a "problem," we tend to divide "objects" from participation in human experience, narrowing our focus to see our way from some thorn in the here-and-now to its removal in the there-and-then. Problems invoke science, and science invokes the need for a method of moving from problems to solutions. Moreover, problems invite us to separate the world into categories of persons and things and to believe that problems are either object-residents of self or object-residents of Others, and not that self and Other can share in or jointly participate in them. By dividing the world into categories, into persons and things, form and content, logic and rhetoric, fiction and nonfiction, reason and emotion, and so forth, and by further inducing in us a deeper division between our experience of and participation in the world, the realm of problems encourages distance, boundaries, monologue, method, and authority.

Mystery, on the other hand, suggests something else, something far more complex and involving. There may be a thorn, but who placed it there? If we remove it, what else is likely to befall us? What "mystery" does is to encourage us to see and to define situations by their unique human and spiritual poetic, the interpenetrations of self, Other, and context, by our complexity and interdependence rather than by some simpler linear or causal logic. Mystery is a "question in which what is given cannot be regarded as detached from the self" (quoted in Gallagher 1975, 32). And perhaps for this reason, as Busch points out, "Scarcely could Gabriel Marcel write a chapter of a book, an article or deliver a paper without becoming autobiographical" (1987, xi).

For Marcel there is a natural correlation between being and creation: "as soon as there is creation, in whatever degree, we are in the realm of being. But the converse is equally true: that is to say, there is doubtless no sense in using the word 'being' except where creation, in some form or other, is in view" (quoted in Gallagher 1975, vii). As evidenced by his life and work as a dramatist, pianist, philosopher, and man, "creation" refers to artistic involvement with the always autobiographical experience of being-in-life, which is to say being aware of the rapture of being alive: "My life is not a succession of images at which I am a spectator. . . . the reality of the self lies beyond its finite and material expression" (quoted in Gallagher 1975, 63). However, it is in the dramatic tension of the experience of one's own being-in-life, and in the realization that the reality of self is beyond that experience, that artistic creation becomes the mediator between the reality of self and the material and finite limits of being. And it is awareness of the possibility of participation in that creation that brings us to confront the experiences of life as mystery and to want, therefore, to enter them, participate in them, be involved in that creative process. Once we own that awareness, not only do we own a vision of the autobiographical self as a questing, experiential phenomenon, but we also learn to see that our quest, our experiences, while necessarily our own, are also connected to, intertwined with, the mysteries and quests and experiences of Others.

In his treatment of the role of language in the construction of self, P. J. Eakin first defines the positions we have elaborated here, then, not surprisingly, suggests that the experience of writing autobiography places "the self finally as a mysterious reality, mysterious in its nature and origins and not necessarily consubstantial with the fictions we use to express it" (1985, 277). With Anderson, following Marcel, and in accord with both the proponents of the first position—who offer an experience of self, albeit necessarily fictional, as the autobiographical quest—and the critics of the second position—who offer the possibility of a quest not for self, but out of the prison-house of language and the politics of hypercapitalism—we find in the positing of *mystery* a new and common ground.

Trying to define the experience of mystery is difficult because mystery lies at the borders and crossroads of self, Other, and context as well as at the intersections of time, space, and the cosmos. However, I believe we can get a sense of mystery by examining a variety of autobiographical texts, each one—to appropriate Joan Didion's powerful emblem—"slouching towards [its own] Bethlehem" in a style, voice, and self of its own making. Particularly close to my own experience of autobiographical and ethnographic writing are the following words from Michael Herr's *Dispatches*, and though the excerpt is taken from a section that deals with the experience of war I read in it a curious, resonant wisdom about the experience of writing self:

> Finding it [the place war makes for you] was like listening to esoteric music, you didn't hear it in any essential way through all the repetitions until your own breath had entered it and become another instrument, and by then it wasn't just music anymore, it was experience. . . . [It was] a complete process if you got to complete it, a distinct path to travel, but dark and hard, not any easier if you knew that you'd put your foot on it yourself, deliberately and—most roughly speaking—consciously. Some people took a few steps along it and turned back, wised up, with and without regrets. Many walked on and just got blown off it. . . . And some kept going until they reached the place where an inversion of the expected order happened, a fabulous warp where you took the journey first and then you made your departure. (1977; quoted in G. O. Taylor 1983, 127)

In Herr's passionate account we feel the borders of self, Other, and context blur into a reading of experience that occurs after the experience has created the reading; at the same time we see the impact of style on how we are persuaded to read the text—to hear its "polyphonic" qualities in the various ways others dealt with the same experiential contexts—and are yet induced through the movement of words through space to arrive at a beginning where an ending "ought" to be. It seems to me that these strategic turns of context are intentional, but that their tactical subtexts, like the experience of self in war that Herr is trying to display for us, exist simultaneously as different polyphonic reads on different planes of experience available to those who come to the words from different angles of approach.

Herr does not define for us the way to read the war; instead, he provides ways into it that liberate our experience of the reading via our own level of engagement of the text, which is to say, via our own engagement of self with the Other through a shared context—in this case, Herr and the words of his text. What he sets up for us through his personally stylized writing is a framework for dialogic engagement, a site for an autobiographical reading of self (his, ours) into the contexts of Others (ourselves as readers of his text, him as the narrative partner to our own).

ENDNOTES

1. This rhetorical illusion is derived from an original treatment by James Olney (1972).

2. Second-person autobiography assumes a different problematic—the appropriation of the experience of the Other as equivalent to the experience of one's self. One effect of this voice choice is to beg identification with the character of the narrator; another may be to alienate the reader.

3. Gunn's argument is better read in the original (1982), but for those readers who may not be familiar with it I will attempt a brief recap. Essentially, she argues for autobiography as a kind of cultural space for reading experience. As such, autobiographical displays of style are part of the creation of that cultural space as well as instructions (or inducements) to the reader about how to engage those experiences. Without the display of style there would be no direct way into the character of the author, and there would also be a denial of the legitimacy of that cultural space.

4. One critique of, and certainly another way to read this contextualization of the fragmentation of personal experience, is that postmodernists did not "discover" the problem of fragmented selves. For example, Friedrich Schiller, at the turn of the eighteenth century, lamented a similar problem in his essay "On the Aesthetic Education of Man." This is certainly true, as Augustine's *Confessions* also offers evidence of fragmented experience through autobiographical expression, but it is too narrow a reading of what postmodernism is about. The fragmentation of postmodernists is not a discovery of a problem of self in culture, but a critique of the determinations, the modes of production, reproduction, and consumption that contribute to it in contemporary cultural life. Here again we find evidence of the tensions between the experience of culture and its institutionalized forms of representation. That is, for me at least, an important and distinguishing aspect of the postmodern condition, and one that speaks directly to the role of autobiography and style in ethnography. To wit: How does one display the fragmentation within "legitimized" styles of discourse that only allow for its naming?

REFERENCES

Aaron, D. 1978. *Studies in biography.* Cambridge: Harvard University Press.
Anderson, C. 1987. *Style as argument: Contemporary American nonfiction.* Carbondale: Southern Illinois University Press.
Ardrey, R. 1967. *The territorial imperative.* Garden City, N.Y.: Doubleday, Anchor.
Bakhtin, M.M. 1984a. *Problems of Doestoevsky's poetics.* Ed. and trans. C. Emerson. Minneapolis: University of Minnesota Press.
Bateson, G. 1936. *Naven.* Stanford, Calif.: Stanford University Press.
Blumer, H. 1969. *Symbolic interactionism: Perspective and method.* Englewood

198 THE REACH OF DIALOGUE

Cliffs, N.J.: Prentice-Hall.

Burke, K. 1969. *A rhetoric of motives.* Berkeley: University of California Press.

Camus, A. 1964. *Carnets.* Paris: Gallimard.

Carbaugh, D. 1988. Cultural terms and tensions in the speech at a television station. *Western Journal of Speech Communication* 52:16-37.

Clifford, J. 1988. *The predicament of culture: Twentieth century ethnography, literature, and art.* Cambridge: Harvard University Press.

Clifford, J., and Marcus, G.E., eds. 1986. *Writing culture: The poetics and politics of ethnography.* Berkeley: University of California Press.

Connor, S. 1989. *Postmodernist culture: An introduction to theories of the contemporary.* New York: Basil Blackwell.

Conquergood, D. 1985. Performing is a moral act: Ethical dimensions of the ethnography of performance. *Literature in Performance* 5:1-13.

De Man, P. 1979. Autobiography a de-facement. *Modern Language Notes* 94:920-30.

Derrida, J. 1976. *Of grammatology.* Trans. G. Chakravorty. Baltimore, Md.: Johns Hopkins University Press.

Eakin, P.J. 1985. *Fictions in autobiography: Studies in the art of self-invention.* Princeton, N.J.: Princeton University Press.

Egan, S. 1984. *Patterns of experience in autobiography.* Chapel Hill: University of North Carolina Press.

Elbaz, R. 1987. *The changing nature of the self: A critical study of the autobiographic discourse.* Iowa City: University of Iowa Press.

Fetterman, D.M. 1989. *Ethnography: Step-by-step.* Newbury Park, Calif.: Sage.

Fish, S. 1980. *Is there a text in this class? The authority of interpretive communities.* Cambridge: Harvard University Press.

Gallagher, K. 1975. *The philosophy of Gabriel Marcel.* New York: Fordham University Press.

Geertz, C. 1988. *Works and lives: The anthropologist as author.* Stanford, Calif.: Stanford University Press.

Goodall, H.L. (1983). The nature of analogic discourse. *The Quarterly Journal of Speech* 69:71-79.

_____. 1989a. *Casing a promised land: The autobiography of an organizational detective as cultural ethnographer.* Carbondale: Southern Illinois University Press.

_____. 1989b. A cultural inquiry concerning the ontological and epistemic dimensions of self, other, and context in communication scholarship. In G. M. Phillips and J. T. Wood, eds., *Studies to commemorate the seventy-fifth anniversary of the Speech Communication Association.* Carbondale: Southern Illinois University Press.

_____. 1989c. On becoming an organizational detective: The role of intuitive logics and context sensitivity for communication consultants. *Southern Communication Journal* 55:42-54.

Gregg, R. B. 1984. *Symbolic inducement and knowing.* Columbia: University of South Carolina Press.

Gunn, J. V. 1982. *Autobiography: toward a poetics of experience.* Philadelphia: University of Pennsylvania Press.

Gusdorf, G. 1986. Scripture of the self: "Prologue in Heaven." Trans. Betsy Wing. *The Southern Review* 22:280-95.

Herr, M. 1977. *Dispatches.* New York: Knopf.

Katriel, T., and Philipsen, G. 1981. "What we need is communication": "Communication" as a cultural category in some American speech. *Communication Monographs* 48:301-17.

Kroker, A., Kroker, M., and Cook, D. 1989. *Panic encyclopedia: The definitive guide to the postmodern scene.* New York: St. Martin's Press.

Lacan, J. 1966. *Ecrits.* Paris: Editions de Seuil.

Levi-Strauss, C. 1955. *Tristes tropiques.* New York: Antheneum.

McHale, B. 1987. *Postmodernist fiction.* New York: Methuen.

Malinowski, B. 1922. *Argonauts of the western Pacific.* New York: Dutton.

_____. 1935. *Coral gardens and their magic.* 2 vols. New York: American Books.

Marcel, G. 1949a. *Philosophy of existence.* Trans. Manya Harari. New York: Philosophical Library.

_____. 1949b. *Being and having.* London: Dacre Press.

_____. 1950. *Mystery of being.* 2 vols. Trans Rene Hague. London: Harvill Press.

Marcus, G.E., and Fischer, M.M.J. 1986. *Anthropology as cultural critique: An experimental moment in the human sciences.* Chicago: University of Chicago Press.

Mead, M. [1928] 1949. *Coming of age in Samoa.* New York: Mentor Books.

Neumann, M. 1988a. Consuming "otherness": The politics of photographic documentary art. *Journal of Communication Inquiry* 12:45-64.

Olney, J. 1972. *Metaphors of self: The meaning of autobiography.* Princeton, NJ: Princeton University Press.

_____. 1980. *Autobiography: Essays theoretical and critical.* Princeton, NJ: Princeton University Press.

Pacanowsky, M.E. 1988. Slouching towards Chicago. *The Quarterly Journal of Speech* 74:453-67.

Philipsen, G. 1977. Linearity of research design in ethnographic studies of speaking. *Communication Quarterly* 25:42-50.

Renza, L.A. 1980. The veto of the imagination: A theory of autobiography. In J. Olney, ed., *Autobiography: Essays theoretical and critical.* Princeton, NJ: Princeton University Press.

Rosaldo, R. 1989. *Culture and truth: The remaking of social analysis.* Boston: Beacon Press.

Rose, D. 1989. *Patterns of American culture: Ethnography and estrangement.* Philadelphia: University of Pennsylvania Press.

Siebenschuh, W.R. 1983. *Fictional techniques and factual works.* Athens: University of Georgia Press.

Stoller, P., and Olkes, C. 1987. *In sorcery's shadow: A memoir of apprenticeship among the Songbay of Niger.* Chicago: University of Chicago Press.

Taylor, G.O. 1983. *Chapters of experience: Studies in modern American autobiography.* New York: St. Martin's.

Trujillo, N., and Dionisopoulos, G. 1987. Cop talk, police stories, and the social construction of organizational drama. *Central States Speech Journal* 38:196-209.

Tyler, S. 1988. *The unspeakable: Discourse, dialogue, and rhetoric in the postmodern world.* Madison: University of Wisconsin Press.

Van Maanen, J. 1981. The informant game. *Urban Life* 9:469-94.

_____. 1988. *Tales of the field: On writing ethnography.* Chicago: University of Chicago Press.

The Polyphony of Experience

Don Ihde

The first movement of a phenomenology of sound and listening has taken its first step in what may be regarded as a preliminary survey of the auditory terrain. It began with first approximations and the center of focal listening. It moved from that listening to the voices of things "outwards" and from there to the listening for the silence of the relative and open horizon of silence. This survey has been attentive to the voices of the World.

This is phenomenologically appropriate, for there is a *primary listening* which precedes our own speech. This is whether one considers the matter as an issue of personal history—I hear the voices of others, of things, of the World long before I speak my own words—or as a matter of the correct phenomenological procedure which begins with noema before taking up noetic acts. Phenomenologically the "self" is modeled after the World which takes primacy in its first appearance.

The movement toward a more detailed review of the auditory terrain is a movement which accelerates the approximations to *existential significations*. The sounds which we hear are not "mere" sounds or "abstract" sounds but are significant sounds. In the first instance listening is a listening to *voices*, the voices of language in its broadest sense.

Existentially things "speak." Heidegger has pointed out, "Much closer to us than all sensations are the things themselves. We hear the door shut in the house and never hear acoustical sensations or even mere sounds. In order to hear a bare sound we have to listen away from things, divert our ear from them, i.e., listen abstractly."[1] The things of the world sound in their own way. Things, others, the gods, each have their *voices* to

From Listening and Voice: A Phenomenology of Sound (pp. 117-121) by Don Ihde, copyright © 1976, Ohio University Press. Reprinted with the permission of the author.

which we may listen. Within auditory experience there is this *primacy of listening.*

Not only do things, others, the gods, and ultimately I "speak" in distinctive voices, but each has its own way with language. For within auditory experience I find myself already *within* language. It is already there. Existentially there is already "word" in the sounding wind which brings things, others, and the gods to me. There is a sense in which within experience a "prelinguistic" level of experience is not to be found. The "prelinguistic" is the philosophical counterpart to the "preperceptual" bare sensation which if found at all is found by diverting one's ears and eyes from the objects.

Sounds which are heard as *already meaningful* do not show us the "lost" beginning. The actual history of man who speaks before he learns to embody word differently in writing and in wordless symbols does not show us the hidden genesis of the word. Nor do prescientific and preliterate languages show us the beginning. Not even the child's "learning" of his first word which contains in itself however latently the "whole" of language reveals the genesis. Long before he has learned to speak he has heard and entered the conversation which is humankind. He has been immersed in the voices and movements which preceded his speaking even more deeply in the invisible language of touch and even that of sound within the womb. Listening comes before speaking, and wherever it is sought the most primitive word of sounding language has already occurred.

The presence of word *already* there for listening is also what I find if I inquire into myself. For wherever I find myself I already stand in the midst of word. My memories do not give me that "first word" which I uttered as a child nor even the "first word" I heard from my parents. This lies beyond the horizon of my memory and appears if at all as an already mythical tale related to me by others.

Nothing gives me the "lost" beginning of word spoken by voice either as that which is built up or as that which occurs at a stroke. Nor is there a need for phenomenology to search for such a beginning. If I listen, I may begin in the midst of word for there is a center to my experience of language. It is that strange familiarity which lies in the very conversation which shows things, others, the gods, and myself. *The center of language is located in the voiced and heard sounding of word.* And from this center I may proceed "outwards" toward the horizons of sound and meaning which embody significance within the World.

The voices of the World find response, an "echo," in my own voice which takes up the languages of the World. My "self" is a correlate of the World, and its way of *being-in* that World is a way filled with voice and language. Moreover, this being in the midst of word is such that it permeates the most hidden recesses of my "self." It is for this reason that the more detailed review of the auditory terrain which follows not only moves ever closer to existential significations, it also takes note of a modality of experience so far barely noticed in the first listening to the voices of the World.

To this point the themes which have been followed could be characterized as *monophonic*. It is as if I, the listener, have been primarily a "receiver" of the voices of the World. As experiencer I have not yet spoken, nor have I yet heard all there is to hear. In particular I have not yet paid attention to that second modality of ongoing experience, the *imaginative mode*. With the introduction of a second modality of experience, in addition to what has been the predominantly perceptualist emphasis, listening becomes *polyphonic*. I hear not only the voices of the World, in some sense I "hear" myself or from myself. There is in polyphony a duet of voices in the doubled modalities of perceptual and imaginative modes. A new review of the field of possible auditory experience is called for in which attention would be focused upon the co-presence of the imaginative.

If the first survey weighted perception, it did so in terms of what has been taken as primary in first phenomenology. Yet even within first phenomenology there is also a counter tendency. Husserl elevated imagination as fantasy to the level of the privileged "instrument" for critical phenomenological reflection itself.[2] His paradigm, at least implicitly, was the thinker such as the logician or mathematician who could reconstruct whole "worlds" by himself. But this elevation of the imagination could equally have been properly modeled after literary or poetic or artistic thinking which also surveys the possible.

Husserl's use of imagination, moreover, often revolved around the reproductive or representational capacities of imagination. Here imagination reproduces what was previously perceptual, but in the assumption that it does reproduce the other modes of experience lies a threat to the primacy of the perceptual itself. In imagination, even at the level of variations, there is already an "excess" which carries it beyond perception. Hidden in this "excess" are both certain aspects of "self-presence" and of a fundamental liaison with the World. The "innermost" is *not* distant from the "outermost."

The imaginative mode, to be considered very broadly as ranging from the "empty" supposings to the most concrete "images" of thought, contains within itself the variations of "self-presence" and "thinking" which pose such difficult questions to philosophy. Of course here the primary question of context is one directed to the various forms of auditory imagination. What is it that I "hear" when my listening is to the "second voice," the imaginative voice? What is that listening which occurs within my self-presence and which accompanies the presence of the things and of others in the perceived World? If the "self" arises phenomenologically strictly as a correlate to the World, a correlate which is in a sense discovered only after discovering the World, it also hides within itself and its imaginative acts (which hide themselves from others) a kind of autonomy.

In the auditory dimension the imaginative mode is a matter of "voice" in some sense. Its center, suggested above, may be located in a clue provided in the history of phenomenology by Merleau-Ponty.

In the discussion of the body as expressive, Merleau-Ponty notes that what is usually taken as an inner silence is in fact "filled with words" in the form of what will here be characterized as "inner speech."[3] *Focally, a central form of auditory imagination is thinking as and in a language.* With and around this phenomenon revolve many of the issues which relate to specific human experience and self-experience.

The second survey which begins its investigation of the polyphony of experience binds what is "innermost," the imaginative, with what is also the broadest in human experience, the *intersubjective.* It is the *voices of language* which assume a focal role in human imagination in its auditory dimension.

Initially there is nothing more "obvious" than the familiarity of human speaking and listening. Wherever humankind is found it is found speaking. Through the polymorphic shaping of sound sing innumerable languages. Languages bind together and separate humankind. Otherness and strangeness is dramatic in the difference of tongues, but there is also the human ability to learn to "sing" in any language.

Language also lies in the interior. Inner speech as the hidden monologue of thinking-in-a-language accompanies the daily activities of humans even when they are not speaking to each other. The voices of others whom I hear immerse me in a language which has already penetrated my innermost being in that I "hear" the speech which I stand within. The other and myself are co-implicated in the presence of sounding word.

Phenomenologically I already always stand in this center. The voices of language surround me wherever I turn, and I cannot escape the immersion in language. The voices of language have already penetrated all my experience, and this experience is already always "intersubjective." And if this experience of the omnipresence of language which comes from others and which settles even into the recesses of myself is "like" the experience of surrounding, penetrating, pervasive sound, it is because its ordinary embodiment lies in the listening and speaking which embodies the voices of language. Voice is the spirit of language.

NOTES

1. Martin Heidegger, *Poetry, Language, Thought,* trans. Albert Hofstadter (New York: Harper & Row, 1971), p. 26.
2. Edmund Husserl, *Ideas: General Introduction to Pure Phenomenology,* trans. W.R. Boyce Gibson (New York: Collier Books, 1962), p. 182.
3. Maurice Merleau-Ponty, *Phenomenology of Perception,* trans. Colin Smith (London: Routledge and Kegan Paul, 1962), p. 183.

■
_____

The Outer Word and Inner Speech: Bakhtin, Vygotsky, and the Internalization of Language

Caryl Emerson

Language is no longer linked to the knowing of things but to men's freedom.

Michel Foucault
The Order of Things

In this statement from *The Order of Things*, Michel Foucault speaks of the nineteenth-century revolution in linguistics that, in effect, rediscovered language and made it the object of systematic study in its own right. Language, no longer seen as a transparent medium, was granted "its own particular density . . . and laws of its own."[1] Yet it is not self-evident how we are made more free by understanding that words are not just a repository of knowledge. The density of language is a troublesome postulate. That postulate, according to Foucault, raises difficult epistemological problems and presents theorists with a choice:

> The critical elevation of language, which was a compensation for its subsidence within the object, implied that it had been brought nearer both to an act of knowing, pure of all words, and to the unconscious element in our discourse. It had to be either made transparent to the forms of knowledge, or thrust down into the contents of the unconscious. (*OT*, p. 299)

The debate on the status of language has been enormous and subtle, but it could seem that these two poles described by Foucault remain constantly in effect. Language is, on the one hand, a transparent medium from which to deduce a metalanguage and on which to build statistical and mechanical models, or language is, on the other hand, a product of the individual psyche and ultimately subject to psychic transformation, to what Foucault calls "dim mechanisms, faceless determinations, a whole landscape of shadow" (*OT*, p. 326).

In the twentieth century, these two poles were reevaluated in the light of Ferdinand de Saussure's celebrated binary oppositions: synchrony/diachrony, syntagmatic/paradigmatic, *langue/parole*. Language had moved from the realm of naming to the realm of relationships—a truly revolutionary shift. But as is so often the case with intellectual revolutions, success tended to institutionalize and finalize the new terminology. One of the most productive (and most quickly canonized) distinctions was that between *langue* and *parole*, between the social-collective institution of language (the code) and the individual act of combination and actualization (the message). Not surprisingly, such an unbridged opposition was not congenial to Marxist dialecticians, and in the Soviet Union of the 1920s Saussure's dichotomy stimulated vigorous debate. Literary scholars, philosophers of language, and developmental psychologists all questioned that opposition in their separate disciplines and were concerned to explain the integration of individual with society in a more benevolent way. It became a central issue in clinical psychology, especially in the branch dealing with language acquisition. And it was a lifelong preoccupation for those members of the Bakhtin circle who were especially interested in language: Mikhail Bakhtin, Valentin Volosinov, and Pavel Medvedev. These various groups, it should be emphasized, worked in and with the termological frameworks of their time, including an experimental and open-ended Marxism that stressed process, change, and the interaction between organism and environment. Among the most eloquent contributions to the debate were two books that appeared under Volosinov's name: *Freudianism: A Marxist Critique* (1927) and *Marxism and the Philosophy of Language* (1929).[2] Each in its own way reassessed the two Saussurian poles and attempted a synthesis. The nature of that synthesis, and the light it casts on the interplay between language and consciousness, is the focal point of this essay.

Members of the Bakhtin circle objected in particular to one fundamental aspect of the *langue/parole* schema, namely, its opposition of the social to the individual. Instead of opposition, they spoke of interaction—and warned the while against understanding this interaction in a mechanical and narrowly rational (by which they meant formulaic) way. As Bakhtin defined the problem:

The idea of the *conventionality,* the *arbitrariness of language,* is a typical one for rationalism as a whole, and no less typical is the *comparison of language to the system of mathematical signs.* What interests the mathematically minded rationalists is not the relationship of the sign to the actual reality it reflects nor to the individual who is its originator, but the *relationship of sign to sign within a closed system* already accepted and authorized. In other words, they are interested only in the *inner logic of the system of signs itself,* taken, as in algebra, completely independently of the ideological meanings that give the signs their content. [*MPL,* pp. 57-58]

This insensitivity to "ideological meanings," Bakhtin suggests, is the ultimate danger behind the fascination with the arbitrary nature of the sign. The corrective, in his view, is a proper understanding of the concept of *ideologija.* Its English cognate "ideology" is in some respects unfortunate, for our word suggests something inflexible and propagandistic, something politically unfree. For Bakhtin and his colleagues, it meant simply an "idea system" determined socially, something that *means.* In this sense of the term, all sign systems are ideological, and all ideologies possess semiotic value (see *MPL,* pp. 9-10). But in contrast to Saussure's claim that a verbal sign is ultimately a mental construct—that the acoustic image and the concept are both contained in an arbitrary closed system— the members of the Bakhtin circle posited four *social* factors that make the understanding of speech and writing possible.

First, they assumed that the sign and its effects occur in outer experience. "[In the] chain of ideological creativity and understanding . . . nowhere is there a break in the chain, nowhere does the chain plunge in to inner being, nonmaterial in nature and unembodied in signs" (*MPL* p. 11). Each ideological product is meaningful not in the soul but in the objectively accessible ideological material.

Second, this outer experience, if it is to register significance, must in some way be organized socially. Signs "can arise only on *interindividual territory.*" But this territory "cannot be called 'natural' in the direct sense of the word: signs do not arise between any two members of the species *Homo sapiens.* It is essential that the two individuals . . . compose a group (a social unit); only then can the medium of signs take shape between them" (*MPL,* p. 12). A social unit is therefore an indispensable aspect of semiotic activity—and for this reason the study of ideologies cannot be grounded in individual psychology. Far from positing a Saussurian tension between society and the individual, Bakhtin posits an individual who actively creates the society in which his discourse occurs. The whole tradition opposing individual to society is misguided: an individual person is simply one biological specimen in a group (see *MPL,* p. 34).

Third, the ideologies that are generated by the material reality of language must be studied *inter*-systemically, not as independent and isolated phenomena. That is, ideology always exists as a relation between (or among) speakers and listeners and, by extension, between or among social groups. According to Bakhtin, each social group—each class, profession, generation, religion, region—has its own characteristic way of speaking, its own dialect. Each dialect reflects and embodies a set of values and a sense of shared experience. Because no two individuals ever entirely coincide in their experience or belong to precisely the same set of social groups, every act of understanding involves an act of translation and a negotiation of values. It is essentially a phenomenon of interrelation and interaction.[3]

Fourth and last, Bakhtin profoundly redefined the Word itself and attempted to infuse it with its original Greek sense of *logos* ("discourse"). For Bakhtin, words cannot be conceived apart from the voices who speak them; thus, every word raises the question of authority. Fully half of *Marxism and the Philosophy of Language* is devoted to an investigation of "indirect" and "quasi-direct" discourse, multileveled speech acts in which more than one voice participates. For Bakhtin, words come not out of dictionaries but out of concrete dialogic situations. He saw the distinction between dialogic words—that is, utterances—and dictionary words as one between *theme* and *meaning.*

> Theme is the *upper, actual limit of linguistic significance,* in essence, only theme means something definite. Meaning is the *lower limit* of linguistic significance. Meaning, in essence, means nothing; it only possesses potentiality—the possibility of having a meaning within a concrete theme. [*MPL*, p. 101]

Words in discourse always recall earlier contexts of usage, otherwise they could not mean at all. It follows that *every* utterance, covertly or overtly, is an act of indirect discourse.

These, then, are the amendments the Bakhtin circle would attach to Saussure: the sign is external, organized socially, concretely historical, and, as the Word, inseparably linked with voice and authority. These four dialectical alterations work a great change in the original distinction between *langue* and *parole.* Bakhtin deals with this dichotomy (in somewhat expanded form) in his discussion of the twin sins of "abstract objectivism" and "individualistic subjectivism" (see *MPL*, pp. 47-63). Abstract objectivism can be seen as the Cartesian extreme, language taken as a code independent of its interpreters. This is an excess to which the Neogrammarians were prone, the myth that language makes poets. Individualistic subjectivism, on the other hand, is the Humboldtian extreme, embodied for Bakhtin in the Vosslerites. They are faulted for grounding the message too exclusively in the individual psyche—thus giving rise to the myth that poets make language. Bakhtin himself does not deny the two poles. But he would synthesize them, and he claims that their opposition in real life, at any given moment, is a fiction. In the Bakhtinian model, every individual engages in two perpendicular activities. He forms lateral ("horizontal") relationships with other individuals in specific speech acts, and he simultaneously forms internal ("vertical") relationships between the outer world and his own psyche. These double activities are constant, and their interactions in fact *constitute* the psyche. The psyche is thus not an internal but a boundary phenomenon. Or to use Bakhtin's political metaphor, the psyche "enjoys extraterritorial status . . . [as] a social entity—that penetrates inside the organism of the individual person" (*MPL*, p. 39).

This concept of the psyche is indeed radical. The assumption that the psyche is, at its base, a "social entity," a space to be filled with ideological signs, sets the Bakhtinian concept of consciousness at odds with much of Western thinking since Freud on the subject. In his remarkable descriptions of the transitions from "social intercourse" to "outer speech," and from "outer speech" to "inner speech" and to consciousness, Bakhtin fundamentally rethinks both the relation of consciousness to the world around it and the relation of the self to others. We read that a poet's style "is engendered from the style of his inner speech, which does not lend itself to control, and his inner speech is itself the product of his entire social life."[4] And in *Marxism and the Philosophy of Language* we read:

> Although the reality of the word, as is true of any sign, resides between individuals, a word, at the same time, is produced by the individual organism's own means without recourse to any equipment or any other kind of extracorporeal material. This has determined the role of [the] word as *the semiotic material of inner life—of consciousness* (inner speech). [*MPL*, p. 14]

When so firmly tied to outer experience, this tripartite equation of inner life = inner speech = consciousness is quite audacious. "People do not 'accept' their native language," Bakhtin insists; "it is in their native language that they first reach awareness" (*MPL*, p. 81). Individuation of the personality is the process of a consciousness working over the "ideological themes" that penetrate it "and there take on the semblance of individual accents" (*MPL*, p. 22). Indeed, a clear distinction between inner and outer speech is impossible, because the very act of introspection is modeled on external social discourse: it is self-observation, communion with the self, "the understanding of one's own inner sign" (*MPL*, p. 36). Thus, the problem of origins in personality is in fact no problem at all, and there is likewise no problem of self-expression:

Not only can experience be outwardly expressed through the agency of the sign . . .
but also, aside from this outward expression (for others), experience
exists even for the person undergoing it only in the material of signs.
Outside that material there is no experience as such. In this sense any
experience is expressible, i.e., is potential expression . . . .

Thus there is no leap involved between inner experience and its
expression, no crossing over from one qualitative realm of reality to
another. [*MPL*, p. 28]

Individual consciousness is a socio-ideological fact. If you cannot talk
about an experience, at least to yourself, you did not have it.

A person's experiences exist "encoded in his inner speech"
(*MPL*, p. 118). Thus the word, Bakhtin affirms, "constitutes the foundation, the skeleton of inner life. Were it to be deprived of the word, the
psyche would shrink to an extreme degree" (*MPL*, p. 29). Purely private,
speechless, isolated experience—the realm of the mystic, the visionary—is
essentially impossible *as experience*. It can only be viewed as erratic, as
something bordering on the pathological. Experience that "lacks a socially grounded and stable audience" cannot "take firm root and will not
receive differentiated and full-fledged expression" (*MPL*, p. 92).

Bakhtin would say, therefore, that we evolve the mechanisms to
express that which our environment makes available for us to experience.
At any given time the fit between self and society may not be perfect, indeed
cannot be perfect, but the mechanisms are always present to engage self
and society in dialogue. In such a model of reality, there is no room for—
and perhaps no conceptual possibility of—an independent unconscious.

Bakhtin develops this argument in his polemical work
Freudianism: A Marxist Critique. For Bakhtin, the teachings of Freud represent a debasing of that already discredited extreme, individualistic subjectivism. As Western culture declines and its social fabric disintegrates,
Freud's star rises. Bakhtin opens his "critical sketch" (see n. 2) on this
comment, and it is no accident: Freudianism is analyzed here not as a
viable scientific theory but as a social symptom. Psychoanalysis saves bour-
geois man by taking him out of history, by explaining him to himself not
as a concrete social entity but as an "abstract biological organism."
According to Bakhtin, Freud would have us everywhere seek the answers
within; we forget the social crisis and "take refuge in the organic warmth
of the animal side of life" (*Fr*, p. 11). The "ideological motif of
Freudianism" is an emphasis on *sex* and *age*, common motifs, Bakhtin
claims, in eras of crisis and decline, when nature (especially "human
nature," in the form of biological drives) is seen as all-powerful and history is seen as impotent (*Fr*, p. 11).

It need hardly be pointed out that Bakhtin is very selective in his
reading of Freud. Nowhere does he engage Freud's most provocative

works, the great sociopsychological essays of the war years and the 1920s. In those works Bakhtin would have found a more complex opponent and, at times, an uncomfortable ally. But it was precisely the early clinical Freud, and his pioneering assumptions and methods of psychoanalysis, that posed a challenge to the Bakhtinian model for perceiving and assimilating reality. Those assumptions and methods had to be confronted. In Bakhtin's model, phenomena originate in the external material world, as do the means to express them. The "unconscious," that is, the part of ourselves that is outside our control and awareness, is best comprehended as merely that portion of the conscious not yet articulate—an "unofficial conscious," if you will, or perhaps a struggle among various motives and voices within the conscious (*Fr*, pp. 76, 85). According to Bakhtin, Freud's projection of autonomous drives and nonnegotiable demands is mere "psychologization of the somatic" (*Fr*, p. 71). It follows that the forces of id and ego that emerge so colorfully during psychoanalysis are not repressed inner realities in the process of discharge but reflections of overt social dynamics, including those between doctor and patient (see *Fr*, p. 79). For Bakhtin, in short, the unconscious in the Freudian sense is a myth—and it functions in society as Roland Barthes has claimed all contemporary myths function: "Semiology has taught us that myth has the task of giving an historical intention a natural justification, and making contingency appear eternal."[5] This evasion of history and the social process is the real sin of the "mythical" unconscious. Eliminate time and society, and a structure cannot be modified. It can only be satisfied or repressed.

Bakhtin's model had to account for the phenomena Freud had observed but do it differently. An alternative system of explanation would have to provide, through experimental work and clinical documentation, specific answers to the key psychological question: How precisely does environment impress a personality, how do outer words become inner speech? One remarkable scholar committed to this project was Bakhtin's contemporary Lev Vygotsky—a man comparable to Bakhtin in productivity and interdisciplinary brilliance. Vygotsky's final work, *Thought and Language* (1934), supplemented by his essays of the 1930s, can be read as an important predecessor and perhaps even as clinical underpinning to Bakhtin's philosophy of language.[6] Soviet scholars such as Vyacheslav Ivanov have made this connection explicitly in discussions of Bakhtin's contribution to semiotics.[7]

It must be said at the outset that this interaction between Bakhtin and Vygotsky is somewhat hypothetical, although none the less intriguing for that. There is no direct evidence that Bakhtin and Vygotsky ever met, and Vygotsky makes no reference to Bakhtin in his work.[8] Interest in dialogic relations and the social context of speech was, of course, rather widespread in the 1920s; both men doubtless pulled upon and were pulled by many of the same social and scholarly currents. Where Bakhtin and Vygotsky intersect is not on the plane of their actual texts, that is, not in the reality of a cross-reference, but in the ultimate implications of their thought. It is this projected intersection that I will now discuss.

Vygotsky's initial inquiry was very similar to that of the Bakhtin circle. Could not the unsatisfactory stalemate between individualistic subjectivism and abstract objectivism—or, as Vygotsky casts the opposition, between idealist and behaviorist psychology—be resolved with a dynamic synthesis focusing on the concrete speech act itself? At both those extremes, the loser had been time: "Whether inclining toward pure naturalism or extreme idealism, all these theories have one trait in common—their antihistorical bias" (*TL*, p. 153). Time, Vygotsky argues, had long been misunderstood and misapplied in the psychological sciences. The development of the child had once been described in terms of botanical models (maturation, "kindergarten") and then in terms of zoological models (the performance of animals under laboratory conditions), but in Vygotsky's view it is precisely what can*not* be learned from plants and lower animals, namely, the uniquely human assimilation and production of language, that psychologists should examine.[9] Language is man's greatest tool; and so it should be seen precisely as a tool, that is, as a means for communicating with and extracting from the outside world. So viewed, language offers special problems to the psychologist. For if language is always a means of interaction with the world, it is perilous to study it in isolated environments or in *traditional* controlled experiments. Vygotsky replaced those conventional locales of science with much looser "task situations," which involved putting subjects in confrontation with real problems in a real social setting.[10] Vygotsky's distrust of the classic psychological experiment (what he derisively called the "stimulus-response framework") should in fact recall Bakhtin's distrust of the classic linguistic model, with its ideal speaker and ideal (or nonexistent) listener. Both were suspicious of modeling, for both insisted that only the concrete historical event could validate a human communication or lead to an act of learning.

Vygotsky created for himself a powerful clinical tool out of two convictions: that psychological events must be studied in history and that external society is the starting point of consciousness. The two are closely allied, for whatever we can perceive in outer reality, we can change, or try to change, through time. In ingenious experiments, Vygotsky extended (and then modified or rejected) the language-learning maps offered by Jean Piaget, William Stern, and Freud. His primary target was Piaget's "egocentric thought," a stage Piaget claimed is intermediate between autistic play and directed (that is, reality-oriented) thought. Piaget had assumed that a child's thought was originally autistic and became realistic only under social pressure; visible here is the direct impress of Freud's pleasure principle and reality principle. Vygotsky was unsympathetic to the idea that an individual is reluctant to adjust to its environment, that reality, work, and social intercourse are somehow not pleasurable." In order to test the opposite assumption, Vygotsky conducted the experiments described in *Thought and Language*—and created his own scenario for language acquisition.

According to this scenario, the child's first efforts at perception result in an isolation of word meanings—but "meanings" only in the sense of verbal stimuli, functioning in context as signals rather than as proper signs.[11] A child cannot translate much of the speech he hears into his rudimentary "signal systems," because the ability to generalize comes slowly. Until the age of two years, language serves the human child much as a thirty-two-"word" vocabulary serves the chimpanzee throughout its life: words—or, better, vocalizations—are purely emotional; they coincide with gestures but exclude any simultaneous intellectual activity. The child passes out of this chimpanzoid stage when he begins to ask for the names of objects, and at this point one of the critical moments in human maturation occurs: "Thought becomes verbal and speech [becomes] rational" (*TL*, p. 44). Vygotsky could not define the precise mechanism linking overt to inner speech, but he assumed—and this, of course, is the crucial point—that this process followed the same course and obeyed the same laws as did other operations involving signs. External experiments could be devised to monitor and refine the seepage between levels.

To this end, Vygotsky isolated four stages of "internalization": the natural or pre-intellectual stage, the stage of naive psychology, the stage of egocentric speech, and the so-called ingrowth stage. The third stage, egocentric speech, was the most conducive to analysis in task situations. Uncomfortable with Piaget's conclusion that this speech is fantasy-talk and generated asocially, Vygotsky ran a series of experiments designed to socialize and complicate the child's environment at precisely the age when the child "talked to himself." He demonstrated that a child talks twice as much when presented with obstacles (see *TL*, pp. 16-17) and that this externalized "conversation with oneself," commenting on and predicting the results of an action, is in fact the natural dynamic of problem solving (see "*TS*," pp. 24-26).[12] Furthermore, this talk turned out to be extremely sensitive to social factors. Piaget had observed similar phenomena: that egocentric speech occurs only in a social context, that the child assumes he is being understood by others, and that such speech is not whispered or abbreviated but spoken as an utterance, that is, as public speech in a specific environment. Vygotsky accepted this data but then devised experiments to detach it from Piaget's conclusions.

When Vygotsky varied the social factors—by isolating the child, placing him with deaf-mutes, putting him to play in a room filled with deafening music—it was found that egocentric speech dropped drastically, to one-fifth its previous rate (see *TL*, pp. 136-37). Vygotsky concluded that egocentric speech was not, as Piaget had suggested, a compromise between primary autism and reluctant socialization but rather the direct outgrowth (or, better, ingrowth) of speech which had been from the start socially and environmentally oriented. Piaget was correct when he observed that private and socialized speech did indeed intersect at this stage. Development, however, was proceeding not along the lines of Piaget's scenario but in the opposite direction. The child was not externalizing his internal thoughts but internalizing his external verbal interactions. That was why egocentric speech is relatively accessible in three-year-olds but quite inscrutable in seven-year-olds: the older the child, the more thoroughly has his thought become inner speech (see TL, p. 134). "Development in thinking," Vygotsky concludes, "is not from the individual to the socialized, but from the social to the individual" (TL, p. 20).

Like Bakhtin, Vygotsky offers us a restructuring of the Saussurian dichotomy. In Vygotsky's model of language acquisition, a child's first speech is social; words evoke specific responses and must be reinforced by adults. Only gradually does language assume the role of a "second signal system," that is, become for the child an indirect way of affecting his environment. When it does, his speech differentiates into two separate though interlocking systems: one continues to adjust to the external world and emerges as adult social speech; the other system begins to "internalize" and becomes by degrees a personal language, greatly abbreviated and predicative (see "TS," pp. 27-28). In this inner speech the sense of a word—a "dynamic, fluid, complex whole"—takes predominance over a word's meaning.[13]

When internalization begins, egocentric speech drops off. The child becomes, as it were, his own best interlocutor. Crucial to this process, however, is the presence of a challenging verbal and physical environment. The descriptive "monologue" of which egocentric speech is composed can be internalized creatively only if questioned and challenged by outside voices. In this way alone is intelligence possible, "intelligence" defined not as an "accumulation of already mastered skills" but as a "dialogue with one's own future and an address to the external world." It should come as no surprise that Vygotsky was unsympathetic to the standard intelligence test, which measured (in a competitive and isolated context) prior achievement and punished children for "cheating." A true test of intelligence, Vygotsky argued, was one that posited problems beyond the capacity of the child to solve and then made help available. How a child seeks help, how he utilizes his environment, how he asks questions of others—all these constitute the child's "zone of proximal development," where all true learning occurs (TL, p. 103). Intelligence is a *social* category.[14]

Speech and behavior interact dynamically in a child's development. First, speech accompanies action, then precedes it, finally displaces it—that is, speech assumes the planning function so essential for the higher mental processes (see "TS," pp. 27-28). Just as children outgrow the need to count on their fingers or memorize by means of mnemonic devices, so do they outgrow the need to vocalize their activities. This final stage of speech development, the ingrowth stage, coincides with the appearance of logical memory, hypothesis-formation, and other mature mental processes.

Vygotsky does not, however, claim a one-to-one fit between thought and speech. There is speech without thought, as in chimpanzees and infants; there is also thought without speech. The two areas overlap in "verbal thought," and this is coincident with language (see *TL*, pp. 47-48). Since we can share only what we articulate and communicate, it is this linguistic dimension alone that has historical validity. In this respect, Vygotsky seems somewhat more modest than Bakhtin, who suggests more strongly that experience can be given absolute expression—inwardly to oneself, outwardly to others—through the word.

For Vygotsky, the Word is a powerful amalgam: part sign, part tool, it is *the* significant humanizing event.[15] One makes a self through the words one has learned, fashions one's own voice and inner speech by a selective appropriation of the voices of others. It would obviously be of great interest to know how this process of self-fashioning takes place. Here we can turn to Bakhtin, to an essay from the 1930s and thus contemporary with Vygotsky's last writings.[16] In this essay Bakhtin mentions two ways of assimilating the words of others. Each plays its own part in shaping the process of inner speech, and each has a ready analogue in the way schoolchildren are asked to learn texts. One may "recite by heart" or "retell it in one's own words." In reciting, the language of others is authoritative: it is distanced, taboo, and there can be no play with the framing context. One cannot even entertain the possibility of doubting it; so one cannot enter into dialogue with it. To change a word in a recitation is to make a mistake. The power of this kind of language, however, has its corresponding cost: once discredited, it becomes a relic, a dead thing. Retelling in one's own words, on the other hand, is a more flexible and responsive process. It is the only way we can *originate* anything verbally. In retelling, Bakhtin argues, one arrives at "internally persuasive" discourse—which, in his view, is as close as anything can come to being totally our own. The struggle within us between these two modes of discourse, the authoritative and the internally persuasive, is what we recognize as intellectual and moral growth.

Both Bakhtin and Vygotsky, as we have seen, responded directly or indirectly to the challenge of Freud. Both attempted to account for their data without resorting to postulating an unconscious in the Freudian sense. By way of contrast, it is instructive here to recall Jacques Lacan—who, among others, has been a beneficiary of Bakhtin's "semiotic reinterpretation" of Freud.[17] Lacan's case is intriguing, for he retains the unconscious while at the same time submitting Freudian psychoanalysis to rigorous criticism along the lines of Bakhtin. By focusing attention on the dialogic word, he encourages a rereading of Freud in which the social element (the dynamics between doctor and patient) is crucial. As Lacan opens his essay "The Empty Word and the Full Word":

> Whether it sees itself as an instrument of healing, of formation, or of exploration in depth, psychoanalysis has only a single intermediary: the patient's Word. . . . And every word calls for a reply.
>
> I shall show that there is no word without a reply, even if it meets no more than silence, provided that it has an auditor: this is the heart of its function in psychoanalysis.[18]

The word is conceived as a tool not only of the external world but also of an autonomous internal world as well. And what emerges, it would seem, is a reinterpretation of the role of dialogue in the painful maturational processes of the child. For Vygotsky, the child's realization of his separateness from society is not a crisis; after all, his environment provides both the form and the content of his personality. From the start, dialogue reinforces the child's grasp on reality, as evidenced by the predominantly social and extroverted nature of his earliest egocentric speech. For Lacan, on the contrary, dialogue seems to function as *the* alienating experience, the *stade du miroir* phase of a child's development. The unconscious becomes the seat of all those problems that Bakhtin had externalized: the origin of personality, the possibilities of self-expression. The *je-moi* opposition in the mirror gives rise to that permanent hunger for "a locus where there is constituted the *je* which speaks as well as he who has it speak."[19] And consequently, the Word takes on an entirely different coloration: it is no longer merely an ideological sign but a potent tool for repressing knowledge of that gap, the face in the mirror, the Other. Lacan's celebrated inversion of Saussure's algorithm, with the line between signifier and signified representing repression, created a powerful but ominous new role for language. The child is released from his alienating image only through discovering himself as Subject, which occurs with language; but this language will inevitably come to him from the Other. Thus, speech is based on the idea of lack, and dialogue, on the idea of difference.

Here the contrast with the Bakhtin circle is especially fruitful, for dialogue between inner and outer speech is central to both approaches. In each case, the gap between inner and outer can be a cause of pain: in Lacan it is the pain of desire, in Bakhtin, the pain of inarticulateness.[20] But Bakhtin defines "the *strife*, the *chaos*, the *adversity* of our psychical life" as conflicts of motives *within* the conscious sphere (albeit an expanded conscious sphere) and this retains for the Word an objective role in a historically concrete context (*Fr*, p. 75). He does not deny the reality of internal conflicts, but he does socialize them, thus exposing their mechanisms to the light of day. If enough individuals experience the same gap, it is re-socialized: there develops a political underground, and the potential for revolution (see, *Fr*, pp. 89-90).

Thus, we see that alienation, if it is to survive at all, must be externalized—at which point it can become the basis for collective rebellion, or for a new dynamic community. One can never, it seems, be existentially alone. In fact, the very concept of solitude is a fiction—or, rather, it is a paradox. When in 1961 Bakhtin returned to his 1929 study of Dostoevsky (then scheduled for republication), he jotted down an eloquent series of thoughts on this question of solitude:

> No Nirvana is possible for a *single* consciousness. A single consciousness is a contradiction in terms. Consciousness is essentially multiple.
>
> I am conscious of myself and become myself only while revealing myself for another, through another, and with the help of another. . .
>
> Separation, dissociation, and enclosure within the self as the main reason for the loss of one's self. Not that which takes place within, but that which takes place on the *boundary* between one's own and someone else's consciousness, on the *threshold*. . . . Thus does Dostoevsky confront all decadent and idealistic (individualistic) culture, the culture of essential and inescapable solitude. He asserts the impossibility of solitude, the illusory nature of solitude. The very being of man (both external and internal) is the *deepest communion. To be* means *to communicate.* . . . To be means to be for another, and through the other, for oneself.[21]

This passage is in part the product of that deep meditation on Christianity that occupied Bakhtin all his life.[22] But it is also an integral part of his philosophy of language. In a world beset with the existential image of no exit, this insistence on community, on true social-ism, gives the Bakhtin circle an aura of almost old-fashioned coziness in an insecure age.[23]

In the Russian model, inner speech is thus a benevolent quantity, a "unique form of collaboration with oneself."[24] Lacan, as we have seen, also depends on the Word to discharge the negative potential of the gap between self and society. But as part of the Freudian model, this word is only with great difficulty available for "collaboration." It is potentially neurotic, the proof of that permanent gap between objectification and identification. It can be mediated only through that structure whose presumed presence makes it possible to pose (and solve) the problem at all: the unconscious. In Lacan, language is a means of expressing the inexpressible. For Bakhtin and Vygotsky, there is, in essence, no inexpressible. In Lacan's world, therefore, the Word is a tool of psychoanalysis. For Bakhtin and Vygotsky, it is a tool of pedagogy.

* * *

The gap between self and society has been, of course, a theme not only of modern linguistics but also of the modern study of literary genres. We may recall that George Lukács defines the epic as a genre embodying the absence of such a gap, as the product of "integrated civilisations" where there "is not yet any interiority, for there is not yet any exterior, any 'otherness' for the soul."[25] Invoking a rather primitive Marxism, Lukács also defines the novel as the opposite extreme: for him, the novel is the product of a fragmented world, a world in which the interior not only exists but is also maximally at odds with the exterior. It would appear that Lukács needed to posit a time when there was no gap between self and society so that he might better describe by contrast the world in which, he thought, we now live.

Two decades after Lukács, Bakhtin addressed the issue of epic and novel in an essay that borrowed some of Lukács' terminology but reversed almost entirely its ethical charge.[26] For Bakhtin, the healthy individual *in life* is the one who can surmount—not deny—the gap, who can break down the barriers between inner and outer; likewise, the healthy *artistic genre* is the one that guarantees a *non*-coincidence between hero and environment. The gap so lamented by Lukács is seen, in Bakhtin's "Epic and Novel," as the beginning of dialogue, of temporal development, and of consciousness. The fullest realization of all three is the novel. For Bakhtin, then, the novel-epic distinction, though historically instantiated, is really trans-historical, a relationship between different *perceived qualities of time*—or, as he would say, "chronotopes"—whenever in history they might occur. When he describes the epic narrative as taking place in an "absolute past" and novel time as truly novel, he is really drawing an ontological distinction. He is speaking of temporal types that are always potential: whenever we talk about a world that does not know time, we are "epicking."

And whenever we talk about a world that fully experiences time, we are "noveling." The novel is alienated from epic wholeness. What results in Bakhtin's construct, however, is not loneliness but freedom. Specifically, characters in novels experience the freedom to be more than their roles in given stories. The epic hero, by contrast, is inseparable from his plot; there is only one way his life could be lived.

> Neither an epic nor a tragic hero could ever step out in his own character during a pause in the plot or during an intermission: he has no face for it, no gesture, no language. In this is his strength and his limitation. The epic and tragic hero is the hero who, by his very nature, must perish. ["EN," p. 36]

Novelistic heroes, on the other hand, are like medieval fools on stage: their roles are temporary, their masks are not their selves. "These are heroes of free improvisation and not heroes of tradition, heroes of a life process that is imperishable and forever renewing itself, forever contemporary—these are not heroes of an absolute past" ("EN," p. 36). A novelistic hero always has a "surplus of humanness" that is not embodied in his biography: thus "there always remains in him unrealized potential and unrealized demands. . . . There always remains a need for the future, and a place for this future must be found. All existing clothes are always too tight, and thus comical, on a man" ("EN," p. 37). When we think away his roles, there is something left: that reminder, that non-coincidence of self and social categories, that capacity to change into different clothes, is freedom.

Novelists rejoice in subjects that are homeless, that is, free to develop. Novels also grant freedom for the *author* to develop, which is to say, freedom for the author to play with his own image on the plane of his own work. The reader (or, for that matter, the creator) of the *Iliad* cannot imagine himself chatting with Hector on the walls of Troy; epic heroes need neither audience nor author. But the writer of novels has an implicated voice. He can enter and manipulate, fuse or distribute his voice among characters. Or he can—and this requires an extra measure of commitment to freedom—grant autonomy to his characters; he can create not just objects but full-fledged *subjects.* This was the "Copernican revolution" that Bakhtin had, in 1929, attributed to Dostoevsky. In Dostoevsky's novels, the author is no longer the creator around whom characters are forced to revolve but is, so to speak, himself but a planet among planets. By the end of his life, Bakhtin had come to see this freedom as characteristic of all true novels. Or to put the point another way, he had come to see the force of "novelness" as the guarantee of freedom.

*   *   *

These, then, are the ways an awareness of the gap between inner and outer might function in both life and literature: as an index of individual consciousness, as a measure of our escape from fixed plots and roles, as a prerequisite for discourse itself. What now remains is for us to return to Foucault's statement that language, de-privileged, is an instrument of man's freedom. In light of this discussion, we can understand this freedom two ways, both valid and both linked to the persistent dichotomy between *langue* and *parole*, between the code and the message.

One way of understanding this freedom can be found in a passage from *The Order of Things* which argues that literature as such could emerge only when language was deprived of privilege and thus made self-conscious (see, *OT*, pp. 299-300). This being so, the purpose of literature could be seen as the preserving, and perhaps even the widening, of this self-consciousness. Through the artistic word we learn who we are. And that knowledge could be harnessed to utilitarian purposes, including, for example, the purpose Freud in "The Relation of the Poet to Day-Dreaming" attributes to literature. In that essay, Freud discusses poetry as a sort of fantasy-play for adults and suggests that our appetite for art has at its base the desire to discharge guilt for such indulgence in play: "The true enjoyment of literature proceeds from the release of tensions in our minds."[27] Literature thus serves as a psychic safety valve, much as, in the Aristotelian view, catharsis serves as a social safety valve. In his role as psychoanalyst, Lacan would probably agree with Freud. If the acoustic image is defined as the repressor of the concept, then human neuroses can be released through, and only through, their identification in the Word. Words have a purpose and a function: they are a code, they can pin down. Definition implies release, and therefore freedom.

In contrast, we might consider Freud's essay as Vygotsky treats it in "Art and Psychoanalysis," a chapter from his early work *The Psychology of Art*. In opposing what he considers a reduction of art, Vygotsky argues that Freud left largely unexplained the effects of the artwork on the audience. Moreover, Vygotsky contends, "such an interpretation of art reduces its social role; art begins to appear as an antidote whose task it is to save mankind from vice, but which has no positive tasks or purposes for man's psyche."[28] Vygotsky began his career as a teacher of literature. The affinities among language, literature, and psychology were never far from his mind, and in studying all three he raised the same question: How might man be kept from closing in on his self? One answer he gives is that we learn, through the word, who we are *not*, who we might yet become. It is precisely this positive task—not identification but liberation—that is taken up by Foucault and by such philosophers of language as Paul de Man. In the modern era, Foucault writes in *The Order of Things*,

> the name ceases to be the reward of language; it becomes instead its enigmatic raw material.
>
> This proper being of language is what the nineteenth century was to call the Word (*le Verbe*), as opposed to the Classical "verb," whose function is to pin language, discreetly but continuously, to the being of representation. And the discourse that contains this being and frees it for its own sake is literature. [*OT*, pp. 118, 119]

The same sentiments are echoed by de Man:

> Here, consciousness does not result from the absence of something, but consists of the presence of a nothingness. Poetic language names this void with ever-renewed understanding and . . . it never tires of naming it again. This persistent naming is what we call literature.[29]

The eternal and inevitable inadequacy of all names permits new meanings to happen and new messages to be created. This permission—or intermission—is Bakhtin's novelistic gap, which not even the author can (nor should wish to) bridge. And it is the lack, the absence at the center, that keeps the outer word and our inner speech in permanent dialogue, out of that danger Bakhtin saw of collapse into single consciousness, which would be non-existence. Inside that gap, it is always worthwhile to try naming it again.

ENDNOTES

1. Michel Foucault, *The Order of Things: An Archaeology of the Human Sciences* (New York, 1973), p. 296; all further references to this work, abbreviated OT, will be included parenthetically in the text.

2. See V.N. Volosinov, *Freudianism: A Marxist Critique*, ed. in collaboration with Neal H. Bruss, trans. I.R. Titunik (New York, 1976); all further references to this work, abbreviated *Fr*, will be included parenthetically in the text. The title has been translated in an unnecessarily misleading way; the Russian is simply *Frejdizm: kriticeskij ocerk* [Freudianism: a critical sketch]. And see Volosinov, *Marxism and the Philosophy of Language*, trans. Ladislav Matejka and Titunik, *Studies in Language*, vol. 1 (New York, 1973); all further references to this work, abbreviated *MPL*, will be included parenthetically in the text. Volosinov's authorship of these two texts is disputed: there is evidence that Mikhail Bakhtin wrote them both, or substantial portions of both. The collaboration between the two men was, at any rate, very close. In the text of this article, I refer to Bakhtin as the author of both works.

3. For a clear and provocative discussion of this aspect of Bakhtin's work, see Gary Saul Morson, "The Heresiarch of *Meta*," *PTL* 3 (Oct. 1979): 407-27. In a note written near the end of his life, Bakhtin emphasized the necessity of difference in any act of understanding: "Understanding cannot be understood as emotional empathy, or as the placing of oneself in another's place (the loss of one's own place). This is required only for the peripheral aspects of understanding. Understanding cannot be understood as translation from someone else's language into one's own language" ("Iz zapisei 1970-1971 godov," *Estetika slovesnogo tvorcestva* [Moscow, 1979], p. 346; my translation). Even understanding, itself, is a threshold phenomenon.

The Tartu school of Soviet semioticians has been very creative with Bakhtinian concepts, which it recognizes as complementary to its own work. For an extension of Bakhtin's insights into the micro-dynamics of the psyche, see Iu. M. Lotman, "On the Reduction and Unfolding of Sign Systems (The Problem of 'Freudianism and Semiotic Culturology')," in *Semiotics and Structuralism: Readings from the Soviet Union*, ed. Henryk Baran (White Plains, N.Y., 1976), pp. 301-9. For an extension of Bakhtin's insights into the macro-dynamics of history, see B.A. Uspenskii, "Historia sub Specie Semioticae," in *Semiotics and Structuralism*, pp. 64-75.

4. Volosinov, "Discourse in Life and Discourse in Art (Concerning Sociological Poetics)," appendix 1, Fr, p. 114.

5. Roland Barthes, "Myth Today," *Mythologies*, trans. Annette Lavers (New York, 1972), p. 142.

6. See L. S. Vygotsky, *Thought and Language*, ed. and trans. Eugenia Hanfmann and Gertrude Vakar (Cambridge, Mass., 1962); all further references to this work, abbreviated *TL*, will be included parenthetically in the text. A more precise translation of the work's title, *Myslenie i rec*, would be "Thinking and Speech": the thinking is specifically a process and not a product, and the language is *uttered*.

An edited selection of Vygotsky's essays has been published in English, with two excellent explanatory essays, as Vygotsky, *Mind in Society: The Development of Higher Psychological Processes*, ed. Michael Cole et al. (Cambridge, Mass., 1978).

7. See Viach. Vs. Ivanov, "The Significance of M.M. Bakhtin's Ideas on Sign, Utterance, and Dialogue for Modern Semiotics (1)," in *Semiotics and Structuralism*, pp. 310-67. I should point out, however, that Ivanov makes very wide claims for Bakhtin's influence; in certain of his cases, parallel development would be a more reasonable hypothesis.

8. For this information I am grateful to James V. Werstch of Chicago's Center for Psychosocial Studies, who read this manuscript and made a number of very astute and helpful suggestions. It is his conviction that Vygotsky's ideas about dialogue are less influenced by Bakhtin than by the formalist linguist Lev Yakubinsky, whose 1923 essay "On Dialogic Speech" Vygotsky does cite (see L. P. Iakubinskij [Lev Yakubinsky], "O dialogiceskoi reci," in *Russkaja rec*, ed. L.V. Scerba [Petrograd, 1923]). In this essay, Yakubinsky advises those who study "practical language" to investigate first the seminal distinction between monologic and dialogic speech (or, better, dialogic processes). Dialogue, he claims, is the prior and more natural form, while monologue requires an artificial structure. Yakubinsky also argues (as Bakhtin does) that dialogue does not depend solely on words: shared context, intonation, visual stimuli are all also powerful carriers of a message.

There are certainly areas of overlap in the thinking of Bakhtin,

Yakubinsky, and Vygotsky on the question of dialogic speech. But Yakubinsky's treatment remains rather naive. For a comprehensive discussion of the Vygotsky-Yakubinsky connection, see chapter 4, "The Semiotic Mediation of Human Activity," from Wertsch's forthcoming study, *Cognitive Developmental Theory: A Vygotskian Approach.* I thank its author for generously sharing with me a draft of this chapter.

9. See Vygotsky, "Tool and Symbol in Child Development," *Mind in Society,* pp. 19-20; all further references to this work, abbreviated "TS," will be included parenthetically in the text.

10. See Vygotsky, "Problems of Method," *Mind in Society,* pp. 58-69.

11. "Signals" and "signal systems" are basic concepts in the Russian school of psychology. The school traces its fundamental assumptions and terminology to Ivan Pavlov and, in particular, to two physiological laws which were worked out for lower animals and then extended to man. The first law provides that all learning is conditional (*uslovnyj*, usually mistranslated into English as "conditioned," as in the phrase "uslovnyj refleks"). In a human context, this means that learning is basically not intuitive but environmental. The second law posits a "second signal system," a derivation and extension of classical conditioning. According to Pavlov, speech introduces a new principle into nervous activity: the ability to abstract and generalize signals from the environment. Whereas animals develop at most a "primary signal system" that links concrete stimuli and visual relationships, speech provides man with a second level of links, by which we inhibit direct impulses and project ourselves in time and space. Through language, man knows time. We can control the strength of stimuli on our senses and thereby modify the rule of force by which all organisms are bound. Thus, man assumes conscious control over his behavior when the word becomes, in Pavlov's terms, a "signal of signals." For a helpful discussion, see Alexander R. Luria, *The Role of Speech in the Regulation of Normal and Abnormal Behavior,* ed. J. Tizard (New York, 1961), pp. 20-42. See also Stephen Toulmin's summary in his excellent review of Vygotsky' work: "The Mozart of Psychology," *New York Review of Books,* 28 Sept. 1978, pp. 51-57.

The distinction between sign and signal is not, of course, exclusively Pavlovian. Vygotsky also incorporated the Husserlian distinction between *meaning* and *objective reference* (the latter term Vygotsky rendered as "the indicatory function of speech"). Although these categories are similar to Charles Sanders Peirce's symbolic sign and indexical sign, there is no evidence that Vygotsky got them from Peirce. I am grateful to James Wertsch for bringing the above to my attention.

12. Vygotsky proceeds to enumerate the advantages of the speaking child over the ape in the area of problem solving: the speaking child is more inde-

pendent of his immediate field of vision, more capable of planning, and has greater control over his actions. Speaking children "acquire the capacity to be both the subjects and objects of their own behavior ("TS," p. 26).

13. Vygotsky, *TL*, p. 146. Vygotsky further states:

> The sense of a word . . . is the sum of all the psychological events aroused in our consciousness by the word . . . . Meaning is only one of the zones of sense, the most stable and precise zone. A word acquires its sense from the context in which it appears; in different contexts, it changes its sense. Meaning remains stable throughout the changes of sense. The dictionary meaning of a word is no more than a stone in the edifice of sense, no more than a potentiality that finds diversified realization in speech. [Ibid.]

Vygotsky's distinction here between *meaning* and *sense* has a nice parallel in Bahktin's distinction between *meaning* and *theme* cited earlier in this essay (see p. 248). Again, I thank James Wertsch, for pointing out this parallel.

14. See Vygotsky, "Interaction between Learning and Development," *Mind in Society*, pp. 84-86. The American educator John Holt seems to have something similar in mind when he writes, with wonderful simplicity: "The true test of intelligence is not how much we know how to do, but how we behave when we don't know what to do" (*How Children Fail* [New York, 1964], p. 205).

15. Vygotsky's distinction between tool and symbol has a parallel in the bifurcating functions of speech. Both tool and symbol involve mediated activity, but tools are externally oriented, aids to mastering nature, whereas signs are internally oriented, ultimately aids to mastering oneself. See his "Internalization of Higher Psychological Functions," *Mind in Society*, pp. 55.

16. See Bakhtin, "Discourse in the Novel," *The Dialogic Imagination: Four Essays*, ed. Michael Holquist, trans. Caryl Emerson and Holquist, University of Texas Press Slavic Series, no. 1 (Austin, Tex., 1981), pp. 259-422, esp. pp. 341-42.

17. See Ivanov, "The Significance of M.M. Bakhtin's Ideas," p. 314.

18. Jacques Lacan, "The Empty Word and the Full Word," in *Speech and Language in Psychoanalysis*, ed. and trans. Anthony Wilden (Baltimore, 1981), p. 9.

19. Lacan, from "La Chose freudienne" (1955), quoted in Wilden, "Lacan and the Discourse of the Other," in *Speech and Language in Psychoanalysis*, p. 266.

20. On this, see Volosinov, *Fr*, p. 89: "The wider and deeper the breach

between the official and the unofficial conscious, the more difficult it becomes for motives of inner speech to turn into outward speech."

21. Bakhtin, "K pererabotke knigi o Dostoevskom" [Toward a reworking of the Dostoevsky book], *Estetika slovesnogo tvorcestva*, pp. 313, 311-12; my translation. The complete text of Bakhtin's 1961 notes for the Dostoevsky book is included as an appendix in my translation of Bakhtin, *Problems of Dostoevsky's Poetics*, Theory and History of Literature Series, vol. 8 (Minneapolis, 1984).

22. In Leningrad of the 1920s, Bakhtin was well known as a *cerkovnik*, a devout Orthodox Christian; it was for his connections with the underground church that he was arrested in 1929. During these years he wrote a huge metaphysical work—only portions of which survive—on the meaning of Christian "responsibility," on "the Word become flesh," and on the implications of the Biblical injunction "In the Beginning was the Word." On this and other points of biography and doctrine, I am indebted to Katerina Clark and Michael Holquist, who have generously shared draft chapters of their *Mikhail Bakhtin*. See also Holquist, "The Politics of Representation," in *Allegory and Representation*, ed. Stephen J. Greenblatt, Selected Papers from the English Institute, 1979-80, n.s. 5 (Baltimore, 1981), pp. 163-83.

23. For an American echo of the voices of Bakhtin and Vygotsky, see Toulmin, "The Inwardness of Mental Life," *Critical Inquiry* 6 (Autumn 1979): 1-16. Very much in their spirit, Toulmin argues that "inner" and "outer" are not on either side of a great divide but that "the moral and emotional ambiguities of our inner lives are simply the moral and emotional ambiguities of our open lives *internalized*" (p. 9).

24. Vygotsky, quoted in Ivanov, "The Significance of M.M. Bakhtin's Ideas," p. 326.

25. Georg Lukács, *The Theory of the Novel*, trans. Anna Bostock (Cambridge, Mass., 1971), pp. 29, 30.

26. See Bakhtin, "Epic and Novel: Toward a Methodology for the Study of the Novel" (1941), *The Dialogic Imagination*, pp. 3-40; all further references to this work, abbreviated "EN," will be included parenthetically in the text. In this essay, Bakhtin posits three generic characteristics of the novel that free it from the strictures of epic: the novel is stylistically multi-languaged ("heteroglot"); it uses time in a way maximally open to the future; and it creates a new zone for structuring images, a zone maximally close to the present. As a result, novelistic heroes are never exhausted by their plots; there is always some other way they might have acted and some other way of understanding their actions. Epics can prophesy; novels only predict.

27. Sigmund Freud, "The Relation of the Poet to Day-Dreaming," trans. I.F. Grant Duff, *On Creativity and the Unconscious: Papers on the Psychology of Art, Literature, Love, Religion*, comp. Benjamin Nelson (New York, 1958), p. 54.

28. Vygotsky, *The Psychology of Art* (Cambridge, Mass., 1971), p. 79.

29. Paul de Man, "Criticism and Crisis," *Blindness and Insight: Essays in the Rhetoric of Contemporary Criticism* (New York, 1971), p. 18.

■ PART THREE

The Trust of Dialogue

■ 9

Existential Homelessness: A Contemporary Case for Dialogue

Ronald C. Arnett
Duquesne University

The new millennium we hope for is not what we are as a people; it is what we could be. The problems before us are enormous. With an estimated debt of two trillion dollars or more and a threatening recession, we are, in anybody's book, a debtor nation. A quarter of the nation's children live in poverty, and a growing number do not live in a home at all. Health care is becoming prohibitively expensive for many Americans. Our environment is threatened and deteriorating quickly . . . in the case of human misery and neglect, things promise only to get worse. . . . The answers do not lie in the traditional, political solutions . . . the solutions and the promise for our new century will come from the collective voice of people who say that it does not have to be this way, that together we can do better, that we are better. (Morse, 1991, p. 4)

Environmental and societal problems plague us as we approach the 21st century. National debt, unemployment, aging cities, and acts of aggression and terrorism are all too commonplace. The struggles are both local and global. Acts of rebellion and repression in China, upheaval in the former Soviet Union, and long-standing hatred in the Middle East are but the tip of the iceberg of contemporary uncertainties. An era of significant uncertainty and mistrust offers a problematic backdrop for human dialogue (Buber, 1967, pp. 306-312). In this chapter, I suggest that trust in existence is a needed foundation for the invitation of dialogue between persons, and such trust is in short supply.

I examine a loss of trust in existence, initiated by the uncertainty and mistrust that surrounds us. I rely on Christopher Lasch's (1977) description of lost "havens of trust," places where certainty and interpersonal trust guide interaction. Agreeing with Lasch's work, I also suggest that we need to put in perspective the challenges we face. Even if our era is one of transition and change, we are hardly unique; mistrust and uncertainty are not new phenomena in the course of human history. Appropriately, Carl Rogers (1961) commented that whatever we consider the most unique is often the most common.

The notion of *trust in existence* is a background foundation for the invitation of dialogue. The experiences and perceptions that compose society, culture, and the individual lay a background foundation that nourishes or inhibits a sense of trust in existence. Smith and Williamson (1985) outline a model of communication based on the importance of background assumptions that surround communicative life (pp. 51-52). They conceptualize communication as grounded in a communication ecology composed of the assumptive background of culture, society, and individual.

Paulo Freire (1968), in *The Pedagogy of the Oppressed*, emphasizes that the larger ecology of a communicative environment has a significant effect on the communicative system invited. Freire suggests that a dialogic relational system is impossible within an environment or communicative ecology of oppression (pp. 46-56). My task is to examine the background of communicative ecology that invites decreased trust between persons and to suggest a communicative answer to this age-old problem of uncertainty and mistrust.

AN ERA OF THE "PARENTHESIS"

The social, cultural, and individual assumptions that frame the background of our communication ecology are under considerable challenge, as outlined by social critics (Lasch, 1965). John Naisbitt (1982) called our current time, an historical moment of the "parenthesis," an era between eras. We are no longer "In stable eras, [where] everything has a name and everything knows its place. . ." (p. 252).

Rapid change can fuel distrust of existence, particularly when some lose faith in an inevitable sense of progress within a paradigm acceptable to one's narrow interests (Lasch, 1991). For some wedded to a particular world view or set of paradigmatic assumptions, such disruption can result in a psychological feeling of being "homeless." The work of Peter Berger on psychological homelessness is supported by both Lasch

(1977) and Bellah (1985). They discuss what occurs when rapid change and uncertainty about the future lessen trust in existence. We begin to lose a feeling of being psychologically "at home."

> If the global effect of modernization can be described as "homeless-ness," then the underlying aspiration of demodernization is a quest for new ways of "being at home" in society. Almost all the significant categories for community in the youth culture bear this out. We need mention only "global village," "tribe" and "family," and we cite only the name of Charles Manson, to indicate that this quest for familial at-home-ness is not without some moral ambiguities. (Berger, Berger, & Kellner, 1974, p. 214)

The feeling of not being at home is encouraged as communities lose a "common center" (Arnett, 1992). The common center is an inherited, understood, and active philosophical and practical set of assumptions and actions that guide a people.

Common Center

The era of the parenthesis is fueled by the loss of a communicative com-mon center (Arnett, 1989, pp. 42-60), an agreed on societal or cultural goal around which our communication can be focused. A communicative common center is a project that gathers diverse people around a com-mon text or center from which a conversation of agreement or disagree-ment can begin. A common center does not imply interpretive agree-ment; it simply keeps people centered on a text accessible to all.

Any organization or society needs to have people disagree on what should or should not be attempted or how a project is actually implemented. However, for the disagreement to be meaningful there needs to be agreement on a common center, a common text under ques-tion. The common center of an organization may vary in commitments to excellence, profit, reputation, honor, or service to the world, to name a few. The particular strategies for accomplishing a communicated project may be in dispute, but a broad-based communicative common center offers a common history and text that binds people together.

Before eliminating a common center that naturally links diverse groups and people together, let us discuss the potential results of such an act. An organization, a culture, or a society can have many subgroups and still work effectively together if a common center can be communicated that propels the actions of the group toward an agreed on project. Any organization or group that does not seek to offer a common center may be subject to sabotage by those attempting to enhance a private individual or group agenda.

Buber's emphasis on common center is similar to the more recent scholarship of Alasdair MacIntyre (1981). In *After Virtue*, MacIntyre stated that what holds people together is agreement on the importance of particular moral stories. People in a community will argue over what the moral stories suggest or imply. The stories are not understood literally. Creativity comes from agreement on a common base and a willingness to permit competing interpretations. Thus, as people argue they use evidence that is publicly known by many in the community. They then must convince others of the viability of their interpretation on a particular issue.

The stories act as a text or base from which agreement can occur. The loss of the common text paves the way for "emotivism," a decision by personal preference without reference to a moral story that another knows and might counter with a contrary interpretation. Emotivism propels us against the grain of one of the major contributions of the Enlightenment—movement of ideas into the public arena where they can be tested and debated. Argument by "I feel" leaves a common public center, in this case a known moral story, and leads to privatized feelings, or emotivism (MacIntyre, 1981).

The perception of lost common centers and moral stories that provide a publicly known base from which conversation can begin contributes to uncertainty and mistrust in an era of the parenthesis. We can, in the words of Lasch, find this uncertainty so demanding that we shift from concern about production, what we might accomplish, to concern about survival of a lifestyle and life we once believed possible.

Directionless

Loss of trust in common centers and moral stories that have offered guidance lays the groundwork for a survival mentality. As we lose optimism in what human beings can accomplish, we open the door to despair, what Lasch (1984) called survivalism (pp. 57-59). Loss of common centers and moral stories result in paradigmatic confusion and mistrust, encouraging a survival impulse. It is the survival view that provides a haven for emotivism. We begin to take care of our own personal preferences.

This survival strategy of following personal preference works until one must make a major decision fueled by multiple and contradictory emotions.

> To avoid confusion, what I have called the culture of narcissism might better be characterized, at least for the moment, as a culture of survivalism. Everyday life has begun to pattern itself on the survival strategies forced on those exposed to extreme adversity. Selective apathy, emotional disengagement from others, renunciation of the past

and the future, a determination to live one day at a time—these techniques of emotional self-management, necessarily carried to extremes
under extreme conditions, in more moderate form have come to
shape the lives of ordinary people. . . . Confronted with an apparently
implacable and unmanageable environment, people have turned to
self-management. (Lasch, 1984, pp. 57-58)

Left with no common center or moral story to offer a beginning for conversation, a person can lose a sense of direction. A person no longer
knows which way to turn and what option to pursue when personal preferences clash.

Most of us take the notion of direction for granted, not noticing
its presence, but rather only the lack of it at particular times in our lives
or organizations. The foundation of a Western commitment to action presupposes the importance of a direction, referred to in classical terms as
teleology, a direction toward a future project (Aristotle, 1985). As we are
divided into what intercultural researchers are calling the increasing
splintering of subcultures with less commitment to a clear superordinate
culture (Samovar & Porter, 1991, pp. 72-74), the chance to discover an
agreed upon direction or future project becomes a more demanding and,
at times, impossible task.

One may not support a number of specific projects that have propelled Western civilization, resulting in the oppression of persons and
exploitation of the environment. But one needs to be wary of the impulse
to reject the notion of teleology. The culprit is not the notion of action or a
teleological direction. The problem rests more with what projects have
been selected. To give up on a teleology or a direction is more often a sign
of decline, rather than health. The importance of teleology is central to
Buber's (1952) understanding of direction and part of his view of dialogue.

A direction can be debated and hopefully modified. But an environment without a clear sense of direction invites the development of
multiple subgroups, similar to feudal Europe. The current events in the
former Soviet Union offer a painful example of what happens when a
direction pointed to by a common center or moral story is taken away or
lost quickly. The people return to ethnic stories and centers to bring
"those like us" together—but a direction with a larger, more complex
common center that can permit different ethnic groups to function
together is no longer present.

Buber (1952) used strong language when discussing the danger
of a lack of direction. He called it a potentially *demonic* act (pp. 126-127).
One of the dangers of lack of direction is the difficulty of debating a particular policy or action that is propelled by emotivism, instead of the more
public commitment to a known common center or moral story. A direction can be modified and changed only when it is understood. A lack of

direction leaves the environment open to massive upheavals and provides an environment for autocratic leaders of ill-will, like Hitler and Stalin, eager to direct (or misdirect) the actions and the lives of others (Hackman & Johnson, 1991, p. 172). A lack of direction can be a sign of what Lasch (1979) called *narcissism*, a preoccupation with survival in the present, with little attention given to the future or the past.

In such an environment, a speaker can become more concerned about preserving a place of status in an organization than in offering a direction that can focus the debate. One is restrained from offering a direction; the large number of subgroups with competing agendas make it impossible to act without offending one constituency or another, thus encouraging a leader to facilitate the debate between the factions without letting his or her position ever be known. Such withholding of comment comes not necessarily from a commitment to group process, but from a survival effort aimed at keeping the warring factions fighting one another and not centered on the leadership.

One then dodges the articulation of a stance, robbing the next generation of a clear position with which to test its own views. In such an environment, a leader avoids leading in order to not offend subgroups. William Whyte, Jr. (1956), in the late 1950s, warned of a survival form of leadership communication: "the whole tendency of modern organization life is to muffle the importance of individual leadership. In studying an organization, one of the most difficult things is to trace a program or innovation back to its origins" (1956, p. 59). Lack of direction in an organization is born as a common center for conversation ceases. We begin to survive by following our own private personal preferences and keeping the focus of attention on others, withholding our ideas from public debate. The focus on private emotions, instead of public common centers or moral stories, can begin to put interpersonal trust at risk. Even when we do not agree with another, if we understand the text from which the other argues we can enter the conversation in a public fashion. However, an emphasis on survivalism that places primary trust solely in one's own personal preferences can lessen trust.

TRUST

It is my contention that the perception of paradigmatic challenge and change makes trust in existence demanding and at times unlikely. Phrases such as "loss of common center," "moral stories," "era of parenthesis," and "survival mentality" point to rapid change that many are not eager to endure. Such a realization of lack of predictability can put trust in existence at risk.

Definitions of *trust* include: "confidence; confident expectation; assured anticipation; belief; hope; reliance or belief without examination" (*Webster*, 1969, p. 899). When trust, as defined by assured anticipation or confident expectation, is not present our communicative ecology is grounded in mistrust in the future. Trust is put at risk when individuals are not convinced they can make a difference—one of the major themes in Ellul's (1964) critique of the latter part of the 20th century.

A Background of Trust

Communication ecology involves the content of a message, background assumptions of the society, culture, individuals in conversation, and the will (James, 1968, pp. 193-213) to speak and listen to another. In gestalt terms, human events are understood through a filter of "background" and "foreground," with the former permitting us to understand the latter.

For instance, if one watches soccer (foreground action) without any knowledge of the rules and plays of excellence (background information), it is unlikely that as much will be understood or appreciated, no matter how much one concentrates on the immediate action in the foreground. The background information permits us to understand the depth of significance of the foreground action.

Another way to examine this background/foreground combination is to explore the intended value of a liberal arts education. The breadth of such an education offers background information that assists in interpreting foreground tasks of immediate technological or social application. For instance, the meaning of casting a vote in a given election, foreground, is best understood when background stories about democracy and the rights of a self-governed people are known. The foreground act can then be conceptualized as a responsibility, as well as an opportunity to voice one's view.

Most often background information goes unnoticed until something startles us into awareness about our taken-for-granted assumptions. Students studying abroad often discover background information that they had not known before, related to their interpretive screens from back home. Frequently it takes an alien interpretation of a foreground action that is accepted by someone we respect or by a large critical mass of people to encourage us to question our own background assumptions.

Such questioning and awareness of unexamined background assumptions is the focus of Stanley Hauerwas's (1981) analysis of the novel, *Watership Down*. He contends that the novel reveals how background stories about how life was to be lived had grown weak and without power; only when the rabbits had to leave their warren did they begin to reflect on the background information necessary for giving meaning to daily foreground activities (p. 18).

My point is that the background set of assumptions has changed from a basic sense of trust in the future to one of mistrust, a fundamental thesis in the work of Lasch. Lasch rejected both the conservative view of a tradition that envisions progress as the maturation of a known paradigm and the liberal view of progress toward ever increasing individual freedom.

The progressive sense of optimism in a better tomorrow is at risk, for both those wanting to perpetuate what is and those wanting to change the world. The conservative envisions change as the maturation of the present; change within the current paradigm. The liberal view of progress envisions a paradigmatic change, but one that the advocate for change can picture and understand (Lasch, 1965). Both conservatives and liberals can invite mistrust as they articulate a view of progress that is questioned by an increasingly cynical public (Arnett, 1992, pp. 104-108).

An Absence of Trust

Most of us are not personally pleased with the prospect of an unpredictable future, a future we cannot trust. We attempt to teach our students that Heisenberg's "uncertainty principle" is a fundamental part of life (Barrett, 1962, pp. 38-40), and we discuss the importance of flexibility in communication (Heisenberg, 1958). It is, of course, easier to discuss the value of change when we are setting the agenda of change for another than to adjust our own lives to unpredictability. Eric Hoffer (1967), in *The Ordeal of Change*, stated what many of us privately feel about change—particularly when we are not setting the agenda.

> It is my impression that one really dislikes the new. We are afraid of it. It is not only as Dostoyevsky put it that "taking a new step, uttering a new word is what people fear most." Even in slight things the experience of the new is rarely without some stirring of foreboding. (p. 3)

We want change, liberals and conservatives, that fits the paradigmatic assumptions of our given values and hopes for the future. Unpredictable change, outside our paradigmatic vision, is likely to generate anxiety.

Lasch suggests that the notion of the "American Dream" is based on trust and confidence. This paradigm of a material and social good life is foundational to the United States and is an example of a common center on which some can no longer depend. According to Lasch (1984), [T]he American dream—no longer has enough foundation in fact to support a social consensus. In a downward mobility, social upheaval, and chronic economic, political, and military crisis. . . [its power has been lost or at the least deeply weakened]" (p. 204).

Lasch (1984) proceeds to insinuate that Robert Smithson's work reveals a feeling that we are at the end of modern society, at least as we have envisioned it to be.

> The minimalist sensibility originates in a mood of retrenchment. It reflects a feeling that there is no place left to go in art and that modern society, like modern art, is approaching the end of the road. "I posit that there is no tomorrow," says Robert Smithson, "nothing but a gap, a yawning gap." With such a view of the future, it is no wonder that artists renounce the hope of permanence. (p. 150)

Lasch was not calling for a romantic return to a past era. His point was that when a major common center is put at risk, a high degree of uncertainty guides the existence of the people.

Sissela Bok (1979) suggests that truthfulness is fundamental for maintaining a quality life. "A society, then, whose members were unable to distinguish truthful messages from deceptive ones, would collapse. But even before such a general collapse, individual choice and survival would be imperiled" (p. 20). My contention is that the word "trusting" could be substituted for truthful in Bok's quotation. A world where truth is in short supply is no more dangerous than one where trust in the future is uncommon.

Lack of trust in the future makes it difficult to meet the next generation with a genuine sense of concern, assistance, and help. It is difficult to help those that will come after us without foreseeing possibilities for the future. Such a time can encourage a romanticizing of our own recent past, instead of focusing on what might be possible. For instance, of all the decades of human history, why do so many colleges and universities center a course around the 1960s?

I do not remember my teachers encouraging me to spend an inordinate amount of time studying the 1920s or the 1940s. My teachers pointed me forward, not back to their immediate past. Their teaching reflected a confidence in the future and a willingness for my generation to carve out a place in that future. When confidence in what might be is at a low ebb, it should not surprise us to find what Lasch (1984) called "a criminal indifference to the needs of future generations" (p. 17). This loss of confidence in the future, as the background of our communication with one another, can begin to influence everyday discourse through a "hermeneutic of suspicion."

INTERPERSONAL CONSEQUENCES

When the background of our communicative ecology is not based in a realistic sense of trust, two major interpersonal consequences are invited: a hermeneutic of suspicion and narcissism.

Hermeneutic of Suspicion

A hermeneutic of suspicion is the result of a generalized lack of trust in existence that encourages us to interpret daily communicative actions from a vantage point of mistrust and doubt. When a lack of trust in the future is fundamental to the background of communication ecology, interpersonal mistrust of one another is likely. Trust in the future assures predictability for oneself and the other. When an agreed on common center of trust in the future is put at risk, the bonds of trust between persons are disrupted as well.

The danger of a lack of trust is made present when it becomes an interpersonal norm, rather than an occasional response. Buber (1969, pp. 195-202; see also Friedman, 1974, pp. 318-331) revealed a hermeneutic of suspicion as a major problem in post-World War II. Buber's concern of 50 years ago is justified today as well. When lack of trust in the future unsettles trust in interpersonal relationships, our interpretive background for everyday communication is disrupted.

When a hermeneutic of suspicion becomes the usual interpretive framework, a person rejects the surface explanation of information and seeks a deeper, more "true" analysis of the information. One begins to question what is stated and looks for an unstated real answer, which begins a cycle of distrust and suspicion in everyday existence. For example, a person is complimented in a public meeting. A hermeneutic of suspicion does not encourage a response of appreciation; instead the complimented person asks a silent question, "What does the other *really* want to gain by such comments?"

Distrust is appropriate, but when it becomes the norm for everyday interaction the foundation for dialogue is at risk. A number of authors have suggested that the test of dialogue is in conflict. However, the examples often cited of Gandhi, King, and Buber reveal dialogue within a particular type of conflict setting—one in which trust between partners is still possible. Gandhi was even criticized for being friends with his opponents, giving them exact information about his upcoming plans for civil disobedience. The test of dialogue may be conflict, but what makes it possible is a foundation of trust between communicative partners or opponents.

Narcissism

The demise of common centers or moral stories pointed to by Buber, MacIntyre, Bellah, and Lasch describe what has happened to the Judeo-Christian philosophical haven. In addition, MacIntyre pointed out that a heroic sense of life as outlined by the Greeks, and lower middle-class values of loyalty and hard work are not being nurtured (Berger et al., 1974; Lasch, 1991). The collective point of these writers is that the philosophical havens of trust that have traditionally held much of life's meaning together are faltering. There seems to be a plaguing sense that "people have lost confidence [trust] in the future" (Lasch, 1984, p. 16), making it more difficult to discover havens of trust, whether in government, the family (Lasch, 1977, p. 165), or on the university campus itself (Boyer, 1990).

Lasch (1979) suggested that damage to havens of trust comes not from people becoming more self-centered, but from the loss of philosophical and practical havens of trust. Without philosophical havens of trust, we begin to live life narcissistically, not because we are self-centered, but out of a feeling that the old moral stories, havens of trust, cannot be counted on.

Lasch's contention is that narcissism is an effort to compensate for a lack of being at home in the midst of a haven of trust that lives by a publicly known moral story. In such a situation, one begins to rely increasingly on "the self," no longer supported by either a geographic or philosophical sense of home that offers meaning for existence. Narcissism is an effort to bolster the self as the core of meaning, in hopes of compensating for the loss of faith in other structures, institutions, and philosophies that had previously offered a sense of home.

An individual begins to ask more and more of "the self," finding that self no longer adequate to meet the changes challenging stable taken-for-granted values. Lasch's (1979) notion of the "minimal self" is not a statement that the modern self is weaker; it is that the institutions that previously gave meaning to life are not as strong, thus placing more emphasis on the self than it can withstand.

Lasch's (1984, pp. 60-99) minimal self lacks confidence in the future and hopes to survive by increasing its strength in a time of lost havens. In *Haven in a Heartless World*, Lasch (1977) summarized the thesis present in his determined writing style.

> The unpredictability of the outer world has become a recurrent theme not only in melodrama but in all of modern literature. The sense of man's isolation and loneliness reflects the collapse of public order. . . the waning of public order. . .the waning of parental authority and guidance. Without this guidance, according to Alexander Mitscherlich, the world becomes "totally inaccessible and incalculable, continually changing shape and producing sinister surprises." (p. 178)

The notion of havens of trust moves from philosophical systems, to concrete places, to our recent overreliance on the self. Instead of looking to philosophical ideals or places like the family, church, and even colleges, we begin to look to ourselves. The self, according to Lasch, is reduced to being a minimal self, without the support of havens of trust. The feeling of the self as minimal or less capable than it was previously is due more to a loss of havens of trust, which previously offered complementary support to the individual self, than to any new personal weakness in the self. We are simply asking the self to do a job it is unlikely to accomplish alone.

DIALOGIC HAVENS OF TRUST

Lasch's notion is that we are losing a significant part of human life when havens of trust no longer offer a foundation of dialogue between persons. The concept of havens of trust is simply a concrete place where a moral story (MacIntyre) or a common center (Buber) guides the daily praxis of a people.

My suggestion is that when such concrete places of trust are not present, communication is significantly affected. First, the loss of havens of trust systemically affects the communication ecology of a culture. Second, change in our communication ecology background from trust to mistrust removes a foundational element needed in dialogue between persons.

Third, a general feeling of mistrust, a hermeneutic of suspicion, begins to permeate remaining places or havens of trust, such as family, church, and college campuses. And finally, as we lose trust in such havens, we begin to spend more time protecting the self. We attempt to bolster a minimal self, trying to compensate for lost havens of trust. In short, the collective work of Berger, Lasch, and Bellah point to a modern world where a sense of home is not present, trust in the future is limited, and an effort to build the self as a form of protection is not working. We are people without a home, turning to self-development as the antidote to the loss of concrete havens of trust.

Dialogue emerges out of a position, a home, a place of trust. Trust is needed as we risk entering dialogue with another; as Buber suggested, "real living begins with two" (Arnett, 1986, p. 77). Without havens of trust to move us toward the arena of dialogue with others, the question is what will or can sustain the impulse or desire to be in dialogue with others?

The demands of dialogue are different when we cannot presume havens of trust that permit dialogue. We must no longer automatically assume that havens of trust exist. Today we are charged with co-constituting foundations for trust in the midst of a communicative ecology that encourages us to live by mistrust.

A *Different Beginning*

Perhaps a first step in inviting trust in such an era is to look into the abyss without the crutches of nostalgia or a belief in the inevitability of progress (Lasch, 1991). This clarity of insight and the courage to withstand the scrutiny of a major social change is a significant theme of William Barrett (1962) in his call to accept the "Furies" of life.

> Greek religion was in deadly earnest here, and perhaps it was never wiser. The Furies are really to be revered and not simply bought off; in fact, they cannot be bought off (not even by our modern tranquilizers and sleeping pills) but are to be placated only through being given their just and due respect. They are the darker side of life, but in their own way as holy as the rest. Indeed, without them there would be no experience of the holy at all. . . .
>
> It would be the final error of reason—the point at which it succumbs to its own *hubris* and passes over into its demoniacal opposite, unreason—to deny that the Furies exist, or to strive to manipulate them out of existence. Nothing can be accomplished by denying that man is an existentially troubled being, except to make more trouble. (pp. 278-279)

We can invite problems if we fail to admit the hard and demanding times we are in and through which we continue to journey. Or, taking Barrett's advice, we can invite new havens of trust if we are willing to look at our own "Furies" without distortion or selective blindness. The "Furies" we need to confront involve the realization that for many the havens of trust can no longer be counted on to supply the foundation for dialogue. To insist on havens of trust—whether the American Dream, the Judeo-Christian ethic, or concrete places like the family, the workplace, or campus—to be able to offer a home for all is no longer plausible for large numbers of people.

Limits and a Home for Dialogue

The early work of Barrett and the recent work of Lasch point to the importance of beginning with the problem as it is, not as we would like it to be. Their advice is consistent with such diverse views in the 20th century as those of Reinhold Niebuhr, who calls for the acceptance of limits, and Carl Rogers, who suggests that change only happens when we can accept who we are at a given time, not what we might want to be. The home or haven of trust for dialogue then becomes an honest statement of the communicative ecology in which we are situated, an era not only of the parenthesis, but a time of psychological homelessness for many no longer able to find havens of trust.

The beginning place of trust I propose in this chapter for dialogue between persons is not a story or narrative protected by havens of trust, but an uncertain honest beginning—an admission that acknowledges that many traditional narratives have lost their collective power and can no longer offer assurance and direction for the future. Such a beginning of trust in dialogue requires acceptance of this reality for many, and simultaneously a willingness to reach out to others in honesty and realistic hope.

> we need to recover a more vigorous form of hope, which trusts life without denying its tragic character or attempting to explain away tragedy as "cultural lag." We can fully appreciate this kind of hope only now that the other kind, better described as optimism, has fully revealed itself as a higher form of wishful thinking. Progressive optimism rests, at bottom, on a denial of the natural limits on human power and freedom, and it cannot survive for very long in a world in which an awareness of those limits has become inescapable. (Lasch, 1991, p. 530)

In short, a better tomorrow will only have a chance to emerge when our hope is realistically tied to the limits and "Furies" of today and the acceptance of common centers not functioning with collective power and influence.

The place or home of dialogue begins with accepting the loss of havens and reclaiming life based on competence and developed skill. Perhaps one could suggest that havens of trust are grounded in competence that has been earned and can be trusted over time. Environments of abundance can be trusted, if earned and cared for over time. Environments of abundance that are not so tended and earned generate little trust—we seem to intuitively know that abundance without effort is precarious.

Working at Trust

Lasch, like a number of authors before him, such as Erich Fromm, William Whyte, and Martin Buber, reminds us of the importance of words such as building, competence, skill, and time. Lasch was interested in reclaiming the importance of work. We can no longer expect to act as *consumers* of common centers, moral stories, or havens of trust. We are asked to be *producers* of new common centers and moral stories within our places of employment and our homes.

Lasch (1991) suggested that a production orientation toward life is tied to "lower middle-class" and "populist" values—based more on phrases such as "honest work for honest pay"—than on a dream of leisure and abundance.

Abundance, they believed, would eventually give everyone access to leisure, cultivation, refinement—advantages formerly restricted to the wealthy. Luxury for all: such was the noble dream of progress. Populists, on the other hand, regarded a competence, as they would have called it—a piece of earth, a small shop, a useful calling—as a more reasonable as well as a more worthy ambition. "Competence" had rich moral overtones; it referred to the livelihood conferred by property but also to the skills required to maintain it. (p. 531)

Dialogue is possible as we accept our homeless state and as we work with others to rebuild places of trust with persistence and tenacity. The foundation for dialogue is invited when havens of trust are co-nourished, using values of building, competence, skill, and time.

Havens of trust are built one relationship, one policy, one task at a time. Admitting the loss of havens of trust is the first movement in the invitation of dialogic trust. A willingness to work to earn trust is the next major step in reclaiming trust for dialogue between persons.

What calls into question previous common centers, moral stories, and havens of trust is the conviction by many that they have been historically and systematically excluded from participation in the story of a people—economically, socially, racially, and ethnically. "Multicultural" education works at outlining new intellectual havens of trust based on inclusion. There are those who applaud the loss of havens of trust for the few that were assisted at the expense of many; such persons will fittingly see opportunity in the midst of the psychological homelessness of the affluent. Others, once committed to havens of trust, will see tragedy in their demise and will no longer be able to support what Bellah, Madsen, Sullivan, Swidler, and Tipton (1985) called, *Habits of the Heart.*

Both those excited about change and those lamenting the passing of old moral stories are called to admit that many are psychologically homeless. My hope is that we can now get down to work and find ways to nourish new havens of trust based on inclusion and access. Maybe acceptance of the "Furies" by those lamenting the era of the parenthesis and a willingness to meet the unknown will permit groups of people previously disconnected to find new and bold ways to slowly invite havens of trust, one relationship at a time. Bellah, in both *Habits of the Heart* (1985) and the *Good Society* (1991), suggests a need for human beings to nourish places of trust that encourage a commitment to the common good.

Finally, I want to emphasize that in the long haul of history, our era of the parenthesis is a minor issue. But for some it is a significant concern that havens of trust, which have carried the meaning of life for so long, are at risk. Perhaps we can benefit from Victor Frankl's (1974) reminder of the importance of being a producer. Meaning comes from what we give, get, and the stand we take against the inevitable. We are accustomed to getting in an affluent culture. Giving and the stand we take against the inevitable are the necessary commitments needed now.

If the foundation of dialogue is trust, perhaps the foundation of trust is courage. I believe that Maurice Friedman (1974) offered important wisdom in *Touchstones of Reality: Existential Trust and the Community of Peace.* Friedman connected dialogue with the "courage to address and the courage to respond." As we prepare to enter the 21st century, I wish to add the "courage to discover with the help of others moral stories and common centers that include us and persons different from ourselves." Such co-created stories might offer the foundation for havens of trust, places where dialogue is invited as we work to find ways to bring differences of religion, race, gender, and nationality together. The "Furies" ask us to fight for old havens. The courage of dialogic trust invites us to reach out to others, not offering answers, but looking for ways to nourish havens of trust in partnership, not just for "my" people, but for anyone willing to roll up their sleeves and work on the problems of our era. Such trust is tied to the importance of the journey in our work and less to romantic images of the past. Producers willing to be in active partnership with one another in the midst of uncertainty need courage—the courage to trust less in old answers and more in the hard work that extends the reach of dialogue to others.

REFERENCES

Aristotle. (1985). *Nichomachean ethics.* Indianapolis: Hackett.

Arnett, R.C. (1986). *Communication and community: Implications of Martin Buber's dialogue.* Carbondale, IL: Southern Illinois University.

Arnett, R.C. (1989). What is dialogic communication? *Person-Centered Review, 4,* 42-60.

Arnett, R.C. (1992). *Dialogic education: Conversation about ideas and between persons.* Carbondale, IL: Southern Illinois University.

Barrett, W. (1962). *Irrational man: A study in existential philosophy.* New York: Doubleday.

Bellah, R., Madsen, R., Sullivan, W.M., Swidler, A., & Tipton, S.M. (1991). *The good society.* New York: Knopf.

Bellah, R., Madsen, R., Sullivan, W.M., Swidler, A., & Tipton, S.M. (1985). *Habits of the heart: Individualism and commitment in American life.* Berkeley: University of California.

Berger, P.L., Berger, B., & Kellner, H. (1974). *The homeless mind: Modernization and consciousness.* New York: Random House.

Bok, S. (1979). *Lying: Moral choice in public and private life.* New York: Random House.

Boyer, E.L. (1990). *Campus life: In search of community.* Princeton, NJ: Princeton University.

Buber, M. (1952). *Good and evil.* New York: Charles Scribner's Sons.

Buber, M. (1967). Hope for this hour. In F.W. Matson & A. Montagu (Eds.), *Human dialogue: Perspectives on communication* (pp. 306-312). New York: The Free Press.

Buber, M. (1969). *A believing humanism: Gleanings.* New York: Simon & Schuster.

Ellul, J. (1964). *The technological society.* New York: Knopf.

Frankl, V. (1974). *Man's search for meaning: An introduction to logotherapy.* New York: Pocket Books.

Freire, P. (1968). *Pedagogy of the oppressed.* New York: Seabury.

Friedman, M. (1974). *Touchstones of reality: Existential trust and the community of peace.* New York: E.P. Dutton.

Hackman, M.Z., & Johnson, C.E. (1991). *Leadership: A communication perspective.* Prospect Heights, IL: Waveland.

Hauerwas, S. (1981). *A community of character: Toward a constructive social ethic.* Notre Dame, IN: University of Notre Dame.

Heisenberg, W. (1958). *Physics and philosophy.* New York: Harper & Row.

Hoffer, E. (1967). *The ordeal of change.* New York: Harper & Row.

James, W. (1968). *Pragmatism and other essays.* New York: Washington Square.

Lasch, C. (1965). *The new radicalism in America: 1889-1963.* New York: W.W. Norton.

Lasch, C. (1977). *Haven in a heartless world: The family besieged.* New York: Harper & Row.

Lasch, C. (1979). *The culture of narcissism.* New York: W. W. Norton.

Lasch, C. (1984). *The minimal self: Psychic survival in troubled times.* New York: W. W. Norton.

Lasch, C. (1991). *The true and only heaven: Progress and its critics.* New York: W.W. Norton.

MacIntyre, A. (1981). *After virtue.* Notre Dame, IN: University of Notre Dame.

Morse, S.W. (1991). Leadership for an uncertain future. *National Forum, 71,* 4.

Naisbitt, J. (1982). *Megatrends: Ten new directions transforming our lives.* New York: Warner Brothers.

New Webster encyclopedic dictionary of the English language. (1969). Chicago: Consolidated Book.

Rogers, C.R. (1961). *On becoming a person.* Boston: Houghton Mifflin.

Rogers, C.R. (1965). *Client-centered therapy.* Boston: Houghton Mifflin.

Samovar, L. A., & Porter, R. E. (1991). *Communication between cultures.* Belmont, CA: Wadsworth.

Smith, D.R., & Williamson, L.K. (1985). *Interpersonal communication: Rules, roles, and games* (3rd ed.). Dubuque: Wm. C. Brown.

Whyte, W.H. (1956). *The organization man.* New York: Doubleday.

■ 10

Friendship and Intimacy

In a fast-paced, complex, and mobile culture, the richness of friendship is put to a serious test. Friendship requires work, patience, commitment, and even a willingness to curb individualistic impulses. Such virtues are not always willingly accepted. In *The Reach of Dialogue* we assume that friendship, no matter how difficult in contemporary society, is still a major component of our humanness. Dialogue may not insure a friend, but an unwillingness ever to enter dialogue with another will make friendship less likely.

Aristotle discussed the notion of polis and the importance of political life, and considered politics to be the most noble profession. However, in *Nicomachean Ethics*, Aristotle (see 1985) suggested true friendship makes politics less necessary. Friendship permits interactions to be enabled by reciprocal good will. Such an environment is guided by friends who ask the question, "How can *we* prosper?" instead of the more contemporary concern, "How can *I* benefit?"

Friendship does not forget the "I"; it is not a form of blind martyrdom. Nor does friendship ignore the needs of others. In the tension of dual concerns, "I" and "other," life is lived with concern for the common good and held together by the bond of friendship.

A teacher and scholar friend of ours initially surprised us when he observed that friendship was the most important part of his life as an academic:

> I never make friendship a goal in teaching. My first and foremost task
> is to teach the information and to be a reliable colleague. But the sur-
> prise of friendship that upon occasion naturally emerges out of my
> work with others makes my life as an academic worthwhile.

Perhaps what makes our colleague open to friendship is his willingness to do his job well, allowing friendship to emerge on its own terms. Our friend enjoys a high level of trust from others because he commits himself to a responsible role, while keeping the notion of the common good as his guide.

The readings in this section remind us of the importance of trust in dialogue. Thomas Merton, who lived his adult life as a Trappist monk deeply interested in the world, asks us to envision love as a project that is active and ongoing, not something that comes to us fully developed. He calls for a thoughtful and active view of love, placing friendship within the realm of action, central to Aristotle's view.

Mary Field Belenky and her colleagues (Belenky, Clinchy, Goldberger, & Tarule, 1986) found in their study of "women's ways of knowing" that trust is important if human conversation is to be significant and valuable:

> In "real talk" domination is absent, reciprocity and cooperation are prominent. Although doubting may still be used to test ideas and may even be described as invigorating or fun, constructivist women are much more likely to replace doubting with believing as the best way of getting the feel of a new idea or a new friend or colleague. (p. 146)

Blind trust makes us naive, but even in a world of domination and deceit, momentary trust is necessary if we are to hear what the other is saying. After a conversation is over, we usually have time to weigh ideas against other perspectives and interpretations. Trust frees persons to listen and yields the potential for friendship as we discover more about each other in the midst of genuine conversation.

REFERENCES

Aristotle. (1985). *Nichomachean ethics* (T. Irwin, Trans.). Indianapolis: Hackett.

Belenky, M. F., Clinchy, B. M., Goldberger, N. R., & Tarule, J. M. (1986). *Women's ways of knowing: The development of self, voice, and mind.* New York: Basic Books.

Love and Need: Is Love a Package or a Message?

Thomas Merton

The expression to "fall in love" reflects a peculiar attitude toward love and toward life itself—a mixture of fear, awe, fascination, and confusion. It implies suspicion, doubt, hesitation, in the presence of something unavoidable—yet not fully reliable. For love takes you out of yourself. You lose control. You "fall." You get hurt. It upsets the ordinary routine of life. You become emotional, imaginative, vulnerable, foolish. You are no longer content to eat and sleep, make money and have fun. You now have to let yourself be carried away with this force that is stronger than reason and more imperious even than business!

Obviously, if you are cool and self-possessed character, you will take care never to *fall.* You will accept the unavoidable power of love as a necessity that can be controlled and turned to good account. You will confine it to the narrow category of "fun" and so you will not let it get out of hand. You will have fun by making others fall without falling yourself.

But the question of love is one that cannot be evaded. Whether or not you claim to be interested in it, from the moment you are alive you are bound to be concerned with love, because love is not just something that happens to you: *it is certain special way of being alive.*

Love is, in fact, an intensification of life, a completeness, a fullness, a wholeness of life. We do not live merely in order to vegetate through our days until we die. Nor do we live merely in order to take part in the routines of work and amusement that go on around us. We are not just machines that have to be cared for and driven carefully until they run down. In other words, life is not a straight horizontal line between two points, birth and death. Life curves upward to a peak of intensity, a high point of value and meaning, at which all its latent creative possibilities go into action and the person transcends himself or herself in encounter, response, and communion with another. It is for this that we came into the world—this communion and self-transcendence. We do not become fully human until we give ourselves to each other in love. And this must not be confined only to sexual fulfillment: it embraces everything in the human person—the capacity for self-giving, for sharing, for creativity, for mutual care, for spiritual concern.

Love is our true destiny. We do not find the meaning of life by ourselves alone—we find it with another. We do not discover the secret of our lives merely by study and calculation in our own isolated meditations. The meaning of our life is a secret that has to be revealed to us in love, *by the one we love.* And if this love is unreal, the secret will not be found, the meaning will never reveal itself, the message will never be decoded. At best, we will receive a scrambled and partial message, one that will deceive and confuse us. We will never be fully real until we let ourselves fall in love—either with another human person or with God.

Hence, our attitude toward life is also going to be in one way or another an attitude toward love. Our conception of ourselves is bound to be profoundly affected by our conception—and our experience—of love. And our love, or our lack of it, our willingness to risk it or our determination to avoid it, will in the end be an expression of ourselves: of who we think we are, of what we want to be, of what we think we are here for.

Nor will this be merely something that goes on in our head. Love affects more than our thinking and our behavior toward those we love. It transforms our entire life. Genuine love is a personal revolution. Love takes your ideas, your desires, and your actions and welds them together in one experience and one living reality which is a new *you.* You may prefer to keep this from happening. You may keep your thoughts, desires, and acts in separate compartments if you want: but then you will be an artificial and divided person, with three little filing cabinets: one of ideas, one of decisions, and one of actions and experiences. These three compartments may not have much to do with each other. Such a life does not make sense and is not likely to be happy. The contents of the separate filing cabinets may become increasingly peculiar as life goes on. Our philosophy of life is not something we create all by ourselves out of nothing. Our ways of thinking, even our attitudes toward ourselves, are more and more determined from the outside. Even our love tends to fit into ready-made forms. We consciously or unconsciously tailor our notions of love according to the patterns that we are exposed to day after day in advertising, in movies, on TV, and in our reading. One of these prevailing ready-made attitudes toward life and love needs to be discussed here. It is one that is seldom consciously spelled out. It is just "in the air," something that one is exposed to without thinking about it. This idea of love is a corollary of the thinking that holds our marketing society together. It is what one might call a package concept of love.

Love is regarded as a deal. The deal presupposes that we all have needs which have to be fulfilled by means of exchange. In order to make a deal you have to appear in the market with a worthwhile product, or if the product is worthless, you can get by if you dress it up in a good-looking package. We unconsciously think of ourselves as objects for sale on the market. We want to be wanted. We want to attract customers. We want to look like the kind of product that makes money. Hence, we waste a great deal of time modeling ourselves on the images presented to us by an affluent marketing society.

In doing this we come to consider ourselves and others not as *persons* but as *products*—as "goods," or in other words, as packages. We appraise one another commercially. We size each other up and make deals with a view to our own profit. We do not give ourselves in love, we make a deal that will enhance our own product, and therefore no deal is final. Our eye is already on the next deal and this next deal—need not necessarily be with the same customer. Life is more interesting when you make a lot of deals with a lot of new customers.

This view, which equates lovemaking with salesmanship and love with a glamorous package, is based on the idea of love as a mechanism of instinctive needs. We are biological machines endowed with certain urges that require fulfillment. If we are smart, we can exploit and manipulate these urges in ourselves and in others. We can turn them to our own advantage. We can cash in on them, using them to satisfy and enrich our own ego by profitable deals with other egos. If the partner is not too smart, a little cheating won't hurt, especially if it makes everything more profitable and more satisfactory for me!

If this process of making deals and satisfying needs begins to speed up, life becomes an exciting gambling game. We meet more and more others with the same needs. We are all spilled out helter-skelter onto a roulette wheel hoping to land on a propitious number. This happens over and over again. "Falling in love" is a droll piece of luck that occurs when you end up with another person whose need more or less fits in with yours. You are somehow able to fulfill each other, to complete each other. You have won the sweepstake. Of course, the prize is good only for a couple of years. You have to get back in the game. But occasionally you win. Others are not so lucky. They never meet anyone with just the right kind of need to go with their need. They never find anyone with the right combination of qualities, gimmicks, and weaknesses. They never seem to buy the right package. They never land on the right number. They fall into the pool and the pool is empty.

This concept of love assumes that the machinery of buying and selling of needs and fulfillment is what makes everything run. It regards life as a market and love as a variation on free enterprise. You buy and you sell, and to get somewhere in love is to make a good deal with whatever you happen to have available. In business, buyer and seller get together in the market with their needs and their products. And they swap. The swapping is simplified by the use of a happy-making convenience called money. So too in love. The love relationship is a deal that is arrived at for the satisfaction of mutual needs. If it is successful it pays off, not necessarily in money, but in gratification, peace of mind, fulfillment. Yet since the idea of happiness is with us inseparable from the idea of prosperity, we must face the fact that a love that is not crowned with every material and social benefit seems to us to be rather suspect. Is it really *blessed?* Was it really a *deal?*

The trouble with this commercialized idea of love is that it diverts your attention more and more from the essentials to the accessories of love. You are no longer able to really love the other person, for you become obsessed with the effectiveness of your own package, your own product, your own market value.

At the same time, the transaction itself assumes an exaggerated importance. For many people what matters is the delightful and fleeting moment in which the deal is closed. They give little thought to what the deal itself represents. That is perhaps why so many marriages do not last, and why so many people have to remarry. They cannot feel real if they just make one contract and leave it at that!

In the past, in a society where people lived on the land, where the possession of land represented the permanence and security of one's family, there was no problem about marriage for life: it was perfectly natural and it was accepted without even unconscious resistance. Today, one's security and one's identity have to be constantly reaffirmed: nothing is permanent, everything is in movement. You have to move with it. You have to come up with something new each day. Every morning you have to prove that you are still there. You have to keep making deals.

Each deal needs to have the freshness, the uniqueness, the paradisal innocence of closing with a brand-new customer. Whether we like it or not, we are dominated by an "ethic," or perhaps better, a "superstition" of quantity. We do not believe in a single lasting value that is established once for all—a permanent and essential quality that is never obsolete or stale. We are obsessed with what is repeatable. Reality does not surrender itself all at once, it has to be caught in small snatches, over and over again, in a dynamic flickering like the successive frames of a movie film. Such is our attitude.

Albert Camus in one of his early books, *The Myth of Sisyphus,* praised Don Juan as a hero precisely because of his "quantitative" approach to love. He made as many conquests as he possibly could. He practiced the "ethic of quantity." But Camus was praising Don Juan as a "hero of the absurd" and his ethic of quantity was merely a reflex response to the "essential absurdity" of life. Camus himself later revised his opinion on this matter. The "ethic of quantity" can take effect not only in love but in hate. The Nazi death camps were a perfect example of this ethic of quantity, this "heroism of the absurd." The ethic of quantity leads to Auschwitz and to despair. Camus saw this and there was no further mention of the ethic of quantity in his books after World War II. He moved more and more toward the ethic of love, sacrifice, and compassion.

Anyone who regards love as a deal made on the basis of "needs" is in danger of falling into a purely quantitative ethic. If love is a deal, then who is to say that you should not make as many deals as possible?

From the moment one approaches it in terms of "need" and "fulfillment," love has to be a deal. And what is worse, since we are constantly subjected to the saturation bombing of our senses and imagination with suggestions of impossibly ideal fulfillments, we cannot help revising our estimate of the deal we have made. We cannot help going back on it and making a "better" deal with someone else who is more satisfying.

The situation then is this: we go into love with a sense of immense need, with a naive demand for perfect fulfillment. After all, this is what we are daily and hourly told to expect. The effect of overstimulation by advertising and other media keeps us at the highest possible pitch of dissatisfaction with the second-rate fulfillment we are actually getting and with the deal we have made. It exacerbates our need. With many people, sexual cravings are kept in a state of high irritation, not by authentic passion, but by the need to prove themselves attractive and successful lovers. They seek security in the repeated assurance that they are still marketable, still a worthwhile product. The long word for all this is narcissism. It has disastrous affects, for it leads people to manipulate each other for selfish ends.

When you habitually function like this, you may seem to be living a very "full" and happy life. You may seem to have everything. You go everywhere, you are in the middle of everything, have lots of friends, "love" and are "loved." You seem in fact to be "perfectly adjusted" sexually and otherwise with your partner(s). Yet underneath there may be a devouring sense that you have nevertheless been cheated, and that the life you are living is not the real thing at all. That is the tragedy of those who are able to measure up to an advertising image which is presented to them on all sides as ideal. Yet they know by experience that there is nothing to it. The whole thing is hollow. They are perhaps in some ways worse off than those who cannot quite make the grade and who therefore always think that perhaps there is a complete fulfillment which they can yet attain. These at least still have hope!

The truth is, however, that this whole concept of life and of love is self-defeating. To consider love merely as a matter of need and fulfillment, as something which works itself out in a cool deal, is to miss the whole point of love, and of life itself.

The basic error is to regard love merely as a need, an appetite, a craving, a hunger which calls for satisfaction. Psychologically, this concept reflects an immature and regressive attitude toward life and toward other people.

■

Real Talk, Silence, and Conflict

Mary Field Belenky
Blythe McVicker Clinchy
Nancy Rule Goldberger
Jill Mattuck Tarule

REAL TALK

Constructivists make a distinction between "really talking" and what they consider to be didactic talk in which the speaker's intention is to hold forth rather than to share ideas. In didactic talk, each participant may report experience, but there is no attempt among participants to join together to arrive at some new understanding. "Really talking" requires careful listening; it implies a mutually shared agreement that together you are creating the optimum setting so that half-baked or emergent ideas can grow. "Real talk" reaches deep into the experience of each participant; it also draws on the analytical abilities of each. Conversation, as constructivists describe it, includes discourse and exploration, talking and listening, questions, argument, speculation, and sharing.

We saw that at the earlier positions women often felt that they had to choose between speaking and listening or that, at best, they might alternate. As a sophomore, Bridget described teetering between these two modes.

From Women's Ways of Knowing (pp. 144-148) by Mary Field Belenky, Blythe McVicker Clinchy, Nancy Rule Goldberger and Jill Mattuch Tarule, copyright © 1986, Basic Books, Inc., a division of HarperCollins Publishers, Inc. Reprinted with the permission of the publisher.

> I am very much of a listener instead of a talker. I will try to contribute things, but I find the moment I start thinking about what I want to say, I stop listening to what everybody else is saying. So I have a tendency to keep my mouth shut, to concentrate on what I am absorbing instead of what I want to throw back out.

Four years later, after having finished college and traveled abroad, Bridget was thinking as a constructivist and described the hard work entailed in bringing listening and speaking into balance.

> I always was the kind of person who felt I had to entertain people or keep the conversation going. I was brought up to be really wishy-washy, at least by my mother anyway. To be the one who entertains, who supports, who perhaps provides the forum for the discussion, but is never a participant in that discussion herself. I'm still finding it difficult in certain circumstances to truly express what I feel or what I want. But I am trying—at least for my own mental health—to be honest and forthright in my communication with people. That is a big challenge—a big, big challenge!

Listening to others no longer diminishes women's capacity to hear their own voices. The capacity for speaking with and listening to others while simultaneously speaking with and listening to the self is an achievement that allows a conversation to open between constructivists and the world.

The devotion of constructivists to "real talk" as a way of connecting to others and acquiring and communicating new knowledge distinguishes them in both their personal and professional lives.* With family and friends they are eager to describe their own experience so that others can understand; they question and listen to others, urging them to speak, so that they might better know the world from the other person's vantage point. At work and in public forums, they believe that people have an obligation to share with others how they know and what they learn when they "jump outside of the given." Kay said, "Somebody can be an expert, but if they do not articulate what they've learned, then that renders their knowledge useless if they can't share it with other people." Alice Koller described the task in other terms: "Once on the other side, [one] must look back and throw down a footbridge . . . for followers to use" (1983, p. 95). In addition to sharing what you know, having a willingness to describe how you got there is important. Adele said, "I tend to trust people who share the process of their thinking."

Political scientist Jean Bethke Elshtain describes a kind of "ideal speech situation"—a term introduced by the philosopher Jurgen Habermas—that is close to what constructivists mean when they refer to "really talking." It is speech of a particular kind: "Speech that simultaneously taps and touches our inner and outer worlds within a community of others with whom we share deeply felt, largely inarticulate, but daily renewed inter-subjective reality" (1982, p. 620).

In "real talk" domination is absent, reciprocity and cooperation are prominent. Although doubting may still be used to test ideas and may even be described as invigorating or fun, constructivist women are much more likely to replace doubting with believing as the best way of getting the feel of a new idea or a new friend or colleague. At times, particularly in certain academic and work situations in which adversarial interactions are common, constructivist women may feel compelled to demonstrate that they can hold their own in a battle of ideas to prove to others that they, too, have the analytical powers and hard data to justify their claims. However, they usually resent the implicit pressure in male-dominated circles to toughen up and fight to get their ideas across.

SILENCE AND CONFLICT

Even among women who feel they have found their voice, problems with voice abound. Some women told us, in anger and frustration, how frequently they felt unheard and unheeded—both at home and at work. In our society, which values the words of male authority, constructivist women are no more immune to the experience of feeling silenced than any other group of women.

Once a woman has a voice, she wants it to be heard. Some women told us that they had arrived at a point in their chosen work where they could "say what they mean and mean what they say," but then they often added that they longed for someone with whom they could genuinely share their visions and problems. They hoped to find understanding and communicative people—people who were invested in "really talking."

For Ruddick, finding her voice and life's work as a feminist philosopher taught her that her intellectual life could "satisfy a deep personal need *and* be intellectually challenging *and* still mean something to an attentive stranger" (1984, p. 148). Constructivist women need and value attentive strangers as well as understanding friends and colleagues. Learning that their ideas can be taken in and put to use—that their ideas can spark interest among unknown others—is an exhilarating and confirmatory experience.

However, many women told us of the anger they felt when no one listened or when their "womanly voice" was dismissed as soft or misguided, a particularly common complaint of women working in a setting where men predominated. One successful professional woman told us, "You know, the older I get the more I realize that I'm willing to talk about things I care about *only* if I know the other person is really listening. If I don't feel that, I find myself falling into a silence, even when I'm at work or in the middle of a professional meeting." She contemplated changing jobs, even changing her career, in the search for a more attentive response from her colleagues. Like many women, she suspected that her ideas might find a more receptive audience among other women. However, as another woman said, "In being a woman, you have to make men see things they haven't had to see. It's not their fault. It's just the way it is."

Most constructivist women feel that women have a special responsibility to try to communicate to both men and women how they view things and why they value what they do, even though they feel that their words may fall on deaf ears.

In addition to the accounts about problems in the workplace, we heard stories about the conflicts and silence between women and the men they cared for. Especially in talk between the sexes, dialogue can stumble on discrepant assumptions and edge toward silence or anger or both.

Donna, a married Hispanic woman in her forties who spent the last seven years finally obtaining her B.A. degree, recognized why she and her husband were heading for difficulties in their marriage. He had supported her in her wish to become "educated" even though he was not; however, she felt they now had very different ways of understanding and dealing with their children and domestic problems.

> We now view events that happen in our lives very differently. He reads them very straightforward, on a superficial kind of level. And I don't. I probe them. I read into them. He says he sees things in black and white and I see all kinds of shades of grays—all these gradations he doesn't see. That's been exacerbated by my education. I think it's a good thing. He thinks it's not so good.

Although she was not contemplating it for the moment, Donna feared an end to the marriage. She was not sure if she could cope with her differences with her husband or if she would have the strength to give up some of the things she only recently discovered she wanted for herself—more education, greater involvement in a career in government, aims that would take her far beyond the boundaries of the home as she and her husband originally defined it. Optimistically, Donna foresaw the beginning of a new phase of her marriage in which she and her husband perhaps could "get to know each other in a different way."

We heard many women describe more negative outcomes in their intimate relationships. Adele, the musician-turned-counselor, told us of the difficulties she had with her ex-husband, difficulties that were beginning to repeat themselves in her relationship with a new man.

> I'm saying as the woman, "I want more—more talk, more sharing, more feeling." And the man is saying, "You're too needy or too demanding" or whatever. I feel like what ends up happening, when the man does that enough, is that I begin not to want to even bother any more. I begin withdrawing a lot, begin feeling angry most of the time.

Adele observed that this was a problem she often came across in counseling couples. As she was well aware, relationships sometimes do not survive the stress of such seemingly unbreachable differences in perspective.

For some constructivist women, particularly those who do not shy away from speaking their minds, enduring, intimate relationships may be hard to establish. The women have difficulties finding companionable and supportive men, and they experience loneliness and discouragement.

> I intimidate many men. It's hard. It means loneliness lots of times. It's necessary to learn to compromise to a certain extent—how much you have to shut up and how much you have to talk. And how to be effective by talking at the right moment.

Social expectations, which shape the behavior between the sexes, continue to exert pressure on constructivist women to accept the status quo. Although persistent in their efforts to be heard and to hold on to their new sense of voice, constructivist women can end up accommodating the needs and ground rules of men out of the sad wisdom that change does not come easily.

NOTES

*Carol Edelsky, based on her study of interactions in mixed-sex professional meetings, distinguishes between two kinds of "floors": the *turn-taking floor* (F1), in which one speaker at a time holds the floor and is center stage, and the *collaborative floor* (F2), which is less formal and is developed by several people "operating on the same wave length." Characteristic of the F1 is a "monologue . . . and hierarchical interaction in which floors are won or lost—and which shares features with other contexts in which women have learned they had best not assert themselves." Women come into their own in the F2 interaction, which results in "high levels of communicative involvement and satisfaction" (1981, p. 416).

REFERENCES

Edelsky, C. (1981). Who's got the floor? *Language in Society, 10*, 383-421.
Elshtain, J.B. (1982). Feminist discourse and its discontents: Language,

power and meaning. *Signs, 7*, 603-621.

Kollar, A. (1983). *An unknown woman*. New York: Bantam.

Ruddick, S. (1984). New combinations: Learning from Virginia Woolf. In C. Asher, L. DeSalvor, S. Ruddick, *Between Women* (pp. 137-159). Boston: Beacon Press.

■ 11

Ethics

Dialogue grounded in interpersonal trust suggests a number of ethical commitments in any exchange: (a) treating communicative partners as persons, not as objects; (b) caring encouraged by mutual good will; (c) permitting each partner to be heard; and (d) taking responsibility for oneself, the other, and the "common good." Such commitments offer a foundation for interpersonal risk taking, for committing one's self to relationships before outcomes are predictable.

This ethical foundation for interpersonal dialogue does not, of course, emerge from a vacuum. Kant, Aristotle, Mill, and Buber are some of the philosophers contributing to these assumed commitments. Even philosophers of this caliber did not invent such ideas in isolation. Their ethical positions emerged from stories of Judaism, democracy, Athenian virtues, and the Protestant work ethic. More recently, Carol Gilligan (1982) reminded us that our choices and evaluations of ethical behavior are tied also to gender. Both philosophical and practical traditions concerned with ethical action call us to respond with genuine attention and respect.

Alasdair MacIntyre suggested that we are storytelling beings. It is out of the stories of philosophical and practical traditions that our ethical lives are shaped. When the stories, for whatever reason, cease to be told, mutual trust is put at risk. Hence, the title of his major work is *After Virtue*—a time after which the stories that give rise to virtue are not told or understood. MacIntyre's critique of "emotivism," or what he called decision by personal preference, is propelled by his concern that ethical decisions become problematic when no story-laden tradition offers guidance. We then follow our own individualistic preferences, unguided and undeterred by any sense of immersion in the dialogue that preceded us.

Nel Noddings believes that an ethic of caring is not necessarily rooted in philosophical tradition. Instead, such an ethic can emerge in everyday acts of service and concern for one another. Noddings reminds us that many women have lived such an ethic of caring in upholding the major responsibility in many relationships.

261

The ethic of caring described by Noddings is based on a praxis of lived experience. People grow and prosper in an environment of care, and those that want relationships to be nourished are naturally called to facilitate care. A relational approach to care does not need rigid adherence to principles. As Noddings (1984) notes, "Many persons who live moral lives do not approach moral problems formally" (p. 8). They just do what is needed within concrete situations to assist those around them, living caring lives.

Charles Brown and Paul W. Keller outlined an interpersonal ethic that encourages care for others. They relied heavily on a democratic tradition and recast "one person, one vote" to imply that each voice has a similar right to be heard. Listening is a key as one responds to the other. Brown and Keller combine some of the concerns of MacIntyre, informing us of democratic tradition and calling attention to practical choices of everyday ethics.

Why should we care about others? Is it really important to invite dialogue with those with whom we disagree? Such questions have guided the work of philosophers from Kant to Buber to Gadamer, and more recently to scholars whose work we have excerpted—MacIntyre, Noddings, and Brown and Keller—who present three variations on the theme of dialogic ethics.

REFERENCES

Gilligan, C. (1982). *In a different voice: Psychological theory and women's development*. Cambridge, MA: Harvard University Press.

Noddings, N. (1984). *Caring: A feminine approach to ethics and moral education*. Berkeley: University of California Press.

The Virtues, The Unity of a Human Life and The Concept of a Tradition

Alasdair C. MacIntyre

I spoke earlier of the agent as not only an actor, but an author. Now I must emphasize that what the agent is able to do and say intelligibly as an actor is deeply affected by the fact that we are never more (and sometimes less) than the co-authors of our own narratives. Only in fantasy do we live what story we please. In life, as both Aristotle and Engels noted, we are always under certain constraints. We enter upon a stage which we did not design and we find ourselves part of an action that was not of our making. Each of us being a main character in his own drama plays subordinate parts in the dramas of others, and each drama constrains the others. In my drama, perhaps, I am Hamlet or Iago or at least the swineherd who may yet become a prince, but to you I am only A Gentleman or at best Second Murderer, while you are my Polonius or my Gravedigger, but your own hero. Each of our dramas exerts constraints on each other's, making the whole different from the parts, but still dramatic.

It is considerations as complex as these which are involved in making the notion of intelligibility the conceptual connecting link between the notion of action and that of narrative. Once we have understood its importance the claim that the concept of an action is secondary to that of an intelligible action will perhaps appear less bizarre and so too will the claim that the notion of "an" action, while of the highest practical importance is always a potentially misleading abstraction. An action is a moment in a possible or actual history or in a number of such histories. The notion of a history is as fundamental a notion as the notion of an action. Each requires the other. But I cannot say this without noticing that it is precisely this that Sartre denies—as indeed his whole theory of the self, which captures so well the spirit of modernity, requires that he should. In *La Nausée*, Sartre makes Antoine Roquentin argue not just what Mink argues, that narrative is very different from life, but that to present human life in the form of a narrative is always to falsify it. There are not and there cannot be any true stories. Human life is composed of discrete actions which lead nowhere, which have no order; the story-teller imposes on human events retrospectively an order which they did not have while they were lived. Clearly if Sartre/Roquentin is right—I speak of Sartre/Roquentin to distinguish him from such other well-known characters as Sartre/Heidegger and Sartre/Marx—my central contention must be mistaken. There is nonetheless an important point of agreement between my thesis and that of Sartre/Roquentin. We agree in identifying the intelligibility of an action with its place in a narrative sequence. Only Sartre/Roquentin takes it that human actions are as such unintelligible occurrences: it is to a realization of the metaphysical implications of this that Roquentin is brought in the course of the novel and the practical effect upon him is to bring to an end his own project of writing an historical biography. This project no longer makes sense. Either he will write what is true or he will write an intelligible history, but the one possibility excludes the other. Is Sartre/Roquentin right?

We can discover what is wrong with Sartre's thesis in either of two ways. One is to ask: what would human actions deprived of any falsifying narrative order be like? Sartre himself never answers this question; it is striking that in order to show that there are no true narratives, he himself writes a narrative, albeit a fictional one. But the only picture that I find myself able to form of human nature *an-sich*, prior to the alleged misinterpretation by narrative, is the kind of dislocated sequence which Dr. Johnson offers us in his notes of his travels in France: "There we waited on the ladies—Morville's.—Spain. Country towns all beggars. At Dijon he could not find the way to Orleans.—Cross roads of France very bad.—Five soldiers.—Women.—Soldiers escaped.—The Colonel would not lose five men for the sake of one woman.—The magistrate cannot seize a soldier but by the Colonel's permission, etc., etc." (quoted in Hobsbaum 1973, p. 32). What this suggests is what I take to be true, namely that the characterization of actions allegedly prior to any narrative form being imposed upon them will always turn out to be the presentation of what are plainly the disjointed parts of some possible narrative.

We can also approach the question in another way. What I have called a history is an enacted dramatic narrative in which the characters are also the authors. The characters of course never start literally *ab initio*, they plunge *in medias res*, the beginnings of their story already made for them by what and who has gone before. But when Julian Grenfell or Edward Thomas went off to France in the 1914-18 war they no less enacted a narrative than did Menelaus or Odysseus when *they* went off. The difference between imaginary characters and real ones is not in the narrative form of what they do; it is in the degree of their authorship of that form and of their own deeds. Of course just as they do not begin where they please, they cannot go on exactly as they please either; each character is constrained by the actions of others and by the social settings presupposed in his and their actions, a point forcibly made by Marx in the classical, if not entirely satisfactory account of human life as enacted dramatic narrative, *The Eighteenth Brumaire of Louis Bonaparte.*

I call Marx's account less than satisfactory partly because he wishes to present the narrative of human social life in a way that will be compatible with a view of the life as law-governed and predictable in a particular way. But it is crucial that at any given point in an enacted dramatic narrative we do not know what will happen next. The kind of unpredictability for which I argued in Chapter 8 is required by the narrative structure of human life, and the empirical generalizations and explorations which social scientists discover provide a kind of understanding of human life which is perfectly compatible with that structure.

This unpredictability coexists with a second crucial characteristic of all lived narratives, a certain teleological character. We live out our lives, both individually and in our relationships with each other, in the light of certain conceptions of a possible shared future, a future in which certain possibilities beckon us forward and others repel us, some seem already foreclosed and others perhaps inevitable. There is no present which is not informed by some image of some future and an image of the future which always presents itself in the form of a *telos*—or of a variety of ends or goals—towards which we are either moving or failing to move in the present. Un-predictability and teleology therefore coexist as part of our lives; like characters in a fictional narrative we do not know what will happen next, but nonetheless our lives have a certain form which projects itself towards our future. Thus the narratives which we live out have both an unpredictable and a partially teleological character. If the narrative of our individual and social lives is to continue intelligibly—and either type of narrative may lapse into unintelligibility—it is always both the case that there are constraints on how the story can continue *and* that within those constraints there are indefinitely many ways that it can continue.

A central thesis then begins to emerge: man is in his actions and practice, as well as in his fictions, essentially a story-telling animal. He is not essentially, but becomes through his history, a teller of stories that aspire to truth. But the key question for men is not about their own authorship; I can only answer the question "What am I to do?" if I can answer the prior question "Of what story or stories do I find myself a part?" We enter human society, that is, with one or more imputed characters— roles into which we have been drafted—and we have to learn what they are in order to be able to understand how others respond to us and how our responses to them are apt to be construed. It is through hearing stories about wicked stepmothers, lost children, good but misguided kings, wolves that suckle twin boys, youngest sons who receive no inheritance but must make their own way in the world and eldest sons who waste their inheritance on riotous living and go into exile to live with the swine, that children learn or mislearn both what a child and what a parent is, what the cast of characters may be in the drama into which they have been born and what the ways of the world are. Deprive children of stories and you leave them unscripted, anxious stutterers in their actions as in their words. Hence there is no way to give us an understanding of any society, including our own, except through the stock of stories which constitute its initial dramatic resources. Mythology, in its original sense, is at the heart of things. Vico was right and so was Joyce. And so too of course is that moral tradition from heroic society to its medieval heirs according to which the telling of stories has a key part in educating us into the virtues.

I suggested earlier that "an" action is always an episode in a possible history: I would now like to make a related suggestion about another concept, that of personal identity. Derek Parfit and others have recently drawn our attention to the contrast between the criteria of strict identity, which is an all-or-nothing matter *(either* the Tichborne claimant *is* the last Tichborne heir *or* he is not; *either* all the properties of the last heir belong to the claimant *or* the claimant is not the heir—Leibniz's Law applies) and the psychological continuities of personality which are a matter of more or less. (Am I the same man at fifty as I was at forty in respect of memory, intellectual powers, critical responses? More or less.) But what is crucial to human beings as characters in enacted narratives is that, possessing only the resources of psychological continuity, we have to be able to respond to the imputation of strict identity. I am forever whatever I have been at any time for others—and I may at any time be called upon to answer for it—no matter how changed I may be now. There is no way of *founding* my identity—or lack of it—on the psychological continuity or discontinuity of the self. The self inhabits a character whose unity is given as the unity of a character. Once again there is a crucial disagreement with empiricist or analytical philosophers on the one hand and with existentialists on the other.

Empiricists, such as Locke or Hume, tried to give an account of personal identity solely in terms of psychological states or events. Analytical philosophers, in so many ways their heirs as well as their critics, have wrestled with the connection between those states and events and strict identity understood in terms of Leibniz's Law. Both have failed to see that a background has been omitted, the lack of which makes the problems insoluble. That background is provided by the concept of a story and of that kind of unity of character which a story requires. Just as a history is not a sequence of actions, but the concept of an action is that of a moment in an actual or possible history abstracted for some purpose from that history, so the characters in a history are not a collection of persons, but the concept of a person is that of a character abstracted from a history.

What the narrative concept of selfhood requires is thus twofold. On the one hand, I am what I may justifiably be taken by others to be in the course of living out a story that runs from my birth to my death; I am the *subject* of a history that is my own and no one else's, that has its own peculiar meaning. When someone complains—as do some of those who attempt or commit suicide—that his or her life is meaningless, he or she is often and perhaps characteristically complaining that the narrative of their life has become unintelligible to them, that it lacks any point, any movement towards a climax or a *telos*. Hence the point of doing any one thing rather than another at crucial junctures in their lives seems to such person to have been lost.

To be the subject of a narrative that runs from one's birth to one's death is, I remarked earlier, to be accountable for the actions and experiences which compose a narratable life. It is, that is, to be open to being asked to give a certain kind of account of what one did or what happened to one or what one witnessed at any earlier point in one's life than the time at which the question is posed. Of course someone may have forgotten or suffered brain damage or simply not attended sufficiently at the relevant time to be able to give the relevant account. But to say of someone under some one description ("The prisoner of the Chateau d'If") that he is the same person as someone characterized quite differently ("The Count of Monte Cristo") is precisely to say that it makes sense to ask him to give an intelligible narrative account enabling us to understand how he could at different times and different places be one and the same person and yet be so differently characterized. Thus personal identity is just that identity presupposed by the unity of the character which the unity of a narrative requires. Without such unity there would not be subjects of whom stories could be told.

The other aspect of narrative selfhood is correlative: I am not only accountable, I am one who can always ask others for an account, who can put others to the question. I am part of their story, as they are part of mine. The narrative of any one life is part of an interlocking set of narratives. Moreover this asking for and giving of accounts itself plays an important part in constituting narratives. Asking you what you did and why, what I did and why, pondering the differences between your account of what I did and my account of what I did, and *vice versa*, these are essential constituents of all but the very simplest and barest of narratives. Thus without the accountability of the self those trains of events that constitute all but the simplest and barest of narratives could not occur; and without that same accountability narratives would lack that continuity required to make both them and the actions that constitute them intelligible.

It is important to notice that I am not arguing that the concepts of narrative or of intelligibility or of accountability are *more* fundamental than that of personal identity. The concepts of narrative, intelligibility and accountability presuppose the applicability of the concept of personal identity, just as it presupposes their applicability and just as indeed each of these three presupposes the applicability of the two others. The relationship is one of mutual presupposition. It does follow of course that all attempts to elucidate the notion of personal identity independently of and in isolation from the notions of narrative, intelligibility and accountability are bound to fail. As all such attempts have.

It is now possible to return to the question from which this enquiry into the nature of human action and identity started: In what does the unity of an individual life consist? The answer is that its unity is the unity of a narrative embodied in a single life. To ask "What is the good for me?" is to ask how best I might live out that unity and bring it to completion. To ask "What is the good for man?" is to ask what all answers to the former question must have in common. But now it is important to emphasize that it is the systematic asking of these two questions and the attempt to answer them in deed as well as in word which provide the moral life with its unity. The unity of a human life is the unity of a narrative quest. Quests sometimes fail, are frustrated, abandoned or dissipated into distractions; and human lives may in all these ways also fail. But the only criteria for success or failure in a human life as a whole are the criteria of success or failure in a narrated or to-be-narrated quest. A quest for what?

Two key features of the medieval conception of a quest need to be recalled. The first is that without some at least partly determinate conception of the final *telos* there could not be any beginning to a quest. Some conception of the good for man is required. Whence is such a conception to be drawn? Precisely from those questions which led us to attempt to transcend that limited conception of the virtues which is available in and through practices. It is in looking for a conception of *the* good which will enable us to order other goods, for a conception of *the* good which will enable us to extend our understanding of the purpose and content of the virtues, for a conception of *the* good which will enable us to understand *the* place of integrity and constancy in life, that we initially define the kind of life which is a quest for the good. But secondly it is clear the medieval conception of a quest is not at all that of a search for something already adequately characterized, as miners search for gold or geologists for oil. It is in the course of the quest and only through encountering and coping with the various particular harms, dangers, temptations and distractions which provide any quest with its episodes and incidents that the goal of the quest is finally to be understood. A quest is always an education both as to the character of that which is sought and in self-knowledge.

The virtues therefore are to be understood as those dispositions which will not only sustain practices and enable us to achieve the goods internal to practices, but which will also sustain us in the relevant kind of quest for the good, by enabling us to overcome the harms, dangers, temptations and distractions which we encounter, and which will furnish us with increasing self-knowledge and increasing knowledge of the good. The catalogue of the virtues will therefore include the virtues required to sustain the kind of households and the kind of political communities in which men and women can seek for the good together and the virtues necessary for philosophical enquiry about the character of the good. We have then arrived at a provisional conclusion about the good life for man: the good life for man is the life spent in seeking for the good life for man, and the virtues necessary for the seeking are those which will enable us to understand what more and what else the good life for man is. We have also completed the second stage in our account of the virtues, by situating them in relation to the good life for man and not only in relation to practices. But our enquiry requires a third stage.

For I am never able to seek for the good or exercise the virtues only *qua* individual. This is partly because what it is to live the good life concretely varies from circumstance to circumstance even when it is one and the same conception of the good life and one and the same set of virtues which are being embodied in a human life. What the good life is for a fifth-century Athenian general will not be the same as what it was for a medieval nun or a seventeenth-century farmer. But it is not just that different individuals live in different social circumstances; it is also that we all approach our own circumstances as bearers of a particular social identity. I am someone's son or daughter, someone else's cousin or uncle; I am a citizen of this or that city, a member of this or that guild or profession; I belong to this clan, that tribe, this nation. Hence what is good for me has to be the good for one who inhabits these roles. As such, I inherit from the past of my family, my city, my tribe, my nation, a variety of debts, inheritances, rightful expectations and obligations. These constitute the given of my life, my moral starting point. This is in part what gives my life its own moral particularity.

This thought is likely to appear alien and even surprising from the standpoint of modern individualism. From the standpoint of individualism I am what I myself choose to be. I can always, if I wish to, put in question what are taken to be the merely contingent social features of my existence. I may biologically be my father's son; but I cannot be held responsible for what he did unless I choose implicitly or explicitly to assume such responsibility. I may legally be a citizen of a certain country; but I cannot be held responsible for what my country does or has done unless I choose implicitly or explicitly to assume such responsibility. Such individualism is expressed by those modern Americans who deny any responsibility for the effects of slavery upon black Americans, saying "I never owned any slaves." It is more subtly the standpoint of those other modern Americans who accept a nicely calculated responsibility for such effects measured precisely by the benefits they themselves as individuals have indirectly received from slavery. In both cases "being an American" is not in itself taken to be part of the moral identity of the individual. And of course there is nothing peculiar to modern Americans in this attitude: the Englishman who says, "*I* never did any wrong to Ireland; why bring up that old history as though it had something to do with *me?*" or the young German who believes that being born after 1945 means that what Nazis did to Jews has no moral relevance to his relationship to his Jewish contemporaries, exhibit the same attitude, that according to which the self is detachable from its social and historical roles and statuses. And the self so detached is of course a self very much at home in either Sartre's or Goffman's perspective, a self that can have no history. The contrast with the narrative view of the self is clear. For the story of my life is always embedded in the story of those communities from which I derive my identity. I am born with a past; and to try to cut myself off from that past, in the individualist mode, is to deform my present relationships. The possession of an historical identity and the possession of a social identity coincide. Notice that rebellion against my identity is always one possible mode of expressing it.

Notice also that the fact that the self has to find its moral identity in and through its membership in communities such as those of the family, the neighborhood, the city and the tribe does not entail that the self has to accept the moral *limitations* of the particularity of those forms of community. Without those moral particularities to begin from there would never be anywhere to begin; but it is in moving forward from such particularity that the search for the good, for the universal, consists. Yet particularity can never be simply left behind or obliterated. The notion of escaping from it into a realm of entirely universal maxims which belong to man as such, whether in its eighteenth-century Kantian form or in the presentation of some modern analytical moral philosophies, is an illusion and an illusion with painful consequences. When men and women identify what are in fact their partial and particular causes too easily and too completely with the cause of some universal principle, they usually behave worse than they would otherwise do.

What I am, therefore, is in key part what I inherit, a specific past that is present to some degree in my present. I find myself part of a history and that is generally to say, whether I like it or not, whether I recognize it or not, one of the bearers of a tradition. It was important when I charac-

terized the concept of a practice to notice that practices always have histories and that at any given moment what a practice is depends on a mode
of understanding it which has been transmitted often through many generations. And thus, insofar as the virtues sustain the relationships
required for practices, they have to sustain relationships to the past—and
to the future—as well as in the present. But the traditions through which
particular practices are transmitted and reshaped never exist in isolation
for larger social traditions. What constitutes such traditions?

We are apt to be misled here by the ideological uses to which the
concept of a tradition has been put by conservative political theorists.
Characteristically such theorists have followed Burke in contrasting tradition with reason and the stability of tradition with conflict. Both contrasts
obfuscate. For all reasoning takes place within the context of some traditional mode of thought, transcending through criticism and invention the
limitations of what had hitherto been reasoned in that tradition; this is as
true of modern physics as of medieval logic. Moreover when a tradition is in
good order it is always partially constituted by an argument about the goods
the pursuit of which gives to that tradition its particular point and purpose.

So when an institution—a university, say, or a farm, or a hospital—
is the bearer of a tradition of practice or practices, its common life will be
partly, but in a centrally important way, constituted by a continuous argument as to what a university is and ought to be or what good farming is or
what good medicine is. Traditions, when vital, embody continuities of conflict. Indeed when a tradition becomes Burkean, it is always dying or dead.

The individualism of modernity could of course find no use for the
notion of tradition within its own conceptual scheme except as an adversary
notion; it therefore all too willingly abandoned it to the Burkeans, who,
faithful to Burke's own allegiance, tried to combine adherence in politics to
a conception of tradition which would vindicate the oligarchical revolution
of property of 1688 and adherence in economics to the doctrine and institutions of the free market. The theoretical incoherence of this mismatch
did not deprive it of ideological usefulness. But the outcome has been that
modern conservatives are for the most part engaged in conserving only
older rather than later versions of liberal individualism. Their own core
doctrine is as liberal and as individualist as that of self-avowed liberals.

A living tradition then is an historically extended, socially embodied argument, and an argument precisely in part about the goods which
constitute that tradition. Within a tradition the pursuit of goods extends
through generations, sometimes through many generations. Hence the
individual's search for his or her good is generally and characteristically
conducted within a context defined by those traditions of which the individual's life is a part, and this is true both of those goods which are internal to practices and of the goods of a single life. Once again the narrative
phenomenon of embedding is crucial: the history of a practice in our

time is generally and characteristically embedded in and made intelligible in terms of the larger and longer history of the tradition through which the practice in its present form was conveyed to us; the history of each of our own lives is generally and characteristically embedded in and made intelligible in terms of the larger and longer histories of a number of traditions. I have to say "generally and characteristically" rather than "always," for traditions decay, disintegrate and disappear. What then sustains and strengthens traditions? What weakens and destroys them?

The answer in key part is: the exercise or the lack of exercise of the relevant virtues. The virtues find their point and purpose not only in sustaining those relationships necessary if the variety of goods internal to practices are to be achieved and not only in sustaining the form of an individual life in which that individual may seek out his or her good as the good of his or her whole life, but also in sustaining those traditions which provide both practices and individual lives with their necessary historical context. Lack of justice, lack of truthfulness, lack of courage, lack of the relevant intellectual virtues—these corrupt traditions, just as they do those institutions and practices which derive their life from the traditions of which they are the contemporary embodiments. To recognize this is of course also to recognize the existence of an additional virtue, one whose importance is perhaps most obvious when it is least present, the virtue of having an adequate sense of the traditions to which one belongs or which confront one. This virtue is not to be confused with any form of conservative antiquarianism; I am not praising those who choose the conventional conservative role of *laudator temporis acti*. It is rather the case that an adequate sense of tradition manifests itself in a grasp of those future possibilities which the past has made available to the present. Living traditions, just because they continue a not-yet-completed narrative, confront a future whose determinate and determinable character, so far as it possesses any, derives from the past.

In practical reasoning the possession of this virtue is not manifested so much in the knowledge of a set of generalizations or maxims which may provide our practical inferences with major premises; its presence or absence rather appears in the kind of capacity for judgment which the agent possesses in knowing how to select among the relevant stack of maxims and how to apply them in particular situations. Cardinal Pole possessed it, Mary Tudor did not; Montrose possessed it, Charles I did not. What Cardinal Pole and the Marquis of Montrose possessed were in fact those virtues which enable their possessors to pursue both their own good and the good of the tradition of which they are the bearers even in situations defined by the necessity of tragic, dilemmatic choice. Such choices, understood in the context of the tradition of the virtues, are very different from those which face the modern adherents of rival and incommensurable moral premises in the debates about which I wrote in Chapter 2. Wherein does the difference lie?

It has often been suggested—by J. L. Austin, for example—that *either* we can admit the existence of rival and contingently incompatible goods which make incompatible claims to our practical allegiance *or* we can believe in some determinate conception of *the* good life for man, but that these are mutually exclusive alternatives. No one can consistently hold both these views. What this contention is blind to is that there may be better or worse ways for individuals to live through the tragic confrontation of good with good. And that to know what the good life for man is may require knowing what are the better and what are the worse ways of living in and through such situations. Nothing *a priori* rules out this possibility; and this suggests that within a view such as Austin's there is concealed an unacknowledged empirical premise about the character of tragic situations.

One way in which the choice between rival goods in a tragic situation differs from the modern choice between incommensurable moral premises is that *both* of the alternative courses of action which confront the individual have to be recognized as leading to some authentic and substantial good. By choosing one I do nothing to diminish or derogate from the claim upon me of the other; and therefore, whatever I do, I shall have left undone what I ought to have done. The tragic protagonist, unlike the moral agent as depicted by Sartre or Hare, is not choosing between allegiance to one moral principle rather than another, nor is he or she deciding upon some principle of priority between moral principles. Hence the "ought" involved has a different meaning and force from that of the "ought" in moral principles understood in a modern way. For the tragic protagonist cannot do everything that he or she ought to do. This "ought" unlike Kants, does not imply "can." Moreover any attempt to map the logic of such "ought" assertions on to some modal calculus so as to produce a version of deontic logic has to fail. (See, from a very different point of view, Bas C. Van Fraasen 1973).

Yet it is clear that the moral task of the tragic protagonist may be performed better or worse, independently of the choice between alternatives that he or she makes—*ex hypothesi* he or she has no *right* choice to make. The tragic protagonist may behave heroically or unheroically, generously or ungenerously, gracefully or gracelessly, prudently or imprudently. To perform his or her task better rather than worse will be to do both what is better for him or her *qua* individual and *qua* parent or child or *qua* citizen or member of a profession, or perhaps *qua* some or all of these. The existence of tragic dilemmas casts no doubt upon and provides no counter examples to the thesis that assertions of the form "To do this in this way would be better for X and/or for his or her family, city or profession" are susceptible of objective truth and falsity, any more than the existence of alternative and contingently incompatible forms of medical treatment casts doubt on the thesis that assertions of the form "To undergo his medical treatment in this way would be better for X and/or his or her family" are susceptible of objective truth and falsity. (See, from a different point of view, the illuminating discussion in Samuel Guttenplan 1979-80, pp. 61-80).

The presupposition of this objectivity is of course that we can understand the notion of "good for X" and cognate notions in terms of some conception of the unity of X's life. What is better or worse for X depends upon the character of that intelligible narrative which provides X's life with its unity. Unsurprisingly it is the lack of any such unifying conception of a human life which underlies modern denials of the factual character of moral judgments and more especially of those judgments which ascribe virtues or vices to individuals.

I argued earlier that every moral philosophy has some particular sociology as its counterpart. What I have tried to spell out in this chapter is the kind of understanding of social life which the tradition of the virtues requires, a kind of understanding very different from those domi- nant in the culture of bureaucratic individualism. Within that culture con- ceptions of the virtues become marginal and the tradition of the virtues remains central only in the lives of social groups whose existence is on the margins of the central culture. Within the central culture of liberal or bureaucratic individualism new conceptions of the virtues emerge and the concept of a virtue is itself transformed. To the history of that trans- formation I therefore now turn; for we shall only understand the tradition of the virtues fully if we understand to what kinds of degeneration it has proved liable.

BIBLIOGRAPHY

This bibliography lists only works directly referred to or quoted in the text, except for classics of philosophy and the social sciences to which reference is made only when there is need to identify a particular translation or edition.

Erving Goffman, *The Presentation of Self in Everyday Life*, 1959.
    Encounters, 1961.
    Interaction Ritual, 1957.
    Strategic Interaction, 1969.
Samuel Guttenplan, 'Moral Realism and Moral Dilemmas', *Proceedings of the Aristotelian Society*, 1979-80: 61-80.
R.M. Hare, *The Language of Morals*, 1951.
Bas C. Van Fraasen, 'Values and the Heart's Command', *Journal of Philosophy*, 70, 1973: 5-19.

The Fundamental Nature of Caring

Nel Noddings

THE FUNDAMENTAL NATURE OF CARING

The main task in this chapter is a preliminary analysis of caring. I want to ask what it means to care and to lay down the lines along which analysis will proceed in chapters two and three. It seems obvious in an everyday sense why we should be interested in caring. Everywhere we hear the complaint "Nobody cares!" and our increasing immersion in bureaucratic procedures and regulations leads us to predict that the complaint will continue to be heard. As human beings we want to care and to be cared for. *Caring* is important in itself. It seems necessary, however, to motivate the sort of detailed analysis I propose; that is, it is reasonable in a philosophical context to ask: Why care about caring?

   If we were starting out on a traditional investigation of what it means to be moral, we would almost certainly start with a discussion of moral judgment and moral reasoning. This approach has obvious advantages. It gives us something public and tangible to grapple with—the statements that describe our thinking on moral matters. But I shall argue that this is not the only—nor even the best—starting point. Starting the discussion of moral matters with principles, definitions, and demonstrations is rather like starting the solution of a mathematical problem formally. Sometimes we can and do proceed this way, but when the problematic situation is new, baffling, or especially complex, we cannot start this way. We have to operate in an intuitive or receptive mode that is somewhat mysterious, internal, and nonsequential. After the solution has been found by intuitive methods, we may proceed with the construction of a formal demonstration or proof. As the mathematician Gauss put it: I have got my result but I do not know yet how to get (prove) it."[1]

A difficulty in mathematics teaching is that we too rarely share our fundamental mathematical thinking with our students. We present everything ready-made as it were, as though it springs from our foreheads in formal perfection. The same sort of difficulty arises when we approach the teaching of morality or ethical behavior from a rational-cognitive approach. We fail to share with each other the feelings, the conflicts, the hopes and ideas that influence our eventual choices. We share only the justification for our acts and not what motivates and touches us.

I think we are doubly mistaken when we approach moral matters in this mathematical way. First, of course, we miss sharing the heuristic processes in our ethical thinking just as we miss that sharing when we approach mathematics itself formally. But this difficulty could be remedied pedagogically. We would not have to change our approach to ethics but only to the teaching of ethical behavior or ethical thinking. Second, however, when we approach moral matters through the study of moral reasoning, we are led quite naturally to suppose that ethics is necessarily a subject that must be cast in the language of principle and demonstration. This, I shall argue, is a mistake.

Many persons who live moral lives do not approach moral problems formally. Women, in particular, seem to approach moral problems by placing themselves as nearly as possible in concrete situations and assuming personal responsibility for the choices to be made. They define themselves in terms of *caring* and work their way through moral problems from the position of one-caring.[2] This position or attitude of caring activates a complex structure of memories, feelings, and capacities. Further, the process of moral decision making that is founded on caring requires a process of concretization rather than one of abstraction. An ethic built on caring is, I think, characteristically and essentially feminine—which is not to say, of course, that it cannot be shared by men, any more than we should care to say that traditional moral systems cannot be embraced by women. But an ethic of caring arises, I believe, out of our experience as women, just as the traditional logical approach to ethical problems arises more obviously from masculine experience.

One reason, then, for conducting the comprehensive and appreciative investigation of caring to which we shall now turn is to capture conceptually a feminine—or simply an alternative— approach to matters of morality.

WHAT DOES IT MEAN TO CARE?

Our dictionaries tell us that "care" is a state of mental suffering or of engrossment: to care is to be in a burdened mental state, one of anxiety, fear, or solicitude about something or someone. Alternatively, one cares for something or someone if one has a regard for or inclination toward that something or someone. If I have an inclination toward mathematics, I may willingly spend some time with it, and if I have a regard for you, what you think, feel, and desire will matter to me. And, again, to care may mean to be charged with the protection, welfare, or maintenance of something or someone.

These definitions represent different uses of "care" but, in the deepest human sense, we shall see that elements of each of them are involved in caring. In one sense, I may equate "cares" with "burdens"; I have cares in certain matters (professional, personal, or public) if I have burdens or worries, if I fret over current and projected states of affairs. In another sense, I *care* for someone if I feel a stir of desire or inclination toward him. In a related sense, I *care* for someone if I have regard for his views and interests. In the third sense, I have the care of an elderly relative if I am charged with the responsibility for his physical welfare. But, clearly, in the deep human sense that will occupy us, I cannot claim to care for my relative if my caretaking is perfunctory or grudging.

We see that it will be necessary to give much of our attention to the one-caring in our analysis. Even though we sometimes judge caring from the outside, as third-persons, it is easy to see that the essential elements of caring are located in the relation between the one-caring and the cared-for. In a lovely little book, *On Caring*, Milton Mayeroff describes caring largely through the view of one-caring. He begins by saying: "To care for another person, in the most significant sense, is to help him grow and actualize himself."[3]

I want to approach the problem a bit differently, because I think emphasis on the actualization of the other may lead us to pass too rapidly over the description of what goes on in the one-caring. Further, problems arise in the discussion of reciprocity, and we shall feel a need to examine the role of the cared-for much more closely also. But Mayeroff has given us a significant start by pointing to the importance of constancy, guilt, reciprocation, and the limits of caring. All of these we shall consider in some detail.

Let's start looking at caring from the outside to discover the limitations of that approach. In the ordinary course of events, we expect some action from one who claims to care, even though action is not all we expect. How are we to determine whether Mr. Smith cares for his elderly mother, who is confined to a nursing home? It is not enough, surely, that

Mr. Smith should say, "I care." (But the possibility of his saying this will lead us onto another path of analysis shortly. We shall have to examine caring from the inside.) We, as observers, must look for some action, some manifestation in Smith's behavior, that will allow us to agree that he cares. To care, we feel, requires some action in behalf of the cared-for. Thus, if Smith never visits his mother, nor writes to her, nor telephones her, we would be likely to say that, although he is charged formally with her care—he pays for her confinement—he does not really care. We point out that he seems to be lacking in regard, that he is not troubled enough to see for himself how his mother fares. There is no desire for her company, no inclination toward her. But notice that a criterion of action would not be easy to formulate from this case. Smith, after all, does perform some action in behalf of his mother: he pays for her physical maintenance. But we are looking for a qualitatively different sort of action.

Is direct, externally observable action necessary to caring? Can caring be present in the absence of action in behalf of the cared-for? Consider the problem of lovers who cannot marry because they are already committed to satisfactory and honorable marriages. The lover learns that his beloved is ill. All his instincts cry out for his presence at her bedside. Yet, if he fears for the trouble he may bring her, for the recriminations that may spring from his appearance, he may stay away from her. Surely, we would not say in such a case that the lover does not care. He is in a mental state of engrossment, even suffering; he feels the deepest regard and, charged by his love with the duty to protect, he denies his own need in order to spare her one form of pain. Thus, in caring, he chooses not to act directly and tenderly in response to the beloved's immediate physical pain. We see that, when we consider the action component of caring in depth, we shall have to look beyond observable action to acts of commitment, those acts that are seen only by the individual subject performing them.

In the case of the lover whose beloved has fallen ill, we might expect him to express himself when the crisis has passed. But even this might not happen. He might resolve never to contact her again, and his caring could then be known only to him as he renews his resolve again and again. We do not wish to deny that the lover cares, but clearly, something is missing in the relationship: caring is not completed in the cared-for. Or, consider the mother whose son, in young adulthood, leaves home in anger and rebellion. Should she act to bring about reconciliation? Perhaps. Are we sure that she does not care if she fails to act directly to bring him into loving contact with his family? She may, indeed, deliberately abstain from acting in the belief that her son must be allowed to work out his problem alone. Her regard for him may force her into anguished and carefully considered inaction. Like the lover, she may eventually express herself to her son—when the crisis has passed—but then again, she may not. After a period of, say, two years, the relationship may stabilize, and the mother's caring may resume its usual form. Shall we say, then, that she "cares again" and that for two years she "did not care"?

There are still further difficulties in trying to formulate an action criterion for caring. Suppose that I learn about a family in great need, and suppose that I decide to help them. I pay their back rent for them, buy food for them, and supply them with the necessities of life. I do all this cheerfully, willingly spending time with them. Can it be doubted that I care? This sort of case will raise problems also. Suppose both husband and wife in this family want to be independent, or at least have a latent longing in this direction. But my acts tend to suppress the urge toward independence. Am I helping or hindering?[4] Do I care or only seem to care? If it must be said that my relation to the needy family is not, properly, a caring relation, what has gone wrong?

Now, in this brief inspection of caring acts, we have already encountered problems. Others suggest themselves. What of indirect caring, for example? What shall we say about college students who engage in protests for the blacks of South Africa or the "boat people" of Indochina or the Jews of Russia? Under what conditions would we be willing to say that they care? Again, these may be questions that can be answered only by those claiming to care. We need to know, for example, what motivates the protest. Then, as we shall see, there is the recurring problem of "completion." How is the caring conveyed to the cared-for? What sort of meeting can there be between the one-caring and the cared-for?

We are not going to be able to answer all of these questions with certainty. Indeed, this essay is not aiming toward a systematic exposition of criteria for caring. Rather, I must show that such a systematic effort is, so far as the system is its goal, mistaken. We expend the effort as much to show what is not fruitful as what is. It is not my aim to be able to sort cases at the finish: A cares, B does not care, C cares but not about D, etc. If we can understand how complex and intricate, indeed how subjective, caring is, we shall perhaps be better equipped to meet the conflicts and pains it sometimes induces. Then, too, we may come to understand at least in part how it is that, in a country that spends billions on caretaking of various sorts, we hear everywhere the complaint, "Nobody cares."

In spite of the difficulties involved, we shall have to discuss behavioral indicators of caring in some depth, because we will be concerned about problems of entrusting care, of monitoring caretaking and assigning it. When we consider the possibility of institutional caring and what might be meant by the "caring school," we shall need to know what to look for. And so, even though the analysis will move us more and more toward first- and second-person views of caring, we shall examine caring acts and the "third-person" view also. In this initial analysis, we shall return to the third-person view after examining first- and second-person aspects.

So far, we have talked about the action component of caring, and we certainly have not arrived at a determinate set of criteria. Suppose, now, that we consider the engrossment we expect to find in the one-caring. When Mr. Smith, whose "caring" seems to us to be at best perfunctory, says, "I care," what can he mean? Now, clearly we can only guess, because Mr. Smith has to speak for himself on this. But he might mean: (1) I *do* care. I think of my mother often and worry about her. It is an awful burden. (2) I *do* care. I should see her more often, but I have so much to do—a houseful of kids, long working hours, a wife who needs my companionship . . . (3) I *do* care. I pay the bills, don't I? I have sisters who could provide company . . .

These suggested meanings do not exhaust Mr. Smith's possibilities, but they give us something to work with. In the first case, we might rightly conclude that Mr. Smith does not care for his mother as much as he does for himself as caretaker. He is burdened with cares, and the focus of his attention has shifted inward to himself and his worries. This, we shall see, is a risk of caring. There exists in all caring situations the risk that the one-caring will be overwhelmed by the responsibilities and duties of the task and that, as a result of being burdened, he or she will cease to care for the other and become instead the object of "caring." Now, here—and throughout our discussion on caring—we must try to avoid equivocation. There are, as we have noted, several common meanings of "to care," but no one of them yields the deep sense for which we are probing. When it is clear that "caring" refers to one of the restricted senses, or when we are not yet sure to what it refers, I shall enclose it in quotes. In the situation where Mr. Smith is *burdened with cares*, he is the object of "caring."

In the third case, also, we might justifiably conclude that Mr. Smith does not care. His interest is in equity. He wants to be credited with caring. By doing something, he hopes to find an acceptable substitute for genuine caring. We see similar behavior in the woman who professes to love animals and whisks every stray to the animal shelter. Most animals, once at the shelter, suffer death. Does one who cares choose swift and merciful death for the object of her care over precarious and perhaps painful life? Well, we might say, it depends. It depends on our caretaking capabilities, on traffic conditions where we live, on the physical condition of the animal. All this is exactly to the point. What we do depends not upon rules, or at least not wholly on rules—not upon a prior determination of what is fair or equitable—but upon a constellation of conditions that is viewed through both the eyes of the one-caring and the eyes of the cared-for. By and large, we do not say with any conviction that a person cares if that person acts routinely according to some fixed rule.

The second case is difficult. This Mr. Smith has a notion that caring involves a commitment of self, but he is finding it difficult to handle the commitments he has already made. He is in conflict over how he should spend himself. Undergoing conflict is another risk of caring, and we shall consider a variety of possible conflicts. Of special interest to us will be the question: When should I attempt to remove conflict, and when should I resolve simply to live with the conflict? Suppose, for example, that I care for both cats and birds. (I must use "care for" at this stage without attempting to justify its use completely.) Having particular cats of my own and *not* having particular birds of my own at the same time are indications of my concern for each. But there are wild birds in my garden, and they are in peril from the cats. I may give the matter considerable thought. I feed the cats well so that they will not hunt out of hunger. I hang small bells on their collars. I keep bird cages ready for victims I am able to rescue. I keep bird baths and feeders inaccessible to the cats. Beyond this, I live with the conflict. Others might have the cats declawed, but I will not do this. Now, the point here is not whether I care more for cats than birds, or whether Ms. Jones (who declaws her cats) cares more for birds than I do. The point lies in trying to discern the kinds of things I must think about when I am in a conflict of caring.

When my caring is directed to living things, I must consider their natures, ways of life, needs, and desires. And, although I can never accomplish it entirely, I try to apprehend the reality of the other.

This is the fundamental aspect of caring from the inside. When I look at and think about how I am when I care, I realize that there is invariably this displacement of interest from my own reality to the reality of the other. (Our discussion now will be confined to caring for persons.) Kierkegaard has said that we apprehend another's reality as *possibility*.[5] To be touched, to have aroused in me something that will disturb my own ethical reality, I must see the other's reality as a possibility for my own. This is not to say that I cannot try to see the other's reality differently. Indeed, I can. I can look at it objectively by collecting factual data; I can look at it historically. If it is heroic, I can come to admire it. But this sort of looking does not touch my own ethical reality; it may even distract me from it. As Kierkegaard put it:

> Ethically speaking there is nothing so conducive to sound sleep as admiration of another person's ethical reality. And again ethically speaking, if there is anything that can stir and rouse a man, it is a possibility ideally requiring itself of a human being.[6]

But I am suggesting that we do not see only the direct possibilities for becoming better than we are when we struggle toward the reality of the other. We also have aroused in us the feeling, "I must do something." When we see the other's reality as a possibility for us, we must act to eliminate the intolerable, to reduce the pain, to fill the need, to actualize the dream. When I am in this sort of relationship with another, when the other's reality becomes a real possibility for me, I care. Whether the caring is sustained, whether it lasts long enough to be conveyed to the other, whether it becomes visible in the world, depends upon my sustaining the relationship or, at least, acting out of concern for my own ethicality as though it were sustained.

In this latter case, one in which something has slipped away from me or eluded me from the start but in which I strive to regain or to attain it, I experience a genuine caring for self. This caring for self, for the *ethical* self, can emerge only from a caring for others. But a sense of my physical self, a knowledge of what gives me pain and pleasure, precedes my caring for others. Otherwise, their realities as possibilities for my own reality would mean nothing to me. When we say of someone, "He cares only for himself," we mean that, in our deepest sense, he does not care at all. He has only a sense of that physical self—of what gives him pain and pleasure. Whatever he sees in others is pre-selected in relation to his own needs and desires. He does not see the reality of the other as a possibility for himself but only as an instance of what he has already determined as self or not-self. Thus, he is ethically both zero and finished. His only "becoming" is a physical becoming. It is clear, of course, that I must say more about what is meant by "ethical reality" and "ethical self, " and I shall return to this question.

I need not, however, be a person who cares only for myself in order to behave occasionally as though I care only for myself. Sometimes I behave this way because I have not thought through things carefully enough and because the mode of the times pushes the thoughtless in its own direction. Suppose, for example, that I am a teacher who loves mathematics. I encounter a student who is doing poorly, and I decide to have a talk with him. He tells me that he hates mathematics. *Aha*, I think. *Here is the problem. I must help this poor boy to love mathematics, and then he will do better at it.* What am I doing when I proceed in this way? I am not trying to grasp the reality of the other as a possibility for myself. I have not even asked: *How would it feel to hate mathematics?* Instead, I project my own reality onto my student and say, *You will be just fine if only you learn to love mathematics.* And I have "data" to support me. There is evidence that intrinsic motivation is associated with higher achievement. (Did anyone ever doubt this?) So my student becomes an object of study and manipulation for me. Now, I have deliberately chosen an example that is not often associated with manipulation. Usually, we associate manipulation with trying to get our student to achieve some learning objective that we have devised and set for him. Bringing him to "love mathematics" is seen as a noble aim. And so it is, if it is held out to him as a possibility that he glimpses by observing me and others; but then I shall not be disappointed in him, or in myself, if he remains indifferent to mathematics. It is a possibility that may not be actualized. What matters to me, if I care, is that he find some reason, acceptable in his inner self, for learning the mathematics required of him or that he reject it boldly and honestly. How would it feel to hate mathematics? What reasons could I find for learning it? When I think this way, I refuse to cast about for rewards that might pull him along. He must find his rewards. I do not begin with dazzling performances designed to intrigue him or to change his attitude. I begin, as nearly as I can, with the view from his eyes: Mathematics is bleak, jumbled, scary, boring, boring, boring. . . . What in the world could induce me to engage in it? From that point on, we struggle together with it.

Apprehending the other's reality, feeling what he feels as nearly as possible, is the essential part of caring from the view of the one-caring. For if I take on the other's reality as possibility and begin to feel its reality, I feel, also, that I must act accordingly; that is, I am impelled to act as though in my own behalf, but in behalf of the other. Now, of course, this feeling that I must act may or may not be sustained. I must make a commitment to act. The commitment to act in behalf of the cared- for, a continued interest in his reality throughout the appropriate time span, and the continual renewal of commitment over this span of time are the essential elements of caring from the inner view. Mayeroff speaks of devotion and the promotion of growth in the cared-for. I wish to start with engrossment and motivational displacement. Both concepts will require elaboration.

NOTES

1. Gauss's remark is quoted by Morris Kline, *Why Johnny Can't Add* (New York: Vintage Books, 1974), p. 58.

2. See Carol Gilligan, "In a Different Voice: Women's Conception of the Self and of Morality," *Harvard Educational Review* 47 (1977), 481-517. Also, "Women's Place in Man's Life Cycle," *Harvard Educational Review* 49 (1979), 431-446. Also, *In a Different Voice* (Cambridge, Mass: Harvard University Press), 1982.

3. Milton Mayeroff, *On Caring* (New York: Harper and Row, 1971), p. 1.

4. See David Brandon, *Zen in the Art of Helping* (New York: Dell Publishing Co., 1978), Chap. 3.

5. Soren Kierkegaard, *Concluding Unscientific Postscript*, trans. David F. Swenson and Walter Lowrie (Princeton: Princeton University Press, 1941).

6. Ibid., p. 322.

■

Ethics

Charles T. Brown
Paul W. Keller

Authentic communication is a mutual struggle for common ground between two distinct and inviolable identities—a loving contest in which each man surrenders his weapons to the other.

Floyd W. Matson and Ashley Montagu*

The trouble with communication is that it works!

Words "bite like a saw into white pine."[1] An exchange of views never leaves the participants unchanged and some encounters "make all the difference" in a person's life. Psychologist Sidney Jourand once painted a picture of what can happen in interpersonal exchanges in these terms: "Some people invite you to live; some invite you to die." A commonsense observation of what happens in everyday life seems to bear him out. Some interpersonal exchanges have the effect of opening doors to growth and creative energy. Other exchanges sow the seeds of despair and defeat.

Does it matter how one human being communicates with another? Is it possible to decide that one case of communication is healthier than another? Do I, as a communicator have any responsibility to the person I talk to? If words are so powerful, are there some principles for their use, a guide to what is right and wrong?

From Monologue to Dialogue: An Exploration of Interpersonal Communication, 2/e (pp. 274-279) by Charles T. Brown/Paul W. Keller, copyright © 1979, Prentice Hall. Reprinted with the permission of the publisher.

A SNAPSHOT OF PAST THOUGHT

Writers at least as far back as Aristotle have been struggling with those questions. One thing virtually all of them agree on is that a communicator does have a responsibility toward those with whom he or she communicates.[2] Beyond that, there is impressive agreement on specific ways in which you can tell whether a communicator is ethical or unethical.[3]

Here is a sampling:

A speaker is unethical if he or she
tells deliberate lies.
knowingly distorts the truth.
pretends to know something he or she does not know.
uses emotional appeals that cannot be supported by reason.
conceals his or her real purpose.
uses tactics designed to block the listener's chance to think
     clearly about the topic.

As a group, these statements say, in effect, "All individuals ought to be responded to in ways that would not deceive them and would strengthen their ability to reason for themselves rather than block that ability." Machiavelli catalogued, and accurately described, many ways in which a prince could influence and control his subjects. But the question he was raising was, What works? and not, What is healthy for all the participants?

The tests of ethics just listed were thought of almost entirely in connection with public speaking because this was the kind of communication the ancients were most interested in. But in a world built on a bill of rights and concern for human potential we now have to ask whether those tests are adequate for describing healthy or unhealthy *interpersonal communication*. Our answer is that all of them apply when we move from public speaking to interpersonal communication, but that our new understandings of the latter require an important shift of emphasis.

AN INTERPERSONAL ETHIC

The tests we have cited have to do chiefly with the content of a message—does it contain lies and distortions? Are the tactics used in presenting it misleading? Is there pretense, exaggeration? *An interpersonal ethic accepts these tests, but is more concerned with the attitude a speaker and a listener show toward each other.* What is wrong with a lie? It is just a different set of words from those that tell the truth. The *ultimate* issue in communication, we are saying, is not the validity of words but the validity of the relationship between the people exchanging words. The reason truth, as we know the truth, is important is that people cannot build bridges between them that crumble when tested.

The *interpersonal* ethic is concerned with the loyalty you have toward the person with whom you are communicating. That ethic can be stated as follows:[4]

> *A's communication is ethical to the extent that it accepts B's responses; it is unethical to the extent that it is hostile to B's responses, or in some way tries to subjugate B. The ethic can best be put to a test when A discovers that B rejects the message A is sending.*

Concretely, if parents or teachers or friends or coworkers try to convince you that something is true, or that a conclusion should be accepted, and you find that you cannot agree with them, how they treat your response to them will reveal whether they are willing to take responsibility for their communication with you.

A *Dig Beneath the Surface*

Does such a test make any sense? Let us try to sketch in the background for it. At one of the many really arresting spots in *The Brothers Karamazov* Dostoevsky has Ivan, an intellectual, trying to convince his younger brother Alyosha, a cleric, of the rightness of his life view. Ivan conjures up a problem to make his point. He says to Alyosha,

> Imagine that you are creating a fabric of human destiny with the object of making men happy in the end, giving them the peace and rest at last, but that it was essential and inevitable to torture to death only one tiny creation . . . . and to found that edifice on its unavenged tears, would you consent to be the architect on those conditions? Tell me, and tell the truth.

"No, I wouldn't consent," says Alyosha. It is tempting to want to stop and pursue the values that are brought into question by Alyosha's firm answer. But we want to use the scene as the basis for a paraphrase we would pose regarding communication:

> Imagine that you have the welfare of another person at heart, and that you are convinced that you know what would be good for him in a given situation. Suppose that you recommend to him the "right" course of action, explaining your reasons fully, developing the reason-

able foundations for your view patiently. And suppose that when you are finished—perhaps after repeated conversations—he rejects your proposal. Would you accept his response without rancor, without an undercover resolution to set him right—in short would you accept his response as the authentic reaction of a free individual?[5]

We take it that the most common way to react, when you think you know what is good for someone else and that person keeps turning down your proposals, is either to turn your back on him or her ("If that's the way he(she) feels, let him stew in his own juice") or to bite your tongue and determine that you will change his or her mind one way or another. If the measure we are proposing of what is ethical is accepted, however, neither of those reactions will pass the test.

Who Should Be Free?

The point we are trying to make is that a communication might pass all of the tests previously proposed—it might be without lies, without distortion, without deceit, without unsupportable emotional appeals—and still prove unethical. For the ethic we are proposing is imbedded in the assumption that *whatever enhances that which is uniquely human in participants is ethical; whatever dehumanizes is unethical.*[6] This assumption finds expression in one of the values held most dear in a democratic society, namely, that conditions *of free choice* be created and maintained in which it becomes possible for *the individual to realize his or her potential.* This is achieved to the extent to which others with whom he or she communicates *do not* try to control, coerce, manipulate, maneuver, or exploit him or her.

Not only is coercive communication unethical because of the injury it does the other. It is unethical for the user also, because it gradually cuts a person off from his or her own creative growth. The constant effort to exercise power over others makes one increasingly dependent on getting defeated responses from others. If the desired responses are not forthcoming, the effort to persuade must be redoubled. And this preoccupation closes the door to one's own personal development. The power of personal competence is given up for the exercise of power over other people.

How Free Is Free?

Any unit of communication, by virtue of its psychological nature, involves *mutual control.* We take this to be self-evident: When a message is sent, the speaker intrudes into the life space of the listener. To the extent that anything is communicated, the speaker determines that the listener shall hear, think, and perceive one thing rather than another. At the same time, the listener to such a message inescapably influences the speaker by virtue of the way he or she either rewards the speaker or withholds rewards. In short, our communicative habits, as speakers, are molded and shaped by the responses we get from our listeners.[7] Thus, even in a one-sided situation in which one person does most of the talking, the speaker and the listener control each other. When we exchange the speaking and listening roles in a conversation, we simply exercise different kinds of control over each other.

Now if this two-way control system is constantly at work in communication, and if it is true that its influence on both the sender and the receiver of messages is profound, then the values each of the communicators regards as important become extremely significant, for both the speaker and the listener are, in part, at each other's mercy.

Why Does Everything Have to Be So Complicated?

If we try to discover through the traditional ethical tests what values communicators hold, the problem turns out to be more intricate than it appears on the surface. Take, for example, the notion that in order to be ethical an argument must be valid. In cases of differences between arguments, who is to say which argument, evidence, or conclusion is valid? What is the truth, and how do we know when we know it? How can we be responsible for believing what is not true? Were people unethical when they believed the earth was the center of the universe? Today there is some suggestion that there are velocities that exceed the speed of light. What are the dangers of taking flu shots or being X-rayed?

Let us make the question even tougher. Is it not true that even a deliberate lie, or the withholding of what is believed, may be justified by the most careful exercise of conscience? Deliberate distortion is surely dangerous, but who has not painfully chosen, as the lesser of two evils determined by conscience, to skirt the facts?

And is it not possible that unconscious distortion is carried in every communication? *How else can we explain the uniqueness of each person's perceptions?* "It's a wise cove as knows wot's wot," says one of Stevenson's pirates.

If both the speaker and the listener are mutually controlling each other's responses, how does either one decide who is right and what is true when they differ?

Where do the waters of the Caribbean Sea and the Gulf of Mexico begin and end? Now tell the truth.

It would seem to us that the loyalty of one person to another is more fundamental than the truth, and that it is easier to answer the question, How do I feel about you? than the question, What is the truth?

How do I, the speaker, react to my listener's reaction? How do I, the listener, react to the speaker? If my listener does not respond in a way that satisfies my goal, or vice versa, if the speaker does not respond in ways that satisfy me, am I angered? Am I despondent, and thus tempted to play for sympathy? Do I, in short, refuse to accept the responses of the other person as those of a free individual? Whatever enhances the basic freedom of response in the individual, we are suggesting, is more ethical; whatever either overtly or covertly attacks that energy is less ethical. A person, we are saying, is likely to know more about his or her feelings than about the truth.

NOTES

*Floyd W. Matson and Ashley Montagu, *The Human Dialogue* (New York: The Free Press, 1967), page 7. By permission of The Free Press.

1. William Stafford, "Lit Instructor," in *Traveling Through the Dark* (New York: Harper & Row Publishers, Inc., 1967), p. 38.

2. See such sources as the following: Henry N. Weiman and Otis Walter, "Toward an Analysis of Ethics for Rhetoric," *Quarterly Journal of Speech*, 43 (1957), 266-270; K. Wallace, "An Ethical Basis for Communication," *The Speech Teacher*, 4 (1955), 1-9; Franklyn S. Haiman, "A Re-examination of the Ethics of Persuasion," *Central States Speech Journal*, 3 (1952), 5-10; Lane Cooper, *The Rhetoric of Aristotle*, (New York: Appleton, 1932).

3. For an especially clear and thorough description of the ways in which communication ethics can be examined, see Richard L. Johannesen, *Ethics in Human Communication* (Columbus, Ohio: Charles E. Merrill Publishing Co., 1975).

4. Much of the material discussed in this chapter comes from the authors' first attempt to find an adequate interpersonal ethic. See Paul W. Keller and Charles T. Brown, "An Interpersonal Ethic for Communication," *Journal of Communication*, 18 (1968), 73-81.

5. *Ibid.*, p. 74.

6. Johannesen, op. cit., Chap. 4.

7. William Verplanck, "The Control of the Content of Conversation: Reinforcement of Statements of Opinion," *Journal of Abnormal and Social Psychology*, 51 (1955), 668-676.

■ 12

Community

The notion of community is currently a significant topic in academic circles. The "communitarian" movement, represented by scholars such as Charles Taylor and Robert Bellah, informs us of the necessity of reclaiming a commitment to the "common good." Commitment to the common good, of course, is not a new issue. Within this tradition of concern, communitarians articulate the importance of community-based issues in contemporary society.

Not all understandings of community, however, involve sincere concern for the common good. Dietrich Bonhoeffer (1954), the martyred theologian who protested Hitler's Third Reich, articulated in *Life Together* (p. 26) that it is possible to use a community solely to promote a single individual or group's own good and growth, ignoring the interdependent importance of community. In such an environment, the rhetoric of community may be spoken, but the reality of selfish concern is the common denominator.

In addition, neither Bonhoeffer nor the prominent Jewish theologian and philosopher Martin Buber equate the notion of community with warm psychological feeling. Instead, they remind readers of the importance of commitment to a common task, a common mission that pulls people together. Buber described a view of community based not just on feelings shared between persons, but on a willingness to participate in a common story. As one of the editors has observed:

> If we are left with voluntary commitment to community and recognition of the importance of a center out of which community can emerge, then narration or communication must carry the essence of our center. For a community to survive, it must have a story. That story must be one that individuals can relate to, feel a part of, and affirm. It is a communicative vision of where they are going and why that keeps a community vibrant and healthy. Time is needed for people to tell their stories and to retell them. (Arnett, 1986, p. 173)

Martin Buber, in "Genuine Dialogue and the Possibilities of Peace," a speech given in Germany in 1953 less than a decade after the Holocaust and World War II, uses the vivid example of an old enemy to illustrate the importance of genuine encounter with those we oppose. A story of our common humanity reminds us of a capacity for both good and evil. We may not always be able to forget or forgive others. However, as we recognize that both good and evil walk in the hearts of all people, including ourselves, we can with genuine empathy identify with others' mistakes. Our common task is to find ways to tame the beast in each of us, opening the doors of dialogue to even our enemies—not naively, but from a conviction that our common humanity is linked not only by our impulses for good and evil, but by the reach of dialogue to one another.

Stanley Hauerwas also connected community to the health of the story-life of a people. Dead stories are just told. Living stories still guide the actions of a people. Our decision making and the structure of our character are shaped by the story-filled life of a community. When we become part of a story and "live into" a story, it begins to shape us. Hauerwas suggested that when we live into a story we contribute and shape the story anew. He ties character development to a dialogic willingness to shape and simultaneously to be shaped by a shared narrative. Such a dual action invites a "community of character."

Paulo Freire's work does not let us associate community solely with the concept of story. Freire is wary of words that are not fully supported by actions. Instead, he wants storytellers who will live the heart of a message. A story becomes worthy of participation when people live what is spoken. Words without the congruence of *praxis* invite lives of lies and deception, not community or dialogue, between persons. Community is nourished by characters willing to tell a story that they attempt to live, simultaneously inviting others to continue to shape the story and the practical life of the community.

REFERENCES

Arnett, R. C. (1986). *Communication and community: Implications of Martin Buber's dialogue.* Carbondale: Southern Illinois University Press.
Bonhoeffer, D. (1954). *Life together.* New York: Harper & Row.

Character, Narrative, and Growth

Stanley Hauerwas

As a way of trying to bring the disparate parts of my argument together I am going to tell a story. It is not a complicated story, but I think it suggests nicely how character and narrative can help us understand how the self can and should be capable of moral growth. Moreover I hope this story will serve to suggest how the convictions peculiar to the Christian story require the development of certain kinds of skills. The story relates an incident between me and my father that occurred in an instant but has stayed with me for many years. In order to make it intelligible, I need to supply a little background.

My father is a good but simple man. He was born on the frontier and grew up herding cows. Living with a gun was and is as natural to him as living with an automobile is for me. He made his living, as his father and five brothers did, by laying brick. He spent his whole life working hard at honest labor. It would have simply been unthinkable for him to have done a job halfway. He is after all a craftsman.

I have no doubt that my father loves me deeply, but such love, as is often the case among Westerners, was seldom verbally or physically expressed. It was simply assumed in the day-to-day care involved in surviving. Love meant working hard enough to give me the opportunity to go to college so that I might have more opportunity than my parents had.

And go on I did in abstruse subjects like philosophy and theology. And the further I went the more unlike my parents I became. I gradu-

From A Community of Character: Toward a Constructive Christian Social Ethic (pp. 145-151) by Stanley Hauerwas, copyright © 1981, The University of Notre Dame Press. Reprinted with the permission of the publisher.

ally leaned to recognize that blacks had been unfairly treated and that the word "nigger" could no longer pass my lips. I also learned that Christianity involved more than a general admonition to live a decent life, which made belief in God at once more difficult and easy. And I leaned to appreciate art and music which simply did not exist for my parents.

Married to a woman my parents would always have difficulty understanding, I then made my way to Yale Divinity School, not to study for the ministry, but to study theology. During my second year in divinity school, every time we called home the primary news was about the gun on which my father was working. During the off months of the winter my father had undertaken to build a deer rifle. That meant everything from boring the barrel and setting the sight, to hand-carving the stock. I thought that was fine, since it certainly had nothing to do with me.

However, that summer my wife and I made our usual trip home and we had hardly entered the door when my father thrust the now completed gun into my hands. It was indeed a beautiful piece of craftsmanship. And I immediately allowed as such, but I was not content to stop there. Flushed with theories about the importance of truthfulness and the irrationality of our society's gun policy I said, "Of course you realize that it will not be long before we as a society are going to have to take all these things away from you people."

Morally what I said still seems to me to be exactly right as a social policy. But that I made such a statement in that context surely is one of the lowest points of my "moral development." To be sure there are ready explanations supplied by the Freudians to account for my behavior, but they fail to do justice to the moral failure my response involved. For I was simply not morally mature enough or skillful enough to know how to respond properly when a precious gift was being made.

For what my father was saying, of course, was someday this will be yours and it will be a sign of how much I cared about you. But all I could see was a gun, and in the name of moral righteousness, I callously rejected it. One hopes that now I would be able to say, "I recognize what this gun means and I admire the workmanship that has gone into it. I want you to know that I will always value it for that and I will see that it is cared for in a manner that others can appreciate its value."

I have not told the story to give an insight into my family history or because I get some pleasure from revealing my moral shortcomings. Rather, I have told it because I have found it illuminating for reflecting generally about moral growth. For the insensitivity of my response to my father did not reflect my failure to grasp some moral principle, or to keep the maxim of my action from being universalized, but showed that I did not yet have sufficient character to provide me with the moral skills to know that I had been given a gift and how to respond appropriately. On the surface my response was morally exemplary—I was straightforwardly honest and my position was amply justified. But in fact what I did was deeply dishonest, as it revealed a lack of self, the absence of a sustaining narrative sufficient to bind my past with my future.[37]

For my response was meant only to increase further the alienation between my father and myself in the interest of reinforcing what I took to be more "universal" and objective morality. I discovered that the person who responded so insensitively to my father was not "who I was" or at least not what "I wanted to be." I was and am destined to be different from my parents, but not in a manner that means I no longer carry their story with me. But my own self, my story, was not sufficient to know how that might be done.

And I am struck by how little I would have been helped by becoming more sophisticated in ethical theory or even by conforming my life more completely to the best ethical theory of our day. My problem was not that I lacked skill in moral argument and justification, but that I lacked character sufficient to acknowledge all that I owed my parents while seeing that I am and was independent of them. Indeed it has taken me years to understand that their great gift to me was the permission to go on, even though they sensed my "going on" could not help but create a distance between me and them that love itself would be unable to bridge.

Equally interesting to me has been the attempt to explain to myself how I could have been so unbelievably self-righteous. My temptation has always been to think that what I said "was not the real me." Moreover there is some good reason to accept that kind of explanation, since I certainly would not have said what I did had I "known better." Therefore, I was not responsible for what I did, though I clearly did it at the time.

But such an explanation is a "temptation," as it is equally clear to me that my moral growth depends on taking responsibility for what I said as something done by me. Not to take responsibility for my response is to remain the person who made that kind of response. Philosophically that seems to be a puzzle, for how am I to explain that I must take responsibility for what "I did 'unknowingly'" in order that I can now claim responsibility for what I am and have become? As puzzling as the philosophical problem is, the moral intelligibility of claiming such an action as mine is just as sure. For retrospectively all my actions tend to appear more like what "happened to me" than what I did. Yet to claim them as mine is a necessary condition for making my current actions my own. Our ability to make our actions our own—that is, to claim them as crucial to our history—even those we regret, turns out to be a necessary condition for having a coherent sense of self—that is, our character. But such a coherence requires a narrative that gives us the skill to see that our freedom is as much a gift as it is something we do.

For our freedom is dependent on our having a narrative that gives us skills of interpretation sufficient to allow us to make our past our own through incorporation into our ongoing history. Our ability to so interpret our past may often seem to require nothing less than conversion as we are forced to give up false accounts of ourselves. Because of the pain such conversions often entail, the language of discontinuity tends to predominate in our accounts of our moral development. But the freedom acquired through our reinterpretations is dependent on our having a narrative sufficient to "make sense" of our lives by recognizing the continuity between our past and present and our intended future. In order to see that, we need a story that not only provides the means to acknowledge the blunders as part of our own story, but to see ourselves in a story where even our blunders are part of an ongoing grace, i.e., are forgiven and transformed for "our good and the good of all the church."[38]

These last claims obviously require a defense more elaborate than I can hope to develop here. Indeed, I am unsure I even know how to defend such a claim or know what defense would or should look like. In fact, I have suggested two related but different points: (1) that the self is a gift and (2) that we need a story that helps us accept it a gift. It is from the story that we gain the skills to recognize the gift on which our life depends, as well as ways of acting appropriate to such a gift. For the language of gift, without an appropriate account of the gift itself, can be just as destructive as the claim that we are our own possession.

Yet the language of gift at least offers us a way to deal with Aristotle's claim that we are responsible for having a careless character. Even though we may intuitively think that to be correct, it remains quite unclear how we can be said to be responsible for our character. For the very condition required to claim responsibility seems to be character itself. Therefore Aristotle seems right in suggesting that it does not just make considerable difference how we are brought up, it makes "all the difference."

And it is certainly true that we need to be trained to acquire certain habits. But it is equally important to be introduced to stories that provide a way to locate ourselves in relation to others, our society, and the universe. Stories capable of doing that may be thought of as adventures, for there can be no self devoid of adventure. What we crave is not dignity as an end in itself, but the participation in a struggle that is dignifying. Without self-respect, integrity is impossible. And self-respect comes from a sense of the possession of a self correlative to our participation in a worthy adventure. Yet my very ability to take on a role in the adventure is dependent on my understanding that there are other roles I am not called on to play or cannot play. But the very existence of these other roles gives me the ability to step back and test my own involvement in the adventure. They provide a standpoint that helps me see the limits and possibilities of my own role. Moral growth comes exactly through the testing of my role amid the other possibilities in the adventure.

Moreover, through initiation into such a story I learn to regard others and their difference from me as gift. Only through their existence do I learn what I am, can, or should be.[39] To be sure, the other's very existence necessarily is a threat to me, reminding me that I could have been different than I am. The truthfulness of the adventure tale is thus partly tested by how it helps me negotiate the existence of the other both as a threat and a gift for the existence of my own story.

The necessary existence of the other for my own self is but a reminder that the self is not something we create, but is a gift. Thus we become who we are through the embodiment of the story in the communities in which we are born. What is crucial is not that we find some way to free ourselves from such stories or community, but that the story which grasps us through our community is true. And at least one indication of the truthfulness of a community's story is how it forces me to live in it in a manner that gives me the skill to take responsibility for my character. That does not mean that there will ever be a point at which I can say "I am now what I have made myself," for the story must help me see that claiming myself as my own is not the same as claiming that I have made or chosen what I am. Rather it means I am able to recognize myself in the story that I have learned to make my own.

This is a particularly foreign perspective for most of us today. For our primary story is that we have no story, or that the stories that we have must be overcome if we are to be free. Thus we demand a universal standpoint so that the self may reach a point from which it can judge and choose objectively between competing particularistic stories; in short, we seek a story that frees us from the adventure. Ironically, the story that we have no story is one that prevents moral growth. For it provides us with a self-deceptive story that fails to adequately account for the moral necessity of having a story and of being a self in the first place.

What we require is not no story, but a true story. Such a story is one that provides a pilgrimage with appropriate exercises and disciplines of self examination. Christians believe scripture offers such a story. There we find many accounts of a struggle of God with his creation. The story of God does not offer a resolution of life's difficulties, but it offers us something better—an adventure and struggle, for we are possessors of the happy news that God has called people together to live faithful to the reality that he is the Lord of this world. All men have been promised that through the struggle of this people to live faithful to that promise God will reclaim the world for his Kingdom. By learning their part in this story, Christians claim to have a narrative that can provide the basis for a self appropriate to the unresolved, and often tragic, conflicts of this existence. The unity of the self is not gained by attaining a universal point of view, but by living faithful to a narrative that does not betray the diversity of our existence. No matter how hard such a people work to stay faithful to such convictions, they never can forget that it is only through a gift that they are what they are.

To argue that what we need is a true story if we are to grow in a morally appropriate way is not to deny the importance of the "universal." But the test of the truthfulness of any story does not reside in its conforming to or embodying a prior universal norm, but rather in how we and others find their lives illuminated and compelled by the accuracy and truthfulness of its particular vision. There is no "story of stories," but only particular stories which more or less adequately enable us to know and face the truth of our existence. Thus, there is no universal point of view, a point of view that does not bear the marks of a particular history. The recognition of that is one of the first indications that we are dealing with a story that should demand our attention for its power to reveal the truth.

3.2 How Can We Be Taught and Grow into the Story?

Every account of moral development must necessarily have educational implications. We must be given some exercises appropriate to the kinds of moral growth desired. That is an incontrovertible risk. The various sets of exercises through which Christians learn to understand and live appropriate to the story of God's dealing with them in Israel and Jesus may be called tradition. The Christian life requires the development of certain kinds of habits, but those very habits require us to face ambiguities and conflicts through which our virtues are refined. Therefore, there is every reason to think that Christians have always been prescribing a form of moral development for training in their own community.

Growth in the Christian life may well involve encouraging a greater conflict between the self and wider society than is generally approved. Thus Christians train or should train their children to resist the authority of the state, not in the name of their "rights" as individuals, but because the "justice" of the state is to be judged against God's justice. Such training is "risky," as it separates the young of the Christian community from powerful support necessary to being "a self." To be trained to resist the state, therefore, requires nothing less than an alternative story and society in which the self can find a home.

Such a society can never be satisfied with external compliance with the story. For the story itself demands that only those who are willing to be the story are capable of following it. That is why it has been the brunt of Christian spirituality through the ages to provide exercises and examples through which Christians might better be what they are. What is crucial is not that Christians know the truth, but that they be the truth. "For if the doctrines of Christianity were practiced, they would make a man as different from other people as to all worldly tempers, sensual pleasures, and the pride of life as a wise man is different from a natural; it would be as easy a thing to know a Christian by his outward course of life as it is now difficult to find anybody that lives it."[40]

I suspect that the insistence on learning to live as you are and be as you live is part of the reason that Christians have maintained that the Christian life finally requires attention to masters of that life. For it is from the masters that we learn skills necessary to have lives appropriate to the claim that we are nothing less than God's people. For the most central of Christian convictions is the assumption that no statement or principle of morality can be sufficient to make us moral. Rather to be moral requires constant training, for the story that forms our lives requires nothing less than perfection—i.e., full participation in an adequate story.

NOTES

37. Of course, it is equally true that every "binding" requires a "loosing," as we cannot and should not be bound to everything in our past. It may even be true that some of use inherit a history so destructive we may rightly wonder how we could ever be bound to it. Yet my freedom from such a history cannot come by having "no history" but by acquiring a narrative that helps me have a stance toward my past without resentment. For resentment would continue to bind me to the destructive, since the self would still be essentially defined by my assumption that I am primarily a creature of injustice. I suspect that one of the reasons growth in the Christian life is described as conversion is that it requires us to learn to live without resentment. And to be able to live in that manner requires us to learn that our life, including the destructive past, is nothing less than gift. I wish to thank Mr. Michael Duffy for helping me formulate this point.

38. I am particularly grateful to James McClendon for suggesting this way of putting the matter.

39. For example, see Enda McDonagh's suggestion that "threat" is always the necessary other side of a "gift." *Gift and Call* (St. Meinrad, Ind.: Abbey Press, 1975), pp. 36-39. That such is the case makes Aristotle's understanding of the centrality of courage for moral wisdom all the more compelling.

40. Law, *A Serious Call to a Devout and Holy Life*, p. 55. There is an unjustified intellectualistic bias in much to the literature dealing with moral development. The assumption seems to be that the more "self-conscious" we are of our "values" and principles, the better chance we have for moral growth. While I suspect any significant tradition must develop some who are "self-conscious," it is by no means clear that all need to be such. We must remember that the Gospel does not require us to be self-conscious as our first order of business. Rather it requires us to be faithful.

■

There is No True Word That is Not At the Same Time a Praxis

Paulo Freire

As we attempt to analyze dialogue as a human phenomenon, we discover something which is the essence of dialogue itself: *the word*. But the word is more than just an instrument which makes dialogue possible; accordingly, we must seek its constitutive elements. Within the word we find two dimensions, reflection and action, in such radical interaction that if one is sacrificed—even in part—the other immediately suffers. There is no true word that is not at the same time a praxis.[1] Thus, to speak a true word is to transform the world.[2]

An unauthentic word, one which is unable to transform reality, results when dichotomy is imposed upon its constitutive elements. When a word is deprived of its dimension of action, reflection automatically suffers as well; and the word is changed into idle chatter, into *verbalism*, into an alienated and alienating "blah." It becomes an empty word, one which cannot denounce the world, for denunciation is impossible without a commitment to transform, and there is no transformation without action.

On the other hand, if action is emphasized exclusively, to the detriment of reflection, the word is converted into *activism*. The latter—action for action's sake—negates the true praxis and makes dialogue impossible. Either dichotomy, by creating unauthentic forms of existence, creates also unauthentic forms of thought, which reinforce the original dichotomy.

Human existence cannot be silent, nor can it be nourished by false words, but only by true words, with which men transform the world. To exist, humanly, is to *name* the world, to change it. Once named, the world in its turn reappears to the namers as a problem and requires of them a new *naming*. Men are not built in silence,[3] but in word, in work, in action-reflection.

But while to say the true word—which is work, which is praxis—is to transform the world, saying that word is not the privilege of some few men, but the right of every man. Consequently, no one can say a true word alone—nor can he say it *for* another, in a prescriptive act which robs others of their words.

Dialogue is the encounter between men mediated by the world, in order to name the world. Hence, dialogue cannot occur between those who want to name the world and those who do not wish this naming— between those who deny other men the right to speak their word and those whose right to speak has been denied them. Those who have been denied their primordial right to speak their word must first reclaim this right and prevent the continuation of this dehumanizing aggression.

If it is in speaking their word that men, by naming the world, trans- form it, dialogue imposes itself as the way by which men achieve signifi- cance as men. Dialogue is thus an existential necessity. And since dialogue is the encounter in which the united reflection and action of the dialoguers are addressed to the world which is to be transformed and humanized, this dialogue cannot be reduced to the act of one person's "depositing" ideas in another, nor can it become a simple exchange of ideas to be "consumed" by the discussants. Nor yet is it a hostile, polemical argument between men who are committed neither to the naming of the world, nor to the search for truth, but rather to the imposition of their own truth. Because dialogue is an encounter among men who name the world, it must not be a situation where some men name on behalf of others. It is an act of creation; it must not serve as a crafty instrument for the domination of one man by another. The domination implicit in dialogue is that of the world by the dialoguers; it is conquest of the world for the liberation of men.

Dialogue cannot exist, however, in the absence of a profound love for the world and for men. The naming of the world, which is an act of creation and re-creation, is not possible if it is not infused with love.[4] Love is at the same time the foundation of dialogue and dialogue itself. It is thus necessarily the task of responsible Subjects and cannot exist in a relation of domination. Domination reveals the pathology of love: sadism in the dominator and masochism in the dominated. Because love is an act of courage, not of fear, love is commitment to other men. No matter where the oppressed are found, the act of love is commitment to their cause—the cause of liberation. And this commitment, because it is loving, is dialogical. As an act of bravery, love cannot be sentimental; as an act of freedom, it must not serve as a pretext for manipulation. It must generate other acts of freedom; otherwise, it is not love. Only by abolishing the situation of oppression is it possible to restore the love which that situation made impossible. If I do not love the world—if I do not love life—if I do not love men—I cannot enter into dialogue.

On the other hand, dialogue cannot exist without humility. The naming of the world, through which men constantly re-create that world, cannot be an act of arrogance. Dialogue, as the encounter of men addressed to the common task of learning and acting, is broken if the parties (or one of them) lack humility. How can I dialogue if I always project ignorance onto others and never perceive my own? How can I dialogue if I regard myself as a case apart from other men—mere "its" in whom I cannot recognize other "I"s? How can I dialogue if I consider myself a member of the in-group of "pure" men, the owners of truth and knowledge, for whom all non-members are "these people" or "the great unwashed"? How can I dialogue if I start from the premise that naming the world is the task of an elite and that the presence of the people in history is a sign of deterioration, thus to be avoided? How can I dialogue if I am closed to—and even offended by—the contribution of others? How can I dialogue if I am afraid of being displaced, the mere possibility causing me torment and weakness? Self-sufficiency is incompatible with dialogue. Men who lack humility (or have lost it) cannot come to the people, cannot be their partners in naming the world. Someone who cannot acknowledge himself to be as mortal as everyone else still has a long way to go before he can reach the point of encounter. At the point of encounter there are neither utter ignoramuses nor perfect sages; there are only men who are attempting, together, to learn more than they now know.

Dialogue further requires an intense faith in man, faith in his power to make and remake, to create and re-create, faith in his vocation to be more fully human (which is not the privilege of an elite, but the birthright of all men). Faith in man is an *a priori* requirement for dialogue; the "dialogical man" believes in other men even before he meets them face to face. His faith, however, is not naive. The "dialogical man" is critical and knows that although it is within the power of men to create and transform, in a concrete situation of alienation men may be impaired in the use of that power. Far from destroying his faith in man, however, this possibility strikes him as a challenge to which he must respond. He is convinced that the power to create and transform, even when thwarted in concrete situations, tends to be reborn. And that rebirth can occur—not gratuitously, but in and through the struggle for liberation—in the supersedence of slave labor by emancipated labor which gives zest to life. Without this faith in man, dialogue is a farce which inevitably degenerates into paternalistic manipulation.

Founding itself upon love, humility, and faith, dialogue becomes a horizontal relationship of which mutual trust between the dialoguers is the logical consequence. It would be a contradiction in terms if dialogue—loving, humble, and full of faith—did not produce this climate of mutual trust, which leads the dialoguers into ever closer partnership in the naming of the world. Conversely, such trust is obviously absent in the anti-dialogics of the banking method of education. Whereas faith in man is an *a priori* requirement for dialogue, trust is established by dialogue. Should it founder, it will be seen that the preconditions were lacking. False love, false humility, and feeble faith in man cannot create trust. Trust is contingent on the evidence which one party provides the others of his true, concrete intentions; it cannot exist if that party's words do not coincide with his actions. To say one thing and do another—to take one's own word lightly—cannot inspire trust. To glorify democracy and to silence the people is a farce; to discourse on humanism and to negate man is a lie.

Nor yet can dialogue exist without hope. Hope is rooted in men's incompletion, from which they move out in constant search—a search which can be carried out only in communion with other men. Hopelessness is a form of silence, of denying the world and fleeing from it. The dehumanization resulting from an unjust order is not a cause for despair but for hope, leading to the incessant pursuit of the humanity denied by injustice. Hope, however, does not consist in crossing one's arms and waiting. As long as I fight, I am moved by hope; and if I fight with hope, then I can wait. As the encounter of men seeking to be more fully human, dialogue cannot be carried on in a climate of hopelessness. If the dialoguers expect nothing to come of their efforts, their encounter will be empty and sterile, bureaucratic and tedious.

Finally, true dialogue cannot exist unless the dialoguers engage in critical thinking—thinking which discerns an indivisible solidarity between the world and men and admits of no dichotomy between them— thinking which perceives reality as process, as transformation, rather than as a static entity—thinking which does not separate itself from action, but constantly immerses itself in temporality without fear of the risks involved. Critical thinking contrasts with naive thinking, which sees "historical time as a weight, a stratification of the acquisitions and experiences of the past,"[5] from which the present should emerge normalized and "well-behaved." For the naive thinker, the important thing is accommodation to this normalized "today." For the critic, the important thing is the continuing transformation of reality, in behalf of the continuing humanization of men. In the words of Pierre Furter:

> The goal will no longer be to eliminate the risks of temporality by clutching to guaranteed space, but rather to temporalize space . . . The universe is revealed to me not as space, imposing a massive presence to which I can but adapt, but as a scope, a domain which takes shape as I act upon it.[6]

For naive thinking, the goal is precisely to hold fast to this guaranteed space and adjust to it. By thus denying temporality, it denies itself as well.

Only dialogue, which requires critical thinking, is also capable of generating critical thinking. Without dialogue there is no communication, and without communication there can be no true education. Education which is able to resolve the contradiction between teacher and student takes place in a situation in which both address their act of cognition to the object by which they are mediated. Thus, the dialogical character of education as the practice of freedom does not begin when the teacher-student meets with the students-teachers in a pedagogical situation, but rather when the former first asks himself what he will dialogue with the latter *about*. And preoccupation with the content of dialogue is really preoccupation with the program content of education.

For the anti-dialogical banking educator, the question of content simply concerns the program about which he will discourse to his students; and he answers his own question, by organizing his own program. For the dialogical, problem-posing teacher-student, the program content of education is neither a gift nor an imposition—bits of information to be deposited in the students—but rather the organized, systematized, and developed "re-presentation" to individuals of the things about which they want to know more.[7]

NOTES

1. Action
   Reflection $\Big\}$ word = work = praxis
   Sacrifice of action = verbalism
   Sacrifice of reflection = activism

2. Some of these reflections emerged as a result of conversations with Professor Ernani Maria Fiori.

3. I obviously do not refer to the silence of profound meditation, in which men only apparently leave the world, withdrawing from it in order to consider it in its totality, and thus remaining with it. But this type of retreat is only authentic when the mediator is "bathed" in reality; not when the retreat signifies contempt for the world and flight from it, in a type of "historical schizophrenia."

4. I am more and more convinced that true revolutionaries must receive the revolution, because of its creative and liberating nature, as an act of love. For me, the revolution, which is not possible without a theory of rev-

olution—and therefore science—is not irreconcilable with love. On the contrary: the revolution is made by men to achieve their humanization. What, indeed, is the deeper motive which moves men to become revolutionaries, but the dehumanization of man? The distortion imposed on the word "love" by the capitalist world cannot prevent the revolution from being essentially loving in character, nor can it prevent the revolutionaries from affirming their love of life. Guevara (while admitting the "risk of seeming ridiculous") was not afraid to affirm it: "Let's me say, with the risk of appearing ridiculous, that the true revolutionary is guided by strong feelings of love. It is impossible to think of an authentic revolutionary without this quality." *Venceremos—The Speeches and Writings of Che Guevara*, edited by John Gerassi (New York, 1969), p. 398.

5. From the letter of a friend.

6. Pierre Furter, *Educação e Vida* (Rio, 1966), pp. 26-27.

7. In a long conversation with Malraux, Mao-Tse-Tung declared, "You know I've proclaimed for a long time: we must teach the masses clearly what we have received from them confusedly." André Malraux, *Anti-Memoirs* (New York, 1968), pp. 361-362. This affirmation contains an entire dialogical theory of how to construct the program content of education, which cannot be elaborated according to what the *educator* thinks best for *his* students.

■
_____

Genuine Dialogue and the Possibilities of Peace*

Martin Buber

I cannot express my thanks to the German Book Trade for the honour conferred on me without at the same time setting forth the sense in which I have accepted it, just as I earlier accepted the Hanseatic Goethe Prize given me by the University of Hamburg.

About a decade ago a considerable number of Germans—there must have been many thousands of them—under the indirect command of the German government and the direct command of its representatives, killed millions of my people in a systematically prepared and executed procedure whose organized cruelty cannot be compared with any previous historical event. I, who am one of those who remained alive, have only in a formal sense a common humanity with those who took part in this action. They have so radically removed themselves from the human sphere, so transposed themselves into a sphere of monstrous inhumanity inaccessible to my conception, that not even hatred, much less an overcoming of hatred, was able to arise in me. And what am I that I could here presume to "forgive!"

With the German people it is otherwise. From my youth on I have taken the real existence of peoples most seriously. But I have never, in the face of any historical moment, past or present, allowed the concrete multiplicity existing at that moment within a people—the concrete inner dialectic, rising to contradiction—to be obscured by the levelling concept of a totality constituted and acting in just such a way and no other.

From Genuine Dialogue and the Possibilities of Peace (pp. 232-239 in Maurice S. Friedman [trans., ed] Pointing the Way) by Martin Buber, copyright © 1957 and 1985, The Estate of Martin Buber. Reprinted with the permission of the Balkin Agency, Inc.

When I think of the German people of the days of Auschwitz and Treblinka, I behold, first of all, the great many who knew that the monstrous event was taking place and did not oppose it. But my heart, which is acquainted with the weakness of men, refuses to condemn my neighbour for not prevailing upon himself to become a martyr. Next there emerges before me the mass of those who remained ignorant of what was withheld from the German public, and who did not try to discover what reality lay behind the rumours which were circulating. When I have these men in mind, I am gripped by the thought of the anxiety, likewise well known to me, of the human creature before a truth which he fears he cannot face. But finally there appears before me, from reliable reports, some who have become as familiar to me by sight, action, and voice as if they were friends, those who refused to carry out the orders and suffered death or put themselves to death, and those who learned what was taking place and opposed it and were put to death, or those who learned what was taking place and because they could do nothing to stop it killed themselves. I see these men very near before me in that especial intimacy which binds us at times to the dead and to them alone. Reverence and love for these Germans now fills my heart.

But I must step out of memory into the present. Here I am surrounded by the youth who have grown up since those events and had no part in the great crime. These youth, who are probably the essential life of the German people today, show themselves to me in a powerful inner dialectic. Their core is included in the core of an inner struggle running for the most part underground and only occasionally coming to the surface. This is only a part, though one of the clearest, of the great inner struggle of all peoples being fought out today, more or less consciously, more or less passionately, in the vital centre of each people.

The preparation for the final battle of *homo humanus* against *homo contrahumanus* has begun in the depths. But the front is split into as many individual fronts as there are peoples, and those who stand on one of the individual fronts know little or nothing of the other fronts. Darkness still covers the struggle, upon whose course and outcome it depends whether, despite all, a true humanity can issue from the race of men. The so-called cold war between two gigantic groups of states with all its accompaniments still obscures the true obligation and solidarity of combat, whose line cuts right through all states and peoples, however they name their regimes. The recognition of the deeper reality, of the true need and the true danger, is growing. In Germany, and especially in German youth, despite their being rent asunder, I have found more awareness of it than elsewhere. The memory of the twelve-year reign of *homo contrahumanus* has made the spirit stronger, and the task set by the spirit clearer, than they formerly were.

Tokens such as the bestowal of the Hanseatic Goethe Prize and the Peace Prize of the German Book Trade on a surviving arch-Jew must be understood in this connection. They, too, are moments in the struggle of the human spirit against the demonry of the subhuman and the anti-human. The survivor who is the object of such honours is taken up into the high duty of solidarity that extends across the fronts: the solidarity of all separate groups in the flaming battle for the rise of a true humanity. This duty is, in the present hour, the highest duty on earth. The Jew chosen as symbol must obey this call of duty even there, indeed, precisely there where the never-to-be-effaced memory of what has happened stands in opposition to it. When he recently expressed his gratitude to the spirit of Goethe, victoriously disseminated throughout the world, and when he now expresses his gratitude to the spirit of peace, which now as so often before speaks to the world in books of the German tongue, his thanks signify his confession of solidarity with the common battle—common also to Germans and Jews—against the contrahuman, and his reply to a vow taken by fighters, a vow he has heard.

Hearkening to the human voice, where it speaks forth unfalsified, and replying to it, this above all is needed today. The busy noise of the hour must no longer drown out the *vox humana*, the essence of the human which has become a voice. This voice must not only be listened to, it must be answered and led out of the lonely monologue into the awakening dialogue of the peoples. Peoples must engage in talk with one another through their truly human men if the great peace is to appear and the devastated life of the earth renew itself.

The great peace is something essentially different from the absence of war.

In an early mural in the town hall of Sienna the civic virtues are assembled. Worthy, and conscious of their worth, the women sit there, except one in their midst who towers above the rest. This woman is marked not by dignity but rather by composed majesty. Three letters announce her name: Pax. She represents the great peace I have in mind. This peace does not signify that what men call war no longer exists now that it holds sway—that means too little to enable one to understand this serenity. Something new exists, now really exists, greater and mightier than war, greater and mightier even than war. Human passions flow into war as the waters into the sea, and war disposes of them as it likes. But these passions must enter into the great peace as ore into the fire that melts and transforms it. Peoples will then build with one another with more powerful zeal than they have ever destroyed one another.

The Siennese painter had glimpsed this majestic peace in his dream alone. He did not acquire the vision from historical reality, for it has never appeared there. What in history has been called peace has never, in fact, been aught other than an anxious or an illusory blissful pause between wars. But the womanly genius of the painter's dream is no mistress of interruptions but the queen of new and greater deeds.

May we, then, cherish the hope that the countenance which has remained unknown to all previous history will shine forth on our late generation, apparently sunk irretrievably in disaster? Are we not accustomed to describe the world situation in which we have lived since the end of the Second World War no longer even as peace but as the "cold" phase of a world war declared in permanence? In a situation which no longer even seeks to preserve the appearance of peace, is it not illusory enthusiasm to speak of a great peace which has never existed being within reach?

It is the depth of our crisis that allows us to hope in this way. Ours is not an historically familiar malady in the life of peoples which can eventuate in a comfortable recovery. Primal forces are now being summoned to take an active part in an unrepeatable decision between extinction and rebirth. War has not produced this crisis; it is, rather, the crisis of man which has brought forth the total war and the unreal peace which followed.

War has always had an adversary who hardly ever comes forward as such but does his work in the stillness. This adversary is speech, fulfilled speech, the speech of genuine conversation in which men understand one another and come to a mutual understanding. Already in primitive warfare fighting begins where speech has ceased; that is, where men are no longer able to discuss with one another the subjects under dispute or submit them to mediation, but flee from speech with one another and in the speechlessness of slaughter seek what they suppose to be a decision, a judgment of God. War soon conquers speech and enslaves it in the service of its battle-cries. But where speech, be it ever so shy, moves from camp to camp, war is already called in question. Its cannons easily drown out the word; but when the word has become entirely soundless, and on this side and on that soundlessly bears into the hearts of men the intelligence that no human conflict can really be resolved through killing, not even through mass killing, then the human word has already begun to silence the cannonade.

But it is just the relation of man to speech and to conversation that the crisis characteristic of our age has in particular tended to shatter. The man in crisis will no longer entrust his cause to conversation because its presupposition— trust—is lacking. This is the reason why the cold war which today goes by the name of peace has been able to overcome mankind. In every earlier period of peace the living word has passed between man and man, time after time drawing the poison from the antagonism of interests and convictions so that these antagonisms have not degenerated into the absurdity of "no-farther" into the madness of "must wage-war." This living word of human dialogue that from time to time makes its flights until the madness smothers it, now seems to have become lifeless in the midst of the non-war. The debates between statesmen which the radio conveys to us no longer have anything in common with a human conversation: the diplomats do not address one another but the faceless public. Even the congresses and conferences which convene in the name of mutual understanding lack the substance which alone can elevate the deliberations to genuine talk: candor and directness in address and answer. What is concentrated there is only the universal condition in which men are no longer willing or no longer able to speak directly to their fellows. They are not able to speak directly because they no longer trust one another, and everybody knows that the other no longer trusts him. If anyone in the hubbub of contradictory talk happens to pause and take stock, he discovers that in his relations to others hardly anything persists that deserves to be called trust.

And yet this must be said again and again, it is just the depth of the crisis that empowers us to hope. Let us dare to grasp the situation with that great realism that surveys all the definable realities of public life, of which, indeed, public life appears to be composed, but is also aware of what is most real of all, albeit moving secretly in the depths—the latent healing and salvation in the face of impending ruin. The power of turning that radically changes the situation, never reveals itself outside of crisis. This power begins to function when one, gripped by despair, instead of allowing himself to be submerged, calls forth his primal powers and accomplishes with them the turning of his very existence. It happens in this way both in the life of the person and in that of the race. In its depths the crisis demands naked decision: no mere fluctuation between getting worse and getting better, but a decision between the decomposition and the renewal of the tissue.

The crisis of man which has become apparent in our day announces itself most clearly as a crisis of trust, if we may employ, thus intensified, a concept of economics. You ask, trust in whom? But the question already contains a limitation not admissible here. It is simply trust that is increasingly lost to men of our time. And the crisis of speech is bound up with this loss of trust in the closest possible fashion, for I can only speak to someone in the true sense of the term if I expect him to accept my word as genuine. Therefore, the fact that it is so difficult for present-day man to pray (note well: not to hold it to be true that there is a God, but to address Him) and the fact that it is so difficult for him to carry on a genuine talk with his fellow-men are elements of a single set of facts. This lack of trust in Being, this incapacity for unreserved intercourse with the other, points to an innermost sickness of the sense of existence. One symptom of this sickness, and the most acute of all, is the one from which I have begun: that a genuine word cannot arise between the camps.

Can such an illness be healed? I believe it can be. And it is out of this, my belief, that I speak to you. I have no proof for this belief. No belief can be proved; otherwise it would not be what it is, a great venture. Instead of offering proof, I appeal to that potential belief of each of my hearers which enables him to believe.

If there be a cure, where can the healing action start? Where must that existential turning begin which the healing powers, the powers of salvation in the ground of the crisis, await?

That peoples can no longer carry on authentic dialogue with one another is not only the most acute symptom of the pathology of our time, it is also that which most urgently makes a demand of us. I believe, despite all, that the peoples in this hour can enter into dialogue, into a genuine dialogue with one another. In a genuine dialogue each of the partners, even when he stands in opposition to the other, heeds, affirms, and confirms his opponent as an existing other. Only so can conflict certainly not be eliminated from the world, but be humanly arbitrated and led towards its overcoming.

To the task of initiating this conversation those are inevitably called who carry on today within each people the battle against the anti-human. Those who build the great unknown front across mankind shall make it known by speaking unreservedly with one another, not overlooking what divides them but determined to bear this division in common.

In opposition to them stands the element that profits from the divisions between the peoples, the contra-human in men, the subhuman, the enemy of man's will to become a true humanity.

The name Satan means in Hebrew the hinderer. That is the correct designation for the anti-human in individuals and in the human race. Let us not allow this Satanic element in men to hinder us from realizing man! Let us release speech from its ban! Let us dare, despite all, to trust!

NOTES

*This address was given on the occasion of the award to the author of the Peace Prize of the German Book Trade at Frankfurt-am-Main, in Paulskirche, September 27, 1953.

Author Index

Subject Index

A

Alienation, 119, 217
America, 270; and "American
Dream," 236
Anonymity, 4, 92, 94-97
Arab-Israeli understanding, xviii
Arts, the, 3
Aspen Movie Map, 100
Athenian virtues, 261
Authenticity, 15, 94
Autobiography, 180, 182-197

B

Being, 25
"Between," the, xiv, xviii, 23, 25
Bulletin board systems, 101, 141

C

Caring, 19, 275-283
Christianity, 293, 297-299
Client-centered therapy, 113, 135,
137
Collaborative orientation, 14, 93
Communication, 1, 3, 11;
models of, 31
Communion, 9, 38-46, 122, 217,
250
Communitarian movement, 291
Community, 3, 26, 42, 100, 141,
217, 231, 270, 291-292, 297
Composition, 3

Computer, 161, 165-166, *see also*
Bulletin board systems; electronic mail
Confirmation, 3, 20, 23-25, 71-72,
81
and acceptance-rejection, 24-25
and disconfirmation, 24-25, 73-
78
and pseudo-confirmation, 75
and schizogenic disconfirmation, 74
Conflict, 86-87, 257-259
and caring, 280-281
and tradition, 271
Congruence, 113, 127, 129-131,
136
Consciousness, 209-210, 220
Constructivists, 255-57
Conversation, 10-11, 13
and constructivists, 255
and conversation analysis, x
and hermeneutics, 112, 114-119
and narcissism, 55, 64-68
with oneself, 213
and peace, 309, 311
Critical theory/theorists, 180, 190
Culture, 54
and America, 17
and cross-cultural theory, 3
and cultural constraints on dialogue, 17-23

319

Printed in the United States
56243LVS00008B/132